HOMER LEA

American Warriors

Throughout the nation's history, numerous men and women of all ranks and branches of the United States military have served their country with honor and distinction. During times of war and peace, there are individuals whose exemplary achievements embody the highest standards of the U.S. armed forces. The aim of the American Warriors series is to examine the unique historical contributions of these individuals, whose legacies serve as enduring examples for soldiers and citizens alike. The series will promote a deeper and more comprehensive understanding of the U.S. armed forces.

Series editor: Roger Cirillo

An AUSA Book

HOMER LEA

*American
Soldier of
Fortune*

LAWRENCE M. KAPLAN

THE UNIVERSITY PRESS OF KENTUCKY

Scholarly publisher for the Commonwealth,
serving Bellarmine University, Berea College, Centre College of Kentucky, Eastern
Kentucky University, The Filson Historical Society, Georgetown College, Kentucky
Historical Society, Kentucky State University, Morehead State University, Murray
State University, Northern Kentucky University, Transylvania University, University
of Kentucky, University of Louisville, and Western Kentucky University.
All rights reserved.

Editorial and Sales Offices: The University Press of Kentucky
663 South Limestone Street, Lexington, Kentucky 40508-4008
www.kentuckypress.com

Page iii: Lieutenant General Homer Lea, circa 1905 (*Bookman*, April 1908, 130);
map, pp. vi–vii: Eastern Asia, 1911 (William Patten and J. E. Homans, *The New
Encyclopedic Atlas and Gazetteer of the World* [New York: P. F. Collier and Son,
1911], 69).

14 13 12 11 10   5 4 3 2 1

Library of Congress Cataloging-in-Publication Data

Kaplan, Lawrence M. (Lawrence Martin), 1954–
  Homer Lea : American soldier of fortune / Lawrence M. Kaplan.
    p. cm. — (American warriors)
  Includes bibliographical references and index.
  ISBN 978-0-8131-2616-6 (hardcover : acid-free paper)
  1. Lea, Homer, 1876–1912. 2. Soldiers of fortune—United States—Biography.
3. United States—Foreign relations—China. 4. China—Foreign relations—United
States. 5. Sun, Yat-sen, 1866–1925. 6. China—History—1861–1912. 7. China—
History—Revolution, 1911–1912. 8. Diplomats—United States—Biography.
9. Generals—China—Biography. 10. Authors, American—20th century—Biography.
I. Title.
  E748.L39K37 2010
  951'.035092—dc22
  [B]   2010023314

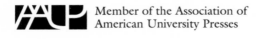

Member of the Association of
American University Presses

CONTENTS

Illustrations follow page 158

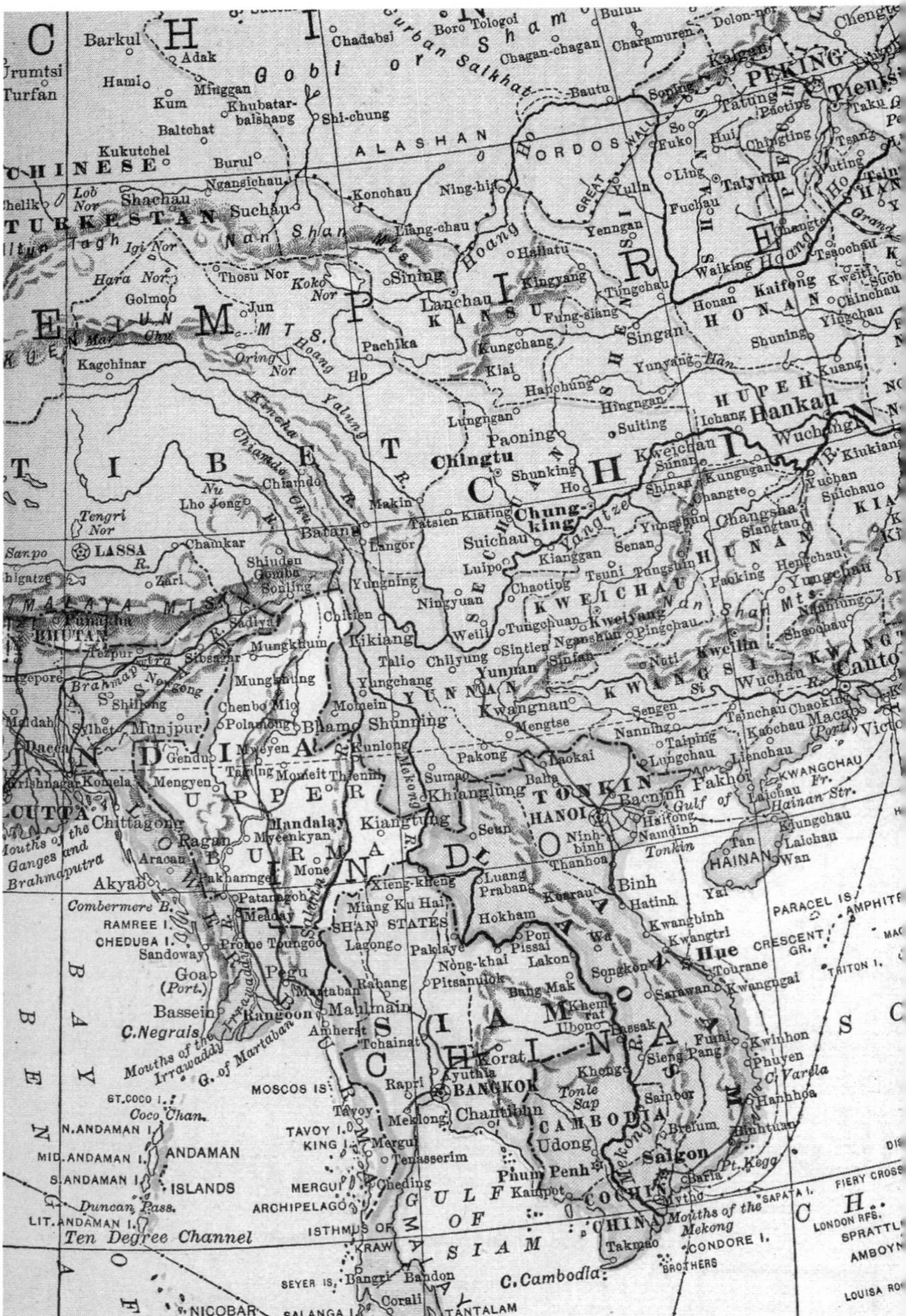

Barkul
Urumtsi
Turfan
Hami
Adak
Kum
Minggan
Khubatar-balshang
Shi-chung
Baltchat
Kukutchel
Burul
Chadabsi
Boro Tologoi
Gobi or
Shamo
Charamuren
Chagan-chagan
Dolon-nor
Bautu
Kalgan
PEKING
Tientsin
Soping
Tatung
Paoting
ALASHAN
ORDOS
GREAT WALL
CHINESE
TURKESTAN
Lob Nor
Shachau
Suchau
Nganslchau
Konchau
Ning-hia
Yulin
Taiyuan
Liang-chau
Nan Shan Mts.
Igi Nor
Hara Nor
Thosu Nor
Koko Nor
Sining
Lanchau
Kingyang
Haifatu
Yenngan
Tungchau
Golmo
Jun
KANSU
Fung-siang
Singan
Honan
Kaifong
HONAN
Kagchinar
Pachika
Kungchang
Kiai
Yunyang
Shuning
Oring Nor
Hoang Ho
Yalung
Hanchung
Hingngan
Lungngan
Paoning
Suiting
Ichang
Hankau
HUPEH
Wuchang
TIBET
Chingtu
Shunking
Kweichau
Sunan
Chiamdo
Lho Jong
Makin
Tatsien
Kiating
Chung-king
Yangtze
Changsha
Siangtau
Tengri Nor
Batang
Langor
Suichau
LASSA
Sanpo
Chamkar
Luipo
Kianggan
Senan
HUNAN
Zari
Shiuden
Gomba
Sonling
Yungning
Chaoting
Tsuni
KWEICHAU
Ningyuan
Kweiyang
Punakha
BHUTAN
Sadiya
Chitien
Lkiang
Weili
Tungchuan
Pingchau
Tezpur
Sibsagar
Mungkhum
Tali
Chilyung
Yunnan
Kweilin
Brahmaputra
Nowgong
Mungkhung
Yungchang
KWANGSI
Wuchau
Canton
Shillong
Chenbo Mio
Momein
YUNNAN
Kwangnan
Sengen
Taipinchau
Chaoking
Macao (Port.)
Victoria
Sylhet
Munjpur
Polamong
Bhamo
Shunning
Mengtse
Nanning
Taiping
Dacca
INDIA
Gendu
Myeyen
Kunlong
Pakong
Laokai
Lungchau
Lienchau
Pakhoi
KWANGCHAU Fr.
Komela
Mengyen
Momeit
Mekong R.
Sumao
Khianglung
TONKIN
Bacninh
Gulf of Tonkin
Hainan Str.
UPPER
Calcutta
Chittagong
Mandalay
Kiangtung
HANOI
Haifong
Namdinh
Mouths of the Ganges and Brahmaputra
Ragan
Myeenkyan
Ninh-binh
Thanhoa
HAINAN
BURMA
Aracan
Mone
Akyab
Pakhangge
Luang Prabang
Binh
Hatinh
Combermere B.
Patanagoh
Xieng-khieng
Miang Ku Hai
SHAN STATES
Hokham
Kwangbinh
PARACEL IS.
RAMREE I.
CHEDUBA I.
Meaday
Kwangtri
Sandoway
Prome
Toungoo
Lagong
Paklaye
Pon
Pissai
Hue
CRESCENT GR.
Nong-khai
Lakon
Tourane
TRITON I.
Goa (Port.)
Pegu
Rahang
Pitsanuok
Bang Mak
Sarawan
Bassein
Martaban
Maulmain
Khemerat
Ubon
Bassak
C. Negrais
Rangoon
Amherst
SIAM
Tchainat
Korat
Mouths of the Irrawaddy
G. of Martaban
Phuyen
C. Varela
MOSCOS IS.
Rapri
Ayuthia
BANGKOK
Tonle Sap
Hanhhoa
ST. COCO I.
Coco Chan.
Tavoy
Meklong
Chantibun
CAMBODIA
N. ANDAMAN I.
TAVOY I.
KING I.
Mergui
Udong
MID. ANDAMAN I.
ANDAMAN
Tenasserim
Pnum Penh
Saigon
S. ANDAMAN I.
ISLANDS
MERGUI ARCHIPELAGO
Cheding
GULF OF SIAM
Kampot
COCHIN CHINA
Duncan Pass.
Mouths of the Mekong
SAPATA I.
FIERY CROSS
LIT. ANDAMAN I.
Ten Degree Channel
ISTHMUS OF KRAW
LONDON RFS.
SPRATTLY
AMBOYNA
CONDORE I.
BROTHERS
Takmao
C. Cambodia
SEYER IS.
Bangri
Bandon
LOUISA
NICOBAR
SALANGA I.
Corali
TANTALAM
Sombrero Chan.
BAY OF BENGAL
MALAY

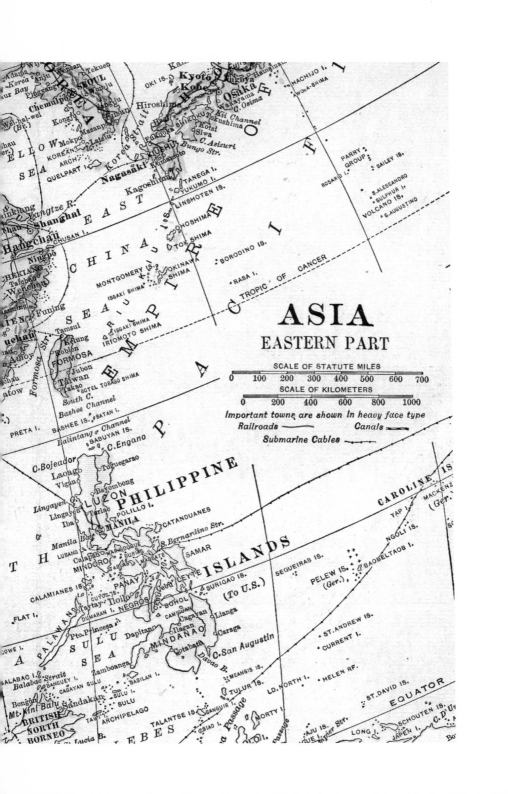

ASIA
EASTERN PART

SCALE OF STATUTE MILES

0   100   200   300   400   500   600   700

SCALE OF KILOMETERS

0   200   400   600   800   1000

Important towns are shown in heavy face type
Railroads ———   *Canals* ▄▄▄
Submarine Cables ———

ACKNOWLEDGMENTS

The research for this work initially began in the 1980s and would not have been possible without the support of a number of individuals and institutions. First and foremost, I wish to thank Joshua B. Powers. He provided me with invaluable insights about Homer Lea and Lea's wife, his mother, when I began my research, and his family graciously allowed me continuing access to his personal papers after his death. Mr. and Mrs. James D. Lea shared with me correspondence between Ermal Lea and Tom Lea Jr. that filled important gaps in the chronology of Lea's life. Dr. Robert G. Wilson supplied me with perceptions and information about Emma Wilson Lea. Dr. Charles E. Pirtle, formerly of Georgetown University, whose expertise in geopolitics has driven his own Homer Lea research, was very helpful in sharing research material I had either missed or not considered. I owe him a huge debt of gratitude, especially for putting me in touch with Mr. Brian Kates and Mrs. LaVonne Perkins. Mr. Kates allowed me access to his father's (Charles O. Kates) personal papers, which are critical to any serious Lea biography, and Mrs. Perkins offered helpful insights on researching Lea family history in Colorado. Mrs. Mabelle M. Selland and her daughter Ms. Julie Selland aided my research on Homer Lea's connection with the Fresno reform Chinese movement. Mabelle Selland also introduced me to Ms. Jane Leung Larson, who furnished me with translated letters from her grandfather, Dr. Tom Leung, about Homer Lea's involvement with the Chinese reform movement.

I would like to extend my thanks and gratitude to the following institutions for their research assistance: Bancroft Library, University of California, Berkeley; California State Archives, Sacramento; Chicago History Museum,; Colorado Historical Society, Denver; Denver Public Library; Fresno City and County Historical Society; Harry Ransom Humanities Research Center, University of Texas, Austin; Historical Center for Southeast New Mexico, Roswell; Holt-Atherton Special Collections, University of the Pacific, Stockton,

California; Hoover Institution on War, Revolution and Peace, Stanford University, Stanford, California; Huntington Library, Art Collections, and Botanical Gardens, San Marino, California; Jackson County Historical Society, Independence, Missouri; Kansas State University Library, Manhattan, Kansas; Library of Congress, Washington, D.C.; Maryland Historical Society, Baltimore; National Archives and Records Administration, Washington, D.C.; National Army Museum, London; Nevada State Library and Archives, Carson City; Occidental College, Los Angeles; Pentagon Library, Washington, D.C.; Public Record Office, Kew Richmond Surrey, United Kingdom; Riverside Cemetery, Denver; Stanford University Registrar, Stanford University, Stanford, California; and University of Iowa, University Libraries, Iowa City.

I could not have completed my research without the assistance of a number of able research assistants. I wish to thank Ms. Polly Armstrong, Special Collections, Stanford University; Mr. Noah Belikoff, independent researcher (Bancroft Library); Ms. Brooke Black, library assistant, Huntington Library; Mr. Ronald M. Bulatoff, archival specialist, Hoover Institution Archives; Ms. Nana Diederichs, Special Collections, University of Iowa Library; Mr. Christopher G. Driggs, archivist, Nevada State Library and Archives; Mr. Elvis E. Fleming, archivist, Historical Center for Southeast New Mexico; Ms. Pam Gorelow, associate production manager, *Stanford Magazine;* Mr. David Kessler, Bancroft Library; Ms. Margaret Kimball, Stanford Registrar Office; Ms. Linda Maguire, Pentagon Library; Mr. John Mills, Pentagon Library; Ms. Maria Ortiz, Fresno City and County Historical Society; Ms. Jean Paule, archivist, Occidental College; and Mr. Michael Wurtz, archivist, Holt-Atherton Special Collections. I also wish to thank my California cousin, Mrs. Pamela Sonnenblick, and her husband, Mr. Robert Sonnenblick, for copying newspaper microfilm articles from the Los Angeles Public Library and tracking down Ansel O'Banion's grave site; and my friends Mr. Brad Wartell and Ms. Christiane Wartell, the former for obtaining material from the Thomas Calloway Lea Papers at the Harry Ransom Humanities Research Center, and the latter for her research assistance at the Bancroft Library and the New York Public Library.

HOMER LEA

INTRODUCTION

Homer Lea's career was stranger than many stories found in romantic fiction. Lea, a five-foot, three-inch hunchback who suffered from debilitating health, overcame his afflictions in pursuing dreams and ambitions such as few achieve. He is best remembered as a somewhat mysterious adventurer, author, and geopolitical strategist who challenged conventional wisdom and confronted significant odds to create for himself a role in world politics. He began his adventures in 1900, after dropping out of Stanford University and going to China during the Boxer Rebellion, and ultimately became the trusted personal military advisor to Chinese revolutionary leader Dr. Sun Yat-sen during the 1911 Chinese republican revolution. In the interim he became a celebrated author and internationally recognized geopolitical strategist. In 1912, poised on the brink of fulfilling a Napoleonic destiny in China, his health gave out. He died later that year, shortly before his thirty-sixth birthday, but the actions of his short life left a profound imprint on the history of his era.

Lea became involved in Chinese affairs while attending Stanford University from 1897 to 1899. In San Francisco he joined a secret Chinese movement, the Pao Huang Hui (Protect the Emperor Society), which had been organized by K'ang Yu-wei, formerly a close advisor to Emperor Kwang-hsu. K'ang Yu-wei was behind the emperor's initiation of a series of liberal reforms in the late 1890s that led to a palace coup d'état by the conservative regent, Dowager Empress Tzu Hsi. She imprisoned the emperor and put a price on K'ang Yu-wei's head. K'ang Yu-wei then established the Pao Huang Hui to restore the emperor to power. Lea recognized a great opportunity for adventure with the Chinese and promoted himself among the reformers as a military expert, claiming to be a relative, which he was not, of the famous Confederate general Robert E. Lee. He dropped out of Stanford and in the summer of 1900 went to China, where he received a lieutenant general's commission in the nascent Pao Huang Hui army. His role entailed training Pao Huang Hui soldiers in Kwangtung and Kwangsi provinces just as China became embroiled in the Boxer Rebellion, although he himself took no part in the fighting. Ultimately, the Pao Huang Hui's military plans to restore the emperor to power failed, but Lea, a valued member of the movement, returned to the United States to continue his work to further Pao Huang Hui goals.

In 1904 Lea masterminded a plan to covertly train a cadre of Chinese soldiers in America. Under his guidance the Pao Huang Hui established a network of military schools, as a cover, in more than twenty cities nationwide. The intent was to have these soldiers return to China, infiltrate the imperial Chinese army, and then take part in a coordinated coup d'état to restore Emperor Kwang-hsu to his throne. Lea hired former U.S. Army soldiers as instructors and commissioned them in the Pao Huang Hui's army. He outfitted his soldiers in altered U.S. Army uniforms, simply replacing the national eagle on the buttons and cap with the imperial Chinese dragon. For himself, he wore an American lieutenant general's uniform, with the altered insignia, along with a modified U.S. Army officer's sword with a dragon handle. His covert training operation nearly collapsed in 1905 when the U.S. Secret Service and several states investigated it for possible violations of neutrality laws. He also fended off the ambitions of another American with ties to the Pao Huang Hui, an opportunist named Richard A. Falkenberg who sought to install himself as the head of the Chinese cadets. Lea's affiliation with the Pao Huang Hui ended by 1908, the year Emperor Kwang-hsu and the dowager empress died (within two days of each other); when they died, so did his commitment to bolstering up the Manchu dynasty.

Lea's next involvement in Chinese affairs brought him into contact with Dr. Sun Yat-sen, whose revolutionary movement was dedicated to the overthrow of the Manchu dynasty. In 1910 Dr. Yung Wing, an eminent Chinese scholar and friend of Lea, arranged for Lea to join forces with Sun Yat-sen, who was in the United States on a fund-raising trip. Sun Yat-sen made Lea his military advisor and promised him an important military position in the Chinese army if his revolutionary movement succeeded. In addition to giving Sun Yat-sen military advice, Lea offered to contact some influential businessmen who might be induced to provide needed financial backing to the revolutionary cause. Lea then helped organize a small covert group of Americans and Chinese, known as the Red Dragon conspiracy, for this purpose. The incentive for the businessmen was great. Sun Yat-sen promised them virtual carte blanche in China's financial affairs if his revolution succeeded in toppling the Manchus. The Red Dragon conspirators believed they could raise enough money for a revolutionary movement that could succeed if it did not act hastily—Sun Yat-sen had a succession of failed revolutionary uprisings behind him. As events unfolded, however, Sun Yat-sen's followers did act hastily. The Red Dragon conspirators dropped out of Sun Yat-sen's plans after an attempted revolutionary uprising, launched by Sun Yat-sen's followers, failed in March 1911.

Despite the financial setback, Lea remained a loyal and valued advisor to Sun Yat-sen. He became instrumental to Sun Yat-sen's success in October 1911. At that time Lea was honeymooning with his new wife, his former secretary, Ethel Powers, in Germany, where he was also being treated for his failing health. He received word from Sun Yat-sen, who was on a fund-raising trip in Colorado, that a new revolutionary attempt had finally succeeded. The days of the Manchu dynasty were numbered. Sun Yat-sen, however, did not travel immediately to China; instead, he cabled Lea for help. He hoped Lea could use his important contacts in Washington and London to try to arrange Western financial backing for a new Chinese republican government. He then met Lea in London, where they both tried to obtain British financial backing. When their efforts to secure such backing failed in Washington, London, and finally in Paris, Sun Yat-sen and the Leas sailed to China. The Western powers believed that General Yuan Shih-k'ai, the leader of the imperial forces, would ultimately resolve China's problems: they had no faith in Sun Yat-sen.

Lea was nonetheless optimistic about his prospects for playing a key role in Chinese affairs as he sailed to China. He informed journalists at one of the ship's stops that he expected to be the chief of staff of the new Chinese republican army. He had already purchased several custom-made military uniforms in London. Furthermore, U.S. State Department representatives covering the progress of the trip reported that Sun Yat-sen, who was slated to become the first president of the new Chinese republic, did not make a move without first consulting Lea.

After Lea arrived in China in December 1911, his immediate expectations began to wane. Sun Yat-sen was elected president but resigned in favor of Yuan Shih-k'ai, in the hopes of unifying the new republic and avoiding a bloody civil war. Although Lea remained a close advisor to Sun Yat-sen, he was an unwelcome outsider in the eyes of other republican revolutionary leaders. They knew very little about him and had no place for him in their plans. Lea's failing health then brought an abrupt end to his involvement in Chinese affairs. In February 1912 he contracted influenza and complications resulted. He went into a weeklong coma from which he awoke blind and partially paralyzed. His doctors advised prolonged rest if he were to recover. He returned to California in his wife's care with hopes of someday rejoining Sun Yat-sen. He never recovered, however. He died in November 1912. His funeral was private and his remains were cremated.

Although Lea's will stipulated that he be buried in China, Ethel Lea felt she could not afford the trip and kept his ashes until her death in 1934, after which she also was cremated. Her son, Joshua B. Powers, finally fulfilled Lea's last wishes in 1969, when the Leas' ashes were received by President Chiang Kai-shek of the Republic of China and temporarily interred in a cemetery near Taipei. The interment was marked by a well-attended formal ceremony to honor "General Homer Lea, American military advisor to Dr. Sun Yat-sen." Chiang Kai-shek envisioned that when the two Chinas were reunited, the Leas' ashes would be transferred to Nanking and interred next to Dr. Sun Yat-sen's mausoleum.

In his rise to prominence, Lea became an internationally known author and authority on military strategy. He first tried his hand as a novelist with *The Vermilion Pencil: A Romance of China* (1908), which received mixed reviews and has largely been forgotten. He then turned his talents to nonfiction. His second book, *The Valor of Ignorance* (1909), examined American defense and in part prophesied a war between America and Japan. It created a minor sensation at home and abroad and instantly elevated his reputation as a credible expert on defense issues and military strategy. Two retired U.S. Army generals, one a former army chief of staff, wrote glowing introductions to the book, which also contained a striking frontispiece photograph of Lea in his lieutenant general's uniform. The unsuspecting reader could easily have assumed Lea was a respected military officer. The book contained maps of a hypothetical Japanese invasion of the Philippines and was recommended reading for many American military officers, particularly those who served in the Philippines over the next generation. His final book, *The Day of the Saxon* (1912), examined British imperial defense and predicted the breakup of the British Empire. It, too, was controversial and received most of its critical attention in Europe.

In *The Valor of Ignorance* and *The Day of the Saxon*, Lea viewed American and British struggles for global competition and survival as the Anglo-Saxon aspect of a larger social Darwinist contest—the "survival of the fittest"—between the races. In the impending clash of races he believed was inevitable, his goal was to promote Anglo-Saxon interests. His affiliation with China figured prominently in his worldview. He ultimately sought to forge an alliance between the Anglo-Saxons and the Chinese in an effort to counterbalance other regional and global competitors.

Lea's writings on geopolitics and military strategy and his political predictions represent his most enduring legacy. After his death, his writings and predictions about the threat of Japanese imperialism and expansionism in Asia and the Pacific Ocean region helped shape the perceptions of many American civilian and military leaders concerned with national security challenges emanating from the Far East. For example, Japan's aggressive policies that led to the establishment of the puppet state of Manchukuo in the 1930s occurred along the lines he predicted. Furthermore, his predictions of an inevitable clash between Japan and the United States appeared vindicated by Japan's surprise attack on Pearl Harbor. In addition there was a startling similarity between his hypothetical picture of a Japanese invasion of the Philippines and the actual events. Although Lea had not been the only writer to warn of a war between Japan and the United States, his predictions came closer to actual events than any of the others and soon established his reputation as an overlooked military genius and prophet.

To date, much of what has been known about Lea has been a mix of fact and fiction. For example, journalist Clare Boothe's lengthy introduction to the 1942 edition of *The Valor of Ignorance* highlighted the book's influence on General Douglas MacArthur, the U.S. military commander in the Philippines, and his staff, and helped elevate Lea to the status of military genius and prophet. Boothe's introduction, however, also unwittingly helped to foster and perpetuate the aura of mystery and myth surrounding Lea. Not unlike medieval monks who copied books verbatim, including their mistakes, Boothe drew on numerous accounts, some accurate and many not, from writers and acquaintances of Lea without discriminating between myth and reality. Boothe made the same mistake as many before her and many after her. The problem began during Lea's lifetime, when he was widely known as an international "man of mystery," in part due to many exaggerated published accounts, rumors, and speculations about his exploits. He did little to set the record straight because the accounts helped advance his career without drawing undue attention to his illegal and covert activities. Furthermore, his papers were intentionally destroyed after his death to protect his former associates from possible legal prosecution. Separating the fact from the fiction of Lea's life became possible in the late 1960s, after the personal papers of Lea's associates surfaced and were made available to researchers. The evolution of the Internet in the 1990s provided access to additional resources previously unavailable through conventional research, and these have been invaluable in better piecing together Lea's career.

CHAPTER 1

CHARISMATIC DREAMER

An obstacle became a challenge, and I never knew him to feel
defeated.

—Ermal Lea

Homer Lea learned early in life that he faced obstacles, challenges, and
an uncertain future. Afflicted with a physically deformed body and an
incurable medical disorder, he grew up in a world that normally would
have destined him to the mundane existence of an invalid. His physical
infirmities were compensated for, however, by a bright, clever mind
and a steadfast determination. Knowing that he could find no happiness in submitting to fate, he took unusual risks and became committed to transcending the constraints of his body and his health.

Homer Lea's grandfather, Dr. Pleasant John Graves Lea, possessed
an adventurous spirit that he wielded in pursuit of accomplishment,
attributes that molded his family's values. A Tennessee native born
in 1807, he became a businessman, physician, and slave owner who
embraced the challenges of settling the American frontier. In 1837 he
helped establish the town of Cleveland in Bradley County, Tennessee,
serving as one of its first appointed commissioners as well as one if its
first merchants. Ten years later his ambitions led him to earn a medical degree from Jefferson Medical College in Philadelphia. Searching
for new opportunities, he and his family moved to Jackson County,
Missouri, in 1849. There he practiced medicine, farmed, and ran the
local post office. He and his wife, Lucinda, had nine children: four
daughters, Elvira, Carrie, Mary, and Annie; and five sons, Thomas,
Joseph, Frank, Alfred, and John. When Lucinda died in 1857, he subsequently met Fanny M. Clark, a music teacher from Ohio, whom he

married in 1859. They, in turn, had a son, Watson. Dr. Lea became a prominent landowner, with a farm encompassing about one thousand acres, and also expanded his business interests to the Colorado Territory after the 1859 Colorado gold rush. In 1860 he ventured into mining and established a sawmill in Boulder, in the vicinity of the area's first major gold discovery. By 1861 he was a leading member of the Jackson County community and his family happily reaped the fruits of prosperity offered by settling the frontier.[1]

But the outbreak of the Civil War in 1861 had tragic consequences for the Leas. When sectional tensions and violence along the Kansas-Missouri border threatened to engulf them, Dr. Lea sent several family members away to safety in December 1861. His wife, pregnant with Watson, went to stay with relatives in Ohio and his daughters and youngest son went to stay with relatives in Tennessee. Of the eldest sons, Thomas, Joseph, and Frank worked various jobs in Colorado, including lumbering, manning freight wagons, and prospecting. In August 1862, Dr. Lea sent his remaining son, seventeen-year-old Alfred, to Colorado to join his brothers in prospecting. The following month Dr. Lea met an untimely and senseless death, most likely at the hands of troopers from Colonel William R. Penick's Fifth Missouri state militia who were on the hunt for Confederate guerillas in the area. No doubt aware of Dr. Lea's southern sympathies, they took him from his home, which they burned down, and shot him to death in cold blood. James A. Shaw, a local resident, later noted there was no known cause for the murder, "as the doctor was highly respected by all" and "was a non-combatant, taking no part in the war."[2]

Alfred Erskine Lea, like his father, possessed a drive and ambition to seek opportunities. After his father's death, Alfred remained in Colorado while his older brothers joined the Confederate army. From 1862 to 1870, Alfred learned assaying and surveying and became a successful gold miner at the town of Black Hawk. During that period he also served briefly in the 1864 Colorado militia campaign against the Indians. He became active in politics and in 1869 won election to the lower house of the territorial legislature, where he achieved a certain notoriety for introducing the "first and only" bill to extend voting rights to women. (It failed.) His progressive political stance may have been influenced partly by his close ties to Colorado's territorial governor, Edward M. McCook, who championed the cause of women's suffrage. Alfred's political ties likely helped advance his prospects. In 1870 he, McCook, and J. U. Marlow, a Denver hotel proprietor, became partners in a mining venture in Boulder County after a significant silver discovery was made there. Meanwhile, Alfred remained active in the community. After winning election in 1871 as the county clerk and recorder of Boulder County, he moved to the city of Boulder, won reelection in 1873, and in the early 1880s served as the treasurer of Boulder County. He earned a comfortable living in the abstract, real estate, and brokerage business, helping to establish several towns in the process. For example, in 1884 he became involved in a venture that established the town of Steamboat Springs, Colorado. The following year he helped his brother Joseph establish the town of Roswell, New Mexico, by surveying and drawing the first plat of the Roswell town site.[3]

Alfred began a family in Boulder. On December 13, 1871, he married Hersa Coberly Soule of Denver, the widow of a Colorado cavalry officer. Their marriage endured early hardships when their first two children, Ivan and Mary, died in infancy. Homer, their third child, was born on November 17, 1876. He derived his name from Alfred's love of Greek mythology, particularly the Homeric epics the *Iliad* and the *Odyssey*. Their family came to include two daughters, Ermal and Hersa. Then tragedy struck on May 16, 1879, about five months after Hersa's birth, when the elder Hersa, in her mid-thirties, unexpectedly died. In poor health for several years, she succumbed to malignant erysipelas while caring for her ailing mother in Denver. Alfred, who had left ten days earlier on a surveying trip to the headwaters of the Gunnison River, did not receive word of his wife's death for some time. After returning to Boulder in June 1879, he decided to divide his family for the time being. He kept Homer and Ermal with him, with the help of a housekeeper and a young Indian servant called Pete who had been brought to Denver by Hersa's first husband after being orphaned in the 1864 Sand Creek Indian massacre, and he sent the infant Hersa to live with her maternal grandmother in Denver.[4]

Unfortunately, other ominous changes were in store for the Lea family, as Homer's health began to decline. The first signs showed at about age four, when he began developing a hunchback. No one in the family knew for sure what caused the affliction. Some family members came to believe that Pete, who nursed Homer, caused his injury. According to Homer's cousin Tom Lea:

> One day when Homer was less than a year old, Indian Pete dropped him; he landed on his spine. It shook the baby con-

siderably and hurt him, but there were no apparent serious consequences of this fall, and the family forgot about it. A few years went by and . . . when Homer was about four . . . he started to complain of a pain in his back.

The little boy was beginning to suffer the consequences of his fall from the hands of Indian Pete. A hunchback began to manifest itself. The family realized that their son was to be a cripple.[5]

Marco R. Newmark, one of Homer's closest friends in later life, explained: "The family was never sure of the cause of the deformity, but thought it was probably due to a fall from a swing in babyhood and also that a fall from the hands of a cousin in infancy might have had something to do with it. They were not sure, however, because in neither case had any sign of the development of a deformity appeared at the time."[6]

Homer, unable to participate in some sports and games with other children, occupied himself by reading and playing with toy soldiers as he grew up. Ermal recalled their father coming home at night and finding Homer "in the library either reading or putting his tin men through all kinds of maneuvers."[7] He was an exceptionally bright child, and as early as the age of four, was reading adventure books such as *Robinson Crusoe* without any help. As he got older, his favorite books included adventure novels about medieval knights and science fiction adventures such as Jules Verne's *Twenty Thousand Leagues under the Sea*. These books fired his imagination. When playing with his sisters and other children, he often pretended to be a medieval ruler or military commander. He particularly enjoyed taking charge and giving orders. Eleanor "Ella" Lea, a first cousin, recalled: "Homer was always the King . . . and we were his ladies and gentlemen in waiting, or vassals, as his fancy dictated. He would sit on his throne ordering us about. No one ever doubted or disputed his authority."[8] On other occasions, such as celebrating the Fourth of July, he and his sisters would build mud forts armed with firecracker cannons and hold mock battles, which he invariably won.[9]

Beyond a love of reading and imagining himself a great military leader, Homer developed a special affinity for animals. When the family's pet dog died, he arranged an elaborate military funeral. Wearing a Napoleonic-style tricorner paper hat and carrying a wooden sword hanging from a rope around his waist, he headed a funeral procession composed of his sisters and neighborhood children. They marched behind the dog's burial box to the grave site and buried it to the tune of the funeral march played on a tin horn. "Our dog was buried with all the pomp and glory which Homer's vivid imagination could portray," recalled Ermal.[10] On another occasion, he and Ermal were visiting their maternal grandmother, who had moved to San Jose, California, where he developed a strong attachment to a rooster. Ermal explained: "One summer he had a pet rooster—and at night when it came time for the chicken to go to sleep he would hunt everywhere for brother—and when he found him would go to sleep on his shoulder. The cook killed him by mistake and when Homer realized it was his pet rooster he left the table and *cried*."[11]

Little is known of Homer's schooling. His early education consisted of home tutoring and periodically attending public schools. He may have attended the Arapahoe School, a public grammar school in Denver. There is evidence he attended the Boulder Central School in 1886 and 1887. Several class photos from Boulder reveal he was considerably smaller in stature than his classmates.[12]

During this period Alfred consulted specialists all over the country to find a cure for Homer's affliction, but to no avail. Finally, Alfred learned that the National Surgical Institute, an institution for the permanently incapacitated in Indianapolis, Indiana, might be able to help. Homer, at about age twelve, went there, remaining for several years. The treatment did not cure his deformity, but did improve his stature while his height increased three or four inches. He stopped growing about this time at a height of about five foot, three inches, weighing about one hundred pounds.[13]

While Homer was away, Alfred rekindled relations with Emma Wilson, an old friend he had known growing up in Missouri. She was a strong-willed, dedicated teacher, whose experience included working with special students at the Deaf Mute Institute in Danville, Kentucky. They were married on July 16, 1890, leading to new hopes for the Lea family.[14] Emma was willing to care for Homer, who returned home from the National Surgical Institute. Alfred had relocated his family to Denver during this period and there the nurturing environment of family life provided Homer with a new means for development. Emma worked closely with Homer, helping to prepare him for entrance into a public high school. Alfred and Emma still hoped he could grow up like other boys his age.[15]

In September 1892, after months of preparation at home, Homer began his freshman year at East Denver High School. He was often shy, frustrated, and disgruntled in public school. He found it diffi-cult to be accepted and lead a normal teenage life among his contem-poraries. Having a deformity and being two years older than many of his classmates did not easily endear him to them. They ridiculed him and called him "little scrunch-neck."[16] Without enough friends or attentive teachers to help him adjust, he became reclusive. His unhap-piness became evident to students and faculty alike. One of those fac-ulty members recalled: "He always seemed to keep rather to himself instead of associating much with the other students, and was rather quiet, and serious, sometimes seeming almost inclined to melancholy. I thought that was probably due to his being a hunchback, and unable to enter into any of the activities of other boys in sports, etc."[17]

Emma helped Homer regain his self-confidence and overcome his isolation. She made a bargain to buy him the best gold watch in Den-ver if he agreed to follow her advice for thirty days. Initially he refused to go along with any plans she had that would cause him to face fur-ther public ridicule, but she persisted. She finally looked him in the eye and said: "Are you crippled in your mind? Which is the most impor-tant, mind or body? Never refer to yourself again, as a cripple."[18] Her counsel worked. It proved to be a significant turning point in his life.

Although Homer's physical affliction limited his ability to take part in many school sports and activities, he found other outlets to occupy his leisure. If something interested him, he would pursue it vigorously, but if a topic held no special interest he tended to ignore it. In addi-tion to reading relentlessly, he loved the outdoors and became an avid hunter and fisherman.[19] In school, Homer often fixed his attentions on avoiding study, with an occasional burst of interest in one par-ticular subject or another. Typically, Emma recalled, he would simply disregard his homework and say to her: "No use me fooling around a couple of hours with this problem. You can do it in a minute. Here."[20]

Homer's first year at Denver High School was also his last. It is unknown why, but Alfred and Emma decided to send him to San Jose, California, to stay with his maternal grandmother. This deci-sion seemed to offer the best opportunity of finding both a school and an environment better suited to his needs. In the fall of 1893, he enrolled for his sophomore high school year in the college prepa-ratory academy of the University of the Pacific, a small Methodist-Episcopal college in San Jose. During his year there he showed aca-demic improvement and a new enthusiasm.[21]

This encouraging news came at time when Alfred's health was giving him trouble. He decided to retire from business and resettle his family in Los Angeles, where he could live comfortably with income from his mining and real estate investments. In the summer of 1894, he moved his family into a nine-room house he had built at 918 South Bonnie Brae Street, near the pleasant surroundings of Westlake Park. Homer rejoined his family in the new home after completing his sophomore high school year.[22]

Homer entered Los Angeles High School for his junior year in the fall of 1894. He became an active student, both in and out of school, and made a concerted effort to take part in school activities. He made new friends, with several of whom he remained close for the rest of his life. One of the most significant of his extracurricular activities was his prominent role in the local chapter of the Lyceum League of America, a national debating society. He excelled in this arena and established a lasting reputation as a skillful, convincing orator and leader.[23] He also seemed to develop an uncanny personal magnetism and charisma that drew others to him. Marco Newmark explained: "Because of his deformity, he was naturally a conspicuous figure in the school, but otherwise it was not generally thought that there was anything outstanding about him. However, at an election of the Lyceum, the school's debating club, one of its members who did sense that he possessed unusual ability nominated him for one of the offices. He declined, but in so masterful and compelling a manner that he immediately became a leader in school activities."[24]

Homer made up for his physical shortcomings in the Lyceum League and became one of the school's most active students. He sharpened his oratorical skills and broadened his horizons. He developed particular interests in civil government and public affairs. The challenge of competition stimulated and excited him. He no longer felt dispassionately aloof from his classmates, being now part of a group that placed a premium on both individual performance and team spirit. The Lyceum gave him a sense of purpose and dedication unmatched by the ordinary school curriculum. Since the league's southern California branch held conventions all over Los Angeles County, he soon gained a widespread reputation for his talents among fellow debaters. He also changed his mind about holding office in the Los Angeles High School's debating club; during his senior year, in 1896, he won election to its presidency.[25]

Homer was no less adept and capable when it came to helping

his friends. When Marshall Stimson, a close friend, ran for the presidency of the Star and Crescent Literacy Society in February 1896, Homer managed the campaign and used his personal charisma at a decisive moment to help clinch Stimson's victory. The entire audience was awed by Lea's powers of persuasion when Stimson was on the verge of losing after a second ballot gave a clear margin of victory to his opponent.[26] According to Stimson, "[B]efore the result could be announced Lea had taken the platform and in his most dramatic manner had charged that the vote of a certain young lady had been changed and asked the presiding officer to question her as to how she voted . . . the entire vote was declared void and later I was elected."[27] Newmark added:

> The point of the story in illustrating his powerful personality is that clearly, since there had been a majority of more than two votes, the ballot referred to should have been declared void and Seyler [the opposing candidate] declared elected. It was only by virtue of the uncanny power of Homer Lea, which overpowered the judgment of both the students and the faculty, including the principals of the high school who were supposed to supervise the affairs of the Star and Crescent Society, that his motion prevailed. . . . Homer was a hunchback, and the combination of his imperturbable poise and the pointing of his lean finger, which his tiny stature made to appear weirdly long, was the hypnotizing influence that overcame the better judgment of students and faculty alike.
>
> It is difficult to portray in words the vivid and dramatic moment that I have described, but I doubt if anyone who was present at that time ever forgot it.[28]

If Homer's prestige in school grew as a result of his abilities and charisma, his personal qualities of loyalty, courtesy, and kindness earned him a special respect from friends and classmates. He never drew attention to his physical deformity or poor health, nor did he permit anyone to make allowances for him on account of his handicaps. Although he could not take part in school sports nor in many ways lead a normal active young man's life, he was not bitter.[29] Ermal later explained: "The fact that he was a cripple hurt him enough, and so deeply that he avoided anything which would draw one's attention to it, and this very deep feeling made him one of the kindest men I have ever known . . . but I have never seen him bitter. An obstacle became a challenge, and I never knew him to feel defeated."[30]

Homer made the best of minimizing his disabilities and maximizing his strong points. These traits not only helped foster romances with several high school girls, some of whom became infatuated with him, but he also rarely lacked something to do or someplace to go after school with his friends. Like some typical high school students, his group of friends often got together in their off hours to smoke, drink, or gamble away from the watchful eyes of their parents. While Homer declined the cigarettes enjoyed by his friends, he indulged in (and occasionally abused) alcohol with them. Many times after their Lyceum Society meetings, he and his friends would meet at Newmark's house and play poker in the stable. On Saturday nights he might be found with some friends playing cards at Stimson's house when Stimson's family was out. He loved the adventure and excitement, especially of gambling, that his not-so-innocent friends offered him.[31] Newmark recalled Homer's enthusiasm for gambling, as well as his carefree attitude toward money, during some of their after-school get-togethers: "One day in a poker game in my home there were four very high hands in one deal, Homer, when the betting was over, proving to have held the highest, namely a straight flush. When the hands were laid down, Homer, in his excitement, jumped up on the table hurraying wildly. I must add that this was not due to the money involved, but only on account of the excitement of the game, as Homer cared very little about money."[32]

When on hunting or fishing trips with his friends, Homer always pulled his own weight, adapting very well to outdoor challenges. What he lacked in skill and abilities as a hunter, he made up for in determination and ingenuity.[33] Stimson related how well Homer came to terms with rugged outdoor life: "In spite of his physical difficulty he was fond of tramping and hunting. He never permitted anyone to refer to his trouble, would carry his gun and perform all the duties around the camp that anyone else did. One very cold night when we were camping in an exposed position and could not keep warm in our blankets, he made a sleeping bag out of old sacks, put a hot rock at his feet, and slept comfortably all night."[34]

Homer developed an appetite for adventure and achievement and found a wealth of popular literature then sprouting in America that appealed directly to his sense of ambition and challenge. Turn-of-the-century America was undergoing diverse changes and improvements in communication, transportation, industry, and business practices that were transforming the country into a fast-paced, urban industrial and commercial society. After the Civil War, aggressive promoters raised business operations to new heights. Rapidly expanding supplies of raw materials and labor, tied to a permissive political environment, opened a national market for exploitation at unprecedented levels. Amid these changes, a revolution in American popular literature produced an unprecedented variety of inexpensive magazines and books catering to a more literate generation.[35]

One outcome of the popular literature boom was a change in the American idea of success. Active, urban industrial or commercial figures became the heroic symbols of this new age. Great leaders, such as Napoleon Bonaparte, and captains of industry and finance, such as Andrew Carnegie and John Pierpont Morgan, became the premier role models of success in a new era that stressed individual initiative and personal ambition. This was a time of opportunity, a time of challenge and triumph for the individual willing to rise to the occasion. Societal pressures of the times required heroes of masterful proportions to lead the country through the maze of doubts, frustrations, and realities of unprecedented power in the hands of a few capitalist giants.[36]

The literary revolution created a national marketplace for ideas, and never before had the American public had such great access to information. The reading public's desire for more details about prominent people and events was insatiable, and no theme was more popular than that of the individual conquering his environment. Popular biographies of military leaders or leaders in industry and finance, and romantic adventure novels of fictional boy heroes in the tradition of George A. Henty and Horatio Alger Jr. took on new importance, exercising a wider function by establishing standards of prestige and success. They offered Homer and other young men lessons in and proof of individual initiative as well as a guide for emulation. Quests for fame and adventure became a moving force of the times. One observer aptly summed it up as the "commendable desire to be honored and envied, to make one's mark in the world and leave a respected name as an inheritance to one's children."[37]

Homer grew up and prepared to go out into the world in this dynamic age, where apparently only one's own limitation of one's goals stood in the way of success. Although restricted by his handicaps, over time he developed the same desires for personal success and fame as countless other impressionable high school students exposed to the same social and literary forces. These desires, in conjunction with his ambition and drive to overcome his handicaps, made him seek opportunities to prove himself.

Homer gave serious consideration to his opportunities and career possibilities and determined that a legal career offered him the best choice. Studying the liberal arts and humanities, he saw his aptitude for literature, poetry, writing, and the rhetorical arts well suited for a career in law. His enthusiasm and success as a debater would enhance a career in that field, which would be ideal for maximizing his abilities and potential. A quick thinker with charismatic qualities, he could excel in law despite his handicaps.[38]

Although he never aspired to be an A student, he excelled academically when it suited his needs to do so. If he sometimes lacked the motivation to apply himself in all his studies, he usually compensated by spending his time reading material not offered in the classroom. He embraced poetry and literature, and also became a devoted student of history, especially the grandeur and glamour of military history. His teachers at Los Angeles High School believed him to be a very bright pupil, albeit an erratic and inattentive one.[39]

Charles Van Loan, another of Homer's friends, recalled his exceptional ability to retain information and his love of military history:

He never seemed to study, but rather to rely upon his power of perception, which was remarkable. He absorbed information rather than acquired it.

It was during this period that he began to read historical works dealing with the life and career of Napoleon, the one character in history who held a fascination for him. This was unquestionably his first impetus to thought along military lines. Before he was eighteen he had mastered every detail, every strategic move in every battle of Napoleon's campaigns, as well as the history of every great engagement of which there was definite record.[40]

Homer admired Napoleon above the other great commanders due, in part, to the exposure Napoleon had received in popular literature and, perhaps more important, because his slight stature was an example of greatness unaffected by physical size. While Homer took vicarious pride in this fact, he did not delude himself into believing he could easily embark on an adventurous military career. However, his self-confidence and his ego stood ready to seize such an opportunity if one arose.

Homer, knowing he could not pursue a military career in the U.S. Army, satisfied himself with being an amateur authority on warfare. He was very interested in the lives of other great military commanders, including Alexander the Great, Julius Caesar, General Robert E. Lee, and General Ulysses S. Grant. He loved discussing their campaigns with his friends. He deeply admired the nobility, honor, and fame enjoyed by these great military men, and above all he believed that martial glory offered the best of opportunities to achieve greatness. He reportedly told family and friends: "I realized then that the only really great careers in history were those made of the sword."[41]

Homer was likely to impress people he met as a well-read, well-informed conversationalist, with a keen memory and a passionate interest in a wide range of topics. In addition to military history, Homer also loved poetry. The *Rubaiyat* by Persian poet Omar Khayyam, for example, ranked among his favorite readings, and he often carried a copy with him. He confided to at least one high school friend: "I have two passions, poetry and war."[42]

From time to time after school Homer and some of his friends would venture into a few of the more mysterious sections of Los Angeles. They acquired considerable exposure to underworld activity and foreign intrigue while attending various trials at the Superior Court of Los Angeles County and wandering into the recesses of the local Chinese quarter. Murderers, thieves, and cutthroats complemented opium dens, bordellos, and tong war violence in educating Homer and his friends about the harsher realities of life. Stimson, a customary companion on these jaunts, explained how the Chinese quarter became particularly seductive to them:

> Chinatown was not far from High School and in those days it was a very picturesque and alluring field of exploration by young fellows of our age. Lea was evidently viewed with a feeling of almost reverence by the Chinese because of his deformity and we were able to penetrate into the most remote places in the Chinese quarter and had a full picture of life that went on there. We made the acquaintance of a very interesting well educated Chinese named Luie Suey. . . . His tales of

life in the Orient and especially China appealed to our sense of adventure and we both decided that we would go there.[43]

Homer's interest in China was also spurred through the influence of a local Chinese missionary friend of his parents. Alfred and Emma had been interested, though not actively involved, in Chinese missionary work since they moved to Denver, and they became acquainted with the Reverend Ng Poon Chew, the pastor of Los Angeles's Chinese Presbyterian Mission Church. Homer got to know the reverend, who occasionally visited his parents, and also paid visits to him on some of his Chinatown jaunts. Homer met other Chinese through Ng Poon Chew and soon began learning their language (Cantonese). Furthermore, when visiting some neighborhood friends he endeared himself to their Chinese cooks by talking with them to practice his language skills.[44]

Nonetheless, he and Stimson overcame their high-spirited, youthful desires to seek adventure in China. Instead, they expected to finish high school in June 1896, and attend Harvard University in the fall, where they both planned to study to become lawyers.[45]

To that end, in June 1896 Homer went to San Francisco, where Harvard conducted its entrance exams for the region. He had not completed enough work to receive his high school diploma, but under the high school's system, in which no specific grades were given other than an endorsement to take higher work in a particular subject, he was eligible to apply to Harvard. He divided his exams into two sections, taking everything but the mathematics and science tests at that time. Not excelling in those areas, he planned on using the summer months to better prepare himself before completing the exams in September. According to Ermal, he placed first in Latin and Greek, and possibly English, out of approximately five hundred students who took the exams. After passing the first portion of the entrance exams, however, he received some surprising and disappointing news about going east to Harvard. His father was experiencing some unexpected financial difficulties and could not afford to send him away to school. As an alternative, he enrolled in Occidental College, a relatively small and fairly new Presbyterian school close to home.[46]

Homer's health continued to be a constant concern and worry to his family. He became periodically plagued by terrible headaches and spells of near-total blindness. It is unclear when his new affliction surfaced. Newmark remembered that "every so often Homer's stepmother would tell me that Homer had one of his headaches . . . he was subject to such attacks in a violent form. When they came he locked himself up in a darkened room and stayed there until the headache passed by."[47] Diagnosis related his condition to a degenerative kidney ailment known at the time as Bright's disease, but his chronic symptoms may also have stemmed from a diabetic condition. In either case, physicians of the period knew very little about the diseases in question. The doctors Homer consulted could at best offer only temporary and limited relief.[48]

Homer attended Occidental College in September 1896, taking classes comparable to those comprising a Harvard freshman's classical course. He hoped to transfer to Harvard as a sophomore the next school year, provided that his family's finances improved; but that was not to be. After completing his freshman year in June 1897, he altered his plans, deciding instead to finish his undergraduate work in California and study law at Harvard afterward.[49]

At Occidental, a school of not many more than a hundred students and faculty, Homer fit in well and furthered his reputation as a well-mannered and charismatic conversationalist. One classmate credited him as "a brilliant student—very genteel in appearance and a most gentlemanly manner . . . [and] well liked by all of the students and faculty."[50] He loved discussing history and world events and was often the center of attention. Another student recalled that it was not uncommon to see Homer sitting "in the center of a group of the 'boys,' during the noon hours, discussing the affairs of state and nation, he seemed to be always well-informed."[51] On other occasions he might be found participating in a spirited debate at nearby Central Square Park.[52]

Homer proved to be a more dedicated and well-rounded student at Occidental than he had proven to be in high school. For the first time he found a school sport, fencing, in which he could participate. He often could be found with a friend or two practicing in his spare time with mask and foil. As his self-confidence continued to grow, he entered school politics and won election to the Senate, the student governing body. Academically, the greater familiarity offered by a small school with small classes had a positive influence on his studies and consequently his grades.[53]

Homer developed a deeper interest in China while attending Occidental, perhaps prompted by his friendship with Theodore S. Chapin, who was born in China of missionary parents. He most likely discussed China at length with Homer.[54]

Debating remained one of Homer's favorite pastimes and he remained a moving force in the Lyceum movement. While at Occidental, he became the president of the Pacific Lyceum League, which included the clubs of southern California. Ermal recalled that he studied *Roberts Rules of Order* and parliamentary procedures "religiously" to prepare for debates.[55] In June 1897 he was honored to preside over the league's semiannual convention with Los Angeles mayor Meredith P. Snyder and other local officials in attendance. The *Los Angeles Times* reported on the event and Homer's leading role: "A pleasant feature of the evening was the presentation to President Homer Lea on behalf of the convention of a handsome gavel made of ebony and silver."[56] Homer may not have realized at the time that meeting Mayor Snyder and several other local officials would prove far more useful to him in the future than receiving an honorary gavel.

After completing his freshman year at Occidental in the spring of 1897, Homer looked for a new school. He had grown eager to experience some of the freedom his friends away at college had found. Although he could not afford to go to Harvard, he found an acceptable substitute at nearby Leland Stanford Jr. University in Palo Alto. There he could continue to prepare for a legal career. Stanford, established six years earlier, had quickly gained a reputation for attracting adventurous spirits, individualists, and eccentrics. Part of its appeal rested in its having one the largest endowments of any American university in that era and thus exacting no tuition fees. Another facet of its appeal was its extensive resources and facilities. All factors considered, it was an ideal choice for Homer. He had a respectable academic record and gained admittance to Stanford without much difficulty. The vice president of Occidental recommended him as an "unusually bright" student.[57]

By the time Homer entered Stanford, he had become adept at capitalizing on his assets and minimizing his liabilities. His involvement with the Lyceum League helped him build self-confidence and establish a widening network of potentially valuable contacts. His passions for poetry, literature, and history, meanwhile, fed his romantic desires for adventure. Whether he found thrill in the competition of a poker game or in vicarious dreams of far-off battlefields, activity was the key to his happiness. As he prepared to leave home, it was then unknown whether he would use his persuasive qualities to become an active leader at Stanford or choose to be a passive follower. He did not suspect that he was approaching a crossroads in his life that would have decisive consequences.

CHAPTER 2

IN THE DRAGON'S LAIR

The oddest career whose unfolding we saw at early Stanford
was that of Homer Lea.

—William Irwin

Lea attended Stanford until his health failed. Repeated absences from
the classroom due to illness and injury dampened his enthusiasm for
college life. He grew impatient during his forced inactivity and recuperation and found more exciting prospects to pursue than college.
The mysteries and intrigue of the Orient beckoned to him.

Lea had barely settled into the first semester of campus life at
Stanford before health issues intervened. Not many weeks after his
twenty-first birthday, and shortly before the end of the fall semester,
his headaches and eyesight worsened. He knew he could not endure
the semester. He also knew that to drop out and go back to Los Angeles and possibly Occidental might be an irreversible step away from his
goals. He decided on a pragmatic but difficult course of action. He
left the university temporarily to recuperate, taking incomplete grades
in half his courses.[1]

The treatment and rest Lea received over the Christmas break
enabled him to return to Stanford undaunted in late January 1898 to
take up where he had left off. By no means cured, however, he began
consulting a San Francisco physician in the hopes of stabilizing his
health enough to remain in school on a regular basis. He redoubled
his academic efforts and managed to handle the new semester course
load while successfully completing most of his delinquent fall course
work. However, even under a physician's care, the strain continued to
take its toll. Toward the end of the semester his eyes were in such a

poor condition that he could not use them for more than a few minutes at a time. Fortunately, he did not have to take a leave of absence again. He was determined to finish the semester. He underwent a series of nasal operations that helped his sight, and although he had to remain confined to his room for several days at a time, he did not have to leave the university.[2]

Lea enjoyed college life at Stanford despite his poor health. He majored in economics, with every intention of becoming a lawyer. He joined the Euphronia Literary Society, one of Stanford's premier debating clubs, and took up fencing again until severe headaches and eye trouble forced him to give it up. As a competitor, he held his own against some of the best fencers on campus. He also established himself with a new group of friends. His enthusiasm for discussion and his love of military history quickly earned him a place as one of Stanford's extraordinary and dynamic personalities.[3] Looking back on those early days at Stanford, writer William Irwin recalled Lea's passion, personality, and enigmatic qualities:

> [T]he oddest career whose unfolding we saw at early Stanford was that of Homer Lea. Pathetically hunchbacked, his torso seemed only a bulb fastened on to his legs and his face had that appearance of a wise child common among people with his affliction. For all that, he carried himself with a defiant dignity. He seemed to repel most advances towards intimacy, probably because he felt that pity prompted them. But he played chess, and so did I; that led to acquaintance. He was always drawing the analogy between chess and war. A clever move with his castle and, "see, I've brought my heavy artillery into action," he would say. I found then, that war was his hobby—our American Civil War especially. . . .
> A good fellow the College called him, but queer. Even his roommates did not pretend to understand him.[4]

While other students adorned their dormitory room walls with pictures of girls or sports figures, Lea preferred huge maps of the world on which he could play out his military fantasies. World events often carried him away to expound on wild ideas of international hemispheric wars and the impending sack of America by expanding predatory powers. He waged great world wars on his maps, using colored pins to mark the day-by-day movements of the military forces at his command. One week he might have masterminded a war between Japan and Germany and the next between China and America. Or another week the players might have been Russia and Great Britain in a contest for India as the prize. He often became so involved in his war games that it affected his moods. One classmate recalled that on the days, for instance, when Great Britain and the United States were ahead, he became "very exhilarated, like he might be Napoleon."[5] Yet on many days, he would be depressed and cynical, explaining, "[T]hings being the way they are with the people, the politicians, the pacifists, the clericalists, the Republic [the United States] and the Empire had to be behind."[6]

At the time, rapidly developing world events added fuel to Lea's burning desires. The sinking of the U.S. battleship *Maine* in February 1898 offered the American yellow press an ideal pretext to stir up war fever. The yellow press struck a responsive chord with Lea, who was already susceptible to the tunes of martial glory. Not only did he actively advocate militarism, he did so with a firm belief in the popular social Darwinist dogma of the day. Insofar as pacifists or clericalists inhibited America's martial development, he viewed them as weakening organisms in the body of the country.

His vigor and reputation as a militarist might have gone unnoticed amid the fevered clamor of the day. Yet, at Stanford, his militant beliefs sharply contrasted with President David Starr Jordan's emphatic and vociferous pacifist preaching. As one of America's leading pacifists and vice president of the newly organized Anti-Imperialist League, Jordan took every opportunity to mold Stanford in his image. He actively sponsored forums and seminars on campus to propagandize and educate the student body toward seeking civilized pacifist solutions to world problems. Against this backdrop, Lea stood out in refuting Jordan's beliefs, while at the same time furthering his own views with the student body.[7]

Lea enjoyed drinking, smoking, and playing cards when he was not fighting global wars on maps in his room or warning that Darwinist militancy was the only answer to America's survival. He became notorious as a poker player.[8] William Irwin's brother Wallace, who also attended Stanford, remembered Lea's reputation for socializing and interest in world affairs:

He was a quiet little chap, and talked rather large, as I recall, bombastic, you might say, but there was an earnestness about him that impressed one. Nobody ever regarded him as a warrior, for how could they? He chummed with what we called the Oregon bunch in college, fellows that came down from that State and kept together a good deal. . . . As it is, what I remember most vividly about him seems to be those poker parties to which he was always inviting the fellows. He was one of the coolest and best poker players I ever knew. He never took any part in sports, of course, except to ride a bicycle, but he loved to talk politics; world politics was his hobby at that time.[9]

While he may have been known as a big talker among his friends, he confided to only a few of them that his devotion to politics and military affairs reflected a new, secret ambition: to attend the U.S. Military Academy at West Point, New York, and become an army officer.[10]

When the Spanish-American War broke out in April 1898, Lea could only stand by and watch as a number of Stanford students went off to war, expecting the glory and adventure for which he longed. He joined a home defense cavalry troop sponsored by some local Palo Alto businessmen. With barely sixty men in the ranks, the Stanford military company drilled under the direction of a retired army officer every evening for about six weeks. Apparently, Dr. Jordan's pacifist influences prevailed on campus enough to inhibit a strong student association with the company. Its membership was far from enthusiastic. According to Wallace Irwin, "[I]t included about a thousand freaks, I think the lame, the halt and the blind and some ex-cowboys."[11] Nonetheless, Lea loved the experience, although it proved a brief one. The semester ended and the university adjourned for summer recess just a few weeks before Spain asked for peace terms in July.

Back in Los Angeles with his family for the summer, Lea devoured news coverage of the war, as well as writings on modern military policy and warfare. He found no shortage in literature and commentary. The war ushered in a wave of arguments justifying American imperialism. Concepts such as Manifest Destiny and Darwinist postulates of natural selection provided ample foundation for militarist and imperialist propaganda.

Representative of the commentary available were the works of Josiah Strong and Alfred Thayer Mahan. America's sense of mission was a dominant theme. In this context, Strong's celebrated 1885 essay

"Our Country," a popular and widely accepted argument for imperialism, depended on the belief that God had prepared the Anglo-Saxon countries of the world to rule all the other races on earth. Similar and often brutally frank views claimed an Anglo-Saxon right—indeed, a duty—to Christianize and civilize the "unpolitical and barbaric races," because the duty of the civilized state transcended all else.[12]

Another, more pragmatic theme won credence through America's premier naval historian and naval philosopher, Captain Alfred Thayer Mahan. He argued convincingly for American naval power and foreign policy tied to modern technology and American global interests. His book *The Influence of Sea Power upon History* (1890) proved to have far-reaching global consequences in describing the great world powers' trend toward an unprecedented naval expansion by the turn of the century. Also, his book *The Interest of America in Sea Power* (1897) specifically advocated an active American pursuit of overseas expansion and empire. While he occasionally resorted to Darwinist metaphors in his arguments, he incorporated such commentary to support his geopolitical security policy, rather than urging imperialism simply for the sake of survival of the fittest.[13]

In the summer of 1898 the economic and strategic potential of the Philippines and the Far East rose to the forefront of American commercial and naval concerns. Even as the war ended and the Monroe Doctrine was used to rationalize a new age in American policy in the Western Hemisphere, the spotlight remained fixed on the Far East. No sooner did Lea return to Stanford for the new fall semester than headlines of Oriental intrigue captured his attention.

A palace coup d'état in mid-September 1898, by the Chinese dowager empress Tzu Hsi, surprised the world by bringing an abrupt end to the rule and reforms of twenty-six-year-old Emperor Kwang-hsu. During that summer, in an effort to modernize China, the emperor instituted a series of progressive Western programs known as the Hundred Days' Reform. He followed the recent Japanese model, as well as the advice and guidance of his close advisor and well-known progressive reform leader and scholar K'ang Yu-wei, in trying to raise China out of the depths to which it had fallen under foreign partition and exploitation during the nineteenth century. These imperial reforms, however, proved too rapid and too liberal for powerful conservative opponents of the policy.[14]

The coup d'état placed the emperor under perpetual house arrest while his advisor K'ang Yu-wei barely escaped China with his life. He

fled the country with a price on his head and began a long and difficult quest for supporters among the world powers and his fellow Chinese with the goal of restoring the emperor to power. While his initial
appeals to the world powers proved fruitless, he found many overseas
Chinese sympathetic to his plans for the emperor's restoration. Yet,
turning their sympathy into constructive action would take time.[15]

Lea followed the events of the coup d'état with great interest.
He befriended Chinese in the vicinity of Stanford and the Bay Area,
including maids and cooks at the university, to discuss their country's events. The Chinese fired his imagination and gave him insights
into China's condition. The intensity of his interest grew. Before long
he began accompanying his new friends into San Francisco's Chinese
quarter.[16]

As the spring semester drew to a close, Lea managed to complete
all but one of his courses before a riding accident forced him to leave
the university prematurely. In early May 1899 he was riding in the
northern California mountains when an unruly horse crushed one of
his testicles, requiring immediate medical treatment. Stanford's school
physician arranged for "Mr. Lea to discontinue his work at once on
account of ill health."[17] Lea checked into San Francisco's Maclean
Hospital and had an operation to remove the damaged organ, but his
convalescence was complicated when he contracted a case of smallpox during an outbreak of the disease in the hospital. The situation
appeared dire, particularly since the outbreak reportedly killed a number of other patients and necessitated burning the infected building
to the ground by order of the Board of Health. According to Dr. Jordan, Stanford's president, Lea's physicians gave him only months to
live, and faced with such a prognosis he determined to seek adventure
in his remaining days. (It is unknown whether he actually did receive
such a prognosis, but it is certain that he did have plans for adventure.)
He recuperated at home, recovering without any scars, but instead of
returning to Stanford, he sued the hospital for negligence in exposing
him to smallpox. He hoped to win a sizable settlement so he could
purchase a yacht and sail around the world with a party of his friends.
Unfortunately, he lost the lawsuit.[18]

With leisure time on his hands, Lea satisfied part of his desire for
adventure by visiting Los Angeles's Chinese quarter, which proved
to have fateful consequences in reorienting his goals toward China.
Through his acquaintance with the Chinese he learned of the existence
of a recently organized secret society whose purpose was to restore the

Chinese emperor to the Ch'ing dynasty throne. K'ang Yu-wei helped establish this secret society, called the Pao Huang Hui (Protect the Emperor Society; also known as the Chinese Empire Reform Association), during the course of his international travels to solicit aid from foreign governments to restore the young emperor to power. While traveling in Canada, he and his followers formed the Pao Huang Hui in July 1899, to mobilize overseas Chinese money and manpower to assist in the emperor's restoration.[19]

Initially, K'ang Yu-wei believed that the Pao Huang Hui's goals could be accomplished only by raising an army to attack his opponents in China if his efforts at international diplomacy failed to restore the emperor to power. He therefore envisioned the Pao Huang Hui merely as a short-term expedient to raise the necessary money and manpower for his plans. K'ang Yu-wei believed that once the emperor had regained power, his own prominence as an imperial advisor, with the resources of the empire at his disposal, would preclude any further need for his secret society. Meanwhile, branches of the Pao Huang Hui gradually spread throughout the world, wherever a concentration of overseas Chinese lived, eventually claiming several million members worldwide.[20]

Lea heard of the society's cause through acquaintance with several of its members and soon saw the opportunity of a lifetime for himself. Here was the chance for Asian adventure that he and Stimson had dreamed of earlier. Now, however, he could go much further and turn his Napoleonic dreams into reality. Excluded from any hope of American military service, either in the Spanish-American War or in the future, he realized he could fulfill his dreams of glory and adventure by helping the Chinese reform party restore Emperor Kwang-hsu to the throne. He was undaunted by his tenuous health and physical restrictions. He was willing to gamble that the adventure would be worth the risk and offered his allegiance and support to the Pao Huang Hui cause. He reportedly formed a group of Stanford students to aid this cause and was not above resorting to duplicity and deception in furthering his ambitions, including keeping his plans secret from his family.[21]

Lea's Chinese contacts in Los Angeles welcomed his offers to help. He succeeded in impressing them with his concern for their cause and assured them that as a student of history and war he could be a valuable asset in the Pao Huang Hui's struggle. He discounted his physical handicaps and convinced them he possessed extraordinary abilities as a military strategist and leader akin to Napoleon. He helped the credibility of his case by falsely claiming the great Confederate army general Robert E. Lee as a relative from whom he inherited his martial insight. Lea's immodest claims notwithstanding, the Chinese reformers appreciated the concern of almost any Caucasian in their cause. At a time when racial bigotry, repressive Chinese exclusion laws, and discrimination marked the treatment of Chinese in America, Lea's interest in their cause appeared extraordinary.[22]

For example, Dr. Tom Leung, an affluent herbal doctor and leading Los Angeles reformer, praised Lea to other Pao Huang Hui leaders such as Chen Lusheng, the leader of the Yokohama, Japan, chapter. Chen Lusheng replied that Lea could be beneficial to their cause:

> In the last few months the Pao Huang Hui has gained much strength and momentum. . . . We need to raise funds and find qualified people. . . .
>
> According to your letter, Kan Ma Li [Homer Lea] is really a talented and rare person. Today we have to utilize strength from abroad. Lea not only understands military matters but also has a mind to help us. Why don't you simply tell him what our party is doing and ask him whether he can recruit American soldiers to help us when the opportunity arises. If our cause succeeds, they will be rewarded with rights in China, such as mines and railroads. If he agrees, ask him to see the Elder [K'ang Yu-wei] to discuss it when he has a chance to travel here.[23]

When not lobbying Chinese reformers, Lea prepared himself for a great adventure. He spent his idle afternoons on Westlake Park's lawns reading military history and occasionally laying out troop formations with toothpicks in the grass. He mentioned nothing about joining the Pao Huang Hui cause to his family, which frowned on his association with the reformers. Instead, he explained that his military books were part of his Stanford course work.[24]

Since the Pao Huang Hui did not yet have a branch in Los Angeles, Lea set his sights on joining its only California branch in San Francisco. Tom Tsai Hin, a prominent Los Angeles reformer, helped arrange Lea's introduction to Pao Huang Hui leaders in San Francisco. His overwhelming faith and confidence in Lea paved the way for a meeting. He provided Lea with letters of introduction singing his praises to the Pao Huang Hui's most important leaders in both San Francisco and Asia (see appendix A). Ironically, when Lea, who did not speak conversational Chinese fluently, arrived in San Francisco in early March looking for the reformers, he could not find them. He turned to Ng Poon Chew, who had recently moved to San Francisco to become the managing editor of a Chinese-language newspaper sympathetic to the Pao Huang Hui. Ng Poon Chew interceded on Lea's behalf and arranged for his introduction and admission to the local Pao Huang Hui chapter.[25] He explained that "after much consultation among the leaders in San Francisco," they decided to send Lea to China secretly as a "foreign advisor" and "paid all his fare to Hong Kong and enough to last him for a few months."[26]

Lea's decision to drop out of Stanford, forego a legal career, and take part in an Asian adventure astonished his family and friends. They found incredible the idea that he would be some type of Napoleon for the Chinese reformers. His sisters pleaded with him not to go off seeking glory when his health was so fragile, and his father threatened to cut off his allowance if he persisted in such a scheme. But Lea's mind was made up. He was determined to have his way. His stock answer to all efforts to restrain him reportedly was: "A man never dies until his work is done."[27]

Lea's friends were no less incredulous than his family when he told them that instead of returning to Stanford, he not only intended to go to China, but he intended to become a general and play an important role in shaping that country's affairs. Wallace Irwin noted: "He was cool and calm when he made this remarkable assertion, as cool as when he held four aces in the poker game that went on much of the time in his room in the dormitory at the university. He was better known as a good poker player at college than for any other quality."[28] Lea dismissed pessimistic warnings from his friends. The thought of potential danger and violence did not concern him. When Newmark warned him that he would probably have his head cut off in China, Lea's reply was curt and flippant: "Fortunately, they'll have a hard time finding my neck."[29]

Lea did not confide his intentions to many people. Those who were his confidants believed he was motivated by a sense of destiny or a desire for military adventure. He was no longer interested in a law career. According to high school friend and journalist Harry C. Carr: "Blackstone [a popular legal text] held no thrill for him. He had determined to be a world figure; and world figures are carved out with swords. He said that he felt that some time in some way, his chance would come."[30] Van Loan speculated:

> Perhaps Homer himself never really understood the influences which drew him eastward. Few of his friends ever heard him speak of them, but once, in a rare burst of confidence, he said: "I knew there would be a chance to get in somewhere. Whenever there is fighting, there are opportunities for leadership. China seemed to me to be the best chance in the world at that time. . . ."
>
> It is certain that the little General's firm belief in destiny played an important part in his life: certain also that in his mind China and his future were closely allied. It was this belief in destiny which drove him.[31]

Carr agreed with Van Loan's observations:

> Lea believed that he was under the protection of a mystic destiny; that he had, in a previous incarnation, been a Chinese in a high position, . . . his military genius a hold-over, perhaps from another life . . . now returning to take up his unfinished work. The Chinese also seemed to share this faith. Homer told me that his life had been largely influenced by a recurrent dream. It first came to his sleep when he was seven years old; perhaps a little younger. In the dream he saw strange men and heard strange sounds and was conscious of the tumult of battle. When he was twelve, the identical dream came again. He was, by then, old enough to recognize the strange men in his dream as Chinese soldiers. The same dream came again when he was about sixteen. This time he identified the terrifying sounds as Chinese war trumpets. He told me that he knew that this dream was the signpost of his destiny. Some day he felt confident that he would see the identical scene of the dream, he would then know that his destiny had been fulfilled.[32]

Newmark believed Lea operated under a belief in the romantic tradition, which helped to rationalize his acquired sense of mission:

> In the first place he was deeply inspired by Lord Byron's romantic adventures in connection with the freeing of Greece.

In the second place he became intimate at Stanford with a Chinese student who passionately desired the release of his people from autocratic rule, and I am inclined to believe that this was the most potent influence which urged him on to his Oriental career. The third factor, however, had a great deal to do with the decision, namely, that Homer believed that all great careers had been carved out by the sword and he thought that somehow he would carve out such a career for himself. In this connection, I recall also that he considered himself to have been marked out by Destiny—an opinion that certainly was not lessened when a Theosophist in his youth told him that he was the reincarnation of a former king.[33]

When Lea arrived in San Francisco in early March 1900, Dr. T'an Shu-pin (known as Tom She Bin), an affluent herb doctor and president of the city's reform association, and other prominent reformers welcomed him with open arms. He stayed at San Francisco's luxurious Palace Hotel, with all expenses paid by the Pao Huang Hui, and received the respect and treatment due a distinguished and valuable member of the organization. Whether guided by destiny or personal ambition, he lived up to the image he created for the Chinese and even started believing in his own fabrications. The Chinese, in turn, viewed him as their American Lafayette and Napoleon rolled into one. Acting in the tradition of the famous British general Charles "Chinese" Gordon, who transformed a Chinese rabble army into an effective fighting force during the 1863–64 Taiping Rebellion, Lea made a strong impression on his Asian benefactors with his assurances of similar success.[34]

The reformers were so impressed by Lea that on the evening of March 16 they gave a banquet in his honor. The Chinese, including Ng Poon Chew, sat in eager silence as Lea laid out his plans through an interpreter. He proposed beginning military operations against China from either the British colony of Hong Kong or the Portuguese colony of Macao, and he offered, if given complete command of all military forces, to train and equip these forces to modern standards, as well as to furnish enough qualified Western officers to lead them to victory.[35]

A little more than a month after Lea joined the Pao Huang Hui and began preparing for his secret trip to China, however, misfortune struck. Word leaked out to the press, possibly from one of Lea's acquaintances, that he and the Pao Huang Hui planned to launch an armed insurrection against the dowager empress. On April 22, 1900, the *San Francisco Call* printed a startling front-page story entitled "Young Californian Is Plotting to Become Commander-in-Chief of Chinese Rebel Forces," which revealed Lea's complicity with the Pao Huang Hui and his military plans as he had outlined them at the banquet. Ho Yow, the Chinese consul general in San Francisco, promptly condemned Lea and the other plotters and warned that his government was taking new precautions against their activities (see appendix B).[36]

The *Call* article seemed to seriously damage Lea's expectations and covert plans by reporting:

> [T]he trump card which the society [Pao Huang Hui] is preparing to play—is its new acquisition, an American citizen. Homer Lea has joined hands with the Chinese revolutionists. Homer Lea, well up in military affairs, claiming a military ancestry back through all American wars, is the masterpiece of conversation. The importance of gaining such a member is so great that the president [K'ang Yu-wei] at Macao is looking at the California achievement. . . . Mr. Lea is about to pack his steamer trunk for Hong Kong. Once inside China he expects to become commander-in-chief of the revolutionary forces and to have 20,000 men turned over to him to be drilled. . . . Homer Lea will be rewarded if he and the revolution are successful. He will be a great man in China and there will be plums in his path to be picked up.
>
> Meanwhile the local leaders feel that their success is now assured—now that an American military man is working with them.[37]

The *Call* article went further than describing Lea as a Stanford University student merely assisting the Pao Huang Hui, elaborating on how Lea, in the highest tradition of soldiers of fortune and filibusters of the period, was planning to organize and lead a regiment of American ex-soldiers in his scheme to restore the emperor to power. Ironically, the publicity generated by the article reportedly resulted in Lea receiving hundreds of letters from those seeking to enlist in his military force, ranging from soldiers of fortune to retired military officers.[38]

Lea and the Pao Huang Hui were not the only proponents of Chinese rebellion and reform in the spring of 1900. K'ang Yu-wei's popular reform movement found ready competition from a revolutionary movement led by Dr. Sun Yat-sen. After devoting his efforts to peaceful Chinese reform in the early 1890s, Dr. Sun Yat-sen, a Western-educated physician, resolved that only a revolution overthrowing the Ch'ing dynasty and establishing a republic could adequately reconstruct China and preserve its independence from internal corruption and foreign domination. After China's disastrous performance in the Sino-Japanese War (1894–95), K'ang Yu-wei's calls for reform and Sun Yat-sen's calls for revolution swept through China. Sun Yat-sen, a Christianized Chinese, at first sought aid primarily from Christian converts, overseas Chinese, and various Chinese secret societies. In late 1894 he sought support among Hawaii's overseas Chinese and organized the revolutionary Hsing-Chung Hui (Revive China Society). Then, shortly after the end of the Sino-Japanese War in September 1895, his new party launched an unsuccessful revolutionary attempt in Canton, China. He thereafter devoted his efforts unceasingly to the revolutionary cause.[39]

When Sun Yat-sen approached K'ang Yu-wei's Pao Huang Hui organization proposing that they unite forces to overthrow the Ch'ing dynasty, he found their ideological differences too wide to bridge. For one thing, K'ang Yu-wei's party, supported by the scholar and gentry classes, looked down on Sun Yat-sen's party, which was composed largely of rural and poorly educated Chinese. In addition, K'ang Yu-wei's party fervently believed that a democratic republic would be disastrous for a largely illiterate and uneducated China. For the most part, K'ang Yu-wei's movement favored reform from the top down while Sun Yat-sen's movement favored revolution from below. With these differences separating them, K'ang Yu-wei boasted wider support and more resources than Sun Yat-sen, and he sharply rebuffed Sun Yat-sen's revolutionary program as excessive and unrealistic. K'ang Yu-wei and his supporters believed that only a reformed constitutional Ch'ing monarchy could solve China's problems.[40]

The publicity from the *Call* article did not cause Lea to cancel his covert mission to China. A few weeks after the article's release, an armed insurrection by a third disgruntled party broke out in China. In May 1900 a Chinese secret society called the I-ho Ch'uan, or the Society of Righteous and Harmonious Fists, launched a campaign of anti-foreign terror in China. Members of an organization that practiced old-style calisthenics, the "Boxers," as they were otherwise known, traced their lineage originally to an eighteenth-century anti-dynastic secret society. However, in the late 1890s they changed their focus to react to an immediate external threat to China's national integrity. In the face of domination and humiliation from foreign powers, strong anti-foreign sentiment permeated the Ch'ing court and China as a whole. High-handed foreign ministers, aggressive missionaries, and the formalization of foreign economic exploitation through the American-inspired Open Door policy served as constant reminders to the Chinese of their national misfortune. Against this backdrop and in light of larger social, economic, political, and religious factors, the Ch'ing court solicited Boxer support in righting the injustice perpetrated by the foreigners and channeling revenge in a Boxer-led anti-foreign movement.[41]

When the Boxer Rebellion broke out, the Pao Huang Hui saw new hope for its plans to restore the emperor to power. With the dowager empress a motivating force behind the uprising and the major world powers sending troops to quell the rebellion and protect their interests, K'ang Yu-wei and the Pao Huang Hui believed that further appeals to the powers to restore the emperor and bring reform to China might at last be heeded. The chaos and confusion in China during the rebellion created an excellent opportunity for the Pao Huang Hui to send a military expedition to depose the dowager empress and restore the young emperor to the throne. Not surprisingly, Sun Yat-sen's revolutionaries also planned independently to take advantage of the chaos to topple the Ch'ing dynasty.[42]

Meanwhile, K'ang Yu-wei and his staff in Singapore had begun planning and coordinating with their overseas Pao Huang Hui branches in preparation for their armed uprising against the dowager empress, which was to be launched in southern China. While funds came in from the overseas Chinese, contacts were made with some of the most powerful secret societies in China, which promised to employ their best fighting men in the uprising. Furthermore, the reformers arranged purchases of secondhand rifles and artillery from the Japanese; and they also negotiated with Philippine revolutionary leader Emilio Aguinaldo to discuss the possibility of enlisting Filipino mercenaries.[43]

The fact that Lea's mission was no longer a secret did not alter his plans to play an active role in the Chinese reform uprising. Exactly what role he would play had yet to be decided by K'ang Yu-wei and the Pao Huang Hui leadership. The decision would be made later in the summer of 1900. Until then, Lea entertained visions of fantasy, hoping to organize and lead a force of American soldiers of fortune in the uprising. With that end in mind, he raised some additional funds by selling some San Jose real estate, which may have been a gift from his grandmother, and he solicited potential recruits from Stanford and filtered through the array of unsolicited offers from adventurers, ex-servicemen, and soldiers of fortune he had received.[44]

It is unknown how many people Lea recruited for his plans. He evidently had some success with his acquaintances at Stanford. In late June another *Call* article revealed: "Many of his fellow students at Stanford, it is stated on reliable authority, and at least one professor, have agreed to follow him to China when the call comes."[45]

Lea boarded the steamship *China* in San Francisco on June 22, 1900, destined for Asia with little fanfare and few good-byes. To the casual observer his departure did not appear different from that of the many other American college students of the day adventuring to far-off lands as idealistic missionaries or aspiring civil engineers. Waving good-bye to a few friends from the deck of the ship, Lea allegedly shouted, "I've got business over there. You'll hear about it later."[46]

The following day the San Francisco *Call* publicized Lea's departure in a front-page article entitled, "Homer Lea, a Stanford Student, Sails for China with a Big Sum of Money Collected for the Purpose of Raising an Army to Outwit the Dowager Empress." The article characterized him as a Pao Huang Hui secret agent, alleging that he carried $60,000 that would be used to outfit a reform army in China. Of particular significance, Lea's notoriety began transcending local and regional news. The *Call* story also ran in the *New York Herald,* which included a photo of Lea with a caption that read, "Secret Agent of Chinese Reform Society."[47]

Lea's decision to leave Stanford and pursue a romantic Napoleonic dream against his family's wishes demonstrated his impatience, his reckless independence, and his determination to fulfill a destiny of his own design. He was not above resorting to deception to further his ambitions and relied heavily on his oratorical skills, powers of persuasion, and keen grasp of military history to promote himself. Despite his military inexperience, the Chinese reformers in California believed he was a military genius who had connections with the Western servicemen and soldiers of fortune necessary to carry out his ambitious plans. Lea was beginning to see his vicarious war games become reality; fulfilling his Napoleonic ambitions, however, would be a different story.

CHAPTER 3

A DON QUIXOTE IN CHINA

Lt. General Homer Lea, Kwangtung China, August 1900.
—Inscription on Lea's military baton

As Lea sailed toward Asia, he aspired to play a significant role in the upcoming Pao Huang Hui uprising. He envisioned that if the uprising succeeded, the reform party might reward his services with a high position in the reformed imperial Chinese army. His enthusiasm helped compensate for his lack of experience, while concurrently there was no place in his thinking for the idea of failure. Although his hopes for glory and adventure in China would fail to materialize as he anticipated, undaunted, he would impetuously embark on another path of opportunity.

K'ang Yu-wei welcomed news of Lea's impending arrival despite the sensational publicity surrounding his covert involvement with the reformers. He wrote Dr. Tom Leung that he was concerned Lea was not getting paid enough for his service since the reformers were low on funds. He believed the Pao Huang Hui uprising, in conjunction with Western forces battling the Boxers, would likely succeed in restoring the emperor to power and improve their finances so they could better compensate Lea.[1]

Lea's ship made port calls in Hawaii, the Philippines, Japan, and China before reaching Hong Kong. During the stop at Yokohama, Japan, on July 11, 1900, he met briefly with Chen Lusheng to receive further instructions. Chen Lusheng gave him $200 at the request of the San Francisco reformers, and a letter of introduction for his intended meeting with K'ang Yu-wei. He sailed the following day for Nagasaki, where a typhoon delayed his journey for several days. There, he unexpectedly crossed paths with Dr. Jordan, Stanford University's president, who was astonished to find him in Japan acting as a Pao Huang Hui representative. Jordan knew little or nothing of his military plans and Lea was not above resorting to deception in explaining his actions. All he would tell Jordan was he that he was going to the American embassy in Tokyo, more than seven hundred miles away, to plead with U.S. minister Alfred E. Buck "to induce the powers of Europe to intervene in behalf of the lawful Emperor of China as against the Dowager Empress."[2] Jordan did not know that Lea had no intention of traveling to Tokyo, or that he was sailing the following day, July 15, on the next leg of his journey.[3]

Lea arrived in Hong Kong a few days later and conferred with the reformers. He next traveled to meet K'ang Yu-wei in Singapore. It is unclear what transpired between Lea and K'ang Yu-wei when they met or how long Lea stayed in Singapore. He evidently returned to Hong Kong in late July to participate in war councils there and at Macao that arranged for raising an army and launching the Pao Huang Hui uprising. Much to his dismay, he may not have received the reception he expected. As they sized Lea up, the reform leaders were evidently more circumspect in their scrutiny of him than had been their enthusiastic California members. They appear to have developed serious reservations about entrusting a self-promoting twenty-three-year-old American without any formal military experience with a prominent leadership role in their army. They were in a delicate position. Unmoved by Lea's claims of military aptitude and competence, they pursued a pragmatic course that avoided offending him and their well-intentioned California members while utilizing his desires to assist their movement. They clearly decided not to adopt his ambitious plans for an uprising, nor did they include him in their own primary operational plans. Instead, they gave him a relatively unimportant assignment in the Chinese interior, which included a promise of a general's commission in their army in return for his services.[4]

Lea may have interpreted his impending promotion to general as an acknowledgment of his military credentials rather than realizing he was being patronized by the reform leadership. Forever eager to prove his worth to the reform leaders, he contrived an alternative military strategy for them to consider after he learned there was no place in the existing plans for him to lead a regiment of American mercenaries. In his new strategy, he proposed forming an alliance with Sun Yat-sen's party and launching an uprising from Macao, using American mercenaries to lead the reform army.

Meanwhile, the Chinese government kept a watchful on Lea and the reformers. On July 29 Ho Yow, the Chinese consul general in San Francisco, revealed additional information about their military plans to the press. Several newspapers across the country reported Ho Yow's revelations: "A few months ago a young man named Lee [*sic*], a graduate of Stanford University, started for China, presumably to lead the revolutionary party. Documents were discovered to prove his mission and to connect him with this Reform Association. . . . The plan of Lee and his Chinese schemers was to raise an army of 40,000 malcontents in the southern treaty ports of the empire and march to Peking. It was not long ago that we succeeded in intercepting at Canton more than 4,000 uniforms intended for this reform army."[5]

It did not take long for news of Lea's presence and provocative proposals to reach Sir Henry Blake, governor of Hong Kong. Lea's nerve in fomenting a rebellion in China astounded Blake, as did his choice of a British crown colony as the site of his machinations. Blake, in his duties as governor, kept abreast of all activities related to Britain's security and interests in the region. Naturally, as the Pao Huang Hui began to rely on the protection and sanctity of Britain's crown colony to plan and organize aggressive operations against the recognized Chinese government, he kept the Foreign Office in London well informed. Lea's entrance into this arena of conspiracy served only to heighten British concern. If the young American adventurer's activities threatened British interests, something would have to be done.

For the time being, however, Lea posed no threat. The Pao Huang Hui listened to his new plans, but again declined to accept them. According to Blake's report to the Foreign Office, Lea proposed uniting K'ang Yu-wei's and Sun Yat-sen's forces in a coalition to seize Canton, the provincial capital of southern Kwangtung province, and from there to annex all the provinces south of the Yangtze River, which divided northern and southern China. American mercenaries would lead a twenty-five-thousand-man Chinese invasion force from Macao, assuming the authorities there could be bribed and an understanding reached with the Portuguese governor based on some type of territorial compensation. Canton's governor and military commander were to be captured and forced to order the surrender of all civil and military authority. After Canton was taken, the reformers planned to notify the Western powers of their goals and guarantee the safety and protection of all foreigners and Christians. Blake added that Lea was pressing for immediate action in the belief that the powers were too engaged with the Boxers in northern China to interfere in the south. He also noted that on July 30, Lea and members of Sun Yat-sen's party met with K'ang Yu-wei's representatives in Macao to discuss organizing a coalition, but the latter refused any cooperation with the former. Blake dismissed the prospects of either party having the necessary forces on hand or ready to conduct such large-scale military operations and concluded that Lea's "plan of campaign is in my opinion mere vapouring."[6]

The British authorities did not detain Lea, nor did they publicly reveal his plot. The potential involvement of an American adventurer was just one more variable for them to weigh in planning their regional security.

Lea's provocative strategy aside, the reformers planned to launch their uprising primarily along the Yangtze River provinces with an army they claimed numbered more than one hundred thousand men, divided into five major commands. The linchpin of their plan was to win cooperation and support from the Western powers and Japan once their military operations offered a probability of success. After seizing portions of China, largely in the south, they would seek assistance from the powers in reinstating the emperor under a joint protectorate.[7]

For all intents and purposes, the reformers' proposal sacrificed much of the emperor's sovereignty to the powers in return for allowing him to reign under their joint protectorate. In July 1900, the Pao Huang Hui sent a petition to President William McKinley and the monarchs of Great Britain, Germany, and Japan. The reformers sought support and elaborated on their offer of a deal to the powers, asserting that "the Emperor Kwang-hsu has published a message in which he proposed that certain of the Powers should aid in reinstating him on the Throne, and should declare a joint Protectorate and undertake the government of the country through the Emperor."[8]

The reform leaders hoped the revolt, scheduled to start simultaneously in the Yangtze River provinces of Anhwei, Hunan, Hupeh, and Chekiang, would swell into a general uprising against the dowager empress's government. Once their main military forces came into play, smaller units of the reform army scattered about the provinces south of the Yangtze River were to assist in sparking a general revolt. Even though many of these smaller units were little more than bands of unarmed peasants and farmers, the reformers understood the political value of building grassroots support for their cause. It was in this arena that Lea was slated to play a minor but potentially significant role within the overall reform plan: his mission was to help generate this grassroots support.[9]

After Lea left Macao at the end of July, the reform leadership sent him into the interior of the southern Chinese provinces of Kwangtung and Kwangsi to help recruit and train any troops he could muster for the intended general uprising. Lea, accompanied by two officers who acted as aides and translators, soon learned the limitations of both his mission and his abilities. Essentially, he was unsuited for the challenge and made poor progress at best. The politically unsophisticated rural Chinese of the interior were slow to join a cause they knew very little about and the new recruits Lea did manage to enlist were handled ineffectively due to his inexperience and ignorance of the local language.[10]

With no practical experience to draw on, Lea's efforts at training and leadership faded in the face of reality. He went through the motions of his job, blaming his problems more on the backwardness of the rural Chinese than on his own shortcomings, of which he took little notice. He later explained:

> The difficulties in massing and drilling troops are great. In town and country both, every available foot of land is put to some use. The houses encroach upon the streets until there is but room for the basket-bearers to pass. In the country the farmers plant their crops up to the edge of the traveled paths, and none of them are wider than is necessary to accommodate the traffic.
>
> A lack of knowledge of recent events on the part of many of the people also renders long and tedious explanations necessary, for they are without exception fond of details and minutiae but with a patience for listening that is consoling.[11]

Lea found some solace in receiving his general's commission on August 13, 1900. The only extant record of the event is an eighteen-inch-long wood and steel baton with both a Chinese and English inscription. The English inscription reads: "Lt. General Homer Lea, Kwangtung China, August 1900."[12] The baton attests to the time and place that Lea earned his general's title. Unfortunately, nothing else is known of the circumstances, except for his dubious claim to have been given responsibility for recruiting and training over the vast area of both the Kwangtung and Kwangsi provinces. In any event, Lea spent barely two weeks at these fruitless duties before a drastic turn of events led him to abort them.

Due to a misunderstanding in orders, one of K'ang Yu-wei's military commanders at Ta'tung in northern Shansi province began fighting prematurely, launching his portion of the reform uprising in early August 1900. While the Boxers laid siege to the foreign legations in Peking, the imperial authorities quickly put down the Ta'tung revolt and soon learned of its counterparts. Furthermore, within a few days of this action, the allied powers' military forces relieved their besieged legations at Peking, forcing the dowager empress and her court to retreat about five hundred miles southwest to the provincial capital of Sian in Shensi province. The immediate results of both these actions proved disastrous for the Pao Huang Hui's plans. With the element of surprise gone, the emperor still remained an out-of-reach captive under the dowager empress's control.[13]

When word filtered down to Lea that the Pao Huang Hui plans for a wide-scale uprising were in jeopardy, he may have realized there was no further point to his recruiting and training mission. Apparently acting on his own, he decided to pursue a bolder plan of action. With his general's baton in hand, he made arrangements to join the Pao Huang Hui's military force at Hankow, the provincial capital of central Hupeh province, while it sought to salvage victory from defeat. Although the chances seemed slim, the Pao Huang Hui command believed the Hankow force might still be able to engage the dowager's forces at Sian and free the emperor. Lea embarked in a palanquin, accompanied by two bearers and his two officers, on the beginning of a nearly eight-hundred-mile trek to join the Hankow force.[14]

Lea hoped to arrive on the scene of battle and help save the day for the reformers. Unfortunately, distance, time, and the rapidity with which events unfolded worked against him. Approaching within one hundred miles of his destination and the reform troops, he learned of the betrayal of the Hankow reform command and the leaders' arrest and execution by the Ch'ing authorities.[15]

Although all seemed lost, Lea's faith in his fantasies and his destiny convinced him there was still a chance to rescue the emperor. He was undaunted, although his efforts to date had been futile and the only information he had with which to formulate a plan was weeks old. As a general, he believed he could assume command of the lead-erless Hankow force and reaffirm the Pao Huang Hui mission to free the emperor. He prepared to embark single-handedly on an adventure he thought would be decisive for China in the outcome of the Boxer Rebellion. He dispatched a courier to the Hankow reform troops in their mountain camps with orders to await his arrival. Again his efforts proved fruitless. The courier arrived at the camp only to discover that the reform force had been dispersed days earlier by the Ch'ing army.[16]

Lea concocted yet another plan. Little is known of its details except that he and his aides believed they might somehow arrange to intercept the dowager's court on its flight to Shensi province and then some-how kidnap the dowager. For whatever reasons, however, Lea and his aides apparently got only as far as Honan province before aborting their scheme. Lea's friend Harry Carr gleaned what little light there is on this episode from a later conversation with Lea. According to Carr: "One of the most dramatic episodes in [Lea's] life in China was when, during the Boxer Rebellion, he and two Chinese determined upon the startling idea of kidnapping the Empress as she was fleeing with scanty escort. . . . The attempt was made, but by the interference of their own men who did not understand the move and who could not be trusted with the tremendous secret the plan failed."[17] In all probability Lea gave friends such as Carr exaggerated and understated accounts of his Asian sojourn to disguise his mistakes and failures.

There is little question that with the Pao Huang Hui uprising a failure, General Lea found himself in a tenuous and potentially dan-gerous situation. Following the destruction of the Hankow reform command, the Ch'ing authorities began a wholesale roundup of K'ang Yu-wei's reform associates in China and any members of the secret societies involved in the uprising. More than one thousand men, ranging from local civil officials down to school students, faced arrest, imprisonment, and possible execution. With this persecution extend-ing through the majority of the southern provinces, Lea's complicity in the attempted regrouping of the Hankow reform force soon earned him the distinction of being a fugitive with a price on his head. It also became clear that the interior of China offered him little hope of successful refuge. The limited evidence available suggests that at this juncture he went farther north toward Peking, where the reformers still had some military forces, before heading south for safety. There is no indication that he ever linked up with the reform forces in the north. Instead, he and his aides probably decided that the international port city of Shanghai in eastern Kiangsu province offered the best chances for their survival. There, Lea could maintain anonymity and thus safety among the numerous European and American residents, at least until pressure from the Ch'ing authorities dissipated.[18]

The length of Lea's stay and his associations in Shanghai are largely unknown. One man, Edward "Tex" O'Reilly, an American soldier of fortune and adventurer, then on the Shanghai police force, recalled thirty-five years later that he had met Lea there. Although O'Reilly's account is sketchy and marred by inaccuracies, it is possible he and Lea met and lived together for a time in Shanghai.[19]

Lea, living in seclusion in Shanghai, knew he could serve no further constructive purpose as a recruiter and trainer for the reform movement, nor hope to remain for long an isolated outlaw without any means of support. The alternative he favored was to return to Kwangtung province, possibly to assist in some further Pao Huang Hui operations there, or at least to receive the organization's assistance in returning to San Francisco.

In October 1900 Lea and his aides returned to Kwangtung province and found a new wave of revolutionary upheaval directed against the Ch'ing regime. This insurrection, however, was sponsored not by the Pao Huang Hui but by Dr. Sun Yat-sen's movement to topple the Ch'ing dynasty. As far as is known, Lea did not witness or take part in any of the engagements between Sun Yat-sen's forces and the dowager's imperial troops. He did, however, survey at least one of the rebel battlefields after a rebel victory. Sometime after the October 11 battle at the city of Po-Lo, about seventy-five miles southwest of Canton, he walked along the deserted battlefield and picked up a souvenir or two before continuing his travels.[20]

When Lea reported to the Pao Huang Hui in Kwangtung province he may have optimistically entertained hopes of getting a new command. Although the failure of the reform uprising to date divided party opinion on the efficacy of using armed force to achieve its goals, certain reform factions advocated rebuilding an army for future military operations. Lea likely conferred with the latter about recruiting and training such a force. Despite its recent military failures, the Pao Huang Hui still enjoyed a large reservoir of sentiment in its favor and support for its cause in the southern provinces. From this reservoir, militant reform leaders and Lea may have believed it was possible to organize a new army.[21]

In the wake of his futile wanderings, Lea was ever anxious for another opportunity to ply his alleged military talents. The political, military, and economic difficulties the reformers faced did not dissuade him. He was prepared to stay in China for an extended period to help organize a new reform army. Unfortunately, mobilizing another army required resources and a consensus of opinion that the Pao Huang Hui now lacked. Lea, however, appears to have kept his romantic visions of adventure alive by pushing for the reorganization of the reform army for a later date. Whatever challenges the future held, he stood ready to assist in organizing a new reform army.[22]

By the end of the year, both reformers and revolutionaries faced an uncertain future if caught and arrested. The remaining reform forces reportedly numbered approximately twelve thousand poorly trained and poorly armed troops, and these were crushed in a final battle on December 18 in a section of central China's Yangtze Valley. The fortunes of Sun Yat-sen's rebels also worsened after their resistance in Kwangtung province ended.[23]

With no further reason for staying in China, Lea knew he had to get out of the country if he was to ever realize his dreams of participating in the organization of a new reform army. Relying on his speaking knowledge of French, he sought to leave from China in the guise of a French missionary to elude detection and arrest by the Ch'ing authorities. His disguise worked. After spending approximately four months in China, he left unhindered.[24]

What transpired next during Lea's travels in Asia remains shrouded in speculation and mystery. His vanity may account for the secrecy that he would forever attach to these exploits. Surviving records offer only glimpses into his Asian sojourn. Aside from the occasional letter to his family or the rare conversation during a chance encounter with a fellow American, Lea allowed little to be known about where he was or what he was doing with the Pao Huang Hui. In addition to meeting Tex O'Reilly, there is evidence that he crossed paths at least twice with other Americans who relayed information about him back to the United States. On both occasions, Lea's secretive nature encouraged speculation about his mysterious activities in China among friends and acquaintances. The Irwin brothers recalled that both episodes involved a Stanford alumnus. Wallace Irwin recounted: "The first news came in a letter from a student who had gone as a missionary. Away back in Honan province a white man had applied for lodging for the night at the mission house. A young missionary went over to see the man and found it was Homer Lea. He could not get a word out of him as to what he was doing in that strange part of the world and the next morning he was gone."[25] William Irwin added:

> I was out in the world when one of our Stanford mining engineers—"Red" Wilson, I think—returned to San Francisco with an odd story. He was exploring formations to westward of Peking when runners brought word that the Boxers had risen against all Europeans. He started for Peking. That night he lodged at the compound of a friendly mandarin. Next morning as he was saddling for what he knew to be the most dangerous stretch of his journey, out of a door came a white hunchback who addressed him by name. "I've never had the pleasure of meeting you," said this stranger, "but I'm a Stanford man myself. Homer Lea, ex-'99—and I know all about you. Don't be worried about your trip to Peking. Word has gone on ahead, and you won't be molested." They chatted a little about acquaintances at Stanford. Then the hunchback, assuring him again that his way to Peking was guarded and greased, excused himself and disappeared.[26]

With his letters of introduction, his commission, and two Pao Huang Hui aides, Lea likely exercised enough influence to travel relatively unhindered in the obscurity of the northern interior as long as he kept his distance from the dowager's imperial authorities.

Lea later told friends what he considered to be some of the most memorable and exciting aspects of his exploits during this journey. One of the people he confided in, Harry Carr, explained:

> He told me that they [he and his two aides] were compelled to take shelter from a furious thunder storm in an old Chinese monastery. . . . While waiting for the storm to pass, some of the monks took to telling palms to while away the time. One of them took Homer's hand, looked at it, and prostrated himself. . . . "What is the matter?" asked one of the other monks in amazement. "This is the hand of a king" whispered the prostrate monk. This amused Gen. Lea very much, but at the same time I think it made considerable impression on his mind.
>
> During this same pursuit they came upon a village which was in the hands of the Boxers and wild riots were in progress. In the natural course of events a white man would have been

torn to pieces. The aides with Gen. Lea were terribly fright-
ened. "I don't know why," said Gen. Lea in telling me about
it, "but I was not in the least alarmed and had not the least
doubt as to the outcome.

"We were traveling in three palanquins. I ordered the other
two to drop behind and I stepped out of mine and went on
foot to meet the mob. At the head of it was an immense Chinaman brandishing a weapon.

"I didn't say anything but walked straight toward him. As
we came close, he came to a sudden stop and the mob behind
him stopped too, so that they faced me like a wall. With what
contempt I could muster in the circumstances, I motioned
for them to stand aside. They parted to the right and left in
dead silence and we passed down a lane of humanity—and
so on through the village. As they were passing through the
crowd, behind me, one of my aides heard the leader of the
mob inform his followers that I had the power of a devil in
my eyes; that I could see nine feet beneath the surface of the
earth; and that they had better be careful."[27]

Lea's friends understood that narratives of his personal exploits
were seasoned with his belief in romantic destiny. On the whole, however, his travels through China skirted the dangerous violence of the
Boxer Rebellion and the dowager's troops.

After leaving China, the Pao Huang Hui did not abandon Lea, nor
did it collapse as a secret society. Defeated on the field of battle, K'ang
Yu-wei's reformers and Sun Yat-sen's revolutionaries both sought to
further their respective causes. Lea spent the next five months in consultation and travel on behalf of the reform movement. Where he
went and whom he saw is largely a matter of conjecture. He may have
spent time in Hong Kong before traveling to Japan.[28]

Lea spent at least three months in Japan after leaving China.
Although little is known of his stay there, he was in Yokohama in
early January 1901, before meeting with Count Okuma Shigenobu,
a former Japanese prime minister and former minister of foreign
affairs. Earlier, in China, Lea had met Baron Yamagata Aritomo, a
former Japanese prime minister and founder of the modern Japanese
army, and he may have helped arrange the Okuma meeting. Okuma
served as Japan's prime minister during the Hundred Days' Reform
in China and proved to be sympathetic to K'ang Yu-wei's reform pro-

gram. Although out of favor with the current government, which was unfriendly toward the reform movement, Okuma still offered the Pao Huang Hui a supportive and valuable voice in Japanese affairs. Lea met with him on January 13, 1901, at his residence outside of Tokyo. He received a polite welcome and a thorough explanation of Sino-Japanese relations, plus a detailed outline of reforms that Okuma and the Chinese emperor had previously agreed to work toward in China.[29]

Okuma also gave his impressionable young guest a brief lesson in international politics. He painted a thorough portrait for Lea, and warned that even though China desperately needed reforms, the key to Pao Huang Hui success was to recognize that Russia, Japan's major adversary in the region, sought to keep China weak. He blamed Russian intrigues for China's misfortunes, adding that Japan's "peaceful and friendly" intentions toward China could help most if Lea focused on containing the "Russian threat."[30]

Okuma's advice most likely opened Lea's eyes to the growing complexities of international affairs and helped him realize that the dowager empress was not entirely responsible for China's ills. Now, thanks to Okuma, Lea may have better understood that international regional alliances would likely play a significant role in furthering the Pao Huang Hui's cause. Okuma also may have opened additional doors for Lea in Japan, including arranging a meeting between Lea and Marquis Ito Hirobumi, another distinguished statesman and former prime minister who was also sympathetic to the reform cause.[31]

Lea's time in Japan yielded no immediate results for the pressing needs of the Pao Huang Hui. He determined to return to California, and after a brief stay there, he planned to go to Washington and London on behalf of the reformers, before finally returning to China and again taking up his military duties. He left Japan in late March 1901 but not without generating some comment in the Japanese press. After his departure, the *Hawaiian Gazette* reported: "The Japanese press discredits the attempts of Homer Lea, a Californian student who has spent some time in China and who is endeavoring to help the true interests of that empire by his influence with the progressives of the southern portion of the Celestial kingdom."[32]

Over the previous nine months Lea had fulfilled his ambition of becoming a general, but his activities had brought little of the glory and glamour he sought. Most of his time was spent fruitlessly trying to accomplish great feats that in actuality were products of an overactive imagination. Only during his stay in Japan, when he was not actively pursuing one of his dreams, did he seem to learn any lessons from his adventure. Nevertheless, if the Pao Huang Hui listened to his recommendations for mobilizing a new army and made him its commander, he still hoped to carve out a career worthy of Napoleon and General "Chinese" Gordon. Although his exploits to date paralleled the fictional Don Quixote battling windmills more than Napoleon conquering empires, Lea believed that destiny still guided him as he continued pursuing his dreams of command and conquest.

CHAPTER 4

GENERAL WITHOUT AN ARMY

This was one of the things to dream romantic dreams about,
but not to take seriously.

—William Irwin

Lea returned to California to find that changes in Pao Huang Hui policies eliminated the need for him to act diplomatically on the society's
behalf or work toward organizing a new reform army in China. With
his chances of playing a leading role in Pao Huang Hui's affairs threatened, he reoriented his goals to coincide with its plans. He could preserve his dreams and ambitions only by devising and selling the Pao
Huang Hui a military plan that conformed to its new policies. Making
such a plan work, however, called for more than imagination and persuasion; it called for perseverance and results.

Lea's ship arrived in San Francisco the first weekend in April
1901. At the dock a few reform party representatives quietly met their
returning general and escorted him to the Palace Hotel.[1] He intended
to stay in San Francisco just long enough to brief his Pao Huang Hui
sponsors, update his plans, and contact some of his family and friends.
He then planned to embark on his intended diplomatic mission to
Washington and London before returning to China.

News of Lea's return soon circulated in the press. He gave interviews to three local newspapers about his Chinese exploits and future
plans with the reform movement. With the exception of a *San Francisco Chronicle* interview, he shrewdly avoided discussing any sensational or revealing aspects of his involvement with the Chinese
reformers, possibly remembering after he spoke to the *Chronicle* how
the press had almost ruined his chances of going to China earlier.

In the *Chronicle,* he related how the reformers had a four-hundred-thousand-man army drilling in China's southern provinces, which would be enlarged, and that he expected to command a large force in the uprising to restore the Chinese emperor to power within two years if there were not international complications. He added: "I traveled over all the southern provinces of China in my absence, organizing our forces. I had four narrow escapes from death, and was laid out once by a blow on the head. The officers of our army include 700 Americans and Europeans, and we are fully armed."[2]

Although Lea's interviews with the *San Francisco Examiner* and the *San Francisco Call* credited him with being a general, he understated his military ties with the reformers and their military capabilities. He portrayed himself more as an intermediary on an important diplomatic mission for the reform party than as a military commander. He made no more than a passing, albeit mysterious, mention of his military activities in China and his status as a general.[3]

He commented largely on the reform party's criticism of the dowager empress and the Russians rather than on himself. Yet when mentioning his involvement, he deliberately disavowed the Pao Huang Hui's sponsorship of his trip to China and generally misled the press about his past connections with the reform movement. As far as the public knew, he simply went to China on his own to help the reformers restore the emperor to the throne. Then, supposedly, only after they realized what an asset he could be to them did the reformers offer to make him a general in their army. To an unsuspecting reader, Lea came across as a true romantic adventurer when he explained:

> I had a fad of studying military strategy and army maneuvers, and my Chinese friends knew it. About a year ago I received a cable from one of them to go to China. . . . I knew that the "Boxer" movement was coming and from advices decided to go to China at once. I paid my own expenses. . . . The Emperor had been made a prisoner and the country was torn with dissention.
>
> The Emperor's strength is in the southern provinces. There an army is being organized. Today about 400,000 men can be mobilized, but it will take time to arm them effectively.
>
> My knowledge of military affairs was of value to the organizers of this force, and as the arrangements progressed I gradually drifted towards the head of it, until I was looked

upon as the commanding officer of the Army of China in the Southern Provinces. We are ready now to support and replace the Emperor on the throne, but only waiting for the time to strike.[4]

Meanwhile, on April 13, 1901, the *Los Angeles Times* printed a front-page story entitled "A Chinese General from Los Angeles," which attempted to explain how Lea, returning with a general's title, became involved in a military venture to restore the Chinese emperor to power. Unlike the San Francisco press articles, which were based on Lea's comments, the *Times* article relied largely on interviews with Lea's friends and acquaintances, who had an incomplete knowledge of his activities, and as a consequence included a variety of exaggerations and misinformation about him. For example, while citing Lea's comment to the San Francisco press that he was "looked upon as the commanding officer of the army of China in the southern provinces," the *Times* added that he participated in "months of hard campaigning and of desperate fighting against the Boxers."[5]

The article did manage, however, to capture a revealing aspect of Lea's personality. It characterized him as being "headstrong" and possessing an "iron determination," but perhaps more important, it attributed to him a magnetic personality and the "peculiar power of making people believe in him that has made him a man of mark at 25."[6]

Whatever Lea actually did in China, there was no escaping the fact that his alleged exploits were well beyond the norm, as the article clearly recognized: "The story of his remarkable career sounds like a fairy tale. Were such things put into a novel, critics would tear it to pieces on the grounds of its absurd improbability."[7]

The exaggerations and misrepresentations in these articles marked the start of a public aura of mystery and myth that continued to surround Lea for the rest of his life. In future articles the press would typically accept Lea's remarks at face value and generally few readers cared enough to dispute the purported facts concerning him. Lea also established early on that he had little interest in setting the press record straight.

Lea had returned to San Francisco at a time when a crucial policy debate raged within the Pao Huang Hui that contributed to factionalism within the party. Although the reformers publicly boasted of a unified front still able to mobilize four hundred thousand supporters in China for military purposes, after their disastrous and costly uprising, K'ang Yu-wei and the moderates were planning to break from the party's more militant radicals. They had learned a bitter lesson from the attempted uprising and now disavowed using direct military force. The growing factionalism soon began to weaken the Pao Huang Hui, especially since many radicals exercised leverage on San Francisco's branch of the influential Chinese Free Mason Society (Chih-kung t'ang). It also left the purpose of a reform army unclear.[8]

Lea's public exposure likely helped elevate his position within the California reform movement, and his status within the Pao Huang Hui took new shape during the party's internal debate. Since his contribution and dedication to the cause were unquestioned and his services were valued by the radicals, the moderates could not ignore him. Although they apparently curtailed his diplomatic duties upon his return, Lea still retained his rank and enough radical support to assume a future role.

Lea likely tried to sway the divided party leadership with visions of success through the mobilization of a new reform army in China. He probably blamed the failure of the reform uprising on poor leadership and proposed that the party could have won victory on the battlefield if his plan to use American officers had been heeded. Now, by offering to produce a group of capable American officers who would serve under him in leading the new reform army, he assumed the moderates might reconsider their opposition to a new reform army.

Lea wasted no time in attempting to persuade some of his old Stanford friends to join the reform army during his two-week stay in San Francisco. He secretly contacted them with offers of reform army commissions in the hope their sense of adventure would rule them as it did him. William Irwin remembered when Lea contacted him:

I received at the *San Francisco Chronicle* a note from Homer Lea. He was at the Palace Hotel; he wanted to see me on important business. I found him established in a suite draped with Chinese hangings, hung with Chinese paintings. He had lost his shyness and acquired an air of authority. First pledging me to secrecy—thereby ruining the interview as a newspaper story—he plunged into business by offering me a commission as captain in the new Chinese army which was going to take over the country and put China on the map as a modern nation. "I'm the generalissimo," he added simply.

Since my military experience was limited to a brief inglorious service with the West Denver High School Cadets, I regarded the offer of a commission as fantastic, and I said so.

"Not at all," he replied. "This isn't any ordinary military situation. You were reared on the frontier. You can ride and shoot. You know how to get on with men. We'd expect you to spend two years in learning to speak Chinese—that's easier than you think—and studying military tactics under European instructors. Then you'd be ready to work. Also, remember this: you write, and China's an untilled field. Everything written about it by a European, so far, is childish—laughable."

This was one of the things to dream romantic dreams about, but not to take seriously. So I declined with thanks, as did several other Stanford men of my acquaintance to whom he offered commissions as captains or majors.[9]

Lea's gamble to sway moderate support for a new reform army ultimately failed. Also, in the wake of the Boxer Rebellion, an invitation to risk and potential violence in China held no special appeal for his old poker-playing Stanford friends. For the moment, he appeared to be a general without an army. Even so, he did not give up hope and settled for the assurance of serving as the party's military expert and advisor should the need arise for his services. Meanwhile, he changed his travel plans, reoriented his goals, and returned home to family and friends in Los Angeles while awaiting a new position within the party.

K'ang Yu-wei, meanwhile, had become increasingly wary of Lea's support. He considered Lea's service of little value and believed his continued ideas for raising, training, and equipping a mercenary army were out of touch and ill suited to the Pao Huang Hui's needs and resources. He later cautioned Dr. Tom Leung:

Kong Ma Li [Homer Lea] does not understand our internal situation, and his idea is not feasible. . . . Those in other places do not know our real situation. Many people . . . have recommended Westerners to come. For example, it has cost us several thousand dollars for Kong Ma Li, who was of no help to us. . . . People like Kong Ma Li and Rong Chunfu [Yung Wing, a prominent Western-educated reformer] all do things in the Western style. They just ask for thousands and millions of dollars from our association. They suggest that such and such arms should be purchased for several million and such and such a steamboat worth several million be purchased. . . . Kong Ma Li's words are merely like someone talking in his sleep. [Association members] in foreign countries do not know the straitened circumstances in China. They cannot donate enough funds but have great expectations. It's ridiculous.[10]

When Lea returned to Los Angeles after a year's absence, most of his American friends and acquaintances dismissed his claims of generalship and Asian adventure as the ravings of an excessive, overdeveloped, and fertile imagination. Yet Lea was bothered more by the prospects of his own inactivity than by what other people thought about him. Harry Carr and Marco Newmark remembered the skepticism Lea encountered on his return to Los Angeles. Carr explained:

We all remember how he reappeared in Los Angeles after the Boxer rebellion and became the "man of mystery" of this continent. He carried a little military "swagger stick" which was beautifully engraved with a dragon and with an inscription denoting its presentation. . . .
What he did in China is only hearsay. The accounts that he gave were touched with mysticism. . . .
None of us knew what he was doing and to tell the honest truth, few believed in him. It was too incredible; to see the boy who sat next to you at school as the lieutenant-general in an Oriental army is altogether too violent an assault upon human probabilities to be taken at one dose.
Homer was serenely indifferent, however, as to whether any one believed in him or not. He had too many other fish to fry—as the saying is—to bother about people's opinions.[11]

Newmark added: "When Homer first began to talk to us in Los Angeles about his Chinese adventures, we found his story somewhat difficult for credence and wondered if he was not a victim of self-delusion. We did, however, hear at the time that the Chinese have a superstitious reverence for hunchbacks and that for this reason as well as because of Homer's personality, it might be possible that he really had become a power in China is spite of the fantastic ascent in a few years of an American school boy to a Lieutenant General in the Chinese army."[12]

Ironically, while Lea faced disbelief and skepticism from many of his Los Angeles friends, his notoriety and public image received a startling boost back in San Francisco. Shortly after his departure from there, the April 21, 1901, issue of the *Call* featured a full-page article entitled "How I Was Made a General in the Chinese Army," which was sensationally illustrated with some of his Chinese photographs. The article largely rehashed his interview with Count Okuma and made brief reference to his travels in China, but it also included a Pao Huang Hui official's letter of praise that Lea had received on his return from China, comparing him to General Charles "Chinese" Gordon.[13] While the article proved to be the last public word on Lea for the next two years, the *Call* apparently received no word from the Pao Huang Hui that his globe-trotting activities had been canceled.

Lea lived at home for the most part, out of the public eye, on an allowance from his father. He clearly had no desire to return to Stanford, study law, or seek conventional employment, which annoyed his father. Ermal recalled that "upon his return home Father treated him as if he were still only a young college boy on vacation. He reprimanded him for his late hours, and his apparent lack of any desire to become a successful businessman."[14] Chinese turmoil, Russian expansionism, the Boer War in South Africa, and the new age of American imperialism dominated the headlines and captured Lea's attention. He became convinced he must learn more about the strategic and geopolitical events that shaped the world. His own experiences in China had revealed some of the practical considerations of warfare, but this was insufficient. Now, with time on his hands, he again turned his attention to reading on Westlake Park's lawn. There he sat for hours on an Indian rug, surrounded by flowers, studying works of military strategy and theory and busily writing in his notebook.[15]

Lea also became a popular speaker with various women's and civic groups. Although he had perfected his forensic skills as a debater, Emma Lea insisted that he follow her advice for his first talks. Unfortunately, her advice hurt rather than helped him. After his second failed speech, he relied on his own instincts and did very well with audiences. Emma remembered:

> He was going to speak before the ladies of the Unitarian Church after his return from China. He said he would speak without notes like William Jennings Bryan. I told him that it

was his first speech and he had better write it out and read it. He argued but did what I said.

It was the dullest thing I ever heard. The ladies sat there for two hours, unsnapping their watches while Homer droned on.

After two wrecked speeches Homer decided to go on as before the Friday Morning Club without notes.

It was brilliant. He had so much dash and fire that they called him back after he had finished.[16]

When Lea appeared in public, he was rarely seen without his most prized possession, his general's baton. He carried it as a badge and symbol of honor wherever he went. Newmark explained:

Even the strongest characters have a weakness. Homer was no exception. He picked up the swagger stick after he dressed in the morning and, except during his meals, it was never out of his hands until he retired.

He was wont, occasionally, to join a boon companion on a spree. During these bibulous adventures, he sometimes became over enthusiastic, and although he lost his sobriety, he never lost his head. He always arrived at his home, swagger stick still in hand.[17]

Meanwhile, the moderates emerged in general control of the Pao Huang Hui during the year or so that it took the party to recover from its reverses and internal problems. By 1902 reform party membership and support began to rise dramatically. The moderate leadership, whose members comprised some of the most affluent and influential overseas Chinese, specifically directed the party's efforts toward building up both organization and finances to sponsor the spread of party newspapers, schools, and bookstores. Furthermore, the restoration of the emperor and reform in China took on new dimensions following the humiliating settlement imposed on China by the powers after the Boxer Rebellion. K'ang Yu-wei's calls for reform and the emperor's restoration began appealing to greater audiences. The reform party grew especially by advocating a popular program of progressive change rather than the provocative revolutionary break with tradition put forth in the more extreme doctrine of Dr. Sun Yat-sen.[18]

A new role for Lea began to emerge with the reconsolidation and expansion of the Pao Huang Hui. During the months he spent reading and conferring with reform leaders, he devised a new military plan beneficial to the Pao Huang Hui and acceptable to both radical and moderate party leaders. Lea's plan centered on training a cadre of reform army soldiers in America that could be utilized to help lead the imperial Chinese army after the emperor was restored to power. The plan offered the party a number of opportunities. Lea's cadre could first infiltrate the dowager-controlled imperial Chinese army and provide important intelligence to the reformers. Then it could work from within the army to weaken the power base of the dowager by soliciting additional recruits to the cause. When efforts to restore the emperor finally succeeded, the cadre's officers could take command of the army and form an elite bodyguard for the emperor, thereby ensuring against further palace intrigues or coup d'états. Finally, the plan offered Lea his chance to contribute to the party's victory and fully realize his own dreams of command in the reform army.

Lea's patience, perseverance, and powers of persuasion paid off. The Los Angeles party leadership ultimately approved his plan, but the questions and complications of putting it into effect remained formidable. American neutrality laws might impede the arming and training of dissident Chinese seeking to overthrow a government on friendly terms with the United States. Also, aside from working out the political and legal practicalities, the actual planning, organization, and execution of such a plan would have to be carried out so as to avoid detection by Ch'ing agents, who already kept watchful eyes on the activities of the reformers. One factor remained certain: for Lea's plan to be effective and worthwhile for the reformers, several hundred or even thousand soldiers would have to be trained and infiltrated into the imperial Chinese army. And no matter what prospects Lea's plan offered, it would still take many months to work out all the necessary details to ensure security and success, and probably several years to train enough soldiers for the reform party's cause.

Lea determined to initiate his plan by establishing cadet cadres in Los Angeles and San Francisco, but he could not begin until he first found capable and qualified drill instructors, especially ones who could be trusted and were discreet. This was not a job that he could offer his Stanford cronies, and finding the right men appears to have taken him more than a year. It is not clear exactly how Lea proceeded. According to U.S. Army first sergeant Ansel E. O'Banion, Troop A, Fourth Cavalry Regiment, then stationed at Fort Riley, Kansas, who eventually became Lea's chief Los Angeles drill instructor, Lea contacted the U.S. Army for assistance in finding a drill instructor among the ranks of seasoned army veterans demobilizing from the Philippine Insurrection (1899–1902). O'Banion claimed that Lea sent a letter to the War Department in Washington, D.C., explaining his needs for a discreet senior noncommissioned officer with an outstanding active service record to assist him in training a group of Chinese in the art of military drill. The War Department reportedly forwarded the request to Major General Adna R. Chaffee, commander of U.S. forces in the Philippines, who replied by suggesting a young cavalry sergeant, O'Banion, as just the man for Lea's needs.[19]

In mid-June 1902, according to O'Banion, he received a call to see his commanding officer, Colonel Camillo C. Carr, who informed him that the War Department believed his qualifications met the criteria for a special request submitted by a Lieutenant General Homer Lea. O'Banion advised his colonel he had never heard of General Lea and that he planned to go into ranching after his upcoming June 18, 1902, discharge from the army. O'Banion agreed, however, to consider the matter further.[20] Some forty years later, O'Banion recalled his meeting with Colonel Carr, and the colonel's following remarks: "[M]y guess is you like adventure and enjoy a good fight too much to settle down quietly on a ranch for the rest of your life. You're not made that way. No romantic, fighting, adventurous Irishman ever is. . . . I've been instructed to give you a letter of introduction to Homer Lea. It is strictly confidential and not to be shown to anyone but Homer Lea. Should you decide not to present it, destroy the letter and forget all about it."[21]

O'Banion headed for California on a train the day after he was discharged and opened the confidential letter given him by Colonel Carr. It was from Major General Chaffee to Lieutenant General Homer Lea, introducing O'Banion as a man with "all the qualifications" that Lea sought.[22] After thinking about the offer, however, O'Banion decided not to pursue the matter further. Although he would later change his mind, he got off the train in Orange, California, putting the letter from his mind and looking forward to the pleasures of ranching.[23]

While Lea worked on his military plans for the reformers, he also became more actively involved in their cause. For example, in August 1903 he wrote President Theodore Roosevelt to call the president's attention to the fate of the editors of a reform newspaper in Shanghai, the *Supao*, who faced arrest by the imperial government for their reform activities. Lea noted that he knew the men in question, members of the Pao Huang Hui. He added that he was in China in 1900 and 1901, and knew from personal experience that the Pao Huang Hui was responsible for maintaining peace in the Yangtze Valley and southern provinces during the Boxer Rebellion. He urged the president to follow the British policy in this affair and refuse to surrender the men in question to the dowager.[24]

Lea returned to the public eye in October 1903, when he began receiving press coverage in connection with the arrival in Los Angeles of Liang Ch'i-ch'ao, a prominent reformer and student of K'ang Yu-wei. This new exposure finally began to convince skeptics there was more to Lea's involvement with the Chinese reform movement than they had credited.[25]

Liang Ch'i-ch'ao was a literary scholar and cofounder of the Pao Huang Hui.[26] During his North American tour, he was often mistakenly described as a royal prince by the American press. While the press also made similar mistakes in describing K'ang Yu-wei as the ex-premier of China, these erroneous representations served the reform party in America very well. They added to the prestige of the party and also helped legitimize Pao Huang Hui activities in the public eye.

Liang Ch'i-ch'ao traveled through Canada and to several American cities to organize branches of the Pao Huang Hui before arriving in Los Angeles. His mission publicly entailed fund-raising and strengthening moderate support within the party. However, there was some press speculation that another reason he was in North America was "to accumulate funds for the rebel movement now going on in Southern China, and to arrange for the shipment of arms and war munitions for the rebels."[27] In Washington, D.C., his distinguished reputation earned him an audience with President Roosevelt and Secretary of State John M. Hay. On that occasion he received tacit American approval for the Pao Huang Hui's peaceful goals of reform in China and for expansion of its activities in America.[28]

In early October 1903 Liang Ch'i-ch'ao unwittingly sowed seeds of discontent between Lea and the reform party during a fund-raising stop in San Francisco. Liang Ch'i-ch'ao privately acknowledged the claims of Richard A. Falkenberg, an opportunistic San Francisco businessman, adventurer, and soldier of fortune, who had evidently acquired a Pao Huang Hui general's commission in 1900, when the reform party resorted to selling commissions and titles to raise money for the reform uprising in China. Lea knew nothing about Falkenberg who, with Liang Ch'i-ch'ao's endorsement, became the second American to claim a generalship in the reform army.[29]

Relatively little is known about Falkenberg. He was born in Louisiana in 1853 and claimed a diverse and remarkable career that included Prussian army service, scouting for the U.S. Army, foreign mercenary service, mining, and amateur boxing. Like Lea, Falkenberg was an unabashed self-promoter and schemer who saw the Chinese reform movement as a stepping-stone to his own success. Apparently marginally successful in business, he hoped that service with the Chinese would be more exciting, and perhaps more lucrative, than other opportunities open to him. Holding a generalship with the Chinese certainly seemed more prestigious and rewarding than any position for which he actually qualified.[30]

Falkenberg had been building a colorful and notorious career for more than a decade before his affiliation with the Pao Huang Hui. His perseverance and audacity were unrivaled. He first came to the attention of the U.S. government in 1891, when he created a minor diplomatic incident by offering to raise a small group of American scouts for service with the Honduran army, in possible violation of U.S. neutrality laws. The *New York Tribune,* which reported on his offer, described him as "Capt. Richard Falkenberg, who has for many years been known as a scout and Indian fighter, both in the Reil rebellion in Canada and in our own far West."[31] In 1893 he began a letter-writing campaign to the War Department seeking recognition for his alleged service as a scout with one of the nation's most famous cavalry commanders during the Indian Wars. Styling himself Captain R. A. Falkenberg of the Arizona Territory, he claimed to be the sole survivor of George A. Custer's legendary last stand at the battle of the Little Big Horn in 1876. He said he joined Custer as his chief scout during the famous battle "independently with my own men outfitted at my own expense."[32] The War Department responded with a refusal to recognize such an outrageous claim, but Falkenberg was undaunted. He wrote back insisting on the veracity of his story. The War Department, likely believing he was a crank, dropped the matter.[33]

Falkenberg next came to the attention of the U.S. government when he began another letter-writing campaign, this time offering to raise and command a private regiment of scouts for service with the U.S. Army during the Philippine Insurrection. He had come close to serving in the Spanish-American War (1898) as the captain of K Troop, Third Squadron, California Volunteer Cavalry Regiment, but his regiment had not been mobilized for national service. In March 1899 he wrote directly to President William McKinley with his offer to raise a scout regiment for the Philippines. In writing the Republican president he blamed "certain Democratic intrigues" for denying him the right to serve during the recent war and hoped the president would balance the scales in his favor. Although McKinley did not reply, that did not stop Falkenberg. He then sent a series of letters to the White House and other government officials repeating his offer.[34]

In letters to McKinley's private secretary, the secretary of war, and the assistant secretary of war, Falkenberg portrayed his past achievements as an "intrepid cavalry officer" and "skillful frontiersman." He told of his service with a "crack cavalry regiment" in Prussia, of his offer to raise an army to fight in Chile in 1891, and last, of being "mortally wounded" at the battle of "La Batouche" in the 1885 Riel Rebellion in Canada. In his efforts to secure government support, his letters quoted laudatory comments from various prominent California men and public officials. The War Department concluded that a number of these endorsements were fraudulent.[35]

Meanwhile, Falkenberg fulfilled his desire of going to the Philippines, but not as an army officer. Instead, he settled for employment by the army post quartermaster at the Presidio in San Francisco. In August 1899 he began serving as a "first-class packer" on board the animal transport *Siam*, traveling between Hawaii and the Philippines.[36]

When Falkenberg returned to California in the fall of 1899, he again wrote the secretary of war, this time requesting permission to serve as "an ordinary scout" in the Philippines.[37] The War Department replied that he could enlist "as a private soldier," which ended his solicitations to serve in the Philippines.[38]

Still undaunted, in the wake of the Boxer Rebellion Falkenberg next unsuccessfully sought a volunteer officer's commission with the U.S. Army in China. In early August 1900, rather than engaging in another of his ambitious letter-writing campaigns, he arranged for California congressman Russell J. Waters to write the secretary of war recommending him for a commission, but the War Department replied that it was not accepting volunteers for service in China.[39]

Falkenberg did not have to wait long for another opportunity to obtain a military commission, but this time it was not with the U.S. Army. In the summer of 1900, he heard of the Pao Huang Hui's need for support and of its sale of titles and commissions to advance its cause. He undoubtedly promoted himself to them as an experienced soldier and leader and, like Lea, he managed to acquire a Pao Huang Hui general's commission.[40]

Not surprisingly, and unknown to Lea in China, by the end of August 1900, Falkenberg began actively representing himself to the U.S. government as a Pao Huang Hui, or Chinese Empire Reform Association (CERA), spokesman. Using his familiar letter-writing tactics, he wrote President McKinley and Secretary of State Hay. This time identifying himself as "General C. E. R. Army and Representative Extraordinary of Emperor Kwong-Hsui [*sic*] and Chinese Empire Reform Association," he claimed to represent the Pao Huang Hui in requesting U.S. government assistance to restore the emperor to his throne.[41] He offered a deal to McKinley in an August 31 memorial; if America would help restore the emperor, Falkenberg maintained that the reform party army, "instructed and led by foreign officers," would protect foreign interests and that "the reward to the United States will be a most substantial one."[42] He wrote this proposition confident that the reform uprising would lead to the emperor's restoration, providing that the powers cooperated. He did not know that the revolt had already failed. He received no acknowledgment or reply from Washington. In an October 6 letter to Secretary of State Hay, he again tried to interest the American government in the Pao Huang Hui's cause. He warned Hay that any agreements made between the powers and the dowager's government would be worthless once the emperor was restored to the throne. This effort to prompt a government response also failed.[43]

When news of the failed reform uprising finally reached Falkenberg in November 1900, he reevaluated his position. Knowing the reform army no longer existed and the emperor remained a prisoner, he curtailed his diplomatic efforts with the U.S. government and retreated with his general's appointment back into the mainstream of American life. Had he adhered to this decision, there would never have been a later clash with Lea for control of the reform army. Falkenberg, however, was not one to pass up an opportunity for furthering his self-interests.[44]

When word reached Falkenberg in early 1903 that the reform party planned to begin rebuilding its army and that Liang Ch'i-ch'ao might be visiting San Francisco in the fall, he moved into action. The San Francisco reformers likely advised him that Liang Ch'i-ch'ao could grant him a reform commission acknowledging his 1900 appointment as a general in the CERA army if he wished to play a role in the party's new army. Falkenberg wanted a commission so badly he would do almost anything to convince the reformers to give it to him. The only problem remained one of convincing Liang Ch'i-ch'ao to grant his request. For the resourceful Falkenberg that problem was quickly resolved. He turned to California governor George C. Pardee for help. His goal was to become a colonel on the governor's staff, which also would assist him in legitimizing his position with the Pao Huang Hui. On January 23, 1903, he wrote Pardee to solicit a commission on the governor's staff "for the grade of Colonel" and signed it "Major" R. A. Falkenberg.[45]

Pardee responded cordially that he was unable to "give attention to this matter at present" but would give it "due consideration" at a later date.[46] Seven months later, on July 21, he turned down Falkenberg's request, but kept open the possibility of considering the appointment at some future date.[47]

Falkenberg did not wait long to press his case. On July 27, in an effort to improve his credentials, he wrote the governor, a Republican, on letterhead of the Standard Rock Oil Company, of which he was president. He explained his intent of using a military appointment on the governor's staff to bolster his position with the Chinese reformers: "I intended asking you for a colonelcy personally for the reason that I have had a position offered me as General in the Chinese Reform Army and they are investigating my military record, which is without a flaw, since 1872. . . . If I could show the Chinese Commissioner [most likely Liang Ch'i-ch'ao] a Colonel's commission on your staff, that would decide the question in my favor, even if I were to resign again almost immediately from your staff."[48]

Falkenberg was not above employing the same self-serving and deceptive tactics with the governor that had characterized his earlier correspondence with Washington, D.C. He alluded to distinguished military service in the recent Spanish-American War and dropped the names of several persons to vouch for him, including those with Republican Party connections. Whether they really knew him or not was academic. It was not the first time Falkenberg had gambled on his story not being checked out. Of those people mentioned, he especially noted that the "Secretary of the L.A. Republican Committee, an old friend of mine, was my Lieutenant during the Spanish war in 1898 in the First California Cavalry Regiment (Provisional)."[49] Again, he signed the letter "Major Falkenberg." He never received the appointment from the governor.[50]

After Liang Ch'i-ch'ao arrived in San Francisco in late September 1903, Falkenberg promptly sought out the reform leader, hoping to revitalize a position for himself in the party's yet-to-be-organized army. By this time he likely had gained the agreement of Dr. T'an Shu-pin to help sway Liang Ch'i-ch'ao to accept his supposed military credentials and previous service to the Pao Huang Hui. Lea's position within the party apparently never entered the discussion. Falkenberg had again done a good job of selling himself: the reformers saw some benefit in his association, valuing the prospect of an American military man's "expert" services once their party came into power in China. At a banquet in San Francisco's Chinese quarter on October 5, Liang Ch'i-ch'ao issued Falkenberg the commission he sought, verifying him as head of the Imperial Reform Army, signed and stamped with the official seal of the reform party.[51]

As far as Falkenberg was concerned, he proposed to make good use of his new command position. He did not mind commanding a ghost army. He took his commission and planned to remain in the background of Pao Huang Hui affairs. Meanwhile, Liang Ch'i-ch'ao and the San Francisco reform leaders understood he would serve the party by compiling a roster of Americans who might be interested in receiving commissions in the reform army once the emperor regained his throne. What Falkenberg failed to tell Liang Ch'i-ch'ao and the reform leadership, however, was that he also planned on using his position to distribute commissions in the Imperial Reform Army to American mercenaries and would-be adventurers for his own personal profit.

When Liang Ch'i-ch'ao left San Francisco to establish a Pao Huang Hui branch in Sacramento, General Falkenberg shrewdly retreated back into his personal affairs, with relatively few party members aware of the role he intended to play in the Pao Huang Hui. Unlike his younger rival in Los Angeles, Falkenberg never received any publicity as a reform general, nor was he publicly linked with the Pao Huang Hui. On the contrary, he shunned publicity and, just as in 1900, probably arranged to have knowledge of his role among the reformers kept in the confidence of as few people as possible.[52]

Liang Ch'i-ch'ao arrived in Los Angeles on the afternoon of October 22 to attend a grandiose reception arranged in part by Lea. The belated arrival of his train did not dampen the expectations of a crowd waiting to welcome a man described by one local paper as the "most distinguished Chinese that has visited the United States since Li Hung Chang," a renowned Chinese statesman of the era.[53] The extent of Lea's influence with the Pao Huang Hui began to come to light in

Los Angeles for the first time. Aside from his standing within the organization as a respected military leader, he appeared to exercise enough clout to court the mayor, a National Guard general, and the Chamber of Commerce in arranging several events for Liang Ch'i-ch'ao's visit. The *Los Angeles Express* helped capture the spirit, flavor, and significance of Liang Ch'i-ch'ao's arrival and Lea's implicit association with the reformers:

> Civic and military dignitaries joined the prominent Chinese in extending a welcome to the eminent reformer. There was Mayor Snyder for the city and a committee composed of John Alton, A. C. Way, Newman Essick and G. G. Johnson for the chamber of commerce; General Prescott and Major Lovett for the National Guard and a detail of the Signal Corps for escort.
>
> After the long and warm wait in the sun Mayor Snyder and General Homer Lea were glad to welcome the visitor who, with his secretary, Dr. Bochee, took seats in the same carriage drawn by four horses and decorated with the American and the imperial Chinese flags. In carriages that followed were the committees, the National Guard officers and representatives of the press. Then followed carriages [approximately fifteen] containing the representative merchants of Chinatown, most of them clad in the silken robes of state.[54]

For the next week, Liang Ch'i-ch'ao and Lea received flattering coverage in the local press. Whenever Liang Ch'i-ch'ao appeared at a banquet or speech among the Chinese, Lea was often the only Caucasian guest. He also enjoyed enough prestige within the local reform party to have the honor of entertaining the reformer one evening at his family's Bonnie Brae Street home.[55]

Lea gained valuable civic and military contacts by handling much of Liang Ch'i-ch'ao's public relations in Los Angeles. On at least two occasions during the visit, Lea arranged for a select group of influential local leaders to attend banquets for the reformer. On the first occasion, a day after Liang Ch'i-ch'ao's arrival, Lea officiated at a banquet at the Angelus Hotel, his residence in Los Angeles. Lea served as the toastmaster and also used the occasion to broaden his personal base of support among guests including Brigadier General Frank C. Prescott and his son Captain Frank C. Prescott Jr. of the California National Guard, Superior Court Justice Waldo M. York, and several Los Angeles Chamber of Commerce representatives. These guests did not have any strong sentiment for or interest in either Liang Ch'i-ch'ao or the reform party, but they later proved valuable contacts for Lea's plan to organize and train a reform military cadre in Los Angeles, particularly the National Guard officers. Whether his guests knew it or not, Lea intended to capitalize on association with recognized public figures.[56]

Lea outdid himself at Liang Ch'i-ch'ao's farewell banquet on October 31, which several National Guard officers and Chamber of Commerce representatives attended. On this occasion, Mayor Snyder also was a guest. He and the other Caucasians were honored by being made Pao Huang Hui members. For their part, Lea's American guests publicly supported Liang Ch'i-ch'ao and the reformers.[57]

Liang Ch'i-ch'ao approved Lea's cadet cadre plan in the course of his visit. The proposal fit in well with his overall mission of strengthening the reform party, particularly since he favored using force in furthering party goals. For example, earlier, in San Francisco, he made his militant views very clear when he cautioned: "There was never a country reformed without a great loss of blood and though we may be accused of being over anxious to cause bloodshed it is only our own blood that we stand ready to see shed. We have shed blood and, gentlemen, we are ready to shed more to the last drop, but we must have a change, and it must take place soon."[58]

Lea's cadet cadre plan came at an opportune time for the reformers. It complemented a new lucrative party financial organization getting under way known as the Commercial Corporation.[59] With Lea's plan offering some chance to weaken the dowager's power base and the Commercial Corporation intending to bolster and help finance party operations, Liang Ch'i-ch'ao ended his tour with promising expectations for the reform party.

When Liang Ch'i-ch'ao left Los Angeles and returned (via San Francisco) to Japan, he left behind the looming problem of Richard Falkenberg.[60] Lea and the Los Angeles reform leaders had heard nothing from Liang Ch'i-ch'ao about the commission given just weeks earlier to Falkenberg. Whether Liang Ch'i-ch'ao believed a conflict of interest would not arise between the two reform generals because they pursued different missions, or whether he did not fully understand the implications of issuing Falkenberg a commission, is not known. Lea, who had not met or even heard of Falkenberg, had no reason to suspect that anything had changed, especially since there was still no Imperial Reform Army.

Lea's expectations appeared to be on the rise. Since his return from Asia he had never given up hopes of future leadership and service within the Pao Huang Hui. Although party instability had seemed to spell an end to his ambitions, his continued determination and perseverance seemed to be paying off. By the fall of 1903 his handling of Liang Ch'i-ch'ao's visit and his proposed military cadre scheme offered viable and valued assistance to the reformers. His revitalized public image also began dispelling the skepticism he had faced upon his return to Los Angeles. Furthermore, Liang Ch'i-ch'ao's visit allowed him to lay the groundwork for gaining the alliance of individuals who might help establish the reform military cadre. His confidence renewed following Liang Ch'i-ch'ao's visit, Lea's organization and training of a reform military cadre appeared to be just a question of time.

CHAPTER 5

THE IMPERIAL REFORM ARMY

[A] great surprise is in store for those who may have looked
upon the establishment of this school by Gen. Homer Lea as
a burlesque.

—*Los Angeles Times*

Liang Ch'i-ch'ao's visit to Los Angeles won useful publicity for the
reform cause. After his departure, Lea seized the initiative to implement his own plans. He needed first to establish a mechanism for
recruiting cadets, and then he must arrange to train them. He envisioned a reform military academy with branches throughout the
United States. After much theorizing, talk, and wishful thinking, he
moved into action, only to find the task more difficult than he had
anticipated.

Lea learned that George W. West, a local civil engineer and recent
dropout from the West Point class of 1902, might be interested in a
part-time job as his chief drill instructor. Lea met with West at the
Angelus Hotel on December 19, 1903, to discuss his plans and offer
West the job. West noted in his diary that "the meeting may mean
worlds to me," and he subsequently agreed to accept an Imperial
Reform Army officer's commission to help train reform cadets.[1]

The addition of West to Lea's plans was an important step, but it
would be several months before Lea was ready to call on him to begin
training. In the interim Lea planned to establish his first two reform
cadet companies, one in Los Angeles and one in San Francisco. He
also sought several more drill instructors for each company before
training could begin.[2]

On January 2, 1904, the reformers showed Lea their gratitude by awarding him a gold medal during dedication ceremonies of their new Los Angeles headquarters. The *Los Angeles Times* reported:

> The new quarters are at No. 417 North Los Angeles street, where dedication exercises were begun at noon. A native orchestra furnished music. Dr. Tom Leung, one of the leading Chinese citizens, read a dedication poem prepared for the occasion. A handsome gold medal was presented to Homer Lea, the young Angeleno who has taken such a prominent part in China, and here, in the reform movement instituted by Liang Chi Chao and associates. The presentation was made by Wong Ping, president of the local society, on behalf of the body as a whole. The medal is inscribed in Chinese to "Gen. Homer Lea, Commander-in-Chief of the reform forces of the Chinese Empire," and refers to his valuable services rendered by him to the cause during the past five years.[3]

Lea's plans for a reform army would have been far better off in the long run had he been aware that the reform party had another opportunistic general in its ranks. In San Francisco word of the reform party's plans to establish a military training program prompted one of its members, Wong Kim, an Oakland postal employee, to organize a company of recruits. This was hardly organized when Richard Falkenberg attempted to use it in furthering his own ambitions. Remembering Governor Pardee's promise to consider him for a future state military commission, Falkenberg believed that it was again time to act. He attempted to persuade Pardee to grant him a commission in the California National Guard by offering to organize Wong Kim's recruits into a company for the guard. On February 17, 1904, he sent Pardee his request, explaining that Wong Kim had "35 Chinese in his company, who are all . . . willing to serve in the National Guard."[4] Although Pardee did not grant the request, Falkenberg kept close ties to Wong Kim's military company, which soon began drawing public attention to the Pao Huang Hui's military plans.[5]

On April 17, Wong Kim's company made a brief public appearance during the visit of Prince Pu Lun, the emperor's nephew, to San Francisco. During welcoming ceremonies at the dock, the company presented the prince with a large flower bouquet inscribed with the members' names. The military contingent later created a minor sensation at the imperial Chinese Consulate when it paid its respects to the prince.[6] Neither the prince nor the press knew quite what to make of the military company. In all probability it presented itself as the vanguard of a future loyal corps to the emperor. The *San Francisco Chronicle* reported:

> Inside the Consulate the Prince was escorted to a large reception room. . . . Then a strange company came filing in, thirty local Chinese, all without the queue and wearing up-to-date American clothes and a yellow ribbon badge which proclaimed them members of the Chinese military company. These untrained amateur soldiers, with a few old Springfield rifles for drill purposes, are the beginning of a military organization started here a month ago. The men all wore campaign hats with a blue cord, and marched proudly in to present their compliments in elaborate bows to the Prince. Then they hurried out, well satisfied to see his highness at close range.[7]

Lea, meanwhile, was taking steps to formalize military training for his cadet company in Los Angeles. With roughly the same number of recruits as its San Francisco counterpart, the Los Angeles cadet company was the first to receive drill instructors. In an April 30 ceremony held in the Los Angeles Pao Huang Hui Hall, Lea installed West as a captain and drill instructor in the reform army and named California National Guard Captain Frank C. Prescott Jr. as a first lieutenant and assistant instructor. The company began training the following week.[8]

News of Lea's cadets quickly spread in Los Angeles. On May 18 the *Los Angeles Times* ran a front-page story about them. Lea took advantage of the opportunity to explain that he was guided by altruism in helping the Chinese:

> I hope nothing will be said that will make this company out to be anything that it is not. It is simply a lot of Chinamen who wish to learn military drill, as a similar number of white young men might do. It is merely the spirit of war that is among them.
>
> Some of the Chinamen came to me a while ago and asked my assistance in getting up a military company. I found Capt. West for them, and helped them organize the company.
>
> Actually that is all there is to it.[9]

Lea also dismissed allegations that he was offering commissions to National Guardsmen as a "ridiculous story."[10]

Lea eventually recruited additional drill instructors to his ranks. He targeted California National Guard soldiers and men with prior military experience. On May 20, for example, he added a friend of West, Floyd G. Dessery, to the Los Angeles cadet company as a lieutenant and assistant instructor. Dessery, a civil engineer and future business partner of West, had attended the December 19 meeting with Lea and West at the Angelus Hotel. Unlike West, who had received some military training at West Point before returning to civilian life, Dessery had active duty military experience. He had served as an army private in the Philippines during the Spanish-American War.[11]

Lea's efforts to attract Spanish-American War veterans led to some unexpected press exposure in early July. For example, a July 10 *San Francisco Call* article entitled "Want Yankees to Drill Them" reported: "The Chinese Reformers are said to be recruiting an army in California. It is reported that they have a company in Oakland, others in Los Angeles and elsewhere, and are now negotiating with Philippine war veterans to drill their men. They offer these soldiers commissions in the Imperial army if they will accompany them to China."[12]

Although it would be years before Lea's plan could bear fruit for the Pao Huang Hui, he went to great lengths to produce a facade of professionalism for his embryonic army. He chose uniforms strikingly similar to those used by the U.S. Army for himself and his cadets, which helped create an appearance of legitimacy.[13] The establishment of his first cadet company also marked a change in Lea's attitude. His days as a young, impetuous adventurer seeking glory on far-off battlefields seemed far removed from his present position within the Pao Huang Hui. He no longer boasted of single-handedly saving China from the dowager empress. He was proving himself to be a skillful manager and strategist.

Lea's search for drill instructors included finding replacements for Prescott and Dessery, who left during the summer for reasons unknown. Fortunately, through his network of friends and associates, he found enough men.[14] One of them, California National Guard sergeant Harvey Waterman, recalled highlights of his experience training the cadets: "The drill taught was close order, U.S. regulations. We had some wooden guns, there was a law that prevented them using regular guns. We used an interpreter, but they soon learned the English commands. It was hard to make them do the drill in a snappy manner."[15]

Lea never told his subordinates more than they needed to know to conduct their duties, nor did they complain or ask too many questions. On the surface, an air of legitimacy covered Lea's small training program. Occasionally U.S. Army officers, National Guard officers, and even visiting foreign officers came by to see the cadet training and consult with him.[16]

In the summer of 1904, West resigned his reform army commission and left Los Angeles when his regular employers sent him to Mexico on a construction project. At this juncture, Lea benefited from a miraculous stroke of good fortune in obtaining West's replacement. By a remarkable coincidence, Lea's friend Dr. A. J. Scott knew about the cadet training and happened to be in contact with former cavalry sergeant Ansel O'Banion, as his physician. When O'Banion complained to Scott of being restless and bored with ranching, Lea's need for a capable drill instructor came up in the conversation. O'Banion now reconsidered Lea's proposal and, at Scott's urging, decided to phone Lea to arrange a meeting.[17]

O'Banion and Lea met in the Angelus Hotel the same day of the phone call. At first the sight of the frail-looking young general startled O'Banion, but he soon overcame his skepticism after listening to Lea. Lea intrigued him with offers and an appeal to his sense of adventure. He decided without hesitation to join Lea. Not long afterward, he became a captain in the reform army at a ceremonial banquet in his honor at the Pao Huang Hui "Armory" in Chinatown.[18]

O'Banion established an excellent working rapport with Lea and the cadets and soon proved to be a valued officer and first-rate drill instructor. When Lea decided to expand the cadet-training program, which necessitated O'Banion being seen around Chinatown more often, O'Banion agreed to open a commercial business, a hay and feed market, in Chinatown as a suitable cover. As an added measure of security, the reform leadership eventually successfully petitioned the City of Los Angeles to appoint O'Banion as a special deputy sheriff to help protect Chinatown. The ploy worked; no one outside of the Chinese community suspected O'Banion's secret intentions in Chinatown. These precautions provided him with a profitable daytime business and afforded him the accessibility to Chinatown and the cadets that his covert services required.[19]

Once O'Banion settled in training cadets, Lea made his next move to expand the organization of his reform military forces, which soon became known as the Chinese Imperial Army (CIA). Lea ultimately intended to train reform cadets across the entire country, and showed O'Banion a national map with red circles drawn around those cities with flourishing Pao Huang Hui chapters. He planned to raise additional cadet companies in these cities and believed he could secure enough drill instructors to make his plan work, with O'Banion's help. He asked O'Banion to find drill instructors among his former cavalry comrades. O'Banion agreed to try, and in a few weeks had compiled a list of former comrades in arms willing to join Lea's venture and receive commissions in the reform army. Lea had enough drill instructors for the additional cadet companies by the late summer or early fall of 1904. He now looked forward to commanding a nationwide army.[20]

While O'Banion's former cavalry comrades would be instrumental in training cadets in the East and Midwest, Lea continued to rely on his California militia contacts to fill his ranks and help add legitimacy to his venture. He recruited several senior militia officers. For example, Lieutenant Colonel William G. Schreiber of Los Angeles, the assistant adjutant general of the First Brigade, California National Guard, served as the adjutant general of the blossoming CIA. He had responsibility for composing the various general regulations governing Lea's army. Thomas A. Nerney of San Francisco, the former commander of the Naval Militia of California, served as the CIA supply officer. Lea also recruited several lower-ranking instructors from the California National Guard's First Brigade Signal Corps in Los Angeles to help form a CIA signal company. Using guardsmen also proved expedient for Lea because they were likely to support him if any allegations surfaced that his training violated federal neutrality laws.[21]

Lea was probably most resourceful in devising a scheme to mask the real intent of his cadet companies. To protect against accusations of violating neutrality statutes, he found a loophole in the law. With the help of his friend and attorney John M. York (Judge Waldo M. York's son), on November 28, 1904, he obtained a charter from the State of California to operate a private school called the Western Military Academy.[22] It served as a legal facade and as a model: Lea envisioned branches of the academy opening under different names in twenty-one cities, with one hundred men to a company, eventually training some two thousand Chinese reform troops nationwide.

Lea next arranged for a reputable board of directors. Five prominent Los Angeles civic leaders—G. G. Johnson, president of the Board of Trade; Roger S. Page, an attorney and high school friend of Lea; and bankers Archibald C. Way, Newman Essick, and John Alton—agreed to sit on the board. Lea's association with some of these men dated back to Liang Ch'i-ch'ao's welcoming reception. He found them willing to support the advancement of the reform movement, although it is uncertain how much they knew of the academy's true purpose. Archibald Way, for one, knew. He directly handled academy finances for the board and was closely involved in the academy's covert activities. For example, on one occasion he reportedly received between $40,000 and $100,000 in cash, concealed in a pillowcase, from Hugh A. Matier, another member of Lea's network, who secretly collected the funds from reformers in Canada. Some of the other board members may have believed they were sponsoring a school that would help uplift the Chinese and educate them to become good citizens. In that case, in return for their moral support, Lea likely assured them they would not be bothered with the affairs of the academy, and there would be no burdensome board meetings, conferences, or requests for money. The Chinese reformers financed the school and Lea likely made occasional progress reports to the board of directors to keep its members informed.[23]

The Western Military Academy was located at 416 Marchessault Street. It occupied two rooms and appeared to be a private school for Chinese reformers. The school charter hung prominently in the front room surrounded by some desks and a few shelves of textbooks. Its course brochure, based on the Stanford University course catalog, announced a variety of courses and credit hours, with all classes scheduled to begin at 8:00 in the evening on various weekdays. O'Banion headed the faculty. The catalogs, books, and the charter were all part of the cover intended to satisfy any curious outsiders. That it was not a school was well known among the Chinese, who already knew it as the "Armory." The larger back room, where cadets drilled, contained several racks of modern Mauser rifles and bayonets.[24]

Even though O'Banion kept the doors locked during "school hours," if the rare occasion involving a too-curious outsider arose, the cadets would appear in the front room pretending to study. Drill instruction lasted from roll call at 8:00 p.m. until 1:00 or 2:00 a.m. every day of the week except the week of the Chinese New Year. Those cadets who had to get to work early in the morning would usually be excused at midnight.[25]

After the Western Military Academy received its charter, Lea began making arrangements for opening branches nationwide. Although little information remains on these other cadet companies, the establishment of the Chicago branch provides a good example of how Lea effectively managed public relations to deceive and downplay the provocative aspects of the academies. In Chicago, Lea also had his officers give the press fictitious stories that the school was for the education and advancement of the Chinese in the American tradition. A December 2, 1904, *La Crosse Tribune* article presented an innocent picture of the Chicago academy:

> Rapid progress is being made by the Chinese Empire Reform Association in the organization of its new academy for the instruction of their countrymen in modern affairs. . . .
>
> Much of the work of the academy will necessarily be done at night, as the majority of the students are employed during the day. Many are merchants who are anxious to advance in American ways. Others are young men who have thus far kept the ways of their fathers.
>
> The corps of instructors thus far engaged includes Thomas E. Milchrist, international and American law; Major George W. Gibbs, late of the Philippine army, instructor in military science; Professor Lineas R. Simpson, instructor in English, and A. F. Woods, instructor in topography and drafting.[26]

What this article could not reveal was that the academy was part of a larger conspiracy to train a covert Chinese military force. Over the course of the next year branches of the Western Military Academy opened across the country.

During this period Lea sought to organize his army along modern lines. Beginning with the training of an infantry branch, he prepared to expand to include branches of artillery, cavalry, engineers, signal corps, and a medical department. He divided his army geographically into four regimental areas, and each regiment was to have twelve companies. The First Infantry Regiment was located in California and included cadet companies eventually located in Los Angeles, San Francisco, Fresno, Sacramento, Oxnard, Ventura, Santa Barbara, Hanford, Bakersfield, San Bernardino, and San Diego. The Second Infantry Regiment eventually included Denver, Phoenix, Chicago, St. Louis, and Pittsburgh. The Third Infantry Regiment eventually included the East Coast cities of Boston, Hartford, Philadelphia, Baltimore, and New York. Finally, the Fourth Infantry Regiment eventually included companies in the Pacific Northwest cities of Portland, Seattle, Spokane, Tacoma, and Walla Walla. Although some of the institutions in the smaller cities trained only fifteen to twenty cadets, a few of those in the larger cities surpassed one hundred cadets. Overall, these regiments made up the Second Army Division.[27]

Part of Lea's success in establishing a nationwide reform army stemmed from the generous salaries he paid. When he employed O'Banion's comrades and various National Guardsmen as part-time drill instructors, many of these former corporals and sergeants had little or no interest in reform party politics. They joined Lea primarily for personal benefit. The Pao Huang Hui paid them the same scale as U.S. Army officers, thereby increasing their incomes dramatically. Instead of earning from $15 to $34 a month as noncommissioned officers, these men received the equivalent of a full-time U.S. Army officer's pay, ranging between $125 and $150 a month.[28]

Lea could afford to pay his instructors well and expand his operations because he established his cadet companies in a period of rising Pao Huang Hui fortunes and membership. Even so, while the party paid for the CIA's major expenses, it did not bear the total cost of Lea's enterprise. Lea's cadets were volunteers who each paid 50¢ a month in dues to the Pao Huang Hui to help finance their training. They also paid for their own uniforms and accessories.[29]

When Lea and O'Banion decided their Chinatown armory was too small for all their training needs, Lea rented supplementary outdoor properties in the small town of Hollywood for his infantry and signal corps units to hold joint maneuvers. There, the cadets could occasionally be seen training on some relatively flat ground north of Norton Avenue, just below Sunset Boulevard, or on some hilly land on the corner of Vermont Avenue and Sunset Boulevard.[30]

Shortly after the Western Military Academy opened, the Los Angeles press began criticizing it as a ridiculous burlesque. Since many Californians treated Chinese with contempt and discrimination, Lea determined to preserve the school's credibility as a cover and orchestrated a public relations campaign. He planned to quiet the cynics and skeptics by having his cadet company participate in the upcoming Tournament of Roses Parade in Pasadena. With the help of his friend John York, a Pasadena resident, he received approval for the cadets to march in the parade.[31]

Lea took a bold step and advised Roger Page, the secretary of the Western Military Academy's board of directors, to seek state authority for his cadets to carry arms in the parade. This would serve three purposes: it would help resolve any legal questions at the highest state levels concerning armed training; it would give the cadets an opportunity to publicly dispel some of the ridicule; and it would show the Chinese community beyond doubt that Lea's covert efforts in training a reform army were working. Governor Pardee and State Adjutant General John B. Lauck approved Page's request for the cadets to carry arms in the parade.[32]

Lea's next step was to generate some favorable pre-parade publicity. He invited a *Los Angeles Times* reporter to witness cadet training at the academy's stockade, a two-and-a-half-acre lot near Chinatown on the corner of Apablasa and Juan streets. He rented this property, a former ballpark surrounded by a ten-foot-high board fence, as a supplementary training area. It was used mostly on weekends, kept locked at all times, and offered improved conditions for training, especially after Lea had electric lights and a rifle range installed. On December 30, 1904, the *Times* reporter watched in amazement as the cadets drilled. The resulting news article served Lea's plans well. It offered a vague explanation of the academy's purpose, it gave an impressive review of the cadets, and it gave Lea his opportunity to address the skeptics publicly. In all, the article promised that "a great surprise is in store for those who may have looked upon the establishment of this school by Gen. Homer Lea as a burlesque."[33]

The Tournament of Roses Parade on January 2, 1905, marked the culmination of Lea's public relations campaign. Seventy-five thousand people crowded Pasadena's streets along the parade's line of march to watch the dazzle and glitter of the pageant. Lea viewed his cadets in the company of Envoy Wong Kai Kah, the Chinese imperial vice commissioner general to the St. Louis World's Fair. Wong Kai Kah, a graduate of Yale University, was fluent in English. He reportedly came to Los Angeles on behalf of his government to investigate Lea's cadets. Lea, in turn, took advantage of the occasion to impress him with members of the emperor's future praetorian guard on the march.[34] Just as Lea had expected, O'Banion and the cadets made a striking addition to the festivities. The *Los Angeles Times* reported: "Perhaps the most interesting among the marching clubs were Gen. Homer Lea's half a hundred Chinese soldiers from Los Angeles. . . . They were very dangerous looking in their new uniforms, and attracted much attention . . . they swung up the street like West Pointers, perfect alignment and cadence, rigid as German dragoons."[35]

The parade marked a significant milestone for Lea and highlighted his initial success in establishing a reform army in America. It also marked a significant advancement in his aspirations and career with the reformers. He was no longer the impetuous, impatient youth searching naively for romantic adventures. At age twenty-eight he demonstrated the characteristics of a skillful manager, guided by patience and determination. His dreams at last were becoming a reality. He had no scruples about his methods, which were often characterized by manipulation and deception; the ends justified the means. With capable subordinates and the reform party behind him, he confidently looked ahead to a bright future as a military leader. He failed to realize, however, that there were some obstacles in his path to glory—Richard Falkenberg was one of them.

CHAPTER 6

THE FALKENBERG COMEDY

Do you think I am a boy that I should believe such a tale?
—K'ang Yu-wei to Richard Falkenberg

Lea may have believed his careful maneuvering and triumphs had cleared the way for the unhindered expansion of his reform career, but to his dismay he soon learned otherwise. The new year brought new challenges to his plans from several quarters. A series of governmental investigations began looking into the cadet training, and his nemesis, Richard Falkenberg, rose to challenge him for control of the reform army. Lea escaped catastrophe, but he came close to losing his academy and his army.

Lea and the reformers had hardly a moment to enjoy the flattering press coverage from the Tournament of Roses Parade before the incidental association with Envoy Wong Kai Kah began casting a shadow over the cadets. Two days after the parade, the *Los Angeles Times* speculated that Wong Kai Kah was an imperial spy sent to investigate the academy. The *Times* also alleged that "Gen. Lea's ambitious plan is to educate officers here from among the Americanized Chinese; and when the time comes, he will pour them into China to take charge of the troops that are to overwhelm the arch adventuress [dowager empress] of all the ages."[1]

Lea soon learned that the unfortunate exposure in the *Times* echoed similar observations being made around the country. During the first week of January 1905 press accounts reported that the U.S. Secret Service was conducting a full-scale investigation of the reform army. The investigation initially focused on several eastern and midwestern cities where cadet training had begun, and it appeared that everything Lea had worked so hard for might suddenly be on the verge of collapse.[2]

Lea and O'Banion were mystified by some of the reports; they had no way of knowing that Richard Falkenberg's dubious military practices as a rival reform army commander had brought on the U.S. government investigation. Falkenberg's latest scheming involved marketing commissions through the mail for his own military organization, called the Chinese Imperial Reform Army (CIRA). This was potentially catastrophic for Lea since there was no way for outsiders to know who was actually in charge of reform military operations. No outsider could know that Lea and Falkenberg were operating independently of each other. The government saw Lea's cadets as possibly part of a larger Chinese military conspiracy under Falkenberg's control, especially since Lea's CIA and Falkenberg's CIRA were easily confused.[3]

Falkenberg's army began taking form in early 1904 after Governor Pardee denied him a commission in the California National Guard. While he remained marginally involved with Wong Kim's recruits, he took his reform general's commission and began organizing his own reform army. Unlike the army Lea was in the process of establishing, Falkenberg's existed largely on paper. He did not need drill instructors, nor did he plan to train a cadet cadre for the reformers. His sole intention was to compile a roster of Americans willing to hold officer commissions in a reform army that would be organized in China at a later date. While the roster was meant to offer a pool of military talent to the Pao Huang Hui for the long term, Falkenberg stood to gain in the short term by soliciting contributions from his prospective officers for the Pao Huang Hui. To assist him in his scheme, he enlisted several acquaintances as subordinate generals in the Chinese Imperial Reform Army. Some of these men had been associates since his Spanish-American War days. Fernand Parmentier, a prominent Los Angeles architect and former member of Falkenberg's volunteer cavalry unit, became a lieutenant general and chief of staff. Edmond F. English of Yankton, South Dakota, a Civil War veteran who was part of Falkenberg's earlier plan to organize a regiment of scouts for Philippine service, became a major general in charge of the Cavalry Division and chief recruiting officer. Falkenberg impressed upon them the secretive nature of their mission and that there could be no newspaper publicity.[4]

English began compiling the roster in April 1904, but despite his attempts at secrecy and discretion, his recruiting efforts soon gained widespread attention. In May 1904, for example, several newspapers across the country reported he was recruiting officers for the Chinese Imperial Reform Army. To add confusion to these accounts, some erroneously reported that Prince Pu Lun had come to America to recruit officers for the Chinese army and entrusted part of the task to English.[5]

At a time that Lea was barely starting to train his CIA cadre, Falkenberg's scheme quickly came to the attention of both imperial Chinese and U.S. government authorities. Prospective officers deluged the Chinese Legation in Washington, D.C., with inquiries about acquiring commissions in the Chinese army. They also wrote their members of Congress asking them to intervene on their behalf with the Chinese minister to obtain commissions. Sir Chentung Liang Cheng, the Chinese minister, categorically dismissed English's recruiting efforts as an unauthorized hoax.[6]

In one case, Massachusetts congressman Ernest W. Roberts asked the State Department if English had authority to offer American citizens Chinese Imperial Reform Army commissions. The State Department, not knowing if the Chinese government was recruiting officers, contacted Sir Chentung Liang Cheng, who chastised English's recruiting efforts. He added that the scheme seemed "to have misled many Americans."[7]

The State Department's confusion about English stemmed from its knowledge that the imperial Chinese government did occasionally contract and commission American militia officers to help instruct and assist the imperial Chinese army's modernization. Since the Chinese minister made clear that English did not enjoy this kind of governmental sanction, the question of who English really represented and whether his operation was legal remained open to question. The State Department concluded it could not take any direct legal action to restrain English since he had not violated any neutrality laws governing recruiting. Instead, since English had used the U.S. mail in his recruiting, the department turned the matter over to the postmaster general for investigation and possible prosecution for violation of mail fraud laws. This marked the beginning of a series of investigations that eventually engulfed Lea and his army.[8]

Shortly after the postmaster general began his investigation in early June 1904, the State Department received a further revelation concerning English's activities. The American minister in Peking forwarded a letter from a Maryland resident, W. T. Neal, asking about the commission he had been offered by English. Neal explained that he had received a letter from English in April, claiming that an acquaintance of Neal, Frank Eberle, had recommended him for service in the CIRA. Neal became suspicious because he did not recall knowing anyone named Eberle. Being a Maryland National Guardsman, he believed someone had probably gotten his name from Maryland state records and suspected that English's letter was "one of many schemes to defraud."[9]

English's correspondence with Neal was representative of his other solicitations. He offered commissions in a Chinese army with pay and benefits equal to what U.S. Army officers received and did not go into great detail about specifics. He advised the prospective officers he did not know when they would mobilize, but indicated they would get at least thirty days' notice before embarking on active service in China. In case applicants had additional questions, he cautioned them to be patient and discreet. In one case he wrote: "There is no hurry about anything except to get yourself in shape so that when you are notified you can go. We will probably make contact with some furnisher so that the officers can get their equipments uniforms etc, at the lowest possible cost and of a uniform texture, and color. All this information will be furnished later. The main thing is to study up and perfect yourself in your duties of the office to which you have been appointed and *have no newspaper notoriety whatever.*"[10]

English's simple approach with applicants may have helped his recruiting, but it proved damaging to Falkenberg's plans. Having no immediate need for officers, no funds to pay them, and no facilities to accommodate them, much less transport them to China, Falkenberg and his associates appeared to be at the center of a sophisticated confidence scheme. Falkenberg, at some point, compounded these beliefs when he began soliciting $5 contributions from new officers under the guise of proposals that included purchasing a gift for K'ang Yu-wei.[11] In late June the postal inspector for Yankton, South Dakota, contacted English at the request of the assistant secretary of state to investigate possible mail fraud. When English informed Falkenberg of the news, Falkenberg delegated Parmentier to contact Secretary of State Hay and explain their innocence. On July 1 Parmentier wrote Hay an explanation: "The postal laws of this country have not been violated in any manner, no money under any circumstances nor even stamps were ever asked for in any communication by any of our officers. No recruiting has ever been indulged in, and only names of Americans are accepted for the commanding General's roster."[12]

In addition to this denial, Parmentier claimed the Chinese envoy's views were not "precise." He admitted English might have been "indiscreet," but insisted that their new army would be purely defensive, protecting the "higher class of Chinese merchants and officials." Above all, he denied all intention to recruit officers through the mail. Parmentier sought to pacify the government by calling Falkenberg "a strong adherent of President Roosevelt" and by claiming high professional and business credentials for the reform army's officers. His most startling and dubious ploy was to suggest that Falkenberg could forestall Japanese influence in China, provided the State Department got Roosevelt's approval for covert cooperation. He also made the fantastic claim that "General Falkenberg has only recently, through personal memorials to the Chinese Empress, been instrumental in securing pardon for all the reformers."[13] Parmentier no doubt hoped these false claims would impress the State Department and garner support for the CIRA. He apparently did not know that Falkenberg's previous correspondence with President McKinley and the State Department had already made some officials in the U.S. government extremely skeptical of his activities.

While the State Department assessed Parmentier's claims, Falkenberg received some unexpected press coverage in San Francisco. A July 25 *San Francisco Call* article entitled "Pig-tailed Warriors Go through Maneuvers" highlighted Wong Kim's cadet company and noted that "Major Falkenberg, formerly of the Filipino Scouts," was assisting in the training.[14] Clearly, neither the State Department nor Lea were aware of the article and Falkenberg's connection to the cadets. For his part, Falkenberg, who undoubtedly had earlier told the Chinese he had served as an officer in the Philippine Scouts, would surely have taken affront at being identified as a major rather than a general.

Although the Chinese minister's denunciation of the CIRA weighed against Falkenberg and his associates, the U.S. government did not have sufficient evidence to arrest and prosecute them. Nor did the government's investigation end Falkenberg's recruiting campaign. For example, on November 14, 1904, the *New York Sun* reported: "American representatives are recruiting throughout the Western States American officers for the Chinese Imperial Reform Army. Seven thousand commissioned officers, it is said, are wanted to officer in a modern Chinese reform army of 200,000, which is being organized in southern China for the apparent purpose of overthrowing the Dowa-ger Empress. A large number of officers have already signed and are going to China this winter as individuals. Secrecy has been maintained marvelously, up to date. The movement is known to army officers."[15]

Falkenberg was stained by the fraud charges and repudiated by the imperial Chinese government, but he retained command of his paper army and seemed safe for the time being.[16] Despite his efforts to shun publicity that might attract attention to his scheme, he and his associates continued to make headlines. In early January 1905, for example, residents of the nation's capital received a glowing account of his work for the Pao Huang Hui in the *Washington Post:* "Foremost in this reform movement in the United States is Gen. R. A. Falkenberg, a full-fledged American, who is commander-in-chief of the Chinese imperial reform army."[17]

Unfortunately for Lea, during that first week of January 1905 the specter of a government investigation quickly engulfed him. He became concerned when news accounts reported that U.S. Secret Service chief John E. Wilkie, who was conducting an investigation into the CIA, believed the military companies to be part of a worldwide conspiracy to overthrow China's dowager empress. The Pao Huang Hui admitted that Chinese companies were drilling throughout the country, but claimed it sought only educational reform and the cadets were no more than a harmless social organization.[18]

Lea and O'Banion redoubled their efforts to portray the Western Military Academy and its branches as a school of educational reform. They knew it was only a matter of time before the Secret Service investigated their academies more closely. Lea instructed his regional drillmasters to hire a real teacher or two and hold some actual classes to help legitimize the academy's academic facade. In Los Angeles, he and O'Banion arranged to help the academy's image by filling the front-room bookcases with an additional wagonload of secondhand books.

Just as Lea suspected, it was not long before Secret Service agents appeared at the various reform cadet academies. O'Banion, acting in his capacity as a special police officer, soon met Secret Service Chief Wilkie in Los Angeles.[19] On four separate occasions, over a six-week period, O'Banion recalled meeting Wilkie and escorting him around Chinatown. They talked a great deal, according to O'Banion, but never discussed anything about the Western Military Academy. O'Banion, however, took no chances and arranged for Wilkie to see for himself how the academy operated. On one of their walks, he guided Wilkie by its open doors, through which it appeared that the cadets were innocently engaged in an English class.[20]

Lea believed his safety precautions were working as the cadet drilling continued across the country. Later, when Wilkie finally completed the Los Angeles phase of his investigation, Lea and O'Banion believed they had forestalled government action and the disbanding of the CIA. Yet they knew that damaging publicity from within the reform ranks might lead to a new series of government investigations. That is the chance they took and eventually lost.[21]

On January 19, 1905, as charges of conspiracy and scandal threatened the CIA, Lea and his Los Angeles cadets made another public appearance. Despite Wilkie's ongoing investigation, Lea refused to be intimidated. His singular position with the Chinese afforded him the privilege of leading a military escort at the funeral of Ah Mow, one of Chinatown's most notable leaders. The funeral was noteworthy for being the largest of its kind ever held in Los Angeles. Ironically, according to a *Los Angeles Times* reporter at the scene, only a few of the thousands of spectators following the procession seemed to know who the cadets were. Spectacular headlines were appearing nearly every day in the press as the Russo-Japanese War captured the attention of America, and many spectators believed the uniformed Asians were some kind of patriotic Japanese group.[22]

Lea and his cadets next planned a grand reception for the upcoming visit of K'ang Yu-wei to America. K'ang Yu-wei's visit was one leg of a world tour he had started in the spring of 1904 to spread and bolster the reform movement. When he entered the United States in February 1905, the rigors of travel and politics, and an attack of bronchitis, forced him to recuperate for almost a month in Portland, Oregon, before visiting California.[23]

Lea played a major role in orchestrating K'ang Yu-wei's reception, as he had done previously with Liang Ch'i-ch'ao. He arranged the welcoming reception at the train station and rented a house on Westlake Avenue, two blocks from his own home, for K'ang Yu-wei and his entourage's planned monthlong stay. Given Lea's growing status in the party and his significant civic, political, and military contacts, K'ang Yu-wei was set to receive an impressive introduction to Los Angeles, one that offered him an excellent opportunity to solicit popular support beyond traditional Chinese audiences.[24]

Poor weather upset Lea's plans for K'ang Yu-wei's reception on March 13. K'ang Yu-wei's train was stormbound for two days before pulling into the Los Angeles Arcade depot on the morning of March 15. Although Lea had received updated information on the train's arrival the previous evening, it was too late for him to arrange for the mayor, several city councilmen, and a Chamber of Commerce committee to get to the depot in time for the welcoming ceremonies. Instead, Lea and a large deputation from Chinatown were on hand to greet the Pao Huang Hui leader.[25]

When K'ang Yu-wei stepped off the train, Lea and a company of cadets acted as an honor guard escort for his carriage procession to Chinatown. The reformer was weary from his journey and still suffering from his bronchial condition, but made a public address that handled questions about the Pao Huang Hui's goals and training reform cadets in America. He tried to defuse any controversy about the cadets by assuring the press the reform military forces were not plotting a revolution. He did indicate, however, that Lea's reform army was intended to be the Pao Huang Hui's principal force for retaining power once the young emperor returned to the throne.[26]

Initially, the Los Angeles press showered K'ang Yu-wei with flattery and praise. It typically referred to him as the former prime minister of China, whose prestige as a scholar, statesman, and reform leader marked him as one of the most important Chinese ever to visit the United States. He was an effective orator and a popular leader. He spoke out against Chinese exclusion laws, which severely restricted Chinese immigration and travel to and from the United States, and continually stressed his desires for the peaceful reform of China based on American ideas. His popularity and that of his reform association were at a high point, especially since the dowager empress was finally beginning to bend to calls for reform.[27]

The first few days of K'ang Yu-wei's visit went very well. In an interview the day after his arrival, he professed an admiration for President Roosevelt that was well received by the press and the American public. On Saturday evening, March 18, he felt well enough to attend a reform banquet given in his honor. Once again Lea handled many of the arrangements, including the guest list, and also presided as toastmaster. The festivities lasted until morning and received notoriety as one of the finest banquets ever given in Chinatown. The elite of the Los Angeles Chinese community attended the event, along with several of Lea's civic, military, and political friends. Even imperial commissioner envoy Wong Tui That attended and astonished the audience with words of praise for K'ang Yu-wei and the emperor.[28]

Lea's importance in the Pao Huang Hui was obvious to all the guests and the invited press. He and his cadets, who acted as an honor guard, made a striking appearance. He wore a specially tailored uniform with a cape that helped obscure his hunchback. His uniform was a slight variation of a U.S. Army lieutenant general's dress uniform, with the cap insignia and buttons ornamented with Chinese dragons instead of American eagles. At twenty-eight years of age, he presented an impressive image, according to the *Los Angeles Times* reporter covering the event

> Kang Yu Wei came in between rigid lines of Chinese cadets, perfectly disciplined and "set up" like West Pointers.
>
> As he entered the banquet hall the Chinese fell back in awe-struck lines, leaving a path through to the table. . . .
>
> Behind him came Gen. Homer Lea in a gorgeous uniform of blue, heavily laced with gold, and with a shoulder cape and spurred riding boots. Then followed the long line of guests.[29]

After the banquet, Lea continued orchestrating events. He arranged meetings for K'ang Yu-wei with prominent people, which included a March 21 visit to Los Angeles mayor Owen McAleer.[30]

These triumphs did not last long for K'ang Yu-wei and Lea. A few days later Richard Falkenberg brought on a storm of discontent and embarrassment to the reformers when he attempted to take command of all reform military training in America. Falkenberg's recent difficulties resulting from his recruiting practices had not dissuaded him from exercising his command prerogative. With reform cadet companies being successfully organized nationwide, he believed the time was ripe to assume command of Lea's CIA. He relied on the help of Dr. T'an Shu-pin and Mr. and Mrs. Albert B. Hotchkiss, Los Angeles society leaders and relatives of his wife, to help him. His immediate goal was to obtain K'ang Yu-wei's confirmation of his general's commission (conferred by Liang Ch'i-ch'ao in 1903), which would grant him a superior rank to Lea's. Once recognized as a four-star general, Falkenberg believed he would outrank Lea, a three-star general, and easily be able to replace him as the CIA commander.

Falkenberg's scheme began taking shape when he arranged for Dr. T'an Shu-pin to visit Los Angeles and meet with K'ang Yu-wei, whom he had invited to be the guest of honor at a luncheon at the Hotchkiss home. Falkenberg did not plan to be present. The luncheon, given on March 22, was a ploy: Dr. T'an Shu-pin and Albert Hotchkiss, a prominent attorney with political and social connections, were to praise Falkenberg and arrange for his introduction to K'ang Yu-wei at a later gathering.[31]

Meanwhile, Falkenberg appeared at the San Francisco headquarters of the CIA announcing that he was the commander-in-chief of the reform army. When he presented his commission, an elaborately ornamented document that was signed and sealed by Liang Ch'i-ch'ao, to Lea's cadets, they were startled but soon accepted him as their new commander. They even hung his picture in their armory. Falkenberg then left San Francisco and repeated his performance for the Sacramento cadet company on his way to assuming complete command in Los Angeles. Before Falkenberg reached Los Angeles, however, Lea received letters from the San Francisco and Sacramento companies describing Falkenberg's visits. Astonished, Lea and O'Banion anxiously awaited Falkenberg's appearance in Los Angeles.[32]

Not long afterward, during an evening drill at the Western Military Academy, O'Banion answered a pounding on the door. He instructed his company to sit down with books and pose as students and opened the door to find two men in uniform. They introduced themselves as General Falkenberg and Lieutenant General Parmentier. The former announced that he had come to take over the training of Chinese troops in America and wanted to inspect O'Banion's cadets. When O'Banion claimed allegiance to Lea and refused to let the men in, Falkenberg chastised O'Banion for impertinence and accused Lea of being an imposter. O'Banion held his ground and closed the door in their faces. Falkenberg responded by threatening to court-martial O'Banion, but for the time being he and Parmentier retreated.[33]

Falkenberg's scheming appeared to be working. On March 29 Lea and O'Banion read with disbelief a report in the *Los Angeles Times* that K'ang Yu-wei had apparently recognized Falkenberg as the reform army commander. Having been denied the courtesy of prior notification, Lea felt angry and betrayed as he read the details of a dinner given at the Hotchkiss home for K'ang Yu-wei and Falkenberg, during which K'ang Yu-wei upheld Liang Ch'i-ch'ao's commission.[34]

Immediately Lea telephoned a *Times* reporter he knew and asked for verification of the news story. Lea's cadets also were bewildered and wanted some answers. The ensuing publicity and uproar led to a favorable resolution for Lea, but at a cost of embarrassing publicity for K'ang Yu-wei and the reform party.[35]

The controversy had actually stemmed from an inaccurate para-phrase of K'ang Yu-wei's comments given by Albert Hotchkiss to the press. In reality, K'ang Yu-wei had never endorsed Falkenberg as Lea's replacement in command of the CIA. On the contrary, when Hotch-kiss's version of K'ang Yu-wei's speech in the *Times* was read to him the following morning, K'ang Yu-wei became so upset and distraught that he quickly sent his secretary to call on Falkenberg and rectify the misunderstanding.[36]

The *Times* reporter then went to K'ang Yu-wei's residence for an interview, though the time seemed inopportune, and later reported:

> Kang Yu Wei was raging. His secretaries were dancing around like hens in coop. One of them explained ingeniously that "the master" was preparing something for the newspapers. . . .
>
> His angry voice was heard on the stairway; he partially appeared, looked over the banisters in evident agitation; then went back. His young secretary, Chew Kok Hean [Chou Kuo-hsien], came down and made excuses for Kang Yu Wei, who sent his respects and said he was sick, but would hear any ques-tions carried to him by his secretary. Thus he was interviewed.[37]

The interview confirmed beyond a doubt that Lea, not Falken-berg, commanded the CIA, although K'ang Yu-wei did apparently recognize Falkenberg's commission as a general in the reform army. This sudden uproar over Falkenberg caught K'ang Yu-wei off guard. When confronted by the *Times* reporter to explain who the fraudu-lent CIA commander was and to make clear what kind of army it was, K'ang Yu-wei was obviously unprepared. The reporter observed:

> The secretary hurriedly ran upstairs and hurriedly ran down again. A look of genuine distress was in his face.
>
> "His Excellency requests that you will not make it too harsh," he said with a scared look, "but Gen. Falkenberg—he—he doesn't know about. . . . If On Won Chew [Liang Ch'i-ch'ao'] appointed him—why—why—maybe something over there," pointing towards China. . . . "Gen. Lea is com-mander of all the military schools in America—of all cadets; they are to respect his authority; he is their commander-in-chief. . . ."
>
> "Then what is Gen. Falkenberg's position?"

"Perhaps in the Imperial army—" began Chew Kok.

"What is the Chinese Imperial Reform Army?"

Chew Kok Hean giggled and said very low; "There isn't any."

"Then these schools scattered over the country are all there is to the Chinese Imperial Reform Army?" . . . "And Gen. Lea is in supreme command of those?"

"Yes."[38]

After the reporter left K'ang Yu-wei's residence, Chou Kuo-hsien (Chew Kok Hean) telephoned Lea and O'Banion to come over immediately to confer with K'ang Yu-wei. When they arrived K'ang Yu-wei was still visibly disturbed over the reporter's questions concerning Falkenberg. Lea acted calm and surprised at K'ang Yu-wei's discontent. He did not accuse K'ang Yu-wei of treachery, but patiently listened as K'ang Yu-wei expressed regret over the entire affair and claimed he had been misquoted and placed in a most embarrassing position.[39]

Although K'ang Yu-wei reassured Lea and O'Banion of his continued support, they left the meeting suspicious and apprehensive. They still did not know much more about Falkenberg than before, or what arrangement he had with K'ang Yu-wei and the reformers. By this time the reform cadets also wanted to know who was in charge. Led by Captain Allen Chung, the general secretary of the local Pao Huang Hui and one of Lea's officers, the entire Los Angeles cadet corps called upon K'ang Yu-wei seeking an explanation. When Chung questioned K'ang Yu-wei about the speech, K'ang Yu-wei denied making any reference to the reform army or ever addressing Falkenberg as commander-in-chief. All K'ang Yu-wei knew was that Falkenberg claimed to have a general's commission from Liang Ch'i-ch'ao and also had made a very generous offer to lend the reformers $10,000,000. K'ang Yu-wei's secretary, Chou Kuo-hsien, confirmed the story and explained that Falkenberg claimed to be the president of the Standard Oil Company and said his proposed loan could be made only after the September dividends came through. Neither K'ang Yu-wei nor Chou Kuo-hsein seemed to realize that Falkenberg's small and obscure Standard Rock Oil Company had no connection with oil magnate John D. Rockefeller's Standard Oil Company. K'ang Yu-wei, in an effort to appease Chung and the cadets, agreed to cable Liang Ch'i-ch'ao to see if, indeed, he had issued Falkenberg a commission.[40]

The whole affair was further aggravated when Chou Kuo-hsien bungled his morning conference with Falkenberg. Instead of clearing up questions regarding the reform army and its command, the meeting left Falkenberg in a confusing position. He agreed to disavow all connections with the cadet companies but still argued that K'ang Yu-wei recognized him as the commander of the reform army.[41]

After the *Times* reporter left K'ang Yu-wei's residence, he went to interview Falkenberg, who was staying at the Hotchkiss mansion. The reporter was satisfied with Chou Kuo-hsien's repudiation of Falkenberg and his Imperial Reform Army, but wanted a statement from Falkenberg about Lea and the cadets. Much to his surprise, Falkenberg granted the interview. He now claimed to be the commander of a different reform army than Lea's. He told the reporter:

> "The fact is he [Lea] is the head of these military schools. I have nothing to do with them. Oh they are just boys' schools; have nothing particular to do with the army."
>
> Asked if Gen. Lea was entitled to military rank, he said, "Why I don't know; I suppose he might be called a captain or major or even a colonel; seven or eight companies, you know these military schools are equivalent to.
>
> "I—Oh—I am supreme in my authority over all the troops of the Chinese Imperial Reform Army. I am the only one who has a commission over them all."[42]

Falkenberg realized his position as commanding general of the paper Imperial Reform Army was in jeopardy and issued a face-saving statement to the press. He explicitly recognized Lea as the commander and organizer of the Chinese cadet companies and stressed that Lea and his cadets had no connection with the CIRA. He also added that "we may possibly in the future, in case of an emergency, accept them individually or as a body for our Chinese Imperial Army depending upon circumstances."[43]

For all his conniving and self-promotion, Falkenberg's prospects as a reform general began to evaporate after the *Los Angeles Times* ran a front-page story based on the interviews of the previous day. When word of the affair reached San Francisco, Falkenberg's credibility and his paper army began crumbling. Officers of the cadet company there, according to the *San Francisco Chronicle*, "turned the picture of their 'General' R. A. Falkenberg, to the wall on Friday night [March 31];

they permitted it to hang in the armory in that position for a few minutes and as it still did not look good to them they are said to have torn it down and thrown it into Sacramento street."[44]

Aside from the San Francisco Pao Huang Hui's discontent with Falkenberg, some of his own CIRA officer corps finally began to suspect something was wrong. When Falkenberg's subordinates in San Francisco began accusing him of running an elaborate confidence scheme, his days with the reformers there were numbered. The *San Francisco Chronicle* added to Falkenberg's public woes, alleging he had defrauded both Chinese and Americans in a scheme involving the distribution of reform army commissions.[45] Falkenberg, despite his reversals and the bad publicity, refused to waver. Unaware that his reform support in San Francisco had vanished overnight, he believed his compromise with K'ang Yu-wei on Lea saved his position as commander of the paper CIRA.

While Falkenberg remained in Los Angeles contemplating his plans, the excitement and embarrassment of the affair began to take a toll on its participants. Albert Hotchkiss had been in ill health for several months, and the anxiety and strain provoked by the accusations of the previous few days were seen as contributing factors to the fatal stroke he suffered on April 1. Then, the following day, K'ang Yu-wei and his entourage abruptly left Los Angeles for a few days to avoid taking any further part in what the press described as the "embarrassing developments in the Falkenberg comedy."[46]

With K'ang Yu-wei gone and Lea the undisputed commander of the cadet companies, the controversy might have died away if Lea and O'Banion had put it behind them. Yet they did not trust Falkenberg, and still wanted to know more about him, his commission, and his connection with K'ang Yu-wei. While waiting for an answer from Liang Ch'i-ch'ao about Falkenberg's commission, and waiting for K'ang Yu-wei's return, they decided to take matters into their own hands. William Sager, an employee of the National Creditors' Association and an acquaintance of Lea and O'Banion, apparently offered to help them gather some information about Falkenberg. Since Sager was not connected with the reformers or their cadets, their plan called for him to approach Falkenberg as a spy, gain his confidence, and find out all he could. Little did they suspect, however, that Sager had his own ideas about resolving the conflict between the two reform army generals. He planned to exploit both parties for his own personal profit. Whether he was an experienced confidence man or a newcomer to the profession, Sager attempted to extort money from Falkenberg in return for secrets about Lea and the promise of favorable press coverage.[47]

On the afternoon of April 6 a mysterious phone caller threatened Falkenberg with injury unless he paid the caller an undisclosed sum of money. The caller warned that he controlled the newspapers and could have them support or oppose Falkenberg in his controversy over the reform army. Falkenberg made an appointment to meet the extortionist alone at a public place, but the extortionist failed to keep the meeting when he saw that Falkenberg came accompanied by a friend. Later that day, Sager went to see Falkenberg at the Hotchkiss house and said he represented another man who could reveal a multitude of secrets about Lea and his army. He tried to blackmail Falkenberg for $5,000 by threatening to unleash a crusade that would drive him from the city if he did not pay. When Falkenberg responded he did not have that much money with him, Sager left, saying that he needed to meet with his accomplice to arrange a meeting the next morning, but would telephone Falkenberg in a few minutes with details of the meeting. At this point, Falkenberg decided to try to lure the blackmailers into a trap. He telephoned the police and explained the situation. The police agreed to send an officer over right away. When Sager then telephoned Falkenberg, Falkenberg told him to come over with his accomplice to receive an immediate down payment of $800. Although Sager agreed to come with his accomplice, when they arrived at the house, the accomplice would not enter. Sager insisted that his accomplice, who did not wish to be seen, had instructed him to pick up the money.[48]

In the meantime, the police officer had arrived and hidden in the doorway of the house waiting to catch the conspirators. When Sager repeated his proposition and demands for money, he was arrested and taken to the police station. There he confessed that his accomplice was none other than Captain O'Banion of Lea's army. At once officers were dispatched to find O'Banion; not long afterward, the police escorted him from the cadet armory in Chinatown to the police station and confronted him with Sager's story. O'Banion admitted that he was the man outside Falkenberg's house, but denied any complicity in Sager's blackmail attempt. He claimed that Lea had recruited Sager to meet with Falkenberg and discover his intentions regarding reform party affairs. When Lea was then called to the police station for questioning, he corroborated O'Banion's testimony and expressed amazement at Sager's attempt to blackmail Falkenberg. Arriving at the truth of the situation was getting so difficult that the chief of police intervened in the investigation to sort it out. In the end, however, the police could not establish anything conclusive against either Sager or O'Banion. Since no money had changed hands, the police decided to release both men. Lea and O'Banion, however, were convinced that Sager had either sold out to Falkenberg to put them in a compromising situation or had contrived the blackmail scheme for his own profit. In either case, Lea and O'Banion denounced Sager and Falkenberg.[49]

Lea wanted the Falkenberg matter cleared up once and for all. The continuing comical references in the press to the rivalry between the two generals and the disastrous Sager incident pushed his patience to the brink. He believed the key to resolving the issue rested solely with K'ang Yu-wei. On April 7, a day after news of the Sager incident brought K'ang Yu-wei and his party back to Los Angeles, Lea and his reform supporters went to see K'ang Yu-wei and put their demands before him. The gravity of the situation was finally forcing a showdown. While K'ang Yu-wei conferred with a house full of reformers and refused to see the press, Lea threatened to stop his work for the party unless K'ang Yu-wei issued a proclamation completely disavowing Falkenberg. K'ang Yu-wei had few options. He wanted to avoid any further damaging publicity, but he also wished to resolve the issue without resorting to harsh tactics. He finally agreed to issue such a proclamation. He and Chou Kuo-hsien worked with Lea on a number of drafts before reaching a version satisfactory to both parties.[50]

In essence, the proclamation represented a weak compromise for K'ang Yu-wei and a triumph for Lea. While it bore no specific mention of Falkenberg, it named Lea as the only bona fide military commander in the reform army, making any other claimant an imposter. That evening copies of the proclamation, written in Chinese on red rice paper, were distributed throughout Chinatown and sent for publication in reform newspapers throughout the United States and Asia. The reformers also provided a copy to the Los Angeles press (see appendix C).[51]

The following day, Chou Kuo-hsien called on Falkenberg to explain the proclamation and K'ang Yu-wei's decision in the affair. A *Los Angeles Times* reporter arrived shortly afterward for a statement and found Falkenberg distressed over the turn of events, but determined to defend the legitimacy of his commission:

Gen. Falkenberg, in the first instance was inclined to doubt the validity of the document. He said that the secretary, Chew Kok Hean [Chou Kuo-hsien], is a friend of Gen. Lea's, and that he believed that he, Chew Kok Hean, wrote the pronouncement without consulting His Excellency, Kang Yu Wei.

Mr. Chew, however, happened to be at Gen. Falkenberg's house at the time and was called in. He said that the ukase was genuine and expressed the sentiments of His Excellency.

He said diplomatically that there was no desire to call Gen. Falkenberg an imposter.

"But," protested Gen. Falkenberg, "you have."

"No," said Mr. Chew softly, "just said that the man claiming to be commander-in-chief of the Imperial Reform Army is an imposter." "And that's me," wailed Falkenberg in an injured tone.

"Perhaps legally," was Chew's vague statement.

Gen. Falkenberg produced an imposing-looking document done in green dragons and red seals and dated at San Francisco which proved to be a commission as "general." . . . He said he would admit that no such army as the Chinese reform is in existence. He said that it is to be organized when the Chinese Dowager Empress dies, to protect the Emperor. . . .

He admits that Gen. Lea is head of the various military scattered over the United States. He says that he (Falkenberg) is just general-in-chief of this army which doesn't exist yet.[52]

Falkenberg did not accept the proclamation and Cho Kuo-hsien's explanation as final. After he had recognized Lea as the leader of the Pao Huang Hui's present military forces, Falkenberg simply did not expect K'ang Yu-wei to repudiate him entirely. He had labored too long to be outdone by Lea. He hoped he could convince K'ang Yu-wei to let him retain his commission, if nothing else. When Falkenberg saw K'ang Yu-wei later he attempted to get back in his good graces. He miscalculated when he made the fatal mistake of infuriating K'ang Yu-wei with unbelievable assertions about his past contributions to the reform movement. Notably, he had the audacity to take personal credit for saving the emperor's life following the 1898 coup d'état. He claimed to have sent hundreds of dollars' worth of cablegrams to the crowned heads of Europe seeking their intercession on the emperor's behalf. He claimed that these cables, in addition to the dispatching of Parmentier to the various European courts at a personal cost of $35,000, were responsible for ultimately saving the emperor's life. The renowned Chinese scholar could only listen in disbelief before losing his temper and remarking with indignation: "What is this you are telling me? Do you think I am a boy that I should believe such a tale?" K'ang Yu-wei's indignation continued to rise when Falkenberg again claimed he could raise $10,000,000 for the reform movement any time he wished. That was all K'ang Yu-wei had to hear to make up his mind about Falkenberg's chances for future service with the Pao Huang Hui. Falkenberg was out of the picture.[53]

Falkenberg, faced with what he considered a temporary setback, packed his bags and returned to San Francisco. Although he was embittered over his humiliating defeat in Los Angeles and never forgave Lea for his downfall, he continued his scheming and recruiting for the CIRA. For the time being he kept his general's uniform and also maintained some connection with Wong Kim and the San Francisco cadets.[54]

There was no question that the damaging publicity from the Falkenberg affair and the Secret Service investigation were almost catastrophic for Lea and his army, but Lea's resourceful handling of the situation lent credence to his managerial skills and increased his prestige within the reform party. Unfortunately, his part in the comical Falkenberg affair eroded some of that prestige and showed him to be naively detached from the inner politics and workings of the party to which he was devoting his career. While he had triumphed over Falkenberg, his success was in part due to Falkenberg making the mistake of going public in a city where he was not well known, and where Lea had friends and patrons in the press. Lea also had wisely avoided a direct confrontation with Falkenberg and gambled that his record and position with the Pao Huang Hui would outweigh Falkenberg's outrageous claims and offers to the party. In the end Lea's gamble paid off, and his position within the party was confirmed, but only at the cost of embarrassment to his, K'ang Yu-wei's, and the Pao Huang Hui's image. Restoring that image would be his next task.

CHAPTER 7

RESOURCEFUL SCHEMER

Who is General Lea, who made him a General, the President
or the Governor of some state?
        —Brigadier General Frederick N. Funston, U.S. Army

Lea's triumph over Falkenberg did not solve all his problems. Governmental inquiries continued to plague the troubled reform army, and Falkenberg, bitter over his defeat, was ready to assist in Lea's undoing. Although some of Lea's own blundering aggravated these problems, he enjoyed sharing the public spotlight with K'ang Yu-wei before a wave of damaging publicity cracked the foundations of his reform army. By the time Lea responded with a resourceful scheme to revitalize his personal and institutional reform party interests, it was too late to undo much of the damage.

After K'ang Yu-wei disavowed Falkenberg, Lea left Los Angeles for a few weeks on an inspection tour of the various California CIA military companies. With his position assured, an inspection tour allowed him to leave the chaos in Los Angeles and explain the Falkenberg affair to his cadet companies. He also hoped to bolster his support within the reform party against future incursions that might threaten his authority.[1]

Much to Lea's chagrin, his troubles as commander of the reform army persisted. Problems arose in Fresno, where California National Guard second lieutenant Edward Curtis Neal was helping train the local Chinese military company. After a member of Neal's Guard unit raised concerns within his chain of command that Neal was neglecting his Guard duties to train the Chinese, Colonel Thomas Wilhelm, the Guard assistant inspector general, sent Lieutenant Jacob A. Alexander to investigate. Not only was Alexander alarmed to find a company of Chinese drilling with arms, but he believed the training was illegal since the Chinese did not have a permit from the governor. He threatened to have Neal court-martialed for his affiliation with the company. William D. Crichton, reportedly the cadets' attorney, was indignant over the charges. He had been assured by Lea that the Fresno cadet company had permission to carry arms, even though Lea advised him there had been "some considerable difficulty in persuading the governor that it was a school."[2] Crichton, a former California National Guard judge advocate officer, denounced the charges and staunchly defended the cadets as drilling within the law and operating with the governor's permission.[3]

News of the Fresno incident in the San Francisco press produced further anxiety for the Pao Huang Hui. It also propelled Lea, who was in San Francisco at that time, into action. He wasted no time in deciding what to do. He planned to resolve the Fresno problem personally, quickly, and diplomatically with Governor Pardee. On April 25 he sent Pardee a telegram with an invitation to meet him and Jing Poo Hai, the imperial Chinese consul general at San Francisco, the following evening for dinner at the Palace Hotel.[4] Lea may also have invited several other distinguished guests to bolster his cause.[5]

Lea and the reformers could not afford to have the governor begin a crusade against them with speculation concerning the reform cadets continually cropping up. The pretense of having Pardee meet Jing Poo Hai offered Lea an ideal opportunity to defend his position to the governor and soften Pardee's attitude toward the reform cadets. Lea was certain he could rely on the consul general's personal friendliness toward the reformers to mislead Pardee into believing that the imperial Chinese government condoned the reform cadets. Furthermore, having the governor attend a meeting with Lea was certain to help restore Lea's prestige in the eyes of the reformers.

While there is no record of the Palace Hotel dinner meeting, Lea likely engaged in careful diplomacy. He evidently did not broach the topic of the Fresno cadets in depth with the governor. Instead, he probably informed the governor about the establishment of the Western Military Academy in Los Angeles and alluded to the fact there were adjunct branches of the academy throughout the state. His goal was to gain the governor's sympathy for the spread of educational reform among the Chinese of his state. It is known that Governor Pardee listened cordially, and Lea left the dinner believing that his subtlety with Pardee had carried the day for the reformers.[6]

Unfortunately, Lea's optimism was short-lived. A week later disaster seemed imminent when he decided to hold a banquet in San Francisco to cement and advance the CIA cause. This time he planned to invite U.S. army brigadier General Frederick N. Funston, commander of the Department of California. Lea already had contacts with several U.S. Army officers sympathetic to his cause, but hoped to add a general among them, which could improve his prestige.

General Funston responded to the invitation in a way Lea did not anticipate. The trouble began on May 2 when two of Lea's officers presented the invitation to General Funston in his office, located in the Phelan Building across from the Palace Hotel. Funston had never heard of General Lea and became enraged when he saw Captains Wong Kim and Ralph J. Faneuf attired in uniforms strikingly similar to those worn by the U.S. Army. A *San Francisco Chronicle* reporter on hand witnessed Funston's ire:

> "Who is General Lea, who made him a General, the President or the Governor of some state?" asked General Funston. The reply was not satisfactory and caused General Funston to look more closely at the man in uniform, and when he saw he was a Chinese the General grew indignant.
>
> "Who on earth gave you the right to wear that uniform," he demanded. "Who made you a Captain?" Again the answer was not satisfactory. The terse and emphatic verbal reply declining the invitation was then delivered and the two made their escape.[7]

When Lea received Funston's reply, he cancelled the planned banquet and cut short his stay in San Francisco. His mistake in approaching Funston had resulted in the one thing he did not need: the distinct possibility of a U.S. Army investigation into the CIA. He knew better than to remain in San Francisco any longer and hurried his departure before the local press could question him and pillory him in the glare of a new and embarrassing series of headlines.[8]

As for Funston, he considered suppressing Lea's companies with a provost guard, but upon further investigation decided no federal neutrality laws had been violated. The academy facade of the CIA companies had saved them once again. All Funston could do was hope state laws were sufficient for Governor Pardee to take appropriate action.[9]

On May 4 the San Francisco press reported Funston's outrage and Lea's hurried departure. Shortly afterward, rumors and speculation about the reform army resurfaced. Informed sources reported the forty-thousand-strong reform party was raising a small army and approximately $500,000 a year for its war chest, with the intention of overthrowing the dowager empress. The reform lobby denied any wrongdoing on the part of its cadets to the governor. It continued to declare that the cadet companies were merely social organizations designed to keep young Chinese off the streets and away from gambling houses.[10]

Pardee, for the most part, accepted the Pao Huang Hui's explanations. Except for Alexander's allegations, he had no grounds to take legal action against the reform military companies. Turning his attention back to Fresno, he wrote to Crichton requesting the document allegedly permitting the cadets to drill with arms. When Crichton suddenly found himself in a growing controversy involving the governor, he had second thoughts about supporting the Fresno cadet company. In replying to the governor, he explained he had no permit, only Homer Lea's word that one existed. He recanted his reported connections with the Fresno military company and clarified that he only represented a group of Chinese merchants in that city. He assured Pardee of his full cooperation and added that the Fresno cadet company would stop drilling if it were in violation of the law. Crichton, who was preparing to leave town for several weeks, also asked Dr. Chester Rowell, an acquaintance and owner of the *Fresno Morning Republican* newspaper, which had reported on the Chinese cadets, to write Pardee a similar pledge on his behalf, which Rowell did. The fact that Rowell was a leading member of the state Republican Party may have helped sway the Republican governor, particularly since Crichton was a well-known Democrat.[11]

By the time Lea reached Los Angeles things looked brighter. He found comfort in knowing that Falkenberg was no longer his rival and that Funston had deferred taking action against the CIA. Lea advised K'ang Yu-wei and the reformers that there was nothing further to worry about concerning the CIA. If Funston did press for some type of action against him, Lea still believed he had support from Governor Pardee and various other political and civic leaders, along with California National Guard officers. He did not know Crichton had chosen to back down in the face of Pardee's inquiry and that the governor was moving closer to action. Lea believed he had successfully sidestepped disaster. His immediate concerns were again in Los Angeles as he prepared to embark on a nationwide tour with K'ang Yu-wei to inspect cadet companies.

K'ang Yu-wei and his party left Los Angeles and on May 15 arrived in St. Louis, their first major tour stop.[12] They had barely settled into the Southern Hotel before receiving startling news that Governor Pardee was closing down the Fresno company. This latest crisis had transpired after the governor received replies from Crichton and Dr. Rowell and decided to act. Earlier, on May 10, Pardee had resolved that the Fresno cadets were drilling in violation of the law and had instructed Fresno district attorney George W. Jones to disband them and "take such action as may be proper for the enforcement of the law."[13] Jones subsequently notified the Fresno cadets, on May 16, of Pardee's decision. Pardee also wrote back to Crichton and Rowell explaining that he had never granted a permit to Lea allowing the Fresno cadets to parade with arms. He went on to express bewilderment at Lea's claim to the contrary, noting that "Homer Lea must be a 'diplomat.' I saw him once, but he did not 'persuade' me to do anything, and he did not even ask for a license for the company in question."[14]

On May 18 Lea received the letter Jones sent to the Fresno Pao Huang Hui ordering it to desist from further drilling or bearing arms until it received legal permission from the governor.[15] Lea replied to Jones that he "was much chagrined to find that there still exists a misunderstanding in regard to this school" and asserted that the governor had granted permission to the Western Military Academy in Los Angeles, which also applied to its branch in Fresno.[16] Lea advised Jones that the Fresno cadets were not an independent company but an adjunct of the main Los Angeles Academy, whose purposes were educational. He added that its articles of incorporation were on file with the Fresno county clerk's office. He also noted that when his cadets had paraded publicly in Pasadena five months earlier, they had obtained the proper permit from the governor. On this occasion, however, he argued a permit was not necessary because the Fresno cadet company drilled privately. Although Lea stood his ground and refused to discontinue the drills, his Fresno cadets complied with Jones's orders until the matter was fully resolved.[17]

Meanwhile, in St. Louis, Lea focused on celebrations, meetings, and banquets while attempting to keep the Fresno publicity to a minimum. He downplayed the importance of Pardee's action, attributing it to a misunderstanding. He also dismissed suggestions that he should abort his tour and return to California. He believed that once Jones found the academy articles of incorporation the matter would be cleared up in his favor. He nonchalantly told a *St. Louis Republic* reporter, "I have not given the matter serious attention. . . . We are conducting these military academies as educational institutions, and to attempt to disorganize them would be the same as attacking any other academy in the State."[18]

Although Jones found the articles of incorporation and forwarded Lea's explanation to Pardee, the matter was far from over. Jones did not accept Lea's explanation. On May 22, in a letter to the Fresno reformers and Governor Pardee, he expressed his belief that all the cadets were in violation of neutrality and international laws and that the federal government should take action to disband them. In his eyes, there was "no question that the established academy in Los Angeles has for an end the training of soldiers. At any rate all the academy does here is to drill in tactics. The contention that there is a branch of an academy in Fresno in the strict sense of the term academy is ridiculous. They do nothing but drill and there are no academic courses in connection with it."[19]

In addition to this continuing trouble, Lea faced a hidden adversary in Richard Falkenberg, who now resurfaced to renew his scheming and accusations against Lea. Falkenberg wasted no time in taking advantage of the situation to distance himself from the reformers and get even with Lea and the reform army. Shortly after the San Francisco press reported on the suppression of the Fresno cadets, Falkenberg began plotting a scheme that would lead to a new series of investigations into Lea's army involving California, New York, and the U.S. Army. Meanwhile, he wrote the first in a series of self-serving letters to Pardee. While disavowing his own connection with the reformers, he implicated Lea in the illegal training of Chinese troops. He denied any connection with the cadets, advising the governor that he believed them to be "entirely illegally organized." He added that when the "the San Francisco boys" had asked his advice a year earlier, "being a military man I at once told them to 'ask permission and a license from our Governor, who himself is a soldier.'"[20] In the face of what appeared to be a blossoming scandal for the reformers, Falkenberg went on record as a law-abiding citizen appealing for a favor from Pardee; he wanted the governor to help protect his good name and stop the press from mentioning his involvement with Lea and the reformers. He also wanted Pardee to know that his own "organization of 3000 American Officers is entirely legal and has nothing to do with these Chinese Military Companies in America."[21]

Although Falkenberg's organization was no more than the paper roster he and English, among others, had been compiling for several years, some of the officers who received commissions in his defunct Chinese Imperial Reform Army were being associated with Lea in the press. Many of those officers who resided outside of California had evidently received no word of Falkenberg's dismissal as the reform army commander. They still expected to ship out to China in July 1905 and take up lucrative positions with the true imperial Chinese army. Their talking out of hand further compounded Lea's problems in Fresno when rumors spread that he was mobilizing a large army on the West Coast to soon overthrow the dowager empress. In the wake of Jones's order shutting down the Fresno cadet company, the *San Francisco Chronicle* reported that a number of Washington state militiamen who had joined the Chinese Imperial Reform Army had begun inquiring about preparations to go to China: "Among the militia soldiers . . . who are in expectancy of battle . . . are Major Fred Llewellyn of Bellingham Bay, First Lieutenant Charles Lindberry of the Second Washington, sergeants and privates without end. They report that they have received marching orders, that by July 1st 50,000 good men will be mobilized in Peking and that then the Dowager had better look out."[22]

Lea, when confronted with these reports in St. Louis, dismissed them as absurd. He continued to claim that his academies were purely educational, adding that "all talk about our preparing for actual war and mobilizing our troops at some place for a Chinese invasion is senseless."[23]

Lea continued to concentrate on building public relations. He had few scruples when it came to courting public opinion. Thus it did not matter that he had a personal aversion to missionaries when he joined K'ang Yu-wei and spoke at an American Baptist Missionary Union meeting. What mattered to him was how well he advanced his interests. Most of all, he wanted the public to believe in his patriotism and progressive commitment to uplift the much-maligned Chinese. His comments on the Orient and world affairs earned him praise in the press as a well-traveled and learned authority, and his proclaimed desire for a great friendship between China and the United States helped explain his reasons for serving in the reform party.[24]

Lea also found an opportunity to promote his cadets at a large public gathering when 135 of them performed a military drill during a fund-raising horse show for the benefit of the East St. Louis Hospital Fund.[25] Lea was particularly proud of the cadets and wanted the public to know how successful their training had been. He told one journalist that "in Los Angeles, where my headquarters are, we have a regiment, which although having been drilled less than a year, can compete with credit with the crack military organizations of California."[26]

Lea offered a particularly candid view of his beliefs in a *St. Louis Post Dispatch* article entitled "American Hopes to Be Lafayette of China; Leads Army." In the course of the interview, he touched on a variety of issues, including his social Darwinist beliefs, his long-term goals, and his desire to foster large-scale American commercial benefits by helping China. He explained:

I had made a study of the military science. Not that I expected at the time to follow the military, but because I loved the science. I realized that no nation was ever in the ascendancy, no powerful dynasty ever fell through the degeneration of its military. The military is and should be the fundamental science of all sciences, for it is this that develops manhood to its highest perfection.

After Empress An had caused the Emperor to be cast in prison, and after she had caused all his councilors to be beheaded, save His Excellency Kang Yu-wei, and after the edicts had been issued changing the customs that had prevailed for thousands of years, I visited China and saw for myself the needs of the great nation.

I saw that China was a nation of dough. What it needed was yeast. That yeast is Western energy. I realized that I could be of vast service to the country. I met a friend who was also a friend of His Excellency.

This mutual friend brought us together. I offered my services and they were accepted. We studied and planned together. We saw that the reformation of China must come from within itself, but there must be help from without. The Chinese Empire Reform Association was organized to furnish this help.

Education is the basis. Our first school was organized at
Los Angeles, California, more than a year and a half ago. Now
in America there are thirty schools, patterned after the first
one. They are not dissimilar from the American military academies. We teach military tactics along with other sciences. It
develops the pupils. The pupils are all Chinese. The instructors and officers are all American. The uniforms appear to be
American, but embrace many Chinese features.

We are working in China, as well as elsewhere. In that
country we already have two-thousand schools established,
but they are not so thoroughly equipped as are our schools in
America.

When the Empress dies and the Emperor is restored to
power, then the schools there will be reorganized on the same
basis as the schools throughout the United States. Until that
time arrives we must work as we are doing now.

Since I have been connected with the movement I have not
drawn one cent of pay, though I have been tendered a large
salary. With this noble band working to get their Emperor
out of prison and to lead their 800,000,000 people from the
darkness into light, I would consider it criminal to accept pay.
When the Emperor is restored, if he had anything to offer I
could then accept.

Americans ought to be interested in our movement for two
reasons. First from a commercial standpoint, for when the
doors of commerce are opened this country will have direct
dealings with more than half the world's population, which
is located in China. And then, for what Americans ever boast,
fair play.[27]

Lea clearly wanted more at this point than a military career in
China. He may have envisioned himself as a modern-day combina-
tion of Lafayette and Napoleon. He foresaw his military role as a necessary step in strengthening China. In his worldview, he wanted a
break with the Open Door policy in China. He believed China needed
to be rescued from the grip of European and Japanese imperialists
and needed to forge new bonds with Anglo-Saxon America and Great
Britain. He wanted American and British finance and industry to assist
China, as he was doing, for the mutual benefit of both parties. He
and K'ang Yu-wei agreed that progressive and educational reform,

as advocated by the Pao Huang Hui, and applied social Darwinism, as he prescribed, were needed for the new China. Lea likely believed he could be an empire builder and his plans were no secret. Once the emperor regained his throne, which in Lea's opinion was just a matter of time, with the dowager in failing health, he planned to return in triumph to China with K'ang Yu Wei. He told a *St. Louis Republic* reporter: "Then there will be no more partitions of China. Powers will cease their greedy glances Eastward. China with her new education and developed resources will become the dominating power of the eastern Hemisphere with the possible exception of England. I hope to live to see a compact among America, England and China. That will be the new 'triple alliance' which will absolutely control the world."[28]

On May 22 Lea and K'ang Yu-wei left for Chicago, their next stop. They had good reason to view their St. Louis visit as a success. They did not suffer any immediate repercussions from the Fresno publicity; and, as Lea noted on their departure: "We have had a most gracious reception and were delighted with everything we saw in the city. Ninety-eight percent of the Chinese here belong to the association and are anxious for the moment to come when they can return to China to teach their less fortunate brethren."[29]

With the Fresno publicity and Governor Pardee's actions in abeyance for the time being, Chicago offered Lea and K'ang Yu-wei a respite from accusations and sensational headlines. They took advantage of the opportunity to improve their public image by downplaying the provocative military aspects of the Pao Huang Hui. While the usual receptions, banquets, and meetings marked their weeklong stay, Lea's military activities with the cadets barely received mention in the press. Lea stepped out of the public spotlight temporarily, but he was still, as one Chicago tabloid noted, "the guide for Kang Yu Wei, and he is considered by the Chinese to be second only to the reform leader."[30]

During the first week in June the reformers visited Pao Huang Hui branches in Ohio before arriving in Washington, D.C., on June 8. At this juncture, Lea realized the potential risk of wearing his uniform in public: it might bring undue scrutiny to reform military affairs. To forestall this he did not share a large part of the spotlight with K'ang Yu-wei and gave few press interviews. K'ang Yu-wei restricted his public comments to denouncing the Chinese exclusion laws and emphasizing his society's goals of peaceful reform in China. Although Lea commented to the local press about his commitment to helping uplift the Chinese, back in Los Angeles, the *Los Angeles Times* reported that he privately "had been telling his friends things that are considered remarkable and that make Chinese exclusionists of the more virulent type shudder."[31]

Neither K'ang Yu-wei nor Lea publicized the fact they had arranged to meet with President Roosevelt the following week. Rather than waiting in Washington for the meeting, however, the reformers decided to make a weekend visit, from June 10 through 12, to Baltimore's Pao Huang Hui chapter. In the course of their visit K'ang Yu-wei gave an address to a Young Men's Christian Association gathering at which Lea kept a relatively low profile and, whether he had intended this or not, the local press referred to him simply as K'ang Yu-wei's interpreter, a duty he assisted Chou Kuo-hsien with during the tour.[32]

After the reformers returned to Washington Lea met first with President Roosevelt. On June 15 he used a letter of introduction from *Los Angeles Times* publisher Harrison Gray Otis, one of his prominent acquaintances, to obtain a brief meeting with the president in the White House. The next day he accompanied K'ang Yu-wei for a discussion with Roosevelt and Acting Secretary of State Francis B. Loomis that focused on the Chinese exclusion laws. Chinese exclusion was the primary issue addressed throughout their tour, and it was a concern that cut across Chinese party lines in America. K'ang Yu-wei's was the second Chinese delegation that week to confer with Roosevelt about the exclusion laws.[33]

The meeting proved beneficial in other ways for the reformers. K'ang Yu-wei impressed upon Roosevelt that the Chinese looked toward America as a model, and he urged the president to assist in allowing Chinese students to come to study in America. When Roosevelt showed sympathy for the idea, both Lea and K'ang Yu-wei were convinced he was indirectly in favor of aiding the Pao Huang Hui. They became more encouraged when, as a result of their lobbying efforts and those of the previous Chinese delegation, the president pledged to ease the rigid enforcement of the existing exclusion laws and to work toward their modification. Last, before embarking for their next tour stop, they arranged another meeting between K'ang Yu-wei and Roosevelt for June 24, when Secretary of State Hay, who was then unavailable, could attend.[34]

Meanwhile, K'ang Yu-wei and his party made another weekend side trip, this time to visit the Pittsburg (as the spelling was from 1890 to 1911) Pao Huang Hui chapter, before returning to Washington for the second Roosevelt meeting. For reasons as yet unknown, Lea did not attend this second meeting. Instead, Dr. Yung Wing, a Yale graduate, notable reformer, and former imperial diplomat living permanently in Hartford, Connecticut, came to escort K'ang Yu-wei and act as his interpreter for the meeting. During the meeting, in which the exclusion question was further discussed, K'ang Yu-wei brought Lea's cadet companies to the president's attention as an example of how the American model was already benefiting his people. According to a statement Chou Kuo-hsien made to the press a few days later, "Mr. Kang said that he told President Roosevelt of the military training the Chinamen in different cities of the United States were receiving and how it was teaching them the English language, to all of which the President said, 'Good!'"[35] Lea took the president's endorsement as a significant stamp of approval. Despite the recent attacks on his army, he now had reason to believe that Roosevelt was not going to stand in the way of the CIA. When the reformers left for Philadelphia later that day, Lea stood at K'ang Yu-wei's side once again.

Philadelphia marked a triumphal tour stop for K'ang Yu-wei and Lea. Following his second successful meeting with Roosevelt, K'ang Yu-wei's stature and prestige within the Pao Huang Hui rose beyond his expectations and Lea again shared the spotlight. The *Philadelphia Inquirer* characterized Lea as "the most skilled military leader of China . . . [whose] ability in military affairs is conceded by experts in all countries."[36] Their reception from the reformers was tremendous and encompassed most of the local Chinese populace. About one hundred CIA cadets from Philadelphia and New York were among the honor guard and escort that welcomed K'ang Yu-wei and Lea at the Broad Street train station that evening. The *Philadelphia Public Ledger* reported that their "blue uniforms and modern rifles attracted as much attention as the society's president."[37]

No sooner had Lea arrived in Philadelphia than he received startling news. He learned that his New York cadets were now involved in a governmental inquiry similar to that in Fresno. Although news of his Fresno and New York problems had so far eluded the Philadelphia press, Lea did not take any chances and quickly distanced himself from inquisitive reporters. He confined his remarks and oratory to Pao Huang Hui meetings and banquets, from which Caucasians were usually excluded. The publicity he received as K'ang Yu-wei's brilliant military commander became more intertwined with exaggeration and blatant falsehoods when Chinese reform spokesmen related whatever rumors they had heard about him as truth to the press. For example, a *Philadelphia Inquirer* story entitled "American May Lead Chinese" reported that Lea was "at the head of a by no means insignificant Chinese army of about 8000 well-drilled men scattered among seventy-two cities."[38] The article went on to offer the following distortions and errors about his background, his affiliation, and his travels with K'ang Yu-wei:

> The General is a small man, suffering from a slight bodily trouble that kept him from attending West Point, but he secured a fine military training at other schools and in the course of his travels investigating military systems he reached China and a study of the army system there.
>
> Kang Ye We was at that time a member of the Chinese Cabinet and personal instructor of the Emperor. He took an interest in General Lee's work and assisted him in every way. While General Lee was visiting in Europe the Chinese reformer had to flee from China to save his life, and the two met later in London and joined hands in taking up the work of spreading the doctrine of reforms for China.
>
> Three years ago General Lee again visited China, and since that time, he and Kang Ye We have traveled through much of the world together.[39]

Since Lea rarely acted to correct inflated and flattering reports about himself, this turn of events further bolstered myths about him. How else could the Philadelphia public view Lea but with awe, when the *Inquirer* speculated that he was earmarked to be the future commander of the imperial Chinese army, and added that "the clear-cut, earnest face of the General, the high brow and piercing eyes together with his small stature, cause many of his acquaintances to see in him a likeness to Napoleon."[40]

As Lea's image underwent distortions in the local press, his reform army became the subject of a new round of sensational charges in Los Angeles. In the wake of the Fresno and New York investigations, the timing could not have been worse. It is unknown if he knew about the charges or how he responded. On June 25 the *Los Angeles Herald* printed a sweeping exposé about his reform army. A front-page article entitled "15,000 Armed Chinese in the United States Preparing on American Soil for War of Conquest," accompanied by a photo of a cadet company, asserted that Lea controlled fifteen thousand well-armed Chinese soldiers who planned the "overthrow of the present Chinese government."[41] The exaggerated size of Lea's reform army may not have been taken seriously in Los Angeles, but other allegations in the exposé, some of which was based on sound investigative reporting, were accurate. For example, the article accurately explained that the Los Angeles cadet academy was really a cover for training Chinese soldiers. John York, the academy's attorney, denied the assertions, but the conspiracy focus of the exposé received additional backing when Sergeant Harvey Waterman, one of Lea's instructors, reportedly stated there were forty-four cadet companies in America with plans to "come together and hold a big encampment in the mountains of California."[42] The exposé also cited George McKeeby, the U.S. district attorney, who indicated that his office had been investigating the cadets since their initial organization, but to date had made no determination on whether they violated neutrality laws.[43] The exposé may have been exaggerated and inconclusive, but it created more unwanted publicity for the reformers and fed further distortions.

On June 27 K'ang Yu-wei and Lea left Philadelphia and attended a reform reception in New York City that was as resplendent as the one in Philadelphia. In New York, however, they received updated information on the Fresno and New York investigations that soon dampened their spirits. Lea finally received the Jones (May 22) letter ruling against the Fresno cadets, as well as a full report on the New York State investigation conducted by Governor Frank W. Higgins. Little did he suspect that Higgins's investigation was not a random coincidence but part of a larger calculated scheme apparently engineered by Falkenberg.[44]

After Falkenberg first wrote to Pardee in early May, he and English likely enlisted the aid of Dr. William H. Eckley of St. Paul, Minnesota, to help implicate Lea in the illegal military training of Chinese in the United States. Not long afterward, Eckley wrote several state governors, including Pardee and Higgins, "that there are a number of Chinamen belonging to an organization, of which Kang-Yu-Wei . . . claims to be Grand President, who are armed and drilling in different cities of this country." Eckley then named Homer Lea of Los Angeles as the commander responsible for the illegal drilling.[45]

Pardee and Higgins responded differently to the Eckley letter. Since Pardee knew about the Western Military Academy, he wrote Eckley back asking for specific information on illegal drilling activities other than in Fresno. When he did not receive a reply, he dismissed the allegations. Falkenberg, meanwhile, did not accept Pardee's passivity. He wrote Pardee another letter, pressing the governor to act against Lea: "[I]n spite of your peremptory strict orders, remarks are made in the different Chinese colonies that 'everything is all right' and the Chinese military companies in Los Angeles, Oakland and San Francisco are still drilling regularly with rifles every week."[46] Again, Pardee replied that action would be taken if the allegations could be proved.[47]

Eckley's letter seemed more effective in New York than California. Governor Higgins forwarded the letter to President Roosevelt's private secretary, William Loeb Jr., to "put it into the proper channels at Washington."[48] Loeb, in turn, forwarded the letter to the War Department, where Lieutenant General Adna R. Chaffee, now the army chief of staff, reviewed the case and decided to have the Los Angeles police chief investigate the allegations rather than the army's regional military commander.[49] The War Department showed no sense of urgency or serious concern. If there was a legal problem, Chaffee had faith that a simple civil investigation could rectify the matter without involving the U.S. Army. Had he been aware of Funston's earlier accusations and lack of action against the cadets, Chaffee might have dismissed the entire investigation out of hand. Fortunately for Lea, William A. Hammel, the Los Angeles chief of police, did not delve too closely into the affairs of the Western Military Academy and gave Chaffee a benign report on the cadets. On June 20 he replied to the War Department: "[A]fter a careful investigation I find that a Company of Chinamen, numbering thirty-six men, under the personal supervision of Homer Lea, and drilled by . . . Capt. Ansel O'Banion, . . . are operating under a Charter, issued by the Secretary of State, under the name of the Western Military Academy. The drill master informs me that they do not drill in public, except with permission from the U.S. Government, and, that their object is the betterment of their condition, as they expect to occupy responsible positions in the Chinese Army at some future time."[50]

While Hammel's report satisfied the War Department, Governor Higgins was in the process of conducting his own investigation. He sent a copy of the Eckley letter to New York City police commissioner William McAdoo, asking him to take action. McAdoo followed up on the case and discovered that the cadets had been drilling with discarded National Guard muskets for some time under the direction of Major George McVickar of the Sixty-ninth Regiment, New York National Guard. McVickar commanded the First Battalion, Third Infantry Regiment, CIA, composed of cadet companies in Boston, Hartford, Philadelphia, Baltimore, and New York. In circumstances similar to those in Fresno, Governor Higgins decided that McVickar's two companies of New York cadets, numbering about 150 men in total, were drilling in violation of state statutes and ordered them to stop.[51]

The New York reformers responded with surprise and indignation to the governor's decision. They insisted that reports of overthrowing the dowager with a secret army were absurd. Sir Chentung Liang Cheng, who received a copy of the *Los Angeles Herald* exposé on the reform army, agreed with the reformers and attributed the latest reports to unnamed persons seeking to take advantage of innocent Chinese for monetary gain:

> I have heard reports of something like that, but I have considered it so unimportant and so unlikely that I have taken no notice of it. The idea that an army for a hostile movement against China could be recruited in a friendly nation like the United States is absurd. In a time of peace, this country would not tolerate the formation here of such an army, but would suppress it at once. Evidence of that can be found in the action taken some time ago by the Governor of California, who had occasion to suppress some such movement which was organized within his jurisdiction. As for this army's going into camp in the California mountains, that, too, is not to be thought of. . . .
>
> Seriously, I suppose that this story and similar ones get a foundation in the fact that efforts are being made from time to time to enlist the sympathies and money of Chinese in this country and political movements which are developing in China. There are numbers of men who through failure to obtain office in China work on the credulity of the poor Chinese in this country and obtain from them large sums of money.[52]

Although Higgins's decision forbade any further armed outdoor drill, the New York Pao Huang Hui chapter president, Chao Wansheng, known by the anglicized name Joseph M. Singleton, applied for and received tentative permission for the cadets to continue their drilling indoors before K'ang Yu-wei and Lea arrived on their tour. In compliance with the police order, McVickar's two companies of cadets carried flags instead of guns when they met K'ang Yu-wei and Lea at the Jersey City ferry and escorted them to New York City's Chinatown. Once inside the confines of the reform headquarters in Chinatown, however, they exchanged their flags for guns and performed a review for K'ang Yu-wei and Lea, albeit a difficult one, since "their gun barrels interfered with the steam pipes on the low ceiling above."[53]

Lea made an effort to keep his cadets out of the public eye and forestall any further controversy for the duration of their weeklong stay. He accompanied K'ang Yu-wei to a meeting with New York mayor George B. McClellan, but there is no indication he broached the topic of his cadets with the mayor.[54] Even so, the New York press, like Philadelphia's, contributed to the Lea mythology by printing exaggerated and misleading accounts of his exploits. For example, a *New York Sun* article entitled "White Leader of Chinese" characterized Lea as "an international man of mystery" who had "covered the whole world twice over in the past six years, and he has been in places which no other white man has ever seen." The article then went on to note: "Three or four times Homer Lea has got into the newspapers as head of the Chinese reform army and leader of a revolution. These reports have come from lands as distant as India. Every time Homer Lea bobs up it is an unexpected spot. In fact, since 1901 he has been in China again, has crossed United States twice and has traveled through Canada, southern Asia, and all Europe. About a year ago he joined Kang Yu Wei on his travels and they have been together ever since."[55]

Lea was guarded in his remarks to the press. He made no effort to correct various "man of mystery" references about his past travels and associations, but continued to completely discount assertions that he was training a revolutionary force to undermine China's government. He explained to one journalist:

It is bosh to say that I am at the head of a revolution. This is not a revolution. Quite the contrary. We are drilling and teaching these young men to help the empire. She needs above all things an army if she is going to work out her own salvation.

It may be ten years, it may not be in my lifetime, but when

China calls we will be ready with a body of native officers who knows something about military discipline and tactics. That's the game. That's all there is to it.

China can't make progress without an army. She needs it to keep the empire intact. I think I know the Chinese now about as well as any white man ever did, and I can say positively that the yellow peril is a myth. They are naturally a peaceful people; the spirit of aggressive conquests is not in them. They are as brave as the bravest, as Gordon found, but they fight naturally only in defense.

Is China awakening? Wait a few years and see.[56]

K'ang Yu-wei, for his part, also continued to dismiss suggestions about an armed uprising. He consistently stated the reformers would achieve their goals through a peaceful revolution. For example, in response to a journalist's inquiry of whether he would use his reform troops to forcibly achieve his goals, he replied: "I anticipate that nothing of the kind will be necessary. In the course of nature the empress dowager, who is now more than 70 years old and feeble, cannot live long. She is also tired of power. Nothing better could be done than for her to accept a pension and retire. With the emperor restored to his own, China will begin her new era."[57]

As the tour neared an end for Lea, he wanted more than ever to return to California as a leader in triumph rather than as one continually under fire. On July 4 he granted an interview to a *New York Tribune* reporter and denied once and for all that his cadets were being trained to overthrow the dowager in China. He continued to assert that America could profit financially after he helped restore China's martial vigor. He also wanted everyone to know that "all efforts of mine for the benefit of China have been misinterpreted by the American people and the Chinese government."[58]

Privately, he still talked in terms of Napoleonic grandeur. Will Irwin, who visited him in his Waldorf Hotel suite, remembered: "Off the record, he talked for hours—almost exclusively of China. The giant was stirring. She could be the most powerful nation in the world. He made it plain that he felt it his mission to lead her to that destiny—to become the Napoleon of the Far East. Someday China would rule all Asia. 'By conquest?' I asked. 'How else does a nation ever achieve empire?' he asked in effect."[59]

Perhaps the summer heat and the continued embarrassing questions about Lea's reform army contributed to a distancing in relations between K'ang Yu-wei and Lea. While traveling to Boston and Hartford during the second and third weeks in July for their final tour stops together, they no longer appeared to be on close terms with each other. Lea reverted to civilian dress and was rarely seen in public at K'ang Yu-wei's side. As his relations cooled with K'ang Yu-wei, however, Lea developed a closer rapport with Yung Wing in Hartford, which would later prove most beneficial in furthering his ambitions. For now, he left the tour in Hartford on July 19 and returned to New York City for reform army business. The *Hartford Courant* reported, "General Lea will meet his aide-de-camp, Captain Ben O. Young, in New York and they will see about what can be done towards keeping up the interest in New York companies of Chinese."[60] The following day, K'ang Yu-wei cut short his stay in Hartford and traveled to New York City after he received word, possibly related to the cadets, to come there immediately. While K'ang Yu-wei continued touring North and South America, he remained in contact with Lea, who next headed to Canada, but the two would never meet again.[61]

It is uncertain if Lea went to Canada for business or pleasure, or exactly where he went and for how long. Although his complete itinerary remains a mystery, he visited Nova Scotia, Quebec, and Toronto for pleasure during his travels. Sir Thomas J. Lipton, the famed British merchant and yachtsman, reportedly entertained him in Nova Scotia; while Sir Bryan Leighton, a distinguished British soldier and journalist, spent time with him in Quebec. A postcard Lea sent Newmark from Toronto, dated August 11, 1905, indicates that his itinerary may have taken him west across Canada on his return to California. An air of mystery surrounded Lea's trip. The *Los Angeles Times* later reported that after leaving K'ang Yu-wei, "Lea was detached on some special service and went abroad for some time; mission not divulged."[62]

When Lea returned to Los Angeles, he planned to revitalize his organization to guard against future accusations and investigations. Instead of having his decentralized army face piecemeal dismemberment while it continued drilling covertly, he proposed to put a greater emphasis on centralizing at least a portion of it in a new and expanded academy. If his plan succeeded, he would train several hundred full-time Chinese students on a regular basis in one new location.

Lea worked out details of his plan with reform leaders, but failed to realize that the investigations into his army were no mere coincidence, or to understand that Falkenberg was determined to ruin him.

Falkenberg, meanwhile, never seemed to be able to bring a coup de grâce against Lea. After hearing about Lea's latest plan, he persisted in urging Governor Pardee to act against Lea and his army. Still lacking any hard legal evidence against Lea, he made a final plea on August 30 to Pardee: "Mr. Homer Lea is going to start a Chinese Military Academy in Los Angeles for the drilling and educating Chinese in military matters. 500 young Chinese will be asked to join and each pay $100 to Homer Lea, who is said to have remarked: 'I don't care what they say up there, I am going to start up anyway, they won't interfere with me.' He says that because the other Chinese military companies in Los Angeles and Oakland are running at full blast."[63]

Pardee was by this time well acquainted with Falkenberg's allegations and did not care to pursue Lea or his Chinese cadets any further. Satisfied with his earlier inquiry, he did not believe Lea's latest plans merited any further attention from the State House. Falkenberg, however, was not through scheming.

Lea's organization did deteriorate as a result of Falkenberg's earlier scheming. It is unclear how many CIA officers and men nationwide resigned or disbanded in the summer and autumn of 1905. Lea's prospects for revitalizing his army in the wake of all the investigations and embarrassing publicity were slim. In one case, Ralph Faneuf, a California National Guard member who headed the Western Military Academy's Oakland branch, not only resigned his CIA captain's commission but then wrote Governor Pardee in late September that he had disbanded the branch and "severed all connection with the nefarious movement."[64] Following their disbandment, a number of Faneuf's cadets reportedly returned to China in small groups to continue serving the reform cause.[65]

As cadets gradually returned to China, Lea also arranged for arms shipments to be smuggled into China for future military operations. The extent of the smuggling and associated bribery is unknown, but on at least one occasion, according to O'Banion, Lea's friend John York reportedly gave a $1,500 bribe to the Portuguese consul in Los Angeles to send a shipment of guns to the Portuguese colony of Macao, where reformers, masquerading as river pirates, took it off the boat before it reached its final destination.[66]

Lea believed the new centralized cadet-training academy would complement his existing companies and provide the Pao Huang Hui with a larger and more efficient pool of future officers. Contrary to Falkenberg's charges, however, he did not plan on making his new academy a showplace in Los Angeles for all to see. Still utilizing his network of contacts, he found a suitable location for his new school in the relatively secluded ocean-side community of Carlsbad. There, a former sanitarium consisting of two large vacant buildings situated on a bluff overlooking the ocean seemed ideal for the new school.[67]

The fundamental problem with Lea's plan remained lack of manpower. He believed he could impress the Pao Huang Hui and regain his prestige in its leaders' eyes only by producing a sizable CIA cadre. Since his cadet contingents could no longer expect to drill without scrutiny, he may have intended to smuggle in enough reformers from China to fill out the ranks of his training program. His plan could not succeed, however, unless he first disarmed the threat of another Pardee investigation.

In a second meeting with Governor Pardee, in early October 1905, Lea apologized for past misunderstandings and emphasized that he helped the Chinese purely to assist and uplift a much-maligned people. Then, in a blatant effort to deceive, he disavowed his association with the reformers completely when he wrote to Pardee a few days later seeking approval for the proposed Carlsbad school. Claiming that the Western Military Academy, its Fresno branch, and the proposed Carlsbad school were in no way connected with the reformers, he asked Pardee to approve the new school and also to reverse his decision on the Fresno cadet company. He claimed: "I am very well aware that misrepresentation has been made to your Excellency and your advisors, connecting this school with a revolutionary party. It is quite true that a political party did claim to have instituted the Academy, in order to gain credit among the Chinese people in the United States, but this is not true."[68]

Lea went on to assure Pardee that, while his new school would be open to all Chinese for a $100 tuition fee per student, "no Chinese have anything to do with the management of this academy; it is solely in the hands of Americans who are trying sincerely to help the deserving youth of the Empire . . . [since] there is in China greater opportunities for military students than in any other line."[69] If he denied ties with any Chinese political party, Lea believed, critics could no longer accuse him of raising revolutionary forces.

Lea was not at a loss in naming distinguished supporters of his plan to Pardee. He listed the Western Military Academy's board of directors as the directors of his new school, and included as references Dr. David Starr Jordan, Harrison Gray Otis, Judge Waldo M.

York, Los Angeles mayor Meredith P. Snyder, and Brigadier General Frank C. Prescott and Lieutenant Colonel William G. Schreiber of the California National Guard. He went beyond trying to impress the governor with local men of prominence and even claimed President Roosevelt's implicit support. He concluded his argument to Pardee by noting: "I expressed all this to President Roosevelt in June, and he expressed his approval."[70]

Pardee's desire to avoid involvement in another round of Falkenberg-Lea charges made him an unwitting accomplice to Lea's latest scheming. After consulting the state adjutant general's office for advice, he informed Lea on October 13 it was not his "duty to issue licenses in cases as that which you call to my attention."[71] His response meant that Lea's military schools did not need special permission for students to drill with arms in private. Lea was clearly confident Pardee would not stand in his way. He had already signed the lease agreement on October 11 for the Carlsbad school.[72]

Just when it appeared Lea could finally carry out his cadet-training program unhindered, Falkenberg attacked one last time. Since Pardee was unwilling to act, Falkenberg wrote to the State Department on October 30 to bring about Lea's undoing. His charges were general in nature. Writing as the president of the Standard Rock Oil Company and representing himself as a "Major" and "member of the present Federal Grand Jury," he enclosed a news clipping about the proposed Carlsbad school and trusted that his impressive credentials would add support to his charge: "After all that has been done to stop the illegal drilling of Chinese soldiers in the United States, here again I find that Homer Lea is still active forming a military academy."[73] Falkenberg did not know that the federal government had resolved its investigation into Lea's activities, and he failed to prompt a new investigation into Lea's affairs. His letter to the State Department marked the end of his campaign against Lea and the reformers, but not his military involvement with the reformers.

In January 1906 Falkenberg presided over the introduction in San Francisco of thirty reform cadets at a well-publicized reception for a visiting delegation of Chinese imperial commissioners. Although the reception appears to have marked his last public appearance with the cadets, not long afterward he returned to his scheme of compiling a roster of would-be candidates for possible future military service in China. Under the guise of a new military organization called the Sinim Order of the Dragon, which still claimed ties to the Pao Huang

Hui, Falkenberg and several of his associates stayed clear of Lea and the reformers and continued recruiting prospective officers. This time, however, instead of soliciting voluntary contributions from his officers, Falkenberg shrewdly levied an $8 initiation fee on each of them, with the understanding they would be subject to additional future assessments, which typically amounted to $25 total. The scheme was lucrative while it lasted, but came to an abrupt halt in August 1906, in the wake of a government investigation into its legality. Bidding farewell to the Pao Huang Hui, Falkenberg took his profits to Nevada, where, for the next several years, he was involved in a mining venture with Nevada governor John Sparks, who gladly made him an honorary lieutenant colonel on his staff. Thereafter, Colonel Falkenberg continued, as always, to look for greener pastures and to exploit them when he found them.[74]

Although Lea no longer faced the unpleasant prospect of Falkenberg's secret plotting against him, and a new wave of government crackdowns failed to materialize, it was too late for him to revitalize the reform army. The damage from all the bad publicity surrounding Falkenberg, himself, and the cadets had taken its toll. By late October 1905, he hoped to oversee some form of cadet training free from outside threats, but his own failures in addition to changes in party policy eventually led to the disbanding of the cadet-training organization entirely.

Chapter 8

THE QUILL AND THE SWORD

If Homer Lea had one distinguishing characteristic it was
his faith in himself and his supreme disregard of all other
contrary opinions.

—Charles Van Loan

Lea's fortunes with the CIA and reformers took an irreversible down-
turn after he and K'ang Yu-wei parted in 1905. By the end of the
year, the investigations and negative publicity surrounding the CIA
culminated in its virtual dismantling and the loss of Lea's position
as its commander. His failure to revitalize the CIA was only the first
problem he faced. A subsequent reorganization of the Pao Huang
Hui signaled the impending demise of the CIA's remnants. As various
factions and leaders broke off for different pursuits, Lea was forced to
do the same. He soon settled on writing as a new vista of opportunity.
This decision, in turn, led to a relationship with a young woman that
would have far-reaching consequences in his life.

K'ang Yu-wei, who continued traveling in the United States and
Mexico after his cross-country trip with Lea, grew increasingly concerned about the CIA and its troubles from reports he received from
Lea and the reformers. It is unclear exactly what information he had
at his disposal, but by late November 1905 he had lost faith in Lea's
ability to oversee any further cadet training. In a November 30 letter
from Mexico, he informed Lea that he had been removed as the head
of the CIA:

> With regard to the military companies I regret very much to
> say that those Chinese merchants who were supporters have

practically disbanded them owing to the recent troubles which you have reported in California. Had it not been for those said troubles the Chinese merchants and students would not have been so discouraged and then our objects sought would have been successfully accomplished; although I have repeatedly persuaded them to resume their work, but they dare not to.

It is a great pity to see this work in which you have taken so much interest die an unnatural death. Now at present those military schools are no longer in existence, hence no further income can be derived. Under such a condition of affairs I feel painful to execute my duty to declare that your office as chief of such military schools in the United States is abolished and the monthly allowance which you have been drawing is hereby ceased from this month (November) on.[1]

K'ang Yu-wei may have fired Lea in the belief that all the cadet companies were disbanded, but that was not the case. It is unknown how Lea responded to his dismissal or if K'ang Yu-wei later reconsidered the decision. Lea, in all likelihood, canceled arrangements for the Carlsbad school, but did not sever his ties with the reformers. On the contrary, he appears to have retained a diminished role with the Los Angeles cadet company, and possibly several others, as the remnants of the few remaining CIA companies graduated and disbanded over the next year and a half. In March 1906, for example, O'Banion told a *Los Angeles Herald* reporter that the "reformists have to a great extent become disheartened over the misinterpretation of their intentions," and "the last few months their guns have remained in their racks while the young men of the regiment have been attending to work."[2] Yet remaining documentation indicates that the Los Angeles cadet company continued operating at least through October 1906.[3]

A reform party reorganization that took effect in early 1907 ensured the demise of the CIA. The reorganization resulted largely from a dramatic shift in Manchu reform policy following Japan's spectacular victory over Russia in the Russo-Japanese War (1904–5). Many Chinese viewed the victory of the small Asian constitutional monarchy over the large autocracy as a sign of the effectiveness of constitutionalism, thereby sparking calls for constitutionalism and reform throughout the Chinese empire. A new wave of Chinese nationalism spread, lending increased support to both reformers and revolutionaries. The aging dowager empress, fearing the growth of Dr. Sun Yat-sen's radical revolutionary party, which called for overthrowing the Manchu dynasty and establishing a republic, responded to domestic pressures and began to shift her support to constitutionalism and reform to ensure the dynasty's survival. The Pao Huang Hui viewed this development as a pivotal opportunity to lead the vanguard of a new movement and unite its forces under the Pao Huang Hui banner. Yet, in so doing, the reform leadership abandoned its goal of restoring the emperor to the throne for the more likely chance of influencing Chinese policy through constitutionalism. There was no place for any of Lea's cadets in the reorganized association, which became known as the Ti-kuo hsien-cheng tang, or the Constitutionalist Association.[4]

It is not clear how many of Lea's soldiers returned to China. Some may have infiltrated the imperial Ch'ing army and waited to take over its command; some may have left the reform party and realigned with Sun Yat-sen's revolutionaries; and some just remained in their respective locales under a shroud of secrecy, waiting for orders that never came. The *New York Times* reported that members of Major McVickar's Chinese regiment held a graduation ceremony upon their disbandment on May 27, 1907. Major McVickar bid his soldiers an encouraging farewell as they prepared to return to China as full-fledged drillmasters: "If the men in China will now do their work as faithfully and as well as you have done yours in the last three years, China will have the best and greatest army in the world."[5] In all, if O'Banion's recollections forty years later are reliable, approximately twenty-one hundred cadets completed their training before the program finally ended. There is no record of when the program actually ended, which was likely in 1907, but Lea's picture continued to hang prominently in Pao Huang Hui assembly halls at least through 1908.[6]

Throughout this final period of cadet training in America, O'Banion served as more than a drill instructor for Lea and the reformers; he also arranged for the smuggling of an uncounted number of reformers and cadets in and out of the United States. Even after he and Lea had broken with the Pao Huang Hui, his continued involvement in smuggling Chinese eventually led to his arrest, trial, and conviction, followed by a brief prison term.[7]

Lea's activities, meanwhile, continued to garner press coverage periodically. In July 1906 his sense of chivalry helped make front-page news when he challenged a visiting salesman to a duel. The incident occurred at an impromptu dinner he hosted for several acquaintances at the Angelus Hotel following a formal dinner he had hosted for Dr.

David Starr Jordan. His guests included two local society women and a friend of theirs, Mr. M. B. Flexner, a traveling salesman from Kentucky who happened to be staying at the hotel. In the course of the evening, Flexner inadvertently offended Lea and one of the women when he left the table and shouted across the room to ask if she was ready to leave. Lea took affront and, getting up from the table, demanded an apology or satisfaction in a duel from Flexner for his rude behavior. He gave Flexner the choice of weapons. Flexner, who later claimed Lea's actions were due to an over indulgence in alcohol, a charge Lea denied, initially responded by leaving the scene without apologizing or accepting Lea's challenge. He later made light of the challenge by contemplating a duel with pastries. The event might have gone unnoticed had it not became front-page news in the *Los Angeles Herald* a few days later. The incident, while trivial, gave the public a further insight into Lea's concept of honor and flair for the dramatic.[8] He commented to a reporter that his family's southern values in defending a woman's honor motivated him to make the challenge:

> I will not fight fist to fist with him, as I am too crippled to do that. But I have given him a great advantage choosing the weapons, and whenever he is ready I am.
>
> He certainly must answer to me for the insult to myself and my guests.
>
> I called his bluff, and I only fear that I shall not have the pleasure of settling the score with him.
>
> In no place in the world is the honor of a woman so little respected as it is by an American man.
>
> When I go down the street I see many things occur that would not be tolerated in any other country. Even in the south a woman receives more protection from men then she does in the west.
>
> An insult to a woman in company with a man is answerable by apology or a fight. It's usually a fight in the south and always one in Europe. I have been brought up that way, and my southern respect for a woman's honor has not in the least been squelched by my residence in the west.[9]

Lea looked for new career pursuits during this period of transition for the CIA and the reformers. He already had an interest in writing, and in late 1905, in the wake of the Russo-Japanese War, had completed a partial draft of a manuscript, eventually entitled *The Valor of Ignorance*, on America's military unpreparedness for a future war with Japan. He put that aside, as he later explained, "in order to allow sufficient time to verify or disprove its hypotheses and conclusions."[10] Now, with the encouragement of a close friend, Robert J. Belford, formerly a senior partner in the New York publishing house of Belford and Clark, he chose writing as offering the best chance for fulfillment and success given his poor health, physical disabilities, and lack of professional qualifications.[11] Some of his family and friends believed his romantic imagination and his affinity for telling tall tales were the perfect attributes for his new career. Lea's stepmother attested to this belief, later recalling: "I always said they weren't lies. They were just good stories. His father used to get so mad at our listening to them. I told him one day, 'Look here. It's pretty dull around here. Homer stirs things up. You'd better listen to them, too.'"[12]

China provided Lea a perfect resource for his literary career. He left Los Angeles in the summer of 1906, accompanied at least some of the time by his sister Ermal and cousin Ella Lea, who was visiting from Roswell, for a cottage in Long Beach, a small southern California resort town. There he busied himself with several literary projects. His writing plans included several nonfiction articles, a book-length history of China, a Chinese adventure novel, and completion of his book on America's military unpreparedness. He also may have planned some articles in Chinese, having by this time become proficient in Cantonese.[13]

In early August 1906 Lea drew up a thirty-chapter outline for "The Re-awakening of China," a proposed book on the political and military history of China. He never progressed beyond the outline, but did manage to complete several articles before the year's end. He reportedly wrote and published an article in Chinese on military science, and he wrote an article on a favorite theme, entitled "Can China Fight?" that appeared in the February 1907 issue of *World Today Magazine*. In the latter article, he criticized Europeans and Americans for grossly underestimating the military qualities of the Chinese soldier, while also giving a brief military history of China. The article brazenly risked renewed public attention to his reform army by including several photos of his Los Angeles CIA company on maneuvers. Although the article implicitly referred to the current Westernized modernization program of the imperial Ch'ing army, Lea had few reservations about misleading his readers with photographs of his own Western-ized troops in action as a pretense to prove his case.[14]

It is unclear how much interaction Ella had had with Lea over the years, but her visit now had an unexpected effect. Lea fell in love with her, but could not tell her of his feelings. Ermal explained:

Eleanor Lea . . . was one of the most beautiful girls I have ever known and Homer fell very much in love with her. Although she had come to visit the family, Homer immediately took over and monopolized her company. I know Cousin "Ella" liked and admired Homer tremendously but as to whether she felt towards him as he did towards her, I don't know, how-ever I do know that the fact they were first cousins prevented Homer from letting Eleanor know just how serious his feel-ings were, for he had told me how much in love he was with Ella, but that "the one girl in the world he would have wanted to become his wife, would turn out to be his first cousin."[15]

Ella had no romantic feelings for her cousin and evidently never realized how he felt about her. Lea spent hours reading poetry to her and telling her about China, but it made little impression on her, though she admired him and his magnetic personality. She later observed:

It has been incomprehensible always to me that Homer, with all his brilliance, could have wasted so much of his valuable time on me. He would read Omar Kahayyem to me by the hour, which I greatly fear went in one ear and out the other. . . . He really did not live on the same level with the rest of us. We simply could not get up to where he was, at least just an ordinary person like myself. . . . When with him, you simply sailed off on a magic carpet onto a "river of crystal light into a sea of dew," and I wasn't in love with him either so don't attribute it to that.[16]

Lea was in his element at Long Beach. Ermal, who adored him, waited on him hand and foot. Ella, no doubt surprised, watched him lie on a couch and "eat as the Romans did," while he declared that "no civilized person should sit up and eat." When venturing out for social visits, Lea wore his uniform and cape and would captivate his friends and admirers. Ella recalled: "Wherever we went his friends, and they were legion, seemed to congregate around him to listen to every word. He was adored by them all."[17]

After Lea completed a draft of his adventure novel with Belford's friendly oversight, he returned to Los Angeles to finalize it and arrange for its publication. He entitled it "The Ling Chee," in reference to a brutal type of Chinese execution by dismemberment. Unfortunately, in Los Angeles his publication plans were delayed when his health again failed. He remained seriously ill from early November 1906 through late January 1907. During this time, he could not put his novel into finished form without help and Ellen Leech, a secretary he knew in Los Angeles, came to his rescue. She had a visiting friend, Mrs. Ethel B. Powers, a young secretary from Tennessee, who agreed to help Lea out. Although it was her first time away from her husband and three children, she seized the opportunity to earn some extra money for her struggling family by typing Lea's final manuscript. Like others who came to know him, she quickly grew to admire him. She may not have realized that her initial work with him was the beginning of a relationship that would later alter both their lives.[18]

Lea contacted his old Stanford friend and writer Will Irwin, then working for *McClure's Magazine,* to see about publishing his novel. Irwin did not believe the manuscript would make a good magazine serial, but he saw in it "a sense of authenticity unique in fiction about China," and recommended it to McClure's book publishing house, which accepted it for publication.[19]

As Lea recovered his health, the *Los Angeles Times* helped launch his new writing career. On January 28, 1907, the *Times* highlighted his debut as an author in a front-page article entitled "Leaves Sword for the Pen," which announced the publication of his first articles and first novel. While Lea no doubt appreciated the exposure, the article also contributed to furthering his mystique. It cited him as having "gained a great and rather mysterious standing" early on with the reformers, as well as giving credence to his military record of having taken part in "several battles against the troops of the Empress" when he was in China.[20]

Lea's success as an author led him to think in patriotic terms of applying his attention to the salvation of America and the Anglo-Saxon race. During this period, America's paranoia and fears of Japan were heightening to a fever pitch, and he began to shift his attentions to the strategic implications of a growing Japanese threat to Anglo-

Saxon interests in Asia and the Pacific. He believed few Americans understood the Asians as he did, and became convinced that Japan's quest for hegemony in the Pacific would inevitably lead to a confrontation with America. He subsequently joined the ranks of America's militant defenders in spreading the call for Anglo-Saxon regeneration as the only key to salvation.[21]

America's policy toward Japan had shifted sharply following the end of the Russo-Japanese War. Prior to the war, U.S. foreign policy interests in the Far East hinged on defending the newly annexed Philippine Islands and supporting the Open Door diplomacy of Chinese political and territorial integrity. President Roosevelt, facing both European competition and growing Japanese militancy and modernization, had sought to counterbalance the ambitions of Russia, Great Britain, and Germany in the Far Fast by supporting Japan. However, two significant events offset Roosevelt's plan, presenting him with an unpleasant shift in the balance of power vis-à-vis Japan. First, Great Britain reduced its naval presence in the Pacific as a result of a 1902 mutual security pact with Japan; then Japan defeated Russia in the war.[22]

While Japan defined its new international mission of expanding economically in China and liberating Asia from Western colonialism, American apprehensions and fears of a confrontation for control of the Pacific quickly surfaced. Yellow journalism, anti-Japanese propaganda, and rumors of a Japanese attack on the Philippines, including a war in the Pacific, spread from coast to coast. It mattered little that Japan's military machine and finances were exhausted as a result of its war with Russia. Many Americans, from the White House down to the general public, began fearing the "Yellow Peril."[23]

The mistreatment of Japanese immigrants in California in the fall of 1906 brought tension between Japan and America to a high point. In January 1907, for example, a front-page *Washington Post* article entitled "Arm against Japan" warned:

> Despite the most vigilant precautions of the President and his advisors in keeping the information to themselves, the fact has leaked out that the relations between the United States and Japan have reached a most critical stage.
>
> According to one of the President's advisers, the two countries seem to be drifting rapidly toward war, and deft and vigorous diplomacy must be exercised if certain new developments are to be disposed of without an explosion.[24]

Although Roosevelt's administration denied the possibility of war with Japan and attempted to calm the fears of the general public, the president privately instructed the military to prepare plans for an eventual war with Japan in the Pacific. Roosevelt's administration, however, could not stem the tide of a war scare spreading across America. In 1907 writers, politicians, and speakers primed America's jingoes for war. Literature appeared offering fictional blow-by-blow accounts of such a war, such as a Sunday *New York Times* feature entitled "The Great War of 1908 Vividly Described," reflecting how fantasy often outweighed reality in arousing the emotions of concerned parties.[25]

Lea, with his hand on the pulse of "Yellow Peril" rhetoric, carefully digested the various arguments and synthesized his own theories. His social Darwinist beliefs made everything quite clear. In light of the Japanese question, America's declining militancy, the growth of finance and commercial capitalism, and astounding technological innovations in transportation and communications, he came to conceive of a global worldview rooted in competition between races. In the case of nations claiming more than one racial group, he believed the consolidation of predominant races within national borders was a prerequisite for ensuring survival of the fittest in a military conflict. He discounted technology and industry, seeing instead individual and group initiative as the keys to success. Modern dreadnought battleships, machine guns, and airplanes could never be more than tools used by both victor and vanquished. Instead, he thought, as his later work revealed, that martial spirit was decisive and could flourish best in a nation that was racially uniform, cohesive, and vigorous. If a nation followed any other course, it faced eventual doom and downfall.[29]

Lea, very much influenced by Brooks Adams's *The Law of Civilization and Decay* (1895), offered a worldview borrowed heavily from Adams's theme of the three stages of cyclical development among nations and races—dispersion, concentration, and dissipation. While also accepting Herbert Spencer's idea that industrialism was gradually displacing militarism, he strongly disagreed with Spencer's conclusion that this was a favorable result. On the contrary, Lea condemned business and commercial interests as posing a grave threat to the survival of the Anglo-Saxon race by eroding militancy and fostering complacency.[27]

Above all, Lea was committed to awakening the nationalist and militant spirit of Anglo-Saxons in a manner similar to America's aspiring archrival in the Pacific. During his years with the reformers, Japan stood as a model for the Chinese to emulate. When that country then emerged as a major power after its war with Russia, Lea saw more than the success of a constitutional monarchy over an autocracy. He saw his militaristic social Darwinist theories proven, and consequently had no doubt of an eventual clash between the Asian and Anglo-Saxon races for control of the Pacific. His respect for and admiration of Japan's martial samurai tradition fueled his fears of America's capacity to compete with the other country in an armed contest over their respective Pacific interests. His confidence in such beliefs was immutable. His friend Charles Van Loan attested to this trait when he later noted: "If Homer Lea had one distinguishing characteristic it was his faith in himself and his supreme disregard of all other contrary opinions."[28]

By the summer of 1907, Lea was determined to complete his book on America's military unpreparedness for a possible war with Japan. Rather than relying entirely on books and articles for his information, he embarked on a camping trip to Bear Valley in the San Bernardino Mountains for his research. During this, and subsequent research trips, he made detailed explorations of southern California's geography and terrain for use in analyzing how Japan might theoretically invade the region.[29]

On one of these trips he almost died. Although he was an accomplished outdoorsman, his independent spirit nearly led to his demise from food poisoning. Newmark recalled how Lea's burro miraculously helped him survive a brush with death:

> For the purpose of these explorations he purchased a burro which he called "Baby." His rations on these trips consisted largely of raisins, grape nuts, sweet chocolate, and he always carried a quart of whiskey for emergencies.
>
> While on this trip he ate some deviled ham from which he got ptomaine poisoning. He was three days on the desert alone. During these days the burro stood with her feet across him, never leaving him. He managed finally to remove the saddle bag. From it he took the bottle of whiskey, broke off the top, and drank the whole quart. To this he attributed his rescue from death.[30]

Lea's affinity for animals may have saved his life on more than one occasion during his research trips. Ermal recalled how he developed an extraordinary bond with a mule that saved him from rattlesnakes:

He stopped at Seven Oaks, a summer resort, to see about getting a horse. There were none available but the owner told him about a wild mule roaming the hills but no one had been able to catch him. But Homer would be welcome to him if lucky to get him. Brother started out and it was days before he even saw him and eventually did and . . . got close enough to pet and talk to the mule—and later followed Homer back to camp—much to the amazement of everyone. This trip took weeks and during that time the animal saved Homer's life several times from rattlers.

When they returned to "7 Oaks" while Brother was getting his notes together the mule would come down from pasture and stay in the cabin all day.[31]

As Lea developed greater expertise from his research, he came to believe that his knowledge and qualifications in making geopolitical judgments were equal to those of respected military men and statesmen. Van Loan, who spent a week with Lea in the mountains, noted how Lea's ego had grown:

One night a talkative stranger introduced the Japanese question. . . . "This Jap scare makes me sick," said the man. "One white man can beat ten brown men. What do you think, General?"

For four hours the General talked and we were treated to a masterly military argument. . . . There was only one man who lacked the sense to refrain from arguing a question beyond his depth—the stranger.

The General drew a rude map of the Pacific Coast, with dots to represent cities and fortifications and burned match-ends to represent bodies of troops and battleship fleets. As he talked he shifted the two forces in illustration of his theory, and it developed that he had a most amazing knowledge of the country over which the land troops were supposed to pass every stream of water, every fertile valley, every mountain pass seemed clear and distinct in his memory. . . .

When the campfire was over it was one o'clock in the morning and there was no more argument left in the stranger. He went away silently, shaking his head. The General retired. Later I heard him chuckling to himself in the darkness and

asked him what was the matter. "Never answer a fool according to his folly," he quoted. "I wasted an argument on that
numbskull that nobody but a commanding general would be
able to appreciate. I should have known better."[32]

While Lea completed his geographic research and worked on his
next book, his literary career seemed to be taking off when he and
Oliver Morosco, the proprietor of the Burbank Theater, arranged to
collaborate on producing a dramatized version of "Ling Chee," which
Lea subsequently renamed "The Crimson Spider."[33] On September
17, 1907, at the outset of their collaboration, Morosco optimistically
told a *Los Angeles Times* reporter: "Mr. Lea's story has in every fiber
that 'element of news' which the American people seem to want, and
if we are successful in translating it to the foot-lights, I believe it will
make a dramatic sensation. We shall certainly afford it every advantage
of cast and all the facilities of production."[34]

Lea's collaborative venture with Morosco, however, never came to
fruition. Morosco reportedly interrupted his work on Lea's drama to
produce another play, *The Society Pilot*.[35] There is no indication that he
ever resumed his collaboration with Lea.

Lea knew that completing his next book would take more work
than his romance novel and decided he again wanted Ethel Powers
to assist him. In December 1907 he contacted her in Chicago, as she
and her family were preparing to move to west Texas, and asked her to
return to California to help him with his new book. By this time Ethel
had become a good friend, despite their different backgrounds. She
was a year older than Lea, and having left her family at fifteen to get
married, did not have a great deal of formal education or training. She
had acquired her secretarial skills from a one-month business college
course that was followed by a job with the Illinois Central Railroad's
branch office in Memphis, Tennessee, the job she left to visit Ellen
Leech in California. She may not have known that Lea wanted her
to return to California partly out of a personal fondness for her but,
according to her eldest son, Joshua, she decided to help him since her
family needed extra money.[36]

Although Lea had had childhood romances, experienced a desire
to marry his cousin Ella, and had feelings for Ethel, at this point in his
life he generally did not have a high opinion of women or marriage,
likely reasoning that entanglements with women would inhibit his
chances of an exciting career. He advised his friend Newmark to break

off his own engagement and forget marriage: "Homer upbraided me somewhat furiously, saying, 'You damn fool.' Here you are getting yourself engaged to be married and depriving the world of a perfectly good humorist and philosopher. Now you will lead a humdrum, monotonous life that you won't enjoy and won't be of any use."[37]

Nor was Lea in the least shy about expressing his bigoted views of women to Newmark's wife. Visiting the Newmarks one evening shortly after his close brush with death in Bear Valley, he startled them with his frankness on the subject, which Newmark recalled: "I very vividly remember that after his return he came to my home one evening for dinner. After dinner, Homer, Mrs. Newmark and I were chatting. He related the experience [of his ptomaine poisoning] . . . and he concluded the story by shaking his . . . weirdly long finger at Mrs. Newmark, looking her straight in the eye and with the utmost complacency saying—'and I want to say to you, Mrs. Newmark, that that burro was the most intelligent female it has ever been my good fortune to meet.'"[38]

Ethel was an exception to Lea's prejudices. She may have worked with him more closely than any other woman he knew. Her kindness, sincerity, and concern made a strong impression on him. She returned to Los Angeles in January 1908, accompanied by her son Joshua, who remained with her, attending the eighth grade in the city. Her relationship with Lea grew closer as she worked with him over the next eight months. She admired him, perhaps much as his cousin Ella had earlier. She saw him as a frail genius who needed someone to look after him. She served as his nurse as well as his literary assistant.[39]

As Lea and Ethel worked on the book, the press continued to help publicize Lea's writing. Lea, who was still reticent about discussing the details of his early military exploits in China, was more than willing to take advantage of any opportunity to advance his geostrategic views. He gave the *Los Angeles Times* an interview for a February 9, 1908, article entitled "Gloomy Foreboding of Gen. Homer Lea" that was accompanied by a photo of him in uniform. The article announced the impending publication of his novel, renamed *The Vermilion Pencil,* and focused largely on his work in progress on America's military unpreparedness for a future war with Japan. In the interview Lea spoke with great authority and advanced for the first time publicly an in-depth argument that a war was impending between Japan and the United States for control of the Pacific. He believed that America's naval and military defenses would be no match against a Japanese invasion, particularly since Japan "will undoubtedly declare war when it best suits her, and without warning." His controversial analysis was predicated on a simple social Darwinist premise: "Japan is going to make war on this country because she must. Wars are not started in hate, or seldom in the bitterness of one race toward another. It is a case of natural expansion."[40]

The publication of *The Vermilion Pencil* the following month brought Lea national fame. Critics overwhelmingly praised him for providing a glimpse of life in Chinese society rarely seen by a Westerner. For example, the *New York Times* reviewer lauded the novel as "the most remarkable piece of fiction the year thus far has brought . . . [and] the most valuable novel on the subject of China as yet penned in the English language." The reviewer added that Lea did for China what the renowned novelist Rudyard Kipling had done for India.[41] Locally, the *Los Angeles Times* declared the novel "remarkable," characterizing it as a powerful "book that defies classification."[42]

Lea drew on both his personal experiences and his vivid imagination to reveal the sights, sounds, and smells of China. The novel's lurid and colorful picture of Chinese rural life centered on the romance between a French missionary and the young wife of a Chinese viceroy. Love, lust, secret societies, gunboat diplomacy, and Chinese customs, rituals, and exotic scenery were part and parcel of his fast-moving and vividly detailed plot. One of his intents was to criticize Western missionaries in China, for whom he had developed an immense distaste.[43] Newmark recounted Lea's feelings about missionaries: "In this novel Homer was, I think, rather too rough on missions and missionaries. These were one of Homer's pet aversions. It was his idea that invariably they were mercenary and self-seeking, and that they conferred on the natives of the lands in which they operated, all the vices of civilization without giving them any of its benefits."[44]

McClure's marketing of *The Vermilion Pencil* contributed further to Lea's mythology. Advertisements for the book sensationalized his position as a lieutenant general in the Chinese reform army and credited him as "one of the most adventurous of living men," who "has fought and toiled in the heart of China for fifteen years."[45]

While Lea worked on his next book he also wrote an article, "How Socialism Failed in China," that later appeared in two parts, in the September and October 1908 issues of *Van Norden's Magazine*. The article was significant as Lea's first public attempt to warn Americans they faced degeneration of their national militancy. In this case he examined the failure of socialism in China during the eleventh-century Sung dynasty, arguing that it had eroded China's militancy, thereby leaving that country susceptible to foreign invasion. His point was that America faced a similar danger from socialism.[46]

Lea decided to leave the distractions of Los Angeles to pursue his writing, and in early April 1908 he took up temporary residence in a small cottage in Laguna Beach, a relatively remote southern California artists' colony, to complete the final chapters of *The Valor of Ignorance*. The task took longer than the three months he had expected and in August he moved to a cottage in Long Beach, situated off the Pacific Electric streetcar line's Vista Del Mar stop, which offered greater accessibility to Los Angeles. Ethel, who appears to have spent this time with him, returned to her family in early September as he put the finishing touches on his manuscript.[47]

Although details are obscure about the time Lea and Ethel spent together, Lea evidently fell in love with her and wanted her to stay with him indefinitely. According to Joshua, her feelings toward Lea were more platonic. Although she admired Lea and would later change her feelings and marry him, she was not yet willing to leave her family.[48] Two weeks after she left, he wrote her of his loneliness and his feelings toward her, signing the letter "with love." "You have no conception how lonely this place is. The coyotes have increased in numbers as have all the other melancholy sounds of night. It is a question how long I will be able to foil the spirit of discontent that is persistently shoving me town-ward. . . . I certainly wish I knew of some way to fix it so you could come back but every thing I lean on breaks; every hope I conjecture up vanishes before the realities of each new day."[49]

Lea's transition from reform army general to successful independent writer marked the beginning of a new career, but it did not fulfill his desires sufficiently to end his military ambitions. Faced with the prospect of losing Ethel, he did not want to live a lonely and complacent life. While he did not abandon his commitment to writing, he realized the time was ripe to seek new adventures and put his resourcefulness to work. Not surprisingly, he looked toward China for the key to his future. He intended to pursue both a literary and a military career, if possible, and ultimately win back the woman he loved, her marriage notwithstanding. The question remained, however, of how to find or create a position in which his singular qualifications would offer him the opportunities he sought.

CHAPTER 9

THE RED DRAGON PLAN

I am ready to do business with any established government
on earth but I cannot help to make a government to do
business with.

—J. P. Morgan

In late 1908 Lea unsuccessfully sought to become a U.S. trade representative to China for the Roosevelt administration. Concurrently,
he contrived an audacious military venture in China called the Red
Dragon plan that attested to his extraordinary imagination and ambition. The plan initially called for organizing a revolutionary conspiracy
to conquer several Chinese provinces and later expanded to include the
entire Chinese Empire. It bordered on fantasy. Yet that did not stop
him from convincing a coterie of supporters to embark on a quest so
risky that it seemed doomed from the outset—but also so potentially
lucrative as to be irresistible to some. By 1909 Lea's continued success as a writer, with the publication of *The Valor of Ignorance,* a geopolitical study that warned of an impending East-West clash, helped
him gain additional notoriety as he made another unsuccessful bid for
a government position in China, this time as U.S. minister to China
for President William H. Taft's administration. Lea was undaunted by
such setbacks. By late 1909 he had reason for optimism as his rising
literary career began opening new doors with important contacts.

When Lea wrote Ethel that he wished there was a way she could
return to him, he also informed her that he planned to offer the
U.S. government his services as a commercial trade representative in
China.[1] At that time a Chinese boycott of American goods had been
in effect for well over a year in reaction to America's exclusion policy.

With this problem weighing heavily on certain American commercial interests, Lea believed he could reap vast economic rewards and help American interests by breaking the boycott. In order to do this, however, he needed to convince President Roosevelt to grant him an appointment as a government trade representative in Canton, China. He chose Canton specifically for two reasons. First, he believed that "there alone would I be able to do the good I believe I am able to accomplish. Canton is the storm center of all anti-Americanism and all boycotts originate in its environs. The Canton merchants are the most active of any in the Empire; their Guild-houses are to be found in every large city from Manchuria to Singapore, the ramifications of their trade interests and power are, in the Orient without end."[2]

Lea also had ulterior motives. After rescuing American commercial interests and reaping lucrative rewards for his service in Canton, he planned to pursue his earlier dreams of liberating China, this time by financing and leading an anti-Ch'ing revolution in southern China.[3]

Lea counted on help from an acquaintance, Charles Beach Boothe, a prominent businessman who had previously lived nearby on Bonnie Brae Street. Among his various pursuits, Boothe was a member of a number of civic and fraternal organizations. For example, he was a leading member of the National Irrigation Association and interested in the history of irrigation in other countries, particularly in China. Earlier, in 1905, Lea had arranged for Boothe, who happened to be in St. Louis during K'ang Yu-wei's cross-country trip, to meet K'ang Yu-Wei, and the two likely discussed irrigation. More recently, in early 1908, Boothe had been after Lea to help arrange another meeting with K'ang Yu-wei, who was visiting America. In the course of their correspondence, Lea approached Boothe with his own plans of getting rich as a trade representative and revolutionary. Although Boothe first hesitated to get involved in such an incredible plot, Lea soon persuaded him to join the Chinese revolutionary venture with promises of financial returns beyond his wildest dreams.[4]

Together they possessed a valuable pool of resources to further Lea's plan. Boothe claimed a career of sound financial experience and also had a number of important financial connections in the East. He was president of the National Irrigation Association, vice president of the National Motor Car Company, a member of the Los Angeles Chamber of Commerce, and one of the driving forces in Los Angeles's prestigious California Club, whose members included leaders in business, industry, and government. It would be his job to handle the arrangements of securing the presidential appointment for Lea. As for Lea, he supplied the all-important Chinese connections. Although isolated from the majority of reformers, he still had the confidence and ear of one of the most prominent Chinese in America, Dr. Yung Wing.[5]

The aging Yung Wing was spending his declining years in Hartford, Connecticut, when Lea approached him with promises of wealth and power in exchange for his support. He had little difficulty gaining Yung Wing's allegiance. The two had initially met in Hong Kong in 1900, and again during K'ang Yu-wei's 1905 tour. They shared similar views on resolving China's problems. They got along very well, especially since the militant Yung Wing had ardently supported the 1900 Pao Huang Hui insurrection in China and also had been closely involved in a 1902–3 failed conspiracy of reformers, revolutionaries, and secret society leaders to start a revolution in Kwangtung province. He thought very highly of "General" Lea, and agreed to lend his esteemed position among the Chinese to Lea's revolutionary conspiracy.[6]

The military strategy Lea intended to adopt for the proposed revolution was essentially a revitalization of the plan he had initially proposed for the 1900 Pao Huang Hui uprising. He also planned to draw upon many of his CIA personnel for a cadre of trained officers. According to Lea's Red Dragon plan, Lea's forces, launching their attack from Macao, would seize first Canton and then the Kwang provinces before the imperial Ch'ing army could be mobilized to stop them.[7]

Yung Wing's assistance was invaluable for the revolutionary portion of Lea's scheme. Through Yung Wing, Lea planned to solicit a united front of various southern Chinese factions and secret societies to organize an army that he (Lea) would command for the revolution. After the successful conquest of the region, Yung Wing would then head a coalition government of these revolutionary forces while Lea and Boothe received wide-ranging economic concessions from the new government for financing and leading the revolution.[8]

The project initially augured well for the conspirators. After Lea enlisted Boothe and Yung Wing, Boothe traveled east in September 1908 on a business trip, during which he met with Yung Wing and began arranging for Lea's presidential appointment as a trade representative. Lea did not sit idly by. He was prepared to call upon a number of prominent people and politicians for an endorsement if Boothe had trouble getting the job done.[9]

Though hopeful, Lea knew his lack of commercial and financial credentials might make President Roosevelt balk at granting the appointment. He reassured Boothe, who was in Washington, that his Stanford coursework in economics and sociology was "the best possible education that one could have as far as academic knowledge is concerned in a position of this kind."[10] He claimed his "knowledge of the Chinese people, on the other hand, is probably equal in all respects to any American who has had long and varied experience in the Orient, while politically and racially, in a personal and sociological sense I do not think it is possible to find any one in this Nation who understands more thoroughly the Chinese."[11]

Boothe accepted Lea's assurances and agreed that their success depended more on having "the proper person see the President," as Lea put it, than on any other single factor. Lea advised Boothe: "That party should be the representative of the largest and most important commercial interests in the south of China. The three principal interests concerned are the Cotton, Cotton-piece goods, the Trans-Continental and Trans-pacific Transportation Companies. . . . You undoubtedly know better what to do than myself but it seems to me that the three principal men to see—or any one of them—are [railroad executive] J. J. Hill, or the president of the Cotton-Growers, or the head of the Cotton-piece Association, all of whom you will find in New York or vicinity."[12]

Although Boothe initially reported favorable progress to Lea, by late October his mission had turned sour. While details are lacking, he clearly failed to get the Roosevelt administration to back the scheme.

Surprisingly, this setback did not put an end to the conspiracy. When it became apparent that Lea was not going to gain an entrée into China and reap the conspirators an economic bonanza, they regrouped and rethought their plans. Lea and Boothe believed the stakes were too great to give up. They decided that if Lea could not orchestrate some kind of financial support for the revolution, then they would seek to put together a syndicate of private American financial backers to do the job.

Boothe brought Walter W. Allen, a reliable boyhood friend and experienced businessman, into the ranks of the conspiracy to help solve their financial woes. Allen was an organizer of the Guggenheim Exploration Company, a member of the exclusive New York Union League Club, and had long been associated with many of the largest financial houses of New York and London. His primary mission was to enlist the eastern financial support that Boothe and Lea believed critical to the success of the Red Dragon conspiracy.[13]

In mid-November 1908, just weeks after Allen joined them, startling news from China added new fuel to the conspirators' dreams. The unexpected and ominous death of Emperor Kwang-hsu indicated that the Ch'ing dynasty might be crumbling. When the *Los Angeles Examiner* approached Lea for comments on the emperor's death, he gave the press a clue to his latest Asian endeavors. He stated that he and others intimately familiar with Chinese affairs expected the dowager to die in the near future, and this event would lead to a civil war. Lea predicted: "It will mean the end of the present dynasty in China, and that a coalition of all the revolutionary forces will be brought about for the purpose of putting on the throne a man of advanced ideas representing the progressive element in China." The *Examiner* added that it might be necessary for Lea "to return to China at once, as the commencement of hostilities may not be far off."[14]

Lea's appraisal was close to the mark. Two days after the emperor's death, the dowager died. Yet, instead of the immediate disintegration of the dynasty and the outbreak of civil war, the dynasty lingered on under the new emperor, two-and-one-half-year-old Pu-yi, with his father, Prince Ch'un, serving as regent. While Lea appeared to have overestimated the immediate consequences of the dual imperial deaths, internal discontent and revolutionary unrest would grow over the next three years and finally bring down the dynasty.

The conspirators believed China's anti-Ch'ing factions would bring on a civil war and the opportunity would soon arise to put their plans into effect. Lea and Boothe agreed that Yung Wing should contact K'ang Yu-wei and members of their proposed anti-Manchu coalition in China to meet, form an "advisory board" as the basis of a provisional government, and plan the revolutionary takeover of Kwangtung province as soon as possible.[15] They also agreed Boothe should urge Allen to hurry in finding financial backers. Boothe, using a prearranged code to guard the most sensitive aspects of their communications, informed Allen on November 18 of these intentions, adding that Lea had all the plans for the takeover worked out: "L [Lea] is confident that with funds of X [$1,000,000] in hands or in such shape that it can be drawn as needed within twelve months after the Advisory Board meets, and another X so pledged . . . to meet any emergencies, that the work can be immediately begun with positive assurances of successful completion within eighteen months at the outside."[16]

Aside from the conspirators' belief in the feasibility of Lea's scheme, which was little more than wishful thinking, their primary problem was funding. Lea and Boothe knew they could not convince K'ang Yu-wei or the Chinese leaders to take part in the conspiracy without money to back the project. Therefore, Allen must deliver these backers. Boothe assured Allen that the generous return for investors would be "either in cash or concessions" less than six months after the Red Dragon plan got under way, and he pressed Allen to "take hold of this matter vigorously and push it to a successful termination. . . . Matters can not progress too rapidly to fit the situation." He then suggested that financier J. Pierpont Morgan, who had conducted extensive business in China, might be just the man to finance their venture.[17] Allen agreed to try.

Meanwhile, Yung Wing also was deliberating on ways to push the conspiracy forward. Debating on how to go about organizing the coalition of forces for the advisory board, he wavered between having the Chinese faction leaders come to America for a meeting, or traveling to China himself to arrange a meeting. With secrecy a fundamental prerequisite for success, he chose to avoid undue attention by sending one of his sons to China as his personal representative. The idea was acceptable to Lea, Boothe, and Allen, but Yung Wing's desire that $10,000 be raised to cover his son's expenses on the trip threw them off guard. Lea, Boothe, and Allen had no inclination to risk their own capital on the project. They did resolve, however, that once Allen could secure American backers, Yung Wing's son could be sent and the Red Dragon plan begun.[18]

January and February 1909 were critical months for the conspirators. During that period they sought to align themselves with forces in both China and America that might well have turned the tide in favor of their venture had they succeeded. In China, after political infighting resulted in the dismissal of General Yuan Shih-k'ai, a former provincial viceroy, imperial grand councilor, and commander-in-chief of the imperial Chinese army, Yung Wing convinced the conspirators that his addition to their ranks would strengthen their cause immeasurably. Of the three men whom Yung Wing considered enlisting to help the conspiracy, Yuan Shih-k'ai, K'ang Yu-wei, and Sun Yat-sen, he believed Yuan Shih-k'ai offered the most likely prospect for success.[19] He assured Lea, Boothe, and Allen that with Yuan Shih-k'ai on their side, victory would be only a matter of time: "He is worth a thousand Kang Yu-Weis. He has gained the respect, and the good opinion of all the foreign representatives in Peking. If he embraces our cause, our battle for the Empire of China is already fought and won."[20]

The conspirators knew Sun Yat-sen had failed in his earlier attempted uprisings and that K'ang Yu-wei's reputation was on the wane as a consequence of allegedly misappropriating reform party funds. They agreed to Yung Wing's proposals.[21] Their next step was for Yung Wing to contact Tang Shau Yi, one of Yung Wing's former students and purportedly the "protégé and right hand man" of Yuan Shih-k'ai, to arrange the necessary negotiations with the latter. The plan appeared promising, especially since Tang Shau Yi was in America at that time making a financial deal with J. P. Morgan. Yung Wing never considered that anything could go wrong.[22]

The prospects of winning Yuan Shih-k'ai over to their cause elated the conspirators, since they hoped the imperial Chinese army would still act at his bidding. With that kind of power at their disposal, they lost sight of their initial goals and expanded their plans to take over the entire Chinese Empire. Although little is known about these plans, Lea, for his part, still remained focused on capturing the Kwang provinces.[23]

Allen did not claim to be a military expert, but he knew he would not remain in the conspiracy long or be able to secure backing for it unless he had a plan that appeared credible on paper. Regardless of Lea's Chinese connections and alleged military expertise, Allen understood enough about planning large-scale operations to discount Lea's assessment of $2,000,000 as sufficient to undertake the Red Dragon plan. Instead of accepting Lea's figures, he advised Lea that his plans and figures needed to be broken down and revised if they were to convince a group of American businessmen to underwrite the Red Dragon venture. His suggestions did not go unheeded.[24]

On February 3, 1909, about two weeks after voicing his criticism, Allen received an updated version of the Red Dragon plan from Boothe:

> L- [Lea] has studied the matter carefully and planned out his campaign and shows that approximately ten thousand combatants and five thousand non-combatants will supply him with all the force necessary to accomplish what he desires. The cost of munitions, subsistence for from six to eight months, accoutrements, transportation, and so forth, will figure out about $2,500,000. This is a close estimate in detail. We believe that a

reserve for contingencies of two million additional, so that the affair shall not die down for want of fuel at a critical moment, will be a conservative and reasonable requirement. Therefore, $4,500,000 is a safe and full estimate for the purposes noted.[25]

Unfortunately for the conspirators, Allen failed to generate the necessary financial backing even after he was armed with both a credible plan and promises of huge returns on investments. Allen's lack of success in obtaining American backers was not surprising. In addition to the impracticalities of the entire Red Dragon scheme, the complexities and discord surrounding Chinese-American relations had a negative effect on the American business community's willingness to get involved in Asia during most of the decade. Roosevelt's efforts to uphold the Open Door policy of equal opportunities for the Western powers in China, while also preserving the balance of power in the region, were both costly and disastrous for American interests. Because the United States attempted to check Russian expansionism by helping Japan, Chinese interests were often jeopardized in the process. America made a series of concessions to Japan unilaterally and without regard for China's territorial or sovereign rights, which included recognition of Japanese hegemony over Korea and southern Manchuria after the Russo-Japanese War. These concessions caused much bitterness among the Chinese.[26]

Other signs of discord between the two nations caused additional irritation to both the Chinese government and the American business community. America's unilateral renewal of the Chinese Exclusion Treaty in 1904 led to the 1905 Chinese boycott of American goods that Lea, in 1908, proposed to end. Although Lea did not get the job, American business interests finally succeeded in pressuring the Roosevelt administration to take action in lifting the boycott. Unfortunately, while threats of employing military force restored American trade and interests considerably, Chinese-American relations suffered further as a consequence.[27]

Under these strained circumstances, American capitalists such as J. P. Morgan were disinclined to risk large sums in an uncertain area. Earlier, when the Russo-Japanese War was still in progress, the Ch'ing government cancelled his American China Development Company's concession to build a Canton-Hankow railway. Despite President Roosevelt's assurance that the U.S. government would "stand by" the company and do everything in its power to protect it from injustice,

Morgan did not wish to be tied down in a struggle with the Chinese government and so gave up the concession.[28]

Allen approached Morgan because the conspirators knew he was interested in exploiting Asian business prospects. They proposed to offer him enormous concessions and guaranteed returns for his backing. What they did not take into consideration, however, was that neither he nor his associates were willing to resort to revolutionary measures to make money. When Allen conferred with Morgan on February 2, 1909, Morgan rejected the proposition, reportedly commenting: "I am ready to do business with any established government on earth but I cannot help to make a government to do business with."[29]

Not long after Allen's meeting with Morgan the conspirators received more disappointing news. Yung Wing's expectations of winning Yuan Shih-k'ai over to their cause also fell through. Apparently, after Tang Shau Yi received Yung Wing's request to meet, he deliberately avoided contacting his former teacher due to fears that involving himself in such a conspiracy was not worth risking his standing in China. This setback left the conspirators back where they had started.[30]

Their lagging efforts at winning over Yuan Shih-k'ai and financial backers led the conspirators to realize the Red Dragon plan was simply going to take much longer than they had expected to initiate. But that still did not dissuade them from forging ahead with the conspiracy. The conspirators, motivated by Lea's dreams, considered some new options.

Lea stepped in with his prescription to remedy the situation during the spring of 1909. By that time he believed he was in a good position to make another attempt at getting an American government post in China to further the conspiracy. The Taft administration had recently come to power, and William W. Rockhill, the American minister to China, was retiring.[31]

There was one new variable working in Lea's favor this time. On this occasion his confidence hinged more on his rising expectations as a writer than on his past Chinese affiliations. He and Boothe arranged to have former U.S. Army chief of staff, retired lieutenant general Adna R. Chaffee, and former U.S. Army chief of artillery, retired major general John P. Story, both of whom had recently settled in California, review Lea's *Valor of Ignorance* manuscript. When both generals lauded Lea's writing as "a remarkable work and marked the author a military genius," Lea and Boothe knew the backing of such prominent men could be very useful in opening important doors for them.[32] At the very least, they had reason to believe that the addition of Chaffee and Story to their list of respected and influential patrons would weight the scales in Lea's favor in Washington.

By arranging to have Chaffee and Story write a foreword and introduction, respectively, to *The Valor of Ignorance,* Lea and Boothe hoped the generals also would throw their support behind recommending Lea to President Taft for the ministerial post in China. Much to their dismay, however, both generals declined to initiate action on Lea's behalf in Washington. They reasoned that as former military officers it would be inappropriate for them to be party to the scheme "on the ground that the Ministership is a political matter and we [Chaffee and Story] should not be originals in recommendations to the President." Instead, they suggested that Lea ask California's two U.S. senators, Frank P. Flint and George C. Perkins, to champion his candidacy. Once that was done, Chaffee said, he and Story would gladly attest to Lea's "very marked and superior equipment for the place when put in comparison with the class of men usually chosen as a reward for services rendered."[33]

Lea fared little better with his other distinguished acquaintances, such as Harrison Gray Otis, and he apparently never received the support of either senator, Flint or Perkins, despite the fact that William A. Bowen, the Lea family attorney, had been employed in Flint's law office prior to his becoming a U.S. senator, and likely would have tried using his influence with Flint on Lea's behalf. As a last resort, Lea had Boothe write to K'ang Yu-wei requesting that he use his influence with Prince Ch'un, the emperor's regent. They presumed that K'ang Yu-wei would soon become an advisor to Prince Ch'un and would thus be in an ideal position to assist Lea. But this too failed since the presumption proved false and K'ang Yu-wei never became an imperial advisor.[34]

For Lea the author, there was a bright side to offset the frustrations of the Red Dragon conspiracy and his two unsuccessful bids at securing a government appointment. With the endorsement of Chaffee and Story, he had little trouble finding a suitable publisher for *The Valor of Ignorance.* Harper and Brothers believed it would do so well, the company serialized portions of it in its popular weekly magazine before publishing it as a book. This decision assured Lea a degree of national fame he had never previously enjoyed.[35] Furthermore, Lea's impending success with *The Valor of Ignorance* also made a marked impression on Ethel Powers. While no records survive, it is likely that Lea wrote her describing his activities and expressing his desire to be with her in the future. She evidently began thinking seriously about returning to him.

The summer and fall of 1909 offered Lea a respite from the trials of the Red Dragon conspiracy. He had planned to take a Hawaiian vacation with his father in September, but his father, who had been suffering from cancer, died unexpectedly in mid-August. The shock of his father's death greatly disturbed him, and he temporarily diverted attention from the Red Dragon conspiracy. Instead, he devoted more time to writing, and at one point Yung Wing complained about his newfound dedication to writing rather than planning campaigns for China. Yet Lea's writing was yielding very favorable results. His attention to geopolitics marked his debut as an internationally recognized global strategist. He had no way of knowing then that above all his other literary works, he would be best remembered for *The Valor of Ignorance*.[36]

The Valor of Ignorance's publication in the fall of 1909 created an international sensation. Lea sent copies of the book, which contained an impressive frontispiece photograph of himself in his lieutenant general's dress uniform, to many prominent persons, statesmen, and military officers. He generally received high praise from the military men. In Great Britain, Field Marshal Lord Frederick Sleigh Roberts, former commander-in-chief of the British army and staunch advocate of conscription and imperial defense, found Lea's work so convincing he bought up all the copies that Harper had there and distributed them to his friends and associates.[37]

In Japan, where *The Valor of Ignorance* was eventually translated and sold two years later, it reportedly went through twenty-four editions and sold twenty-six thousand copies in a month's time. The Japanese were far from alienated by the book; they were flattered. Lea considered them a worthy and honorable enemy, and in the tradition of the samurai spirit they respected his views on discipline and the military way of life. His work also impressed the Japanese as being the first Yellow Peril literature by an American they considered more realistic than imaginary.[38]

The Valor of Ignorance became one of America's most controversial books of the period. Some waved it as a lantern shedding light on America's martial weakness, while others condemned it as the alarmist ravings of an overactive imagination that added unnecessary fuel to the Yellow Peril fires. In one case, the book led a Los Angeles playhouse to perform an invasion drama depicting how the Japanese would capture California.[39] Lea, however, was not the only thinker to criticize America's military weakness or advocate Darwinist prescriptions for the salvation of Western civilization. On the contrary, the moving force of his arguments rested more on his presentation than on his originality. His experience in debate and attention to minute details helped make his case.

In *The Valor of Ignorance* Lea justified militaristic imperialism and gave an analysis of the conflict between American and Japanese interests in the Far Fast. In the first section of the book he presented an exposition of general principles concerning the struggle for national supremacy and concluded with a case study of two countries involved in such a struggle. Lea argued that nations were Darwinist organisms engaged in a struggle for survival in which war was not only a biological and political necessity, but an inevitable facet of man's and nations' evolutionary growth. He believed war and expansion were equivalent to national greatness and that commercialism and racial diffusion were eroding America's vitality. He warned that America faced disintegration through decadence and then complete defeat in an international struggle when the East clashed with the West, if his warnings were not heeded. He believed that in the ensuing clash, Japan, imbued with a martial spirit and stronger armed forces than America, would be better equipped to prevail than America. He theorized that Japan could conquer the Philippines and Hawaii with little difficulty before capturing America's Pacific coast. He drew an ominous picture of a defeated America:

> The inevitable consummation that follows the investment of San Francisco becomes apparent in the utter helplessness of the Republic. In the entire nation there is not another regiment of regular troops; no general, no corporals. Not months, but years, must elapse before armies equal to the Japanese are able to pass in parade. These must then . . . [attempt] the militarily impossible; turning the mountain-gorges into the ossuaries of their dead, and burdening desert winds with the spirits of their slain. The repulsed and distracted forces to scatter, as heretofore, dissension throughout the Union, brood rebellions, class and sectional insurrections, until the heterogeneous Republic, in its principles, shall disintegrate, and again into the palm of reestablished monarch pay the toll of its vanity and its scorn.[40]

One literary reviewer aptly observed that Lea "says that Americans will read his book with bitterness, and he is no doubt right."[41] Lea, guided by a strong sense of mission, discounted most negative criticism of his book, especially when pacifists such as Norman Angell and Dr. David Starr Jordan continually referred to it as the worst example of rampant militarism. Conversely, when Lea began receiving positive feedback from those who supported his views, he started to formulate notes for a companion volume.[42]

The success and notoriety Lea gained from *The Valor of Ignorance* could not have come at a more opportune time for the troubled Red Dragon conspiracy. From the outset his revolutionary conspiracy had seemed more a fantasy than a reality, and as such, doomed to failure. Now there would be new faith in Lea and his plan. Although *The Valor of Ignorance* did not help him get the Chinese ministerial position, it helped elevate his credibility with his fellow conspirators enough to keep the Red Dragon conspiracy alive, and would prove valuable in luring a new potentially powerful ally, Dr. Sun Yat-sen, into their ranks.[43]

Alfred E. Lea, circa 1880. (*History of Clear Creek and Boulder Valleys, Colorado*, facing 342)

Hersa Lea, circa 1875. (Personal Papers, Mr. and Mrs. James D. Lea,
Houston, Tex.)

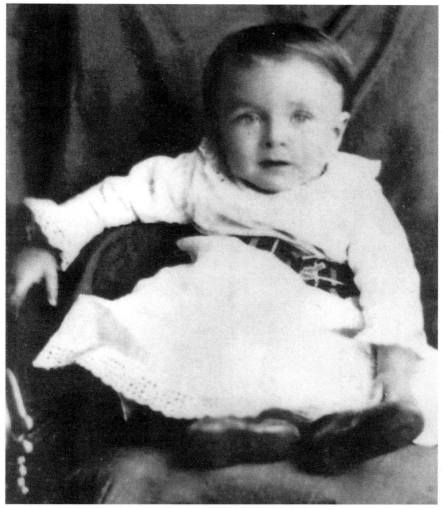

Homer Lea in infancy. (Charles O. Kates Personal Papers, Mr. Brian Kates, Pomona, N.Y.)

Homer Lea, age twenty, as a high school senior. (Kates Papers)

K'ang Yu-wei, circa 1898. (Philip W. Sergeant, *The Great Empress Dowager of China* [New York: Dodd, Mead, 1911], facing 176)

Liang Ch'i-ch'ao, circa 1903. (Kates Papers)

Lieutenant General Homer Lea, CERA, circa 1904. (Author's collection)

Homer Lea in Chinese attire, circa 1904. (Author's collection)

First Sergeant Ansel E. O'Banion, U.S. Army, circa 1902. (Courtesy of U.S. Cavalry Museum, Fort Riley, Kans.)

Ansel O'Banion (white shirt) and Western Military Academy cadets training at Sunset Blvd. and Vermont Ave., Los Angeles, August 12, 1904. (Kates Papers)

CERA cadets, Fourth Infantry Regiment, Portland, Oregon, circa 1905. (Kates Papers)

Unidentified CERA officer, St. Louis, circa 1905. (Kates Papers)

General Richard A. Falkenberg
and Captain Wong Kim, CIRA,
1904. (*Philadelphia Inquirer*,
January 15, 1905, 3)

Unwanted publicity for Lea and the reformers, 1905. (*Los Angeles Herald*,
June 25, 1905)

Ethel B. Powers, circa late 1890s. (Joshua B. Powers Personal Papers, Powers Family, South Royalton, Vt.)

Charles Beach Boothe, circa
1909. (Moody, "Makers of
Los Angeles," 322)

Dr. Yung Wing,
circa 1910.
(*World's Work*,
July 1910,
13105)

Dr. Sun Yat-sen, 1912. (photograph by K. T. Thompson)

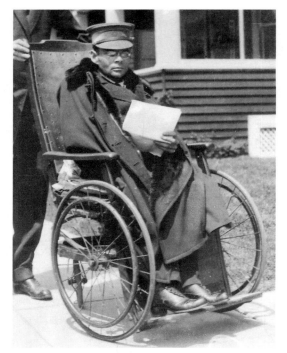

Homer Lea convalescing, Los Angeles, 1912. (Kates Papers)

Military honor guard with the Leas' ashes followed by Joshua B. Powers and daughter, Mrs. Carolien P. Maynard, Taiwan, April 19, 1969. (Powers Papers)

CHAPTER 10

FINAL CRUSADE

Sun is going to make him his Chief of Staff so he is wild with delight.

—Ethel Lea

Lea's fame from *The Valor of Ignorance* and his growing reputation as a military strategist led to his becoming a confidential advisor to Dr. Sun Yat-sen and his revolutionary movement. He had long shown his revolutionary fervor in words and action with the covert CIA and the Red Dragon plan. Now, he faced the ultimate test. Could he be of any actual political or military service to the Chinese revolution and its leader while at the same time crusading for a revival of Anglo-Saxon militancy? He came close to realizing his dreams, but tragically, while at the crossroads of achieving his destiny and dreams, his health ultimately gave out and sidelined him until his untimely death, just days before his thirty-sixth birthday. He also gained further fame as a military strategist with *The Day of the Saxon*, the companion volume to *The Valor of Ignorance*, but Anglo-American society failed to accept his concepts of world order.

Sun Yat-sen came to America in the fall of 1909 on a fund-raising tour for his revolutionary movement, which had plans for a Chinese uprising in the near future. While details are lacking, it is known that in the course of his tour he met with Yung Wing, who convinced him that Lea and the Red Dragon conspirators could benefit his revolutionary movement. Yung Wing intended Lea and Boothe to meet with Sun Yat-sen, but Lea was in such poor health for most of December he could not do so, and Boothe was too busy to travel east. Instead, Boothe advised Yung Wing that it would be best if Sun Yat-sen met with them in California.[1]

Sun Yat-sen, Lea, and Boothe met twice in California in 1910: first during February and again in March. They spent many hours combining their revolutionary plans at Lea's Long Beach cottage and a nearby hotel. After working out the details, they planned to conquer all China. They decided on several means to do it. First, they agreed to an alliance whereby Sun Yat-sen would receive $5,000,000 in private American backing to underwrite his anti-Ch'ing revolution. They then agreed that Lea, Boothe, Allen, and Yung Wing would receive generous financial concessions or possibly key positions in the new Chinese republican government if their efforts succeeded. Finally, they devised a contingency plan whereby Sun Yat-sen would head an interim military government, with Lea as his army chief of staff, until the mechanism for establishing a stable Chinese republic could be put into place.[2]

Lea and Boothe also shared in planning Sun Yat-sen's revolution. Lea urged Sun Yat-sen to establish a covert base in China where foreign officers could train partisans for the revolution. Whether he envisioned an active role for himself in such a venture is unclear. The question, however, became academic. His fellow conspirators rejected the plan owing to the difficulty in finding a training area that would not arouse the suspicion of the Ch'ing government.[3]

Boothe's recommendations carried more weight. He persuaded Sun Yat-sen to restrict all revolutionary outbreaks until financial arrangements were complete, so potential backers would have more faith in the leadership, organization, and coordination of the revolutionary movement. Even so, Sun Yat-sen stipulated that he could hold back his next uprising only until winter. If by that time Boothe had failed to raise the money, Sun Yat-sen warned that he would take independent action that might lead to modifying the conditions of their agreement.[4]

Meanwhile, when Lea was not devoting his time to revolutionary activities, he was busy writing and lecturing. With the assistance of Ethel Powers, who returned to him after her divorce in late 1909, he resumed writing about future aspects of Western civilization. He now focused his attention on the controversy surrounding aviation in modern warfare.[5]

After the Wright brothers' spectacular invention of the airplane in 1903, writers began speculating about the potential value of aircraft in military operations. Some believed it would soon become a decisive weapon of mass destruction. Lea offered his views in "The Aeroplane in War: Some Observations on a Military Delusion," published by *Harpers Weekly Magazine* in August 1910. He took a pragmatic approach, dismissing the popular concept that the airplane would be the next wonder weapon. He believed there could be no real substitute for the foot soldier, particularly with the present limitations of aircraft. However, he underestimated how the airplane might alter future warfare. He allowed that the airplane might become a devastating military tool, but he discounted its value as a decisive instrument of war on the premise that the great powers would band together to prohibit it rather than allow the technology to fall into the hands of a small nation and upset the balance of power.[6] He also believed there was a correlation between developing new decisive instruments of war and the decline of racial militancy. He returned to a social Darwinist condemnation of modern society: "The superstition of the inanimate is still upon man. . . . Whenever militancy goes from the spirit of a race, there enters into it, in a proportionate degree, a racial aversion to pain and subordination; in other words, moral and physical cowardice has come upon it, and it is then, in that period of evasion and subterfuge, that it seeks succor in the inanimate; in gods, in inventors, or what not."[7]

During this period Lea was captivated by his role as a military strategist and he became more intolerant of other opinions and views. Whether in his writing or simply in discussing issues over a drink with friends, he did not spare his scorn of anyone who ventured to disagree with him. His greatest impatience may have been with American military officers. He thought the average U.S. Army officer had scant strategic sense and he held many of them in contempt.[8] Harry Carr recalled an episode in which Lea demonstrated such intolerance:

The force of Lea's personality was overwhelming. I remember how he used to sit in an alcove of the old Alexandria Bar in Los Angeles and hold what amounted to a royal levee. Actors, soldiers, distinguished lawyers, journalists, came to listen with respect. His manner was imperious. I happened to be sitting with him one day when an army major ventured to contradict some of his conclusions. Homer hitched around in his chair, the way cripples do, and looked him over with contempt.

"Major," he said "I am a consulting strategist by profession. If our country goes to war—as it will—I shall be too busy to suggest a role for you to play; so I will tell you now. When war comes, I want you to drive a mule in a pack-train. Don't try to drive the lead mule because your mental capacity is not equal to the job. Select a mule somewhere in the middle of the train." The major faded away.[9]

Lea occasionally lectured to various social and civic groups on defense matters when not drinking and dispensing wisdom at the Alexandria Bar or conferring on matters of revolutionary strategy with his fellow conspirators. On August 13, 1910, for example, he created a minor uproar in an address to the City Club of Los Angeles on *The Valor of Ignorance*. He underscored the defenselessness of the Pacific coast and advanced the probability of a Japanese war and invasion within five years. He urged the mayor to take action and enlist the support of high army officials in properly defending the Pacific coast. One press account noted: "The utterance caused a mild sensation in this city, owing to the prominence of General Lea, and it is likely that a movement may be launched for the purpose of having the Government render more material protection to the Pacific coast cities and towns."[10]

Lea's inflated status as a military authority may have resulted partly from the influence *The Valor of Ignorance* was having in Congress and on the American military establishment. On May 19, 1910, California congressman James McLachlan submitted a resolution to the House of Representatives calling for the secretary of war to provide a detailed report on the nation's defenses. He followed the resolution by a fervent speech, "Defenselessness of the Pacific Coast," in large part inspired by *The Valor of Ignorance*. He sought to rectify deficiencies in American defense policy and praised "General Lea" and *The Valor of Ignorance,* suggesting "a wide reading of this book by the Members of this body."[11] U.S. Army major George H. Shelton, editor of *Infantry Journal,* seized upon McLachlan's speech and reprinted it in the *Journal*. He also communicated with Lea that he would use the *Journal* to spread Lea's message. The U.S. Military Academy at West Point added *The Valor of Ignorance* to its recommended reading list for graduates, including a mistaken reference to Lea being a major general in the Chinese army. Lea's arguments likely also were a contributing factor to army war games and maneuvers based on his scenarios. Yet he failed to awaken the general public to the extent that he hoped. The American people at large remained unresponsive to his dire warnings.[12]

His determination to bring about the salvation of Western civilization convinced him to redouble his efforts and write another book. During the spring and summer of 1910, he and Ethel worked on a second volume, which dealt with British imperial defense and also included an exposition on the general decline of militancy in the entire Anglo-Saxon race. Lea sought to make all English-speaking peoples see that they were in a global competition for supremacy against the Teutonic, Slavic, and Asian races. He believed that once awakened, they would embrace his militant doctrines and prepare for the coming global onslaught. His missionary zeal was clear. He responded to flattering remarks from Field Marshal Lord Roberts about *The Valor of Ignorance* by explaining:

> This book *The Valor of Ignorance* is but introductory to a general work I have in mind to bring about:
> (1) a change in form & spirit of this government
> (2) conscription
> I now realize the full meaning of this job. It is an Augean stable business, only here we have to do with that human manure of bigotry, ignorance, vanity, graft, venality, cowardice and the general rottenness of a vast and heterogeneous mass. It seems hopeless at first sight but is not . . . it is our duty to preserve at all costs, our racial integrity and Anglo-Saxon domination over the world. Let there once be reached a certain point in its disintegration and the rule of the race is lost.[13]

In the summer of 1910 Lea also returned to writing drama. He began a collaborative effort with U.S. Army major Richard C. Croxton, then stationed overseas. It is unclear how he and Croxton met, and little is known about Croxton. At the time he was an infantry officer stationed at the Headquarters, Department of Luzon, Manila, in the Philippines. He had done some writing and likely corresponded with Lea, probably praising *The Valor of Ignorance*. He helped Lea promote *The Valor of Ignorance* with his brother officers, including his superior, Major General William P. Duvall, commander of the Philippines Division. Croxton even arranged for General Duvall to forward a copy of *The Valor of Ignorance* to former president Roosevelt on Lea's behalf. Lea and Croxton hoped their drama would be completed by the fall of 1911. They initially had difficulty coming up with a topic, but eventually decided on an adaptation of *The Vermilion Pen-*

cil entitled *The Great Symbol.* Ultimately, two versions of the drama emerged; one by Homer and Ethel Lea, later copyrighted on February 13, 1913; and one by Homer Lea and Major R. C. Croxton, copyrighted on June 13, 1913, which included Ethel as a copyright holder.[14]

Lea's star continued to rise as he made more public appearances. California governor James N. Gillett invited him to be a delegate to the first Pacific Coast Congress, which convened in San Francisco in November 1910. It comprised approximately three hundred civil, military, and commercial representatives who discussed specific problems affecting the region. Lea addressed the congress as an authority on the potential Japanese threat and the question of coast defenses.[15]

In December Lea spoke at a public dinner in San Diego. A local newspaper reported: "General Lea is an earnest speaker. His words carry the force of his conviction. Military and naval men listened with rapt attention to every utterance. His sentences came like the thundering roar of artillery." Military audiences, in particular, liked Lea. The *Army and Navy Journal* reprinted his San Diego speech with the title "An Eloquent Note of Warning."[16]

Lea's increased notoriety also earned him a place in the prestigious *Who's Who in America: A Biographical Dictionary of Notable Living Men and Women of the United States.* His ego got the best of him when he submitted his entry for inclusion in the 1910–11 volume. It included the following highlights about his military credentials, which appeared impressive to the unsuspecting reader: "Undertook relief of Kwang Hsu, Emperor of China, 1900, 1901; raised and comd. 2d Army Div., 1904, holding rank of lt.-gen. over these forces."[17] The entry furthered his myth by giving the strong impression he had returned to China in 1904 to command an army division instead of accurately portraying his command of Chinese cadets in America.

Lea's attention was sharply drawn back to Chinese revolutionary affairs when he received some startling news. On December 16, 1910, Sun Yat-sen wrote Lea and Boothe he would no longer hold back his revolutionary forces: "We are now taking independent measure of our own to start the great movement in the coming few months. But we are in great need of help at present. Can you do anything for us by your own means? Another few hundred thousand could make us carry out everything perfectly through. But at any case whether we have the money or not, I am sure of our success in the next move."[18]

Sun Yat-sen's letter prompted Boothe to find someone other than

Allen to help raise capital quickly for the conspirators. Boothe turned to C. B. Hill, a Montclair, New Jersey, lawyer and business associate with sound financial connections. He enlisted Hill's assistance with the same promises and dreams that had kept the conspiracy alive so long, including the prospects of financial rewards "beyond the dreams of avarice."[19]

Despite Boothe's last-ditch efforts to help Sun Yat-sen and salvage the conspiracy's interests, Sun Yat-sen's revolutionary uprising occurred and failed in late March 1911, before Hill could mobilize financial backing. Had the uprising succeeded, Lea, Boothe, Hill, Allen, and Yung Wing may well have reaped some rewards for their efforts. Unfortunately, the failure of Sun Yat-sen's revolutionary forces, his tenth attempt, ended his chances of securing any future private American backing, and sealed the fate of Lea's conspiracy. Boothe, Allen, and Hill would have nothing more to do with such risky ventures. As for Sun Yat-sen, the March revolutionary failure meant it would simply take longer to topple the Ch'ing dynasty.[20]

Lea remained committed to Sun Yat-sen, but his delicate health kept him from giving much real help. At the height of his literary career, the thirty-three-year-old Lea was going blind. He knew his future was uncertain. His California physicians offered few hopes for recovery. Even if he did recover, they advised him, it would be dangerous to attempt active work.[21]

Yet Lea still had cause for some optimism. Although his doctors could do little for him, he learned of an eye specialist in Wiesbaden, Germany, who had been successful in treating cases similar to his and arranged for treatment. By this time, he and Ethel had decided to marry and use the trip as a honeymoon.[22]

With his health failing, Lea was forced to curtail his socializing, drinking, and occasional lecturing, but he refused to give up his dreams of greatness. While considering the prospects of a more passive life and possible employment as a typewriter salesman in a friend's company, he continued working with Sun Yat-sen and writing the companion volume to *The Valor of Ignorance*. He also formulated ambitious plans to expand his 1908 *Van Norden's Magazine* article "How Socialism Failed in China," into a short book that would be followed by a multivolume history of China.[23]

Sun Yat-sen was traveling in America on a fund-raising tour during most of 1911 while Lea continued trying to raise funds for the Chinese revolution. Lea may have contributed earlier to the Red

Dragon conspiracy and revolutionary cause out of his own pocket; it is unknown if he did so. Now, however, he arranged for Sun Yat-sen to receive the copyright and royalties for a Japanese edition of *The Valor of Ignorance*. This unselfish gesture set the stage for renewing their alliance and earned him Sun Yat-sen's implicit trust.[24]

In early June 1911 Lea and Sun Yat-sen met again in Los Angeles to continue their revolutionary planning. They were partially successful in keeping their meeting secret. As far as the public knew, Lea was meeting with a Chinese businessman named Y. S. Sun, not the revolutionary leader Sun-Yat-sen. The *Los Angeles Times* reported on June 10: "Y. S. Sun, a retired Chinese capitalist of Singapore, who has been touring Europe and has just crossed the continent, is at the Lankershim [Hotel], the guest of Homer Lea. Lea will leave soon for a five or six-year sojourn in the capitals of Europe."[25]

Lea and Sun Yat-sen reached several new resolutions concerning the next uprising in China, scheduled for March 1912. Aside from confirming their earlier plans of jointly heading an interim military government in China, Sun Yat-sen granted Lea wide latitude in formulating Chinese foreign policy after the revolution. Lea thought a strong China would help preserve Anglo-Saxon hegemony in the Far East. He believed that granting America and Great Britain special status over the other powers in return for their immediate support of Sun Yat-sen's new government would achieve three major goals. First, with Anglo-American financial support and military advisors, China could develop into a strong regional power. Second, China could then become the bulwark of Anglo-American security interests in Asia and the Pacific by counterbalancing Russian and Japanese interests. Finally, with a special status, Anglo-American interests would reap vast economic concessions at the expense of the other powers in China. Lea proposed to implement his geopolitical agenda by using his contacts to gain entrée into American and British governmental circles. He hoped to convince both countries of the impending downfall of the Ch'ing regime and garner their support for Sun Yat-sen's democratic program to liberate China.[26]

As Lea and Sun Yat-sen finalized their plans, Lea invited one of his closest high school friends, journalist Harry Carr, to have breakfast with him at the Lankershim Hotel and meet Sun Yat-sen. In the course of their meeting he confided in Carr that he might be dying. Carr recalled: "He told me, as we sat at the table, that he had been informed by his physicians that he had Bright's disease in an advanced stage and had not long to live. He seemed more affected by the disgust of being put on a milk-toast diet than by the fact that the Grim Reaper was beckoning. It was the first time during our long friendship that he had ever spoken about his affliction. He spoke of the terrible handicap under which he had lived; and how it had debarred him from commanding troops in the field."[27]

After Lea and Sun Yat-sen parted, Lea left Los Angeles. He reportedly took a train on June 14 for San Antonio, Texas, where he met Ethel. From there they headed to Memphis, Tennessee, where Ethel had family, to be married. As a special gesture, Lea may have given Ethel his mother's wedding ring, which he treasured and always wore. The Leas kept their marriage a secret for the time being. Their friends in Los Angeles would learn the news later, after the Leas arrived in Wiesbaden.[28]

The Leas next visited Washington, D.C., where they obtained passports and Lea tried to solicit government support for a Chinese revolution. It is unclear for the most part whom Lea visited in Washington, but it is known that he approached Senator Elihu Root, a former secretary of war and champion of military reform, to whom he had dedicated *The Valor of Ignorance*. Lea warned him of an imminent revolution and change of government in China, but Root made no promises. He was courteous and attentive, and personally favored the right of the Chinese to self-government, but he advised Lea there was nothing he could do at that time for Sun Yat-sen's cause. Root may have arranged for Lea to meet with Secretary of War Henry L. Stimson, who likely gave Lea advice similar to Root's. The U.S. government recognized the Ch'ing regime, and the Taft administration's aggressive Asian commercial policy of "Dollar Diplomacy" was firmly rooted in the concept of equal opportunity in the region. Root, at least, agreed he would keep in touch with Lea in Wiesbaden if there were any new developments.[29]

The Leas next traveled to New York City, where their ship sailed for Europe. They arrived in Wiesbaden in July 1911, and Lea began receiving treatment from Dr. Karl Meurer, a famed eye specialist. His eyes began improving and his future looked brighter when he wrote a friend in August about his health and future travel plans: "I am doing a little work every day now, so you know that my eyes have improved a great deal—I hope to be completely well by the first of November, when we leave Wiesbaden. We will visit Nuremberg, Munchen and Berlin, then go to Paris for the winter, with the exception possibly of a few weeks in London some time during the winter."[30]

That summer, while traveling and sightseeing with Ethel through Germany, Lea patiently avoided overtaxing himself. With his eyes very sensitive to light due to his medical treatment, he could work only periodically on his next book, *The Day of the Saxon*. Aside from having a few social drinks with some German army officers, and arranging through the U.S. military attaché in Berlin to see Kaiser Wilhelm II review troops on maneuvers in Mainz in mid-August, he had nothing to do or say in his capacity as a "General," or as a military authority. Ironically, he was probably unaware that a week after the maneuvers, the *New York Times* Berlin correspondent reported that Kaiser Wilhelm and Prince Henry of Prussia had recently read *The Valor of Ignorance* and "have expressed themselves about it to American friends in most enthusiastic terms."[31]

Lea might very well have recovered his health, completed his trip, and returned to a comparatively quiet life with Ethel in California if dramatic events had not unfolded in China. Much to the world's surprise, on October 10, 1911, Sun Yat-sen's revolutionary forces prematurely launched a revolt in Wuchang, Hupeh province, which finally ushered in the long-expected revolution that would topple the Manchu dynasty. The revolutionaries initially gained a significant foothold and their ultimate success seemed assured, as the Ch'ing army began crumbling in the wake of defeats and wholesale desertions. The prince regent, in a desperate effort to save the dynasty, recalled Yuan Shih-k'ai, the one man in the empire believed capable of saving it, and granted him full authority over the government to quell the revolution. These unexpected events forced Sun Yat-sen and Lea to react immediately.[32]

Sun Yat-sen learned of the revolution while on his American fundraising trip. He received word he would likely be elected president of the provisional government and realized that Western diplomatic and financial backing were all the more imperative for his plans. He and Lea had already agreed that they would seek Anglo-American support to form the bedrock of the new China. Sun Yat-sen later explained:

> At that time, I could have come home in disguise by way of the Pacific Ocean, and I could have reached Shanghai in twenty days. Then I could have directed the revolutionary war myself; that would have given me the greatest satisfaction of my life. But my second thought was that my contribution to the revolutionary work was not in the battle field but in diplo-

matic circles. So I decided to devote myself to diplomatic work and not return until the diplomatic questions were solved. . . .

In brief, of the six Foreign Powers that have most intimate relations with China, America and France were sympathetic with the Chinese Revolution. Germany and Russia were opposed to us. The people in England were sympathetic toward us, but the government policy was not definite. So the key of our diplomacy would be the attitude of the British government because it would determine in a large measure the success or failure of our Revolution. If the British government was for the revolution, the Japanese government would not need be feared.[33]

As Sun Yat-sen prepared to seek support, he cabled Lea in Wiesbaden to go to London as soon as possible and open negotiations with the British government. Whatever their success, Sun Yat-sen would then join Lea and they would both return to China together.[34]

On October 18 Lea left Ethel in Wiesbaden and hurriedly traveled to London to act on Sun Yat-sen's behalf. He planned to be gone only a few days. In that time, he was confident his distinguished British acquaintances could arrange an introduction for him to governmental circles.[35]

Checking into London's elegant Savoy Hotel, Lea first planned to see Lord Charles Beresford, a former admiral who had served in the Orient and presently a Conservative member of Parliament. Beresford, whose party was out of power, was a personal friend of Yuan Shih-k'ai. Lea believed he might help rally parliamentary and governmental support for a loan to Sun Yat-sen's revolutionaries. Lea then planned to see Prime Minister Herbert Asquith and Foreign Secretary Sir Edward Grey. Yet his plans began going awry when Sir John G. Tollemache Sinclair, a friend he had made from writing *The Valor of Ignorance,* informed him that due to bitter partisan politics, introductions from Conservatives, with the possible exception of Field Marshal Lord Roberts, would not be of any use to him in Labour government circles. In any case, Beresford was away and could not be reached, and Roberts could not see him before October 23.[36]

Lea grew frustrated and impatient that weekend. Rain, constant since his arrival, made London dark and cold. He did not leave the hotel, fearing he might miss someone's call. As much as he missed Ethel, he could not afford to send for her for the few more days he expected to be in London. He was spending almost all of his money on cables to Sun Yat-sen and to revolutionary leaders in China. So far, Sun Yat-sen's only replies were vague urgings to do something at once.[37]

When the weekend finally ended, Lord Roberts visited Lea to discuss the first chapters of *The Day of the Saxon* and revolutionary affairs in China. Roberts praised the book so highly that a few days later Lea used it to his advantage in getting a $1,500 advance and a 50 percent increase in royalties from Harper and Brothers' London office. As for Lea's prospects of getting a quick loan for the revolution, Roberts was not as enthusiastic. He believed it would take much longer than Lea expected. Lea wrote Ethel: "I must stay here for some weeks, as nothing could be done in less time on a matter of such great importance."[38]

After accepting Roberts's advice, Lea decided it was not worth continuing his lone efforts to finance the revolution. He wrote Ethel: "I made up my mind I would not stay here longer alone. I have never been so miserable and lonesome in my life." He added, "You must not worry. I have not entered a bar or taken a drink with anyone."[39] With his own finances replenished, he sent Ethel a £60 money order and asked her to explain his departure to Dr. Meurer. With that money she was to buy Lea's necessary prescriptions and learn the method of treatment if possible. His most pressing concern, however, was for his bride, Ethel. "Come at once," he urged. "I have been dreaming of you every night. I certainly will devour you with kisses as soon as I get you here."[40]

On October 31, three days after Ethel arrived in London, Sun Yat-sen cabled Lea enthusiastically: "Organization everywhere excellent. All looking for me to lead. If financially supported, I could control situation absolutely. No strong government could be formed until we get there. Therefore loan is necessary. You are given full power to negotiate such."[41]

The following day Sun Yat-sen was even more optimistic. After learning that his revolutionary forces were making outstanding progress against the Manchus, he and an entourage of supporters prepared to leave New York for London. He cabled Lea: "Things much improved. I may take Mauretania tommorrow."[42]

Lea took Sun Yat-sen's cables as the proof he had been waiting for to convince skeptics the revolution was succeeding. With financial negotiations at a standstill, he wrote Roberts with news of Sun Yat-sen's impending arrival in London and enclosed the cables. He urged that the time was now ripe to "at least formulate some plan whereby we can proceed to secure the loan immediately."[43] He also contacted Elihu Root, hoping that Root could help arrange a loan from Washington. With the Manchu dynasty faltering, he wrote Root: "As I told you in Washington such a result was inevitable. We could hold it down no longer. You will remember that the sole purpose for which I desired the money was to secure perfect cohesion and unity amongst our forces scattered over so vast an area as China." If money had been available, he added, "we would have accomplished this revolution without any bloodshed whatever." If Sun Yat-sen lacked money to stabilize his revolution, Lea warned, "it means an indefinite prolongation of warfare" that could harm both Chinese and Anglo-American interests. Since Anglo-American interests faced such grim prospects, in Lea's view, he wanted Root to get a secret note from the U.S. government indicating support for the revolutionaries. He was "confident that . . . [such a note] would turn the scale and by a secret acquiescence [with the British] I would be able to secure money" from them. He also reminded Root that the issue of support transcended helping the Chinese. Underlying his master plan, he still proposed to "bring about . . . a tacit amalgamation of the Anglo-Saxon race in the Orient." To carry out this plan, he urged Root to see President Taft and Secretary of State Philander C. Knox for their "immediate support." He then promised to keep the American government informed of his progress in establishing a new government in China.[44]

Nothing came of Lea's proposals to Root, largely because the Taft administration was committed to a policy of neutrality until the revolution was settled. Lea, meanwhile, still sought to influence American foreign policy to fit his world vision. He may not have realized the extent to which both the American and British governments, as well as a good part of the anti-Ch'ing camp, believed that Yuan Shih-k'ai, not Sun Yat-sen, would bring about a negotiated settlement in China.[45]

Lord Roberts did not share Lea's enthusiasm either. Having already made inquiries on Lea's behalf, he discovered that the British government shared similar views with Washington. When he returned Sun Yat-sen's cables to Lea, he offered a sobering response: "I see no way by which a loan could be started in this country, and I fear Sun will be greatly disappointed when he arrives."[46] A few days later he gave Lea more regrettable news. Prime Minister Asquith and Foreign Secretary Grey refused to see Sun Yat-sen. Roberts did, however, manage to arrange a meeting for Lea and Sun Yat-sen he believed might be helpful with Lord George N. Curzon, a member of the House of Lords and former viceroy of India. Roberts also added he would keep his schedule open to see Lea and Sun Yat-sen any time during the upcoming week at his Berkshire country house.[47]

Britain's Imperial Maritime League, prompted by Sir John G. Tollemache Sinclair, offered Lea a membership when he was in Wiesbaden. The league, founded in 1908, was dedicated to safeguarding British naval supremacy in the world. Once Lea was in London, the league invited him to attend a meeting on the evening of November 10, but Sun Yat-sen's arrival that day demanded his attention and prevented his attendance. Lea regretted his absence, but did not let the opportunity pass of preaching his crusade for Anglo-Saxon hegemony in the world. He sent a letter that was read at the meeting, which elaborated on his world vision:

> It is, I believe, and should continue to be, the policy of my country to do everything possible to increase the power of the British Empire. While we have enunciated a doctrine of American immunity from Continental Europe, yet it is not so much this doctrine as it is the power of the British Empire in its mastery over the Atlantic that conserves to my country her suzerainty over the Western Hemisphere, and anything I can do to aid in the increase of the strength of Great Britain I will feel that I am directly contributing to the welfare of my own country.[48]

With Sun Yat-sen now in London, Lea appeared to be making some inroads into British governmental circles through the assistance of his friend, Sir Arthur Trevor Dawson of the armaments firm Vickers, Sons, and Maxim. Dawson, believing that Sun Yat-sen would soon be the president of China and Lea would be his army chief of staff, agreed to approach Sir Edward Grey on their behalf in the expectation of receiving lucrative orders from them for arms and munitions. On November 14 Dawson submitted a proposal to Grey from Sun Yat-sen and Lea that strongly reflected Lea's partisan hand:

> Sun Yat-sen's party wish to make an Anglo-Saxon alliance with Great Britain and the United States of America. They are now in close touch with the United States through Senators Root

and Knox. General Homer Lea is Chief of Staff responsible only to Sun Yat-sen. . . .

Sun Yat-sen requires the friendship and support of the British Government and will act under the advice of the British Government, and would accept the appointment of a Political Officer on his Staff for that purpose.

He will agree, in the event of his party coming into power and his becoming President—which he believes to be a certainty—to make an agreement with the British Government and with the United States of America by which they shall have favoured nation terms over all other countries.

He will further place the new Navy under the command of British Officers, subject to his orders.

In regard to any agreement China may make with Japan they would act under advice of the British Government.[49]

Sun Yat-sen and Lea, in addition to seeking an Anglo-Saxon alliance, also wanted Grey's assistance on three other points. First, they wanted his help arranging financial backing for their revolutionary government. Second, they wanted him to block loans to the Ch'ing government from a Four Power bank consortium. Finally, they wanted the British government to instruct its colonial authorities in Malaya and Hong Kong to rescind a long-standing travel ban on Sun Yat-sen so he could return to China without encountering undue difficulties.[50]

Grey was not persuaded by Sun Yat-sen's proposal, nor taken in by his generous offers. The Foreign Office had already made up its mind about Sun Yat-sen, considering him an "armchair politician and windbag."[51] Furthermore, by this time, it was no secret to Sun Yat-sen and Lea that Grey expected Yuan Shih-k'ai to emerge as the commanding figure in China. Grey did grant one of Sun Yat-sen and Lea's requests. He decided to raise the travel ban, fearing that doing otherwise might tarnish Britain's image. He also needed no prompting to stop loan payments going to Peking. The consortium bankers had already made up their minds earlier, on November 8, not to continue the loan payments until a responsible government emerged.[52]

Meanwhile, as Lea's reputation continued to open doors for him with Conservatives, and reports of the revolution's growing success in China reached him, he believed he was finally on the verge of realizing his grand military dream. On the evening of November 14, he gladly participated at the opening meeting of the Royal Colonial Institute, where Lord Roberts presided over a discussion of British imperial unity and defense.[53] Two days later, on the eve of his thirty-fifth birthday, several newly tailored military uniforms he had ordered arrived at his hotel. Ethel wrote her sister: "Sun is going to make him his Chief of Staff so he is wild with delight."[54] The press in London further fueled Lea's ambitions when the *Daily Graphic,* after interviewing Sun Yat-sen's entourage, reported that General Lea was going to China with Sun Yat-sen to establish an interim military government until a republic could be organized.[55]

News of Lea's prospective place in the Chinese army did not surprise everyone. He had already informed some friends and associates of his plans and had begun inquiring if they knew any British officers interested in service with the new Chinese republican army. Although the extent of Lea's military contacts is unknown, both Roberts and Sinclair came through with some recommendations. One of the recommended men, a retired Royal Artillery colonel named Callivele, regretted that his health would not permit him to go to China, but he was willing to help Lea find other capable officers. Another retired officer, former Royal Engineers colonel Frederic N. Maude, an internationally recognized author on military affairs, was very interested in going to China and helping Lea find other officers, but only after the issue of pay had been worked out. For the time being Lea could only take names. Once he got established in the Chinese republican army, he advised Callivele and Maude, he would be able to work out the details of awarding commissions.[56]

After Sun Yat-sen and Lea failed to arrange a $5,000,000 loan through the Hong Kong and Shanghai Bank, they determined there was no point remaining any longer in London. Sun Yat-sen, still desperate for money, wanted to stop in Paris to consult with the French government, as a last resort, about soliciting financial support before sailing for China. The possibility of a Franco-Chinese alliance clearly violated Lea's world vision, but he acquiesced under the urgency of Sun Yat-sen's dilemma.[57]

Before leaving London, Sun Yat-sen gave an interview to *Strand Magazine* that highlighted significant aspects of his career. The interview also contributed to furthering both mystery and misconceptions about Lea's Chinese endeavors. In explaining how Lea became his chief military advisor, Sun Yat-sen carefully avoided any references to their meeting through Yung Wing and the illegal Red Dragon conspiracy. Instead, he fabricated an account for popular consumption, possibly with Lea's complicity, which shrewdly claimed Lea had been his chief military advisor since the days of the Boxer Rebellion in China.[58]

On November 20, Sun Yat-sen, his entourage, and the Leas left for France. They spent four days in Paris before traveling to Marseilles and sailing for China. There is no evidence to suggest that Lea had anything to do with Sun Yat-sen's French negotiations. He and Ethel spent their first leisure time in a month sightseeing and were likely pleased when a member of the local Chinese revolutionary committee declared to the French press that Lea was China's Lafayette. Sun Yat-sen, meanwhile, held fruitless talks with French bankers and politicians. His apprehension over returning to China without Western financial backing led him to doubt whether he should become China's first republican president. He cabled revolutionary leaders in Shanghai indicating that either Yuan Shih-k'ai or Li Yuan-hung, the commander of revolutionary military forces, both of whom had been considered for the presidency, would be acceptable to him as presidential candidates.[59]

The strain and excitement of assisting Sun Yat-sen began to show on Lea shortly after they set sail. Being anxious to play an influential role in the revolution and also to complete *The Day of the Saxon* before reaching China, he pushed himself too hard to maintain his fragile health. On November 26 Ethel wrote her sister: "Am afraid he will have to dictate the last of [the book] for he cannot use his eyes for any length of time now."[60] But Lea would not let up. Throughout the voyage, Ethel later noted, "[P]lans were completed for carrying on the revolution, and all cables sent to the leaders were revised by Homer Lea and in many cases were dictated by him entirely."[61]

Sun Yat-sen could not have been happier with Lea. Rumors abounded that Lea's advice had been instrumental in helping to topple the Manchus. When other passengers met them on board ship, it was not uncommon for Sun Yat-sen to introduce his American companion as "the greatest military theorist under heaven."[62] When they arrived at Penang, the Straits Settlements, on December 14, Sun Yat-sen declined to speak to the press about the Chinese revolution, but Lea granted an interview explaining why it was important for Great Britain and the United States to support the establishment of a strong post-Manchu China. He asserted that the new China could help protect British interests in the Pacific and India against possible Russian expansionism and repeated his belief that it could counterbalance Japanese dominance in the Pacific to help protect America's commercial interests in the region. There were even several press reports from Asia that Lea's arrival there would surely tip the scales in favor of the revolutionaries. For example, the *Singapore Free Press* reported: "It will not encourage Peking to know that they have only YUAN SHIH-KAI to pit against the brain of HOMER LEA."[63]

On December 21, after making a brief stop in Singapore, Sun Yat-sen and Lea arrived in Hong Kong. A Chinese gunboat with Governor Wu of Canton was on hand, along with revolutionary leaders from all over south China, to greet Sun Yat-sen and his soon-to-be army chief of staff. At that point, as the Manchu dynasty neared its end, Lea reportedly received a commission as a "Major General in the Kwangtung Army."[64] Despite Yuan Shih-k'ai's efforts to negotiate a settlement to save the dynasty, the revolutionaries would not compromise. Plans were under way to establish a republic and provisional government, with Sun Yat-sen its first president.[65]

In Hong Kong Lea called at the American Consulate to pick up his mail and update Consul General George E. Anderson on Sun Yat-sen's latest plans. Anderson, however, wanted more than that. He wanted to talk the situation over with Sun Yat-sen, Governor Wu, and the other revolutionary leaders before reporting back to Washington. He also wanted "to have some authoritative statement of such plans."[66]

Anderson got his meeting and then drew up a statement with Lea that was carefully scrutinized and approved by Sun Yat-sen and his party before being cabled to the State Department "as a direct expression from this head of the revolutionary movement of his plans and purposes as to the government of China." The statement read:

> We propose on arrival at Shanghai to organize consolidated provisional government; Sun Yat-sen, President. A cabinet, governors, provinces will be appointed by him. Homer Lea, chief of staff, will negotiate direct Manchus; will demand complete relinquishment of all power. Manchus will be allowed full enjoyment property; pension imperial class. Provisional government to establish peace; then call constitutional convention. We propose if necessary to request the President of the United States mediate with Manchus but offer no compromise or conditions but the above mentioned. We propose to select the best provisional administrators independent of present officials. Provisional Government military. Permanent Government strongly centralized Republican Government

modified American plan. We propose employ eminent American jurist to assist framing constitution.[67]

Anderson's report added that the dominant idea behind the entire Lea–Sun Yat-sen plan was the anticipation of Anglo-American guidance and assistance. Aside from appealing to President Taft to act as a mediator, the plan expected that American and British advisors would play a pivotal role in shaping the new China. In all, Anderson's appraisal of Lea could not be taken lightly by the State Department. He cabled Washington: "It is evident that General Lea has a great influence over him [Sun Yat-sen], almost a controlling influence in matters of relations with other powers."[68]

Journalist Linton Wells of Shanghai's English-language *China Press* was on hand for the arrival of Sun Yat-sen and Lea in Shanghai on December 25, a bleak and chilly Christmas Day and he, like Anderson, clearly recognized the extent of Lea's influence on Sun Yat-sen. He recalled: "I was among the mob at the customs jetty to greet Doctor Sun when he landed in Shanghai. . . . I interviewed him a few hours later, but first I had to pass a Cereberus in the form of an amazing little man . . . Homer Lea, who was closer to Sun than any other individual on earth. . . . Sun came to rely upon his advice more than that of anyone else; therefore Homer, whose intimate I later became, examined visitors carefully before permitting them to enter the leader's presence."[69]

The anticipated ascension to power of Sun Yat-sen and Lea soon came to the test. To many of the revolution's newer followers, Sun Yat-sen was a leader about whom they knew little. With a Ch'ing price on his head, he had not been in China for more than a decade. Now, appearing without the finances he so desperately needed to defeat the Ch'ings and stabilize China, he realized his prospects for achieving these goals would be difficult at best. His one overriding desire, to unify and stabilize China, continued to guide his actions. A National Convention in Nanking unanimously elected him the first president of the Chinese republic the day of his arrival, but his presidency was short-lived. He accepted the presidency and on January 1, 1912, was inaugurated in Nanking, but only with the provision that he would resign in favor of Yuan Shih-k'ai once the Ch'ings abdicated, to spare China a protracted civil war and unify the new republic.[70]

As events continued to unfold, Lea's prospects quickly diminished. He became the unfortunate victim of revolutionary party rivalries and

178 • Homer Lea

American legal technicalities. Because he stood out as the most prominent person in Sun Yat-sen's entourage, his influence over Sun Yat-sen soon caused resentment among other revolutionary leaders. With most of the fighting over, they regarded Lea as an unwelcome interloper seeking to exploit their hard-earned victory. Journalist Frederick McCormick observed that Lea was the "star in his [Sun Yat-sen's] galaxy of satellites," but "remained an unnecessary enigma to many foreigners and Chinese."[71] Dr. Wu Ting Fang, the revolutionary party's foreign minister, was indignant on the subject. He not only wanted Sun Yat-sen to drop Lea, he wanted Lea out of China at the earliest opportunity.[72]

Part of Lea's problem was that he was a foreigner and was relatively unknown in China. Apparently the press reports lauding his arrival in the Singapore and Hong Kong newspapers had not been printed in China's newspapers. Also, since his books had not been published there, his reputation as an acclaimed author and military strategist did not precede him as he might have hoped. Nor was he known for his years of service with the Pao Huang Hui.

On December 27, before Lea fully realized there would be pressure from within the revolutionary party to cast him aside, he gave an interview to Wells that revealed his expectations. The *China Press* story appeared the next day, entitled "'Gen.' Homer Lea Says He Is Chief of Staff," and was accompanied by a photo of him in his lieutenant general's dress uniform, the same photo used as the frontispiece in *The Valor of Ignorance*. Lea did not go into detail, but briefly explained that he was the chief of staff of the republican army, that he had his government's support, and that he expected to be assisted in the future by American and British generals:

[Wells]: How can you act as chief of staff of the revolutionary army when you are an American citizen?

[Lea]: That has been arranged. A number of American generals are coming out to help us.

[Wells]: That is very interesting, that generals of the United States Army should be allowed to come out to China to take part in fighting like this.

[Lea]: Then I suppose you would be surprised to know that English generals are also coming out to help us.

[Wells]: When are they coming?

[Lea]: I can't divulge that, but they will be here.[73]

During the interview Lea made some startling revelations about his past. For the first time since the *San Francisco Call*'s 1901 article "How I Was Made a General in the Chinese Army," Lea commented publicly on his early military career. In discussing how he first became a general, his ego would not allow him simply to say that he received the title for attempting to train some Pao Huang Hui military forces, in which endeavor he subsequently failed. Instead, he gave Wells a self-inflated and misleading response, possibly to embellish his credentials, as he expected to soon be the republican army chief of staff. He explained that eleven years earlier, he had single-handedly organized and commanded four divisions in China, "commanded by American officers," for the rescue of Emperor Kwang-hsu.[74] The reference to American officers, possibly the first and only time the claim had ever been made, probably referred to those Americans who were willing to join him in his original Chinese exploits.

The *China Press* interview did not help Lea in the eyes of Amos P. Wilder, American consul general in Shanghai. Wilder contacted William J. Calhoun, the U.S. minister in Peking, concerning Lea's involvement in the revolution. Apparently, neither Wilder nor Calhoun had received prior information on Lea from the State Department. To them he was clearly in violation of a federal statute that forbade American nationals from aiding revolutionary movements. Calhoun wasted no time. On the afternoon of December 28 he cabled the State Department seeking approval for Wilder to publish the statutory articles in the Shanghai press. Meanwhile, Nelson Johnson, the U.S. vice consul in Shanghai, warned Lea in no uncertain terms that he could face arrest, trial, and even the death penalty if he continued assisting the Chinese revolutionaries.[75] Lea was furious. He told the Chinese press:

I came to China to join the Chinese Revolution of my own personal decision and it has nothing to do with the American government. . . . I am not an American army officer so I am not under restrictions of American military law. I joined the Chinese revolution based on my personal qualifications and due to humanitarian reasons as an aim. Today China's millions of people are under torture by a repressive system. How could I just sit there and do nothing? I was invited by the Chinese revolutionary party to come to China to relieve this depression and stop them from sinking. I am a world wide supporter of fair play . . . there is no reason why they [the U.S. government] should interfere.[76]

In Shanghai Lea chanced to meet Charles L. Boynton, a former Los Angeles High School classmate, who was then secretary of the National Committee of the Young Men's Christian Association of China. Boynton was well aware of Lea's controversial outspokenness and antimissionary zeal, and was no great admirer of him. Privately, he considered Lea a "fake and an adventurer." In the course of a three-hour lunch together at the elegant Astor House Hotel, Lea made a persuasive effort to moderate his views and appease Boynton. For instance, when the subject of missionaries came up, Lea now credited them as "the best friends of the Chinese" who "have contributed more than any other one factor to the success of the present revolution." Lea also used his powers of persuasion to challenge Boynton's skepticism about the role he intended to play in China. After the lunch, Boynton wrote his mother:

> He is here as chief military adviser to the new President Sun Yat-sen. They apparently take him very seriously, though the newspapers have done everything that could be done to make fun of him and his pretensions, printing a very foolish interview which he repudiates root, stock and branch. . . . He certainly takes himself seriously and has persuaded others to the same view. If he is as able as he thinks and as devoted as he professes, he may do some good to the cause, unless held up by the United States for the violation of neutrality; for which the penalties are severe.[77]

Johnson's warning about violating neutrality undoubtedly influenced Lea's decision to end his hopes of serving as the republican army chief of staff. There also is an unconfirmed report the U.S. District Court in Shanghai issued an injunction prohibiting Lea from aiding the revolutionaries.[78] However, Lea had no intention of cutting himself off from Sun Yat-sen or China. After all he had been through and all he thought he had done to help both the United States and China, he felt betrayed and cheated by the American government. He bitterly resented the loss of his opportunity to serve the revolution in an official military capacity and still planned to act as Sun Yat-sen's unofficial advisor. Sun Yat-sen, for his part, supported Lea's course of action, and Lea remained his confidant.

Lea's writing career still held promise, although he had to reconcile himself to playing a diminished role in building an Anglo-Saxon alliance with China. Harper and Brothers had been bombarding him for some exclusive articles on the situation in China, in return for which the publishers promised him handsome fees. He also had just completed the draft of his book on British imperial defense, *The Day of the Saxon,* and sent it to Harper and Brothers.[79]

Although Lea faced official marginalization in China, his ties with Sun Yat-sen remained firm. On January 1, 1912, he allegedly held the distinction of being the only foreigner present at Sun Yat-sen's presidential inauguration in Nanking, the republic's capital. Sun Yat-sen took the oath of office in the viceroy's yamen (government offices) as a "foreign-fashion" band played "Behold, the Conquering Hero Comes" and "God Be with You till We Meet Again." The official photographer took a picture, which showed Lea as the only Caucasian in the group.[80]

During Lea's stay in Nanking as Sun Yat-sen's unofficial advisor, he may have performed some service or been an observer with the republican army. Although his relations with the army remain unclear, he participated in at least one military operation aimed at consolidating republican positions between Nanking and Peking. He later described part of these experiences to a friend: "As I remember it was the later part of January 1912 or the first part of February that our armies were advancing in three parallel columns north, the left column following the Hankow-Peking railway, the right proceeding along the grand canal, while the center proceeded along the Pukow-Tientsin railway. I was with the center column. In the latter part of January of this year, I moved my headquarters from Peng Fu on the railroad to a village northeasterly in direction of the grand canal."[81]

In Nanking the Leas resided in a stately yamen, described as a "foreign two-story brick building with wide porticos," in the vicinity of the foreign consulates.[82] According to one rumor, Lea could often be found in the bar of the Bridge House Hotel, "discussing the thesis of '*The Valor of Ignorance*' animatedly and interestingly with whomever happened to be present at the time."[83] His imperious manner and brazen outspokenness did not help his reputation. His presence near Sun Yat-sen still aroused critics to raise questions and speculate about his influence in republican affairs. One foreign resident in Nanking, who believed many of the rumors circulated about Lea by his detractors, observed:

The only foreigner I know of is Homer Lea and I guess I understand about him now. He has no position, is a personal friend of Sun Yat-sen, a delightful little man, and more than a little mad. He is possessed of the idea that he is behind all the military organization, and that he is responsible. I think the truth is that he does not know what is going on and has no say at all. He is just cracked about the movement, and about high strategy and such things, and is, I believe bitterly disappointed that he was not given command of one of the armies . . . it was possible that he was consulted sometimes about military things, but only as Sun's personal friend. He may be quite left out of account.[84]

Sun Yat-sen's negotiations with Yuan Shih-k'ai to end the revolution and unify China reached a resolution a few weeks after he took office. In early February 1912, after the Manchus finally announced their intention to abdicate, Sun Yat-sen prepared to hand the reins of the new republic over to Yuan Shih-k'ai, as he had promised earlier. Sun Yat-sen would still hold a post in the republican government, but Lea would be removed from the limelight and center of power that he had waited so long to be near.[85]

Lea's outspokenness soon incurred the ire of British and Japanese diplomats. On February 7 he reportedly received additional pressure to sever his advisory role with China's republican leaders after British and Japanese diplomats unofficially protested his public criticism of the 1902 Anglo-Japanese Treaty, which bound both nations by a military alliance. He allegedly stated his beliefs that Britain and Japan had plans to exploit China for their benefit at the expense of the United States, a statement that the diplomats of the two nations found unacceptable.[86]

It is unclear how Lea would have responded to this latest effort at curtailing his involvement with China's republican leaders because he suddenly collapsed from a stroke on February 11, three days before Sun Yat-sen resigned the presidency. He had contracted influenza in January, possibly from the rigors of military campaigning, but recovered by the end of the month. This attack came without warning.[87] Lea later recalled the fateful events: "I was struck stone blind. . . . One morning directly at reveille, at about six o'clock, I mounted for inspection and rode across parade. Suddenly, I was in darkness, inky blackness. I halted my horse, ran my hand across my eyes, rubbed them hard, with the idea that I was fainting and would fall. I dismounted, groped my way in the direction whence I had come. I must have wandered ten minutes, it seemed an eternity, before they found me and led me back. The doctors explained that I had burst a blood vessel in my forehead."[88]

Initially, Lea was not expected to live. The physician called in to treat him, Dr. M. Urbanek, a neighbor, diagnosed the cause of the stroke as a blood clot in the brain. Lea's diabetic condition very likely contributed to the stroke. He remained in a deep coma for three days, and as his condition worsened, Dr. Henri Fresson, a French physician and surgeon working in Shanghai, rushed to Nanking on a special train to help care for him. Lea eventually regained consciousness, but was left completely paralyzed on the left side of his body. His vision also was severely impaired. As he showed signs of improvement, Dr. Urbanek's prognosis turned optimistic, especially since Ethel's careful nursing appeared to help. Dr. Urbanek, aware of Lea's controversial reputation, observed, "[T]here are no symptoms of any great defect in intellect, though the patient has many maniacal ideas, but all of them are to a person acquainted with the extremely imaginative mind of General Homer Lea, easily explainable."[89]

Lea's doctors believed he would be better off returning to California for his recuperation. When he was well enough to begin the long journey back home, he and Ethel traveled to Shanghai, where on April 12 they departed for San Francisco on the Japanese ship *Shinyo Maru*. When the ship stopped at Japanese ports, delegations were on hand to greet and welcome Lea. Ethel, meanwhile, made arrangements to keep their impending arrival in San Francisco secret to avoid the unnecessary excitement of reporters and welcoming delegations. Lea was still in no condition to receive either. He was confined to a wheelchair, almost blind, and had no desire to explain his Chinese adventures to inquiring crowds. The ship arrived in San Francisco on May 6 with little fanfare.[90]

Lea and Ethel took up residence at a small Santa Monica cottage overlooking the ocean, at 135 South Wadsworth Avenue, for his recuperation.[91] At first he believed he was going to die and became especially concerned about Ethel's future. He contacted his old friend Marco Newmark for help. Newmark explained:

A day or two after their arrival, Homer sent for me. I found him sitting in a wheel chair. He said to me, "I know, Marco, that I am going to die. I called you here for two reasons.

"Do you remember that time when you became engaged

to be married, I told you you were a damn fool, that now you will have a family, that you will lead a monotonous life and be of no use to anybody? Well, I wanted to say to you that I made a mistake.

"The second reason is that after I have gone I want you to keep in touch with Ethel and watch over her."[92]

Ethel's devotion and support no doubt helped Lea alter his outlook on life and raise his spirits for recovery. He soon began looking forward to the day when he could smash his wheelchair and return to China. The atmosphere of China pervaded his cottage. It was furnished with Chinese décor and Lea entertained distinguished Chinese visitors along with his closest friends on a regular basis. His visitors also occasionally accompanied him along the waterfront in his wheelchair.[93]

As he anxiously awaited the publication of *The Day of the Saxon*, he began dictating several literary projects to Ethel. His plans included writing a twelve-volume history of China, five books on governments of the world, and at least one romance novel. In one case, he began dictating a book on China, but later became dissatisfied with it and tore it up. He commented: "I can do better a little later, and I will soon commence on the twelve volumes of history."[94]

In *The Day of the Saxon,* published in June, Lea broadened his vision of doom and announced his intension to complete a third volume for a trilogy, but offered no details about it. In *The Day of the Saxon* he expressed his belief that the entire Anglo-Saxon race faced a threat from German (Teuton) and Russian (Slav) expansionism. He believed that while Russia moved against India, the Germans, operating under the inspiration of Bismarck, would strike at England, the center of the British Empire. He thought the Anglo-Saxons faced certain disaster from their militant opponents. Only a rejuvenation of the race could save the English-speaking peoples in the coming racial war. If they failed to do this, then, according to Lea, theirs would be the "fate of nations as they have laid themselves down to sleep throughout the ages . . . in all their glory and hope and vanity, only to awake at a predetermined hour to find themselves upon a savage dawn, stripped and desolate."[95]

Lea had hoped that *The Day of the Saxon* would be his crowning work to date, but it was not received as well as *The Valor of Ignorance* had been. It lacked immediate relevance to awaken interest in the American public. There were no plans or maps foretelling a German invasion on the Atlantic coast to grab the attention of Americans. Moreover, many reviewers agreed that Lea had simply gone too far with his dogmatic and pessimistic appraisals. The Japanese remained interested in Lea's writings, and at least one of Japan's largest booksellers later placed orders with Harper and Brothers for copies of the book. Even though it eventually went into a German translation, its popularity in Germany was not comparable to that of *The Valor of Ignorance* in Japan. If anything, it only added to the antagonisms and tensions that were already growing between Anglo-American and German interests.[96]

Lea's prognosis brightened considerably after three months of recuperation. He began planning his return to China when his physicians expressed confidence that he would fully recover. On July 27 he wrote Sun Yat-sen of his intentions:

> I will be able to return to China about the middle of September and will again devote myself to whatever tasks you have for me there.
> This has been a very severe sickness but I now feel almost quite recovered.[97]

On August 3 Lea granted his first interview since returning from China to Willard Huntington Wright, literary editor of the *Los Angeles Times*. Wright greatly admired Lea and had recently written a flattering review of *The Day of the Saxon*. Now he went further, considering Lea's writings masterpieces. He called Lea "the greatest military strategist in America . . . one of the greatest men in America and one of the most remarkable minds of this decade." He also contributed to the growing mythology surrounding Lea, characterizing him as a man of mystery and "dominating power" behind the scenes in China.[98]

In the interview Lea elaborated on his plans for a third volume to complete a trilogy with *The Valor of Ignorance* and *The Day of the Saxon*. In the new book he wanted to advance his social Darwinist beliefs by discussing the spread of democracy among nations. He explained: "The principle of democracy is the principle of weakness, of the disintegration of power; that is why the Saxon race is daily evolving into a race of weakness. . . . My next book, the third of the trilogy will deal with this phase of government as it pertains to the interrelation of world powers."[99]

Lea's plans to return to China coincided with a visit in mid-August from General Lan Tien Wei, one of the Chinese republican revolution's most distinguished commanders. General Lan Tien Wei had worked with Lea in China, and in the course of visiting Los Angeles, called on him to pay his respects and thank him for his work on behalf of the revolution. They no doubt discussed Chinese affairs and Lea's intended return as Sun Yat-sen's advisor.[100]

During Lea's recuperation, Ethel's son, Albert H. Powers, often wheeled Lea along the boardwalk at Santa Monica Beach, where they enjoyed fishing from the pier. Occasionally, inquisitive onlookers stopped to talk, but Lea had little patience with their questions. Albert recalled:

Every day that I wheeled the general down the beach in Santa Monica, one or two people stopped us to ask various foolish questions of his experiences in China. Most of these queries were about the manner in which he became paralyzed. As these questions annoyed him his answers were short and they generally put an end to the conversation.

One day a well-dressed man, about 25 years old asked, how did you get hurt, General?

The reply was, "Well it was this way. I was standing on a street corner, one day and a lady ran into me with a baby buggy and knocked me down. The shock paralyzed me in my left side."

The silence was oppressive for a few seconds and then the man walked away.

Another answer was, "A black cat jumped on me one day and scratched me in the face. Since then, I haven't been able to use my left arm or leg."[101]

In October Lea appeared to have won his fight for survival. He was finally strong enough to walk and thought about working with Sun Yat-sen and returning to China. Although still in pain, he would not let that stand in his way. He confided to Van Loan: "Physical pain—that is a mere trifle when you are used to it. I cannot remember that I have ever passed a day in my life which was free from pain."[102] He was guardedly optimistic about his health and wrote Belford: "This is now the tenth month of convalescence and for the first time have [the word "definite" is crossed out] hopes of complete recovery although it may take some time yet."[103] When Marshall Stimson dropped by for a visit on October 27 he found that "partly blind, and in a wheelchair, Lea still had something of his old fire. He . . . denounced commercialism and political corruption of the United States, the lack of wisdom in her leaders in failing to prepare for the great wars that Lea said were coming on and expressed his contempt for the softened, luxury and vice, of American living."[104]

In the year since the revolution began Lea's reputation may have improved in China. The republican government reportedly accorded him a distinct honor by prominently displaying his picture at the inauguration of a hall of fame in Peking commemorating the one-year anniversary of the October Revolution. Furthermore, Sun Yat-sen wrote in mid-October that he hoped to meet Lea in Paris in about two months.[105]

Unfortunately, Lea and Sun Yat-sen would never meet again. On October 27, after spending an evening entertaining some friends, Lea unexpectedly suffered another stroke, from which he did not recover. Ironically, during the evening's entertainment he remarked to Ethel he was confident about soon returning to China.[106] The *Los Angeles Tribune* reported on Lea's sudden decline: "Entertaining a party of writers and other friends . . . General Lea was unusually brilliant and seemed to enjoy the occasion thoroughly. He retired in good spirits but was stricken that night and could not rally."[107]

Lea died at his cottage on November 1, 1912, shortly before 2:00 in the afternoon. Ethel, his sister Hersa, and Robert Belford were at his side.[108] It was eleven days before his thirty-sixth birthday. When news of his death reached Chinatown in Los Angeles, the Chinese community immediately acknowledged its great loss. According to the *Los Angeles Examiner:*

> Within an hour after the news of General Lea's death had been received in Chinatown yesterday, the Chinese Chamber of Commerce, Chinese-American League of Justice and Chinese Protective Association, three of the largest Chinese organizations in the United States, called a special meeting and adopted resolutions of regret, extending to General Lea's widow the condolences of the three societies. The resolutions, as translated, stated that General Lea had "devoted considerable of his life and energy to the cause of freeing China from the Manchu yoke, and that his death was a blow that would be deeply felt by the Chinese people throughout the world."[109]

Lea's funeral, held on the afternoon of November 2, was private and quiet. He had expressed wishes that he be dressed in his general's uniform and that there be no ceremony of any kind. In the morning, his body, dressed in his uniform, lay in state at his cottage while friends called to pay their respects. Only his immediate family and most intimate friends attended the funeral. Ethel, Hersa, O'Banion, Newmark, Van Loan, Belford, and Isaac O. Levy, a high school friend, gathered at his cottage to bid him a final farewell.[110] Newmark described the scene:

> He lay on a bed, clad in the uniform of a lieutenant general of the Chinese army, his cherished swagger stick beside him.
>   There was no service. Two men came in with a casket, placed in it the wasted little body that had been the home of so mighty a spirit and conveyed it to a crematory.[111]

In the afternoon a hearse from the Bresee Brothers funeral home, escorted by the funeral party, slowly drove Lea's body to the Rosedale Cemetery crematory in Los Angeles. The funeral party arrived at the crematory about 4:00 and attendants placed Lea's plain black casket, adorned with several simple wreaths, in the chapel. After the funeral party took seats in the chapel there was a moment's silence, some whispered consultation, and then the mourners left to return to Santa Monica. A *Los Angeles Times* reporter covering the event observed it was "impressive in the extreme from its absolute simplicity in the absence of any services or last rites."[112]

Lea gambled on his health against the advice of his doctors and suffered the ultimate consequences of pursuing his ambitions. He believed the end justified the means and often took undue risks to achieve his goals. The Red Dragon conspiracy, if discovered, could have landed him and his cohorts in jail. Yet, driven by a strong sense of destiny and mission, he consistently refused to accept defeat or be swayed from his course by adversity. When contacted by Sun Yat-sen to solicit British and American support for the republican revolution, he did not think twice. With no prior experience in diplomacy, he played a commanding role on Sun Yat-sen's behalf, conferring with British and American diplomats. Even after the U.S. government shattered his dream of serving as the republican army chief of staff, and even when his health collapsed, he was still determined to return to Sun Yat-sen's side, and also to continue his writing career.

CONCLUSION

THE MAN AND THE MYTH

[T]he full story of the accomplishments of Homer Lea will
probably never be told, and may never be known.
                    —Major George H. Shelton, U.S. Army

Unraveling the man and the myth has been a topic of debate since
Lea first went to China in 1900. He has been revered as a genius by
some, vilified as a charlatan by others, and considered a man of mystery by many. Not even his family or closest friends were privy to a
full account of his adventures. Ermal, who was very close to him,
acknowledged that "the actual details of his work in China were very
sketchy."[1] Newmark claimed he had "never heard the full account,"
and he did not believe anyone else ever had either.[2] Van Loan considered the possibility of someone writing Lea's life story, but dismissed
such prospects, noting: "I doubt that it will be, for he was singularly
silent upon the question of his career."[3] If Lea left any authoritative
record of his associations and exploits, they will probably never be
known because many of his papers were intentionally destroyed after
his death by Ethel and O'Banion to protect associates who had been
involved with his covert and sometimes illegal activities.[4]
    Lea rarely took steps to correct exaggerations and speculation
about himself in the press, possibly because such rumors and speculation helped divert attention from his covert activities, or possibly
because he may have been sensitive to ridicule from those who would
have dismissed him as a romantic dreamer. Whatever his reasons, with
the exception of his remarks to the Shanghai *China Press* in which he
discussed how he became a general, he may never have confided to
anyone the true details of his career. Van Loan, who spent a week in

the mountains with Lea during his research for *The Valor of Ignorance,* recalled an episode in which Lea resisted pressure to discuss his Chinese exploits:

> At night, when the campfire was lighted, acquaintances would drop in to chat, and it was then that the General was at his best, for he was, above everything else, a companionable soul and fond of company. Most of the visitors were curious to hear of his experiences in the Chinese campaign. They wanted to know how he came to be called "General Lea," and why, but the most persistent questioning never succeeded in making Homer talk about himself or his experiences.
>
> "Oh, what's the use?" he said one night, after his visitors had departed. "It seems strange to me sometimes and how then could I expect them to believe it?"[5]

Of the newspapers and magazines that printed obituaries of Lea, few accurately portrayed his life. Most added to the myth and mystery that surrounded him. Of all the obituarists perhaps no one gave a better insight into him than Major George Shelton, who came to know and admire him:

> Few men probably knew Lea intimately. Not many more than casually. To know him at all one had to break through the little shell of curious vanity that surrounded him. One had moreover, to realize that the man moved in a mental world where most of us seldom venture. On brief acquaintance he startled most men with ideas that seemed almost preposterous for advancement in this age of sanity and longed-for peace. In the general shock of opinions so unacceptable, yet so frank and well informed, the casual acquaintance was likely to forget the mentality behind which inspired their expression. Closer acquaintance always changed this. Pity for the wasted and crippled body changed to admiration for the powerful intellect and the tremendous will which kept both in operation. Shock at surprising ideas gave way to wonderment over the logic which gave them form. The almost pathetic vanity of the man was lost to sight in the comprehension of the innate modesty which it disguised. Some weaknesses that one perhaps should not admire were easily forgiven when the full pathos of

his lonely life was realized, and they made the man more likable. And even though with all one could not come to know him, one came irresistibly to respect him.[6]

Several of those closest to Lea confirmed many of Major Shelton's observations and offered additional insights into Lea's character. Ethel, in her private diary, later wrote of her admiration for Lea, her "dear one," a man possessed of a "wonderful intellect and that sweetness of character we so seldom see."[7] Albert Powers fondly remembered Lea's "gorgeous sense of humor" and "keen sense of the ridiculous."[8] Ermal too recalled that he "had a wonderful sense of humor and delighted in teasing father and me."[9] While Lea may have been intolerant of other's opinions and views, Newmark noted that he "never hated anyone," or possessed "the faintest spirit of revenge."[10] Fred A. Knight, an attorney Lea befriended in Long Beach in 1910–11, recalled him as "one of the most brilliant and convincing speakers I've ever met," and "one of the strangest and most unforgettable personalities I have ever known." He added that despite Lea's deformity, he was very popular with women and enjoyed their company.[11] Belford, who knew Lea as well as anyone, saw him as a genius with "an inordinate passion or ambition for possession of power" that led him in pursuit of far-reaching goals he could never satisfy.[12] Van Loan characterized him as a courageous "example of what a weak body may do when driven by a will that never admitted defeat."[13]

Certainly, some of Lea's attributes and behavior seemed unconventional, enigmatic, or eccentric to others. For example, the April 13, 1901, *Los Angeles Times* article "A Chinese General from Los Angeles," which reviewed his background, noted he had a good many "eccentricities."[14]

While the Lea family evidently valued its ties to the Presbyterian Church and its relationship with the Reverend Ng Poon Chew, Lea followed a divergent path, one that subsequently led to his break with his family's religious traditions. As an adult, he was not an adherent of any religion, but did study the Bible and evidently explored various religious faiths. Ermal recalled that after he returned from China in 1912, "someone persuaded him to take up Christian Science," but it is unclear to what extent it informed his religious beliefs.[15] She added that "a person's creed meant nothing to him, and he had friends among all faiths."[16]

Major Shelton was mistaken about Lea leading a lonely life. He led an active social life among a wide range of Caucasian and Asian friends and acquaintances. He shared a wide variety of interests with them. For example, in addition to discussing politics and world events, he considered himself an expert on football and loved to discuss the game. The *Los Angeles Herald* characterized him as a "well known clubman and society favorite."[17] He also appeared to be an active member of both the Mason and Shriner fraternal organizations.[18]

Among his many attributes, Lea was well known for his wit. A journalist friend from the *Oakland Tribune* noted that he readily made friends by his clever wit and sense of the ridiculous. The friend recalled an episode at San Francisco's Palace Hotel, in which Lea, who was a regular guest, masqueraded as a baggage clerk to win a wager:

On one occasion, a foreigner, a blustering guest at the Palace, mistook him for the house's baggage man. Not at all disconcerted, Lea encouraged him in that opinion.

"See here, my man," he remarked to General Lea, "I'm in a hurry to catch the limited for New York this morning. Here's my ticket. See that my three trunks are properly checked."

Lea hunted up the baggage man and gave him the same order, the latter thinking he was the owner of the tickets and trunks. When the job had been performed, he handed the ticket back to Lea and got a dollar tip. The guest rushed up at this juncture [and] in getting his ticket from Lea proffered the latter $3 as a tip.

"Hand the money to my subordinate," was the reply as Lea pointed to the real baggage man.

The latter's eyes bulged with astonishment on hearing the remark. The guest did as directed, and went off none the wiser. Lea had successfully carried out his role on a wager with a friend for a dinner for six.

And it was a jolly repast the sextet enjoyed that day.[19]

Joshua Powers recalled that Lea was reckless behind the wheel of an automobile. He appears to have purchased a new, top-of-the-line Chalmers-Detroit touring car in 1909, which the *Oakland Tribune* characterized as "the finest automobile in the city."[20] He reportedly had a chauffeur, but sometimes drove himself. His interest in motoring included car racing, and he reportedly knew many of Los Angeles's racing men. He also joined the Automobile Club of Southern California, a motor club dedicated to improving driving conditions.[21] He may have prided himself on owing a new car, and according to Joshua was fortunate in never having any serious auto mishaps. Joshua, who came to live with his mother and Lea at Long Beach in 1910, during his tenth-grade school year, remembered how Lea liked to race with other drivers. Once Lea almost caused a catastrophic accident: "I rode in that car with him one day and damn near got killed. He was a terrible driver. He drove just like the firefly that flips in the summer breeze—on inspiration. When somebody would come along side of him on the road they would race and then suddenly he would get a notion and switch in front of the other guy and turn in some side street and damn near kill everybody. But he never had an accident because he was fast."[22]

Lea's friends may never have heard the full account of what he did in China, but he was evidently more forthright in discussing his romances with some of them. His amorous adventures at Los Angeles High School included several sexual relationships, and his excursions into Chinatown more likely than not included visits to Chinese prostitutes.[23] He was considerably concerned about his virility after his horse accident injury and operation; years later he described his fears to Edwin Janss, a Los Angeles High School friend, who observed: "He confided his worry to no one, but determined to test his impaired virility on the first opportunity. He was still not satisfied as to his capabilities up to the time he left for China, but some years after his return remarked once to me, "Ed, I was worried about myself because of that damn horse accident, but I can tell you now that I scattered bastards from Peking to Shanghai—and back!"[24] After he returned from his first China trip, he proudly showed photos to several of his friends of two Chinese sisters he claimed had been his mistresses.[25]

Despite Lea's sometimes imperious and sarcastic behavior, there were occasions when he was particularly considerate of other people's feelings. Ermal recalled two occasions, in particular, that illustrated her brother's sensitivity in delicate situations:

> One evening Homer was having dinner at the Alexandria Grill, a man came to his table, introduced himself, and told Homer how much he had enjoyed reading "The Vermilion Pencil," and how much he admired Homer, and he wanted to present him with a small token of his admiration, and with these remarks, he handed him a ring whose stone appeared to

be a ruby. Homer naturally thanked him and said he couldn't think of accepting the gift. The conversation continued for a few moments, when another man appeared and whispered to Homer that he was the man's secretary, and as he had been drinking, would Homer please humor him, by taking the ring, and then leave it at the hotel desk when he left. Homer agreed, put the ring in his pocket and forgot about it until the next morning, when he immediately went to the hotel and was advised that the man and his secretary had left for San Francisco. Homer wired the hotels there, and inserted advertisements in papers up and down the coast and in the eastern cities, but to no avail. He never received any reply, nor any response to his inquiries. The ring was appraised at $1,000.

While in New York, awaiting passage for [Europe], Homer and [Ethel] were stopping at the Waldorf Astoria. Before Homer had left Los Angeles, Mr. Phillips, a friend of the family's and to whom he had dedicated his "Vermilion Pencil" had given him a lovely emerald stick pin, and also stopping at the same hotel was a very attractive young girl and her family. She had admired the pin and asked Homer if she could take the pin and show it to her mother and father. Homer gave her the pin, and each day following she would tell him that she had forgotten to bring the pin down but would do so the next day. The time was drawing close for him to leave for [Europe] and he didn't want to cause an embarrassment by insisting that she return the pin so he went to a novelty jewelry store, and purchased a paste diamond set in what would appear to a casual observer, old gold, and wore it to dinner. The girl remarked how beautiful that pin was, and could she show it to her family, Homer said of course she could, but as he had only brought two pins with him, this one and the emerald, he would have to have the other one to wear while her family looked at this one. The exchange was made, and Homer left for [Europe] the next day.[26]

To those who knew him well, Lea was a down-to-earth, approachable friend. Harry Carr, who wrote the obituary of Lea that appeared in the *Los Angeles Times*, entitled, "Death Overpowers Odd World Figure," fondly observed: "In the course of newspaper life one gets to know many men of many manners; but I have never known a more lovable, kindly, simple-hearted gentleman than Homer Lea. Kings, great generals, statesmen, were his friends; but they did not impress him at all. In the whole course of his career there was never one minute his head was turned."[27] Newmark had similar observations to make about Lea: "One of his most marked qualities was loyalty—either to a friend or to a cause. He became very famous; he reached to high places; but to the end, his favorite companions were four or five high school mates."[28]

Through all his endeavors and despite his usual practicality, Lea cared little about his own finances or acquiring wealth. He handled great sums of cash while working for the Pao Huang Hui, and received ample rewards for his service, including a number of valuable Chinese artifacts. He also received similar gifts for his service from Sun Yat-sen.[29] Yet money was not nearly as important to him as his dedication to a cause. In 1905 he told a St. Louis reporter: "Since I have been connected with the movement I have not drawn one cent of pay, though I have been tendered a large salary."[30] Later, in 1908, when he and Charles Boothe began the Red Dragon conspiracy, Lea offered to sell a very rare Chinese plate, reportedly valued as worth between $5,000 and $15,000, to help finance their venture.[31] He made a similar gesture when he signed over the rights to the Japanese edition of *The Valor of Ignorance* to Sun Yat-sen. Albert Powers characterized him as being "very practical in most ways—outside of money."[32] O'Banion added: "Homer cared nothing about money. When I first knew him he had a sizable fortune. He spent it all in getting the revolutionary movement underway and organizing the Pao Wong Wei society—and when the money started coming in he did not want any of it for himself."[33]

Lea's indifference to acquiring wealth did not dampen his interest in surrounding himself with the trappings of luxury. The *Oakland Tribune* reported that he "spent money lavishly, and it was nothing unusual for him to take a few friends out for an evening and give them a $100 dinner."[34] Ermal recalled how he "enjoyed luxury in all forms. Luxurious surroundings, fine wood, expensive clothes, and he liked having a retinue of Chinese servants."[35]

Lea admired Chinese art and collected in particular embroideries and sculpture. For example, when he returned to San Francisco from China in 1901 and met with Will Irwin, Irwin noted that he was "established in a suite draped with Chinese hangings, hung with Chinese paintings."[36] After his death the *Los Angeles Times* reported that his "collection of rare vases of 'crackle' Ming ware" contained rarities that rivaled or exceeded those in the collection of J. P. Morgan, one of the world's top collectors of this ware.[37] Many of these items remained in Ethel's hands; she later sold them at public auction or handed them down to her family.[38]

After Lea's death no one came forward to write a truly definitive and authoritative account of his exploits. Some of his writer and journalist acquaintances wrote obituaries about him, but here, too, fact and fiction became inextricably intertwined as these reminiscences unintentionally included speculation and exaggerated accounts. Several of these writings, such as Van Loan's full-page article "General Homer Lea," which appeared in the January 4, 1913, issue of *Harper's Weekly,* simply perpetuated the "man of mystery" myth already associated with Lea.[39]

In at least one case—that of Stanford University president Dr. Jordan—a commentator went on the attack to curb the growth of a Lea mythology. It was no secret that Jordan's staunch antiwar beliefs contrasted sharply with Lea's militant views, but despite their differences the two had gotten along together, at least until *The Valor of Ignorance*'s publication. Jordan had accepted invitations from Lea for various social functions and dinners at which they could exchange their views and he had heard some of Lea's adventure stories. Lea even sent Jordan a copy of *The Valor of Ignorance,* for which Jordan, in December 1909, offered a courteous and diplomatic reply to "Gen. Homer Lea" that noted: "The book is cleverly written, and contains many truths, but I also hope it contains some errors."[40] Some time later, however, Jordan went on the attack. Not only did he denounce Lea's militant views in *The Valor of Ignorance,* he went so far as to refer to Lea as a "crippled dwarf."[41] It is not known if or how Lea responded to Jordan, but he did confide to his friend Marshall Stimson that although he did not mind what Jordan said about his ideas, he believed the demeaning personal reference was unwarranted.[42]

Lea's heightened popularity in the press, which gave added weight to his militant views in *The Valor of Ignorance,* and some erroneous public references crediting him as being a former U.S. Army officer, including the misleading *Who's Who* biographical citation, were too much for Jordan to take any longer. In late December 1911 Jordan began to act. He initially wrote letters to newspaper, journal, and periodical editors, cautioning them about exaggerating Lea's accomplishments and military credentials. On December 28 he wrote a short letter to the editor of the *San Francisco Chronicle* pointing out that Lea had no connection with any recognized army and that *The Valor of Ignorance* was "strictly a work of fiction."[43] His annoyance grew in January 1912 when he learned that the recently published Japanese edition of *The Valor of Ignorance* had been entitled *The Future War between Japan and America* to popularize it in Japan, and that it referred to Lea as being an American army officer. Jordan wrote Robert Young, the editor of the *Japan Chronicle* in Kobe, condemning the book as "worthless," and cautioned that "this so-called 'General' Lea has not and never had any connection with the United States Army, nor with any other recognized army." He added: "It would be unfortunate if anybody in Japan should consider him as a representative of the American army."[44] In February Young wrote a scathing commentary on Lea and *The Valor of Ignorance* in the *Japan Chronicle* entitled "The Impudence of Charlatanism" that echoed Jordan's criticism.[45]

Meanwhile, Jordan continued his crusade. In April 1912 he warned another editor: "In your next edition, if you quote from Homer Lee, you can make it very clear that he was only a college sophomore who went in search of adventures, that he has had no connection with the American Army, and that his title which he translates as 'Lieutenant General of the Second Division of the Chinese Troops' refers to his drilling of Chinese school boys and waiters on the fields about Los Angeles."[46]

In May Jordan reached out to members of the World Peace Foundation, which he headed. He arranged for a reprint of "The Impudence of Charlatanism" in the World Peace Foundation Pamphlet Series, which included a copy of his letter to Robert Young. The article also contained additional commentary from the series' editor, who explained the rationale for attacking Lea and *The Valor of Ignorance:* "The publication of a Japanese translation of this absurd and pestiferous book in Tokyo makes this a proper occasion to expose more widely its real character and that of its writer."[47]

In at least one case someone rose to Lea's defense. Jordan's efforts to discredit Lea and his bellicose anti-Japanese warnings eventually came to the attention of the editor of the *Army and Navy Register,* who took issue with Jordan's attack on Lea through *The Impudence of Charlatanism* pamphlet. He wrote an editorial in the August 24, 1912, issue of *Army and Navy Register* that defended Lea and *The Valor of Ignorance.* He concluded that "the best indorsement of its value and the best encomium of its author . . . is Dr. Jordan's diatribe and the hysterical 'exposure' and warning of the World Peace Foundation."⁴⁸

Jordan did not remain silent. He fired off a critical response to the editor. He again stressed that Lea's questionable military "rank and achievements" gave undue weight to his arguments in *The Valor of Ignorance*, adding:

> [T]o the average public, its value depends on the authority behind it. Its positive assertions as to war, and especially as to the unfriendly designs of Japan and her ability to carry them out, seem to have weight through the author's supposed rank and achievements. . . .
>
> Mr. Lea has never been an officer in any recognized army, and any stress laid to his work from his military standing should be discounted. Certainly no man of military training could take seriously his account of the power or purposes of Japan, or his estimates of the cost, which the war measures he describes twitching tail on that country.⁴⁹

Jordan next decided to set Lea's military record straight, as he saw it, by writing a critical and comprehensive review of *The Valor of Ignorance* that he hoped would be published quickly by his friend, sociologist Charles Zueblin, the editor of *Twentieth Century Magazine*. The review observed: "This work deserves more attention from actual students of public affairs because it is cleverly written, perfectly sincere, and because it has been taken as the last word of military experience by a very large number of good people who suppose that 'General Homer Lea' is in some degree the spokesman for the American Army."⁵⁰ Zueblin, however, returned the review in early September with regrets: he was resigning the editorship and would not be with the magazine long enough to get it published.⁵¹

In mid-September Jordan's *The Unseen Empire: A Study of the Plight of Nations That Do Not Pay Their Debts*, a book that discussed war, disarmament, and the relation of nations, was published; it contained a lengthy footnote reprising his criticism of Lea and *The Valor of Ignorance*. Jordan gave a brief biography of Lea that dismissed him as "a boy with dreams of Empire" and added that his book "has no value from the military or political point of view."⁵²

After Lea's death, Jordan changed his strategy. He now concentrated on exposing Lea as a self-promoting schemer with delusions of grandeur by publicizing the commentary of Lea's former acquaintances. He may have contacted people such as Charles Boynton, who later recalled joining Jordan "in an attempt to deflate Lea's newspaper reputation."[53] However, Jordan soon found just the right ally in Ng Poon Chew, the former Chinese reformer and acquaintance of Lea. He had had little or no contact with Lea after 1900, but claimed an inside knowledge of him. On December 5, 1912, Jordan wrote Ng Poon Chew to gather ammunition for his attack and Ng Poon Chew willingly obliged. It is unclear why he cooperated with Jordan. He may have harbored resentment against Lea for his harsh treatment of missionaries in *The Vermilion Pencil* or he may have grown disenchanted with Lea for some other reasons over the years. He was clearly no friend of Lea when his newspaper, the *Chung Sai Yat Po,* reportedly announced Lea's return from China in poor health with the headline, "The Hunchback Returns with Weakened Knees."[54] Now, he responded with a blunt characterization of Lea as a "schemer pure and simple" who was "never a general in the reform army," who had "created all the titles he bore" by himself, and who had few legitimate connections to any Chinese movement.[55] Jordan sent the response to the *New York Evening Post* and the *Oriental Review* with a cover letter that was simple and to the point. He explained: "In view of the mythology growing up about the name of the late Homer Lea, author of the 'Valor of Ignorance' and advocate of war, the following information . . . may be of value." The *Post* printed the defamation on December 19, and it subsequently appeared in the January 1913 issue of the *Oriental Review.*[56]

Ethel quickly came to her deceased husband's defense when she learned of the attack in the *Post.* She wrote Jordan that she was "at a loss to understand why you should go out of your way to make so uncalled for and cowardly [an] attack on General Lea."[57] She and Jordan exchanged several letters concerning his allegations about Lea, but Jordan refused to apologize for the attack. The best she could do was to advise Jordan that Ng Poon Chew was a Manchu sympathizer and enemy of Lea. She also provided Jordan information about Lea's exploits that were easily verified. For the time being, her efforts seemed to have convinced Jordan to cease any further public attacks on Lea.[58]

Ten years later, when Jordan published his memoirs, he again criticized Lea. By this time, with Lea largely forgotten by the public, Jordan was not as motivated to defame a growing Lea mythology. Now, he chastised Lea as an overambitious, if somewhat likeable, dreamer who "was never taken seriously" by himself or Lea's former Stanford colleagues.[59] Despite the criticism, he acknowledged a fondness for Lea as an extraordinary individual: "Though a hunchback dwarf, he was a youth of extraordinary parts—ready memory, very vivid imagination, imperturbable coolness, and an obsession for militarism and war. . . . One could hardly help a kindly feeling for the ambitious little romancer trying to make the most of his short life, limited physique, and boundless imagination."[60] Ironically, despite Jordan's concerns to stem a growing Lea mythology, he unwittingly contributed to that mythology in his memoirs when he repeated assertions about Lea's life and exploits based on unreliable information.[61]

Unfortunately, Ethel's limitations as a writer also contributed to the Lea mythology. In August 1913, while she was touring Europe, J. Russell Kennedy, an Associated Press correspondent Lea had worked with a year earlier in China, approached her to write some articles, but she declined because she did not have confidence in her abilities as a writer.[62] Kennedy made the same request again the following month, but she noted in her diary, "[I]t's hopeless—realized long ago that this is something that I can't do."[63] In October 1918 Sun Yat-sen wrote her: "I think it would be a good idea for you to write a biography of the General . . . The life of such a brilliant man must not remain ignorant to the world."[64] Ethel agreed and assembled a number of remaining letters and documents with the intention of undertaking a biography, but again, nothing substantive resulted. This may help explain why her only written record concerning Lea's career was a brief summary of his accomplishments written in 1929 for the authors of a book about China. However, her summary's lack of detail suggests Lea may not have confided in her about his exploits to the degree one would have expected.[65]

Lea's reputation was partly based on a keen, absorbing, disciplined intellect and partly on his charisma and abilities as a self-promoter. His acquired knowledge of military history and the Chinese language, coupled with his powers of persuasion, earned him valuable credentials with the Chinese. His writings earned him international recognition with military men and statesmen, among others. Conversely, the element of the self-promoter in Lea contributed to assertions that he was a charlatan. Charles Boynton, for example, believed: "He was a remarkable illustration of what an inflated ego can do to advance a man's reputation and to build a reputation for genius on a very slender foundation of fact."⁶⁶ These types of charges, however, may have had more merit when Lea began his quest for adventure and self-fulfillment as a university student. There was a vast difference between the youthful, brash self-promoter of 1900 and the wiser author-advisor of 1912. Between those years Lea matured in his outlook, gained invaluable experience as a planner and organizer, and became a central figure in a crusade to influence the outcome of a new world order.

The Valor of Ignorance, Lea's most important work, generated much debate and controversy about his theories. For instance, one critic believed he would be remembered as "either a master of strategy or a dreamer."⁶⁷ Although *The Valor of Ignorance* opened doors for him, his biggest disappointment in life was its failure to awaken the Anglo-Saxon world to his warnings. Ermal explained: "His most important accomplishment, I know, he felt was his 'Valor of Ignorance,' and I know his deepest disappointment was that his warnings were ignored, for he felt that his country was destined to be among the great countries of civilization and he felt that every precaution should be taken to ensure this, and to protect herself from any invasion, particularly from the Far East."⁶⁸

Several of Lea's startling and controversial geopolitical predictions, particularly those regarding Japan, were later borne out by events. He erred in the timing of these predictions, but not in their general consequences. For example, in a November 1908 *Los Angeles Examiner* interview following Emperor Kwang-hsu's death, he predicted that the Manchu dynasty "would break up in war and bloodshed" and "Japan will take part in this succession to the throne."⁶⁹ He envisioned that China might become enmeshed in a civil war in which the international community would likely allow the establishment of a Japanese-controlled Chinese puppet state to emerge. While this failed to materialize after the deaths of the emperor and dowager empress, or after the Manchu abdication in 1912, his prediction eventually came true in the 1930s. Civil strife plagued China through the 1920s and created the conditions for Japan, in 1932, to establish the puppet state of Manchukuo along the lines Lea predicted, headed by Pu-yi, the last Manchu emperor.⁷⁰

Furthermore, as early as 1908 Lea believed there would soon be a war between Japan and the United States in which Japan would initiate hostilities by a surprise attack. In a 1910 speech to the Los Angeles City Club, he suggested the war would begin no later than 1915. The time frame proved to be inaccurate, but eventually the Japanese surprise attack on Pearl Harbor in December 1941, and the country's subsequent successful invasion of the Philippines, vindicated Lea's prophesy in part. He accurately forecast that the main Japanese invasion would take place with landings at Lingayen Gulf and the Lamon Bay coast on the island of Luzon.[71]

Lea's writings remain his most enduring legacy. His work drifted into obscurity in America, but remained more popular in parts of Europe and Asia. When Ethel visited Berlin in June 1913, the *New York Times* noted that she "has learned with pleasure that high German military and naval authorities, including the Kaiser and Prince Henry of Prussia, are admirers of her husband's book, 'The Valor of Ignorance,' which has such timeliness at this hour."[72] *The Day of the Saxon* also held a strong interest in Germany. Graf Ernst zu Reventlow, a writer on international subjects, produced a German translation of it in 1913 with the revised title *Des Britischen Reiches Schicksalsstunde: Mahnwort eines Angelsachsen,* which translates as "The British Empire's Fateful Hour: The Warning of an Anglo Saxon General," to popularize it with German readers. The translation inspired retired German army lieutenant colonel Hermann Frobenius to write *Des Deutchen Reiches Schicksalsstunde (The German Empire's Hour of Destiny),* which appeared just prior to the outbreak of World War I in 1914. Frobenius took issue with Lea's assertions that Germany threatened the British Empire and instead envisioned a coalition including France, Russia, and Great Britain launching a massive war on Germany in 1915 or 1916.[73]

Writer-biographer Valeriu Marcu saw firsthand Lea's influence on several leading figures during the First World War. He observed:

Even during the first World War, Lea's books (and books about him) were published by the German General Staff. One of the most prominent exponents of German expansionist politics, Count Reventlow, introduced the American prophet of total war to the German public in a long foreword. Lea's ideas were discussed at length in German military periodicals, and he became a recognized authority on military politics. More than that, a definite effort was made to popularize his theories, especially his slogan: "To speak of the end of all wars is like speaking of the end of all earthquakes." His theory that the convergence and intersection of lines emanating from centers of power enable us to foresee the theaters of future wars is regarded as the ABC of their science by the professors of "geo-politics."

To the writer's personal knowledge, leading Europeans interested in the problems of war had Homer Lea's works readily at hand. In 1916, I saw Lea's *The Valor of Ignorance* on the desk of Lenin [Vladimir Ilyitch Ulianov] in Zürich. "This book will someday be studied by thousands of people," Lenin told me. I saw it on the desk of General [Hans] von Seeckt, the great German general. "This Lea is astounding," he told me. "Do you know who he is? I have rarely encountered a writer who made one feel so strongly that he carried the burden of a whole continent on his shoulders."

According to Marcu, Lea's writings also spread among the postwar Nazi school of geopolitics in Germany, whose proponents credited him as one of their "major prophets."[74]

Lea's influence was evidently no less profound on the Japanese military establishment. The Japanese edition of *The Valor of Ignorance* sold well. For example, Lea claimed the book went through twenty-four editions in the first month of its publication. The *New York Times* book review added, "[T]he publisher there expects it to go to 100 editions in six months—an absolutely unprecedented sale in that country."[75] Not surprisingly, *The Valor of Ignorance* remained popular with some Japanese military officers through the post–World War I period and during World War II. In 1920, for example, Lieutenant General Kojiro Sato wrote a series of articles, influenced by *The Valor of Ignorance,* which discussed the military possibilities of a Japanese-American war. Sato also published his arguments in a book, translated into English as *If Japan and America Fight* (1921), which cited Lea several times as a military authority.[76] Other senior officers, such as Admiral Isoroku Yamamoto, the commander-in-chief of the Japanese Combined Fleet during World War II, Vice Admiral Shigeru Fukudome, chief of staff of the imperial Japanese navy during the war, and General Tomoyuki Yamashita, commander of Japanese forces in the Philippines during the war, also respected Lea's writings and acknowledged his influence. Yamamoto was clearly influenced by *The Valor of Ignorance*'s premise that Japan would control the Pacific and occupy California when he wrote a friend in January 1941: "Any time war breaks out between Japan and the United States I shall not be content merely to capture Guam and the Philippines and occupy Hawaii and

San Francisco. I am looking forward to dictating peace to the United States in the White House at Washington."[77] Yamashita, in a post-war interview, called Lea "a very great soldier."[78] Fukudome acknowledged Lea's influence when he wrote a postwar article on the Pearl Harbor attack and singled out the year 1909, the year of *The Valor of Ignorance*'s publication, as the point in time when "the Japanese Navy had made the U.S. Navy its sole imaginary enemy."[79] Furthermore, with a resurgence of Japanese interest in *The Valor of Ignorance* during the war, the Hokuseido Press, one of Japan's oldest publishers of English-language books, published an abridged version of it entitled *If America Fights with Japan: The Pacific War Foretold Thirty-three Years Ago* (1942).

The Valor of Ignorance had a following among American military men, particularly those concerned with defending the West Coast and America's Pacific possessions against possible Japanese aggression. The book, for example, made a "deep and lasting impression" on U.S. Army captain George Van Horn Moseley, who "studied it" and carried his impressions to the Army War College, where he matriculated in 1910.[80] In August 1910 the *New York Times* reported that the book "has stirred up military circles in the Philippines" and "a new edition has just been issued in order to meet the demand for it from Manila."[81] It remained popular reading for officers stationed in the Philippines through the beginning of the Second World War. Although Lea's prediction of a war with Japan by 1915 failed to materialize, in March 1917 U.S. Navy commander Ward Winchell cited Lea's dire warnings about defending the West Coast from a naval invasion in a *Los Angeles Times* article urging men to join the navy.[82] *The Valor of Ignorance* also attracted interest among some officers stationed in Hawaii. In 1935, for example, U.S. Army lieutenant colonel George S. Patton Jr., stationed at the Headquarters, Hawaiian Department, Office of the Assistant Chief of Staff for Military Intelligence, cited Lea in assessing the probability of a future conflict with Japan. He outlined his assessment in a paper entitled "The Causes of War: A Comparative Study of the Similarity of Conditions Existing in 1913 and 1935," which included a reference to a warning in *The Valor of Ignorance* about potential Japanese aggression against Hawaii.[83]

General Douglas MacArthur, commander of U.S. forces in the Far East at the time of the Japanese attack on Pearl Harbor, was particularly familiar with Lea's writing. According to Major General Charles A. Willoughby, MacArthur's chief of intelligence in the southwest

Pacific during World War II, MacArthur's defense of the Philippines rested in part on his "encyclopedic knowledge of previous campaigns in the Philippines, with particular reference to what Homer Lea had written about them." Willoughby elaborated:

> If MacArthur knew what the Japanese would do in general, he also had a fairly clear notion of what they would do in the Philippines in particular. . . . He knew what Homer Lea had written in The Valor of Ignorance as long ago as 1909. He knew that general staffs everywhere, including the Japanese, had read Lea's extraordinary forecast.
>
> In many a pre–Pearl Harbor staff conversation at the General's Manila military headquarters in gloomy old Fort Santiago, Lea's "invasion map" of the Philippines—a pincer movement on Manila beginning with landings at Polillo Bight—was discussed.[84]

The Pearl Harbor attack also rekindled national interest in Lea as a military prophet. Secretary of War Henry L. Stimson, who had met Lea in 1911, made the following entry in his personal diary on February 10, 1942: "The people of the United States have made an enormous mistake in underestimating the Japanese. They are now beginning to learn their mistake. Many times during recent months I have recalled meeting Homer Lea when I was Secretary of War under Mr. Taft. He . . . wrote a book on the Japanese peril entitled 'The Valor of Ignorance.' In those days the book seemed fantastic. Now things which he prophesied seem quite possible."[85]

Of all the books published in the previous half century foretelling a war between Japan and the United States that were reexamined after Pearl Harbor, *The Valor of Ignorance* arguably stands out. *Washington Post* book reviewer Robert E. Runser observed: "The parallels with actual events are startling and uncanny. On this account alone, Homer Lea has a good chance of being hailed as an inspired prophet."[86]

Newspapers, magazines, and radio programs discussed Lea's writings, while several of his former friends wrote articles and gave talks about him.[87] No one did more to publicize him, however, than journalist Clare Boothe, who visited the Philippines prior to the outbreak of the war and heard about him from Willoughby, among others. She became an ardent admirer of Lea and unwittingly contributed to his fictional mythology when she wrote two articles about him in March

1942. The articles subsequently became introductions to new editions of *The Valor of Ignorance* and *The Day of the Saxon*. Originally appearing in the March 7 and March 14 issues of the *Saturday Evening Post,* the articles repeated earlier misinformation and exaggerations about Lea.[88] Ermal took issue with some of the errors and wrote the magazine recommending several corrections: "I enjoyed Miss Boothe's articles concerning my brother, Homer Lea, very much. I realize that material concerning him is difficult to obtain, and, as a consequence, the information is not always accurate or true. For this reason, and because my brother and I were very close, I would like to make the following corrections. . . ."[89]

One of Ermal's corrections, for example, related to an episode in which Lea allegedly sat "piggyback on O'Banion's shoulders" to address a crowd.[90] Ermal responded that he was "never carried in Captain O'Banion's arms, as Miss Boothe states. Nor did he ever sit 'piggy-back' on his shoulders."[91]

Albert Powers also found fault with Boothe's portrayal of Lea. Yet he evidently did not contact the magazine recommending corrections. He later wrote O'Banion concerning his recollections of Lea:

> There seems to be a lot of confusion as to whether Homer Lea was a genius or a bluffer. Clare Booth did not help much in her articles. She pictured Homer not at all as I knew him, and in her first draft she had you down as a giant half-wit who carried Homer piggy-back over the mountains. As I remember Homer he was pretty tough, even if not strong. I know he did a lot of tramping in the mountains with me. He certainly wasn't a crack-pot cripple, but had a gorgeous sense of humor, and was very practical in most ways—outside of money. . . . I remember how kind he was to me always, and what an interesting mind he had. . . . the keen sense of the ridiculous he had, as well as his strong convictions, and also how much he knew about so many things.[92]

O'Banion agreed with Powers. He replied, "Homer was not a cracked pot in any sense of the word."[93]

Unfortunately, Ermal's corrections came too late for Boothe to revise the articles before they appeared as introductions to the new editions of *The Valor of Ignorance* and *The Day of the Saxon*, published March 18 and April 1, 1942, respectively.[94]

In March Tom Lea Jr., a war artist for *Life Magazine*, tried to arrange a meeting with Clare Boothe, who was married to *Life* publisher Henry Luce, to discuss his famous cousin. They did not meet because she was overseas, but shortly afterward *Life* commissioned Tom to write an article about his cousin. He believed the request "to write about Homer doubtless grew from my inquiry about seeing Mrs. Luce."[95] He agreed to tackle the project and contacted Ermal for assistance. He then completed a draft article, but for reasons unknown, *Life* did not publish it.[96]

Ironically, in the course of Tom Lea's correspondence with Ermal, she indicated that she was writing her own biography of her brother. Because her husband had recently lost his job, she and her family were having financial problems and she saw a biography as a potential source of income. She also knew there was the possibility of a film being made about her brother and believed her biography would serve as its basis. Her biography, however, never came to fruition.[97]

Albert Powers and O'Banion, dissatisfied with Clare Boothe's characterization of Lea, saw an opportunity to influence his portrayal in a Hollywood film being made about Sun-Yat-sen. In early 1943 they discussed the prospect of O'Banion writing about his experiences with Lea to set Lea's record straight, and recommending the result to the film's producers. Although the film never materialized, Powers and O'Banion decided to forge ahead on a book about O'Banion's experiences. Powers arranged for O'Banion to collaborate with writer Carl Glick, resulting in *Double Ten: Captain O'Banion's Story of the Chinese Revolution,* published in 1945. Unfortunately, Glick based his narrative largely on O'Banion's recollections, of which many were flawed, and added his own dramatizations to the book. The end result was a work combining the attributes of a poor-quality history and a mediocre romance novel that contributed to Lea's mythology rather than set the record straight.[98]

Charles O. Kates, a U.S. Army Reserve officer, undertook the most ambitious effort to write a Lea biography. In 1939 he began collecting information about Lea from Lea's friends and family, including Joshua and Albert Powers and Ermal. He transcribed some of his notes and shared them with Joshua Powers, who later permitted Clare Boothe access to them when she was writing her articles. Kates set the biography aside while he served on active duty in the army from 1941 to 1947, writing military manuals instead, and when he left the army he realized that his need to earn a living would not permit him to devote time to writing the Lea biography: someone else might be better suited to the task. Looking for a collaborator, he approached Carl Glick with the proposition in early 1947, believing that Glick "was infinitely more qualified" than himself. Glick, however, was not interested, as he was already busy on his next book. Kates dropped the matter until Joshua Powers contacted him in early 1948, inquiring about the biography's progress. Kates still wanted to write the work, but knew it might be a long time before he could complete it. He again solicited Glick's cooperation, but to no avail. Glick remained uninterested, particularly since his publishers saw no merit in a Lea biography. Kates finally found a willing collaborator later that year, Frederic L. Chapin, a college student who planned to write a thesis about Homer Lea. Their cooperative project received a boost when Joshua Powers, who had recently discovered several boxes of correspondence and documents his mother had assembled for her planned Lea biography, shared the material with them. Chapin took the lead in writing and produced an A.B. honors thesis about Lea at Harvard in 1950. He completed a longer draft manuscript in early 1952, while working overseas for the State Department. Kates, meanwhile, returned to active duty after the outbreak of the Korean War in 1950. When he returned to civil life in early 1952 he sought to improve Chapin's manuscript and find a publisher, but was unsuccessful on both counts.[99] Despite all his efforts, he could not resolve the manuscript's deficiencies. He later explained why to Joshua Powers: "The problem, as you know, is not one of doing nearly routine research and writing. Had it been, I could have turned out a biography of sorts, long before this. There is a great lack of personal information about Lea, as well as serious gaps in the chronology of his life."[100]

The challenges Kates and others confronted in writing a Lea biography were partly eased when significant research materials started becoming available. In the late 1960s Joshua Powers and the relatives of Charles Boothe donated their respective collections of papers related to Lea to the Hoover Institution on War, Revolution, and Peace at Stanford University. These papers provided the basis for a new generation of researchers contemplating a Lea biography, including Eugene Anschel, whose *Homer Lea, Sun Yat-Sen and the Chinese Revolution* (1984) was the first significant, well-documented published account of Lea's exploits. Anschel, however, made no claim to writing a definitive Lea biography, noting in his prologue: "There remain . . . many gaps in the story that cannot be filled and many uncertainties that cannot be dispelled."[101] Anschel also fell victim to the perennial problem of separating fact from fiction. His biographical account contained numerous historical errors and continued to perpetuate several Lea myths. Fortunately, by the 1990s, the advance of the information age and evolution of the Internet opened additional and unprecedented avenues of research to help narrow the gap between fact and fiction in researching a Lea biography. Yet many unanswered questions about Lea's exploits would invariably remain.

Filmmakers first became interested in Lea and his writings in the early 1920s. In 1922 Japanese-born Sessue Hayakawa, a leading Hollywood film star and movie producer, adapted the *Vermilion Pencil* to the screen. The film, among several with Asian themes Hayakawa both starred in and produced in the 1920s, received mixed reviews.[102]

Interest in a film biography of Lea arose during World War II. In 1942 Clare Boothe's interest in him, combined with his renewed popularity, generated several efforts to produce a film biography. One of the first indications of the idea came when movie columnist Louella O. Parsons reported on February 27, 1942: "The dramatic story of the late Homer Lea, the hunchback who was denied entrance into West Point because of his affliction, is attracting the attention of several movie companies."[103] In mid-April the *Los Angeles Times* noted: "'The Life of Homer Lea' is being written by Upton Close and Mary Baker, with the films in mind, and Paramount and Warners are reported interested."[104] Not surprisingly, Boothe had her own plans for a film biography. She and writer Elizabeth Cobb worked on a fictionalized screenplay about Lea with the suggested title "Foreign Devil." Louella Parsons reported that the "particular version of the Homer Lea story the studios are interested in is the one coauthored by Clare Boothe."[105] However, nothing came of either project. Later that year there were plans to make a film about Sun Yat-sen with actor Paul Muni in the starring role, which impelled Powers and O'Banion to write about Lea, but as previously noted, nothing came of that project either.[106]

Interest in a Lea film resurfaced sporadically after the war, but had subsided by the late 1950s. In 1947 director Lester Fuller considered making a film version of *Double Ten*, but dropped the idea, remarking that because of "the restricted hysterical state of the market today as a result of the 'Un-American investigation' and the studio's fears of a depression, this story, dealing as it does with a part of the Chinese revolution sounds like poison to the story departments."[107] In 1948 and

1949 film producer Lester Cowan looked into the possibility of making a *Double Ten* film, with no result. In 1953 the Twentieth Century Fox studio briefly investigated the prospect of making a *Double Ten* film, also with no result.[108] In 1955 Hollywood film producer William Schorr reportedly considered making a Lea biography starring Mickey Rooney as Lea and William Holden as a newspaperman. When Charles Kates heard about the planned film, he wrote Schorr that he had the "full story of Lea, based upon careful research, and largely in the form of original, exclusive material," with hopes of collaborating on it, but the film never came to fruition. Joshua Powers claimed the rights to a life story of Homer Lea and Schorr had failed to purchase them. Furthermore, Powers was apprehensive that the film would not do Lea justice, particularly as Rooney, in his opinion, would be miscast as Lea. He explained: "I could not consent to a picture being made about him unless I knew the work is being properly done and did not belittle him or misrepresent him."[109] In 1958 the Hal Roach Studio considered making a television version of *Double Ten* for its *Telephone Time* series, and then possibly making a feature-length film, but as with earlier endeavors, nothing came of either project.[110] Finally, in 1959 film and television producer Julian Lesser proposed doing a television episode about Lea's amazing predictions for an intended series called *The Unexplained,* which would have been devoted to examining unusual happenings for which satisfactory explanations have never been forthcoming. There is no evidence, however, that the project advanced beyond the concept stage.[111]

After Lea's death, an obituary in the *Christian Science Monitor* astutely noted, "[H]is intimate associations with the revolutionary movements in China that led to the formation of a republic will always make him an important secondary figure in that historic event."[112] Eight years later, the Honorable Juming C. Suez, consul of the Republic of China in New York, singled Lea out for public tribute for assisting Sun Yat-sen during the Chinese republican revolution in a *Far Eastern Fortnightly* article that commemorated the anniversary of the revolution and reflected on Chinese-American ties. Suez hoped that "when the history of the Chinese Republic comes to be written his [Lea's] services would be suitably recognized and recorded."[113]

In Lea's own estimation his greatest legacy may have been his contributions to Sun Yat-sen and the Chinese revolution. His will stipulated that he be buried in China, but Ethel, although she remained in contact with Sun Yat-sen until his death in 1925, evidently did not seek his assistance or those of any other Chinese in the matter. Furthermore, she never thought she could afford the trip to China and kept Lea's ashes with her in Los Angeles. Lea's cremation, in turn, came as a shock to the Chinese. In 1914, when members of a delegation of Chinese Nationalist League officials visited Ethel and asked to visit Lea's tomb, they were horrified to learn that he had been cremated and his ashes were in her home. They believed he deserved a more fitting resting place. After Ethel died in 1934, and her remains also were cremated, the Leas' ashes remained in the possession of her son Joshua. Although aware of Lea's last wishes, he too believed he could not afford the trip to China, particularly before the establishment of the communist People's Republic of China in 1949. Finally, in 1968, the year he donated Lea's surviving papers to the Asian collection of the Hoover Institution at Stanford University, he made the fulfillment of Lea's burial wish one of the conditions of the donation. Dr. John Ma, the collection's curator-librarian, assisted in fulfilling Lea's final wishes by contacting the Republic of China (Taiwan) and arranging for the fulfillment of Lea's will.[114]

Taiwan recognized Lea as a national hero. The ashes of both Leas received the government's highest attention. President Chiang Kai-shek, Sun Yat-sen's brother, took a personal interest in the arrangements. He considered Lea "the first foreign adviser to the Republic of China and was delighted to know that he willed to have his ashes buried in China."[115] He also believed the interment of Lea's ashes in Taiwan should only be temporary, until such time as they could be transferred to Nanking and interred by Sun Yat-sen's mausoleum, when Taiwan and mainland China were finally reunited. On April 18, 1969, Powers, several family members, and Dr. Ma escorted the Leas' ashes to Taiwan. The American ambassador, Dr. Sun Fo (Sun Yat-sen's son), and several Chinese dignitaries were on hand at the airport to honor the arrival of the ashes.[116] The *China Post* described the solemn scene:

> Two Chinese Army guards of honor climbed up the ramp into the jetliner, brought down the ashes of the Leas and placed them on an altar.
>
> Presidential Secretary-General Chang Chun led ranking Chinese government officials to pay one minute of silent respect to the man who helped Dr. Sun Yat-sen overthrow the Manchu Dynasty.[117]

The following day more than a hundred government officials and admirers of Lea attended burial services at the Yangmingshan cemetery near Taipei, which was reserved for very important persons. Vice President Yen Chia-kan presided over the services, which included several speakers and lasted an hour and a half. President Chiang Kai-shek had arranged for a plaque to hang above the temporary altar reading: *Yung Huai Feng Yi* (Probity and heroism will be long remembered). At the conclusion of the services, the *China Post* reported,

> Yen laid a wreath before the ashes of the Leas and bowed deep three times. Four Chinese Army guards of honor carried the ashes to the grave, which was sealed.
>
> Then, all notables at the ceremonies stood at attention as the taps was blown to lay the Leas to rest.[118]

During the visit Powers presented Lea's dragon-head sword to Chiang Kai-shek as a final gesture of Lea's commitment to China. However, the gift of Lea's sword and the burial did not mark the final chapter in Lea's ties to China. The Taiwanese press reported on the government's (Chiang Kai-shek's) position that the interment was temporary, and Joshua Powers noted on his return to the United States: "The Generalissimo made me promise to come back to Taiwan to accompany the ashes when he takes them back to the mainland and puts them alongside those of Sun Yat-sen."[119] Chiang Kai-shek and Joshua Powers, who both had personal connections with Lea, have since passed from the scene, and it remains speculative whether a reaffirmation of Lea's historical role in Chinese affairs may someday lead to his ashes being placed alongside those of Sun Yat-sen.

Lea's life was stranger and more exotic than romantic fiction. He overcame afflictions of deformity and poor health to pursue grand ambitions. As a highly talented college dropout, he leveraged his skills to a remarkable extent in forging for himself a role on the world scene. In the pioneering tradition of his grandfather, father, and uncles, he welcomed adventure and the challenges of conquering new frontiers. He had few scruples about how he achieved his goals; to Lea the end justified the means. He relied on situational ethics in pursuing his adventures and was not above resorting to duplicity in some cases while abiding by a traditional code of honor and integrity in others. He earned a reputation as a mysterious adventurer through his affiliation with the Chinese reform and revolutionary movements partly because he never set the record straight or confided the truth about his exploits to those closest to him.

When Lea began his adventures, while still a Stanford student, his love of military history, combined with claims of kinship with General Robert E. Lee, helped pave the way for his acceptance into the Pao Huang Hui reform movement, though he was an untested military "expert." His initial hopes of playing a leading role in restoring the Manchu emperor to his throne were not realized. During his trip to China in 1900, his grand schemes and epic wanderings produced little more than a general's title and the beginnings of a mythology he did little to curb. Remaining committed to the reform movement, he demonstrated a genuine capacity for organizing and planning the covert training of Chinese military cadets in America. His reputation with the reformers was on the rise until a series of government investigations, compounded by the rivalry of Richard Falkenberg for control of the reform army, brought his cadet-training scheme to the brink of collapse. By the time of the emperor's death in 1908, his Pao Huang Hui ties and commitment to the Manchu dynasty had withered.

Lea remained inextricably linked to China. He organized the Red Dragon conspiracy, a fantastic plan to seize control of the Kwang provinces, and subsequently allied with Sun Yat-sen's revolutionary movement to topple the Manchus. As Sun Yat-sen's trusted advisor he hoped to play a key military role in the new Chinese republic. He also intended using his position to help shape a new world order, wherein China would be a counterweight employed to preserve Anglo-Saxon regional interests. When the Chinese republican revolution succeeded, he played an instrumental role in Sun Yat-sen's return to China, but U.S. government intervention and a catastrophic failure in his health curtailed his involvement with China's new republic. There can be little question that his revolutionary fervor and loyalty to a cause were sincere. No other American was as closely involved in the establishment of the Chinese republic than Lea. Had he recovered his health, he would certainly have rejoined Sun Yat-sen to help mold a new China.

Lea's writings, which challenged his generation to consider the rising forces of geopolitical change, unquestionably remain his most enduring legacy. His militant social Darwinist views generally created a polarizing effect on his audiences, who either embraced him as a genius or dismissed him as a charlatan. Undeterred by his failure to convince the Anglo-Saxon race to embrace his militant doctrines, or his failure to preside more actively over molding a new China, he remained determined to continue his crusade until his death. In the end, however, political and social circumstances did not allow him to play the role that he sought. Anglo-American foreign-policy makers were unwilling to discard the Open Door principle in China, and the English-speaking peoples of the world were unprepared to divest themselves of their business and commercial pursuits to take up the sword and the shield for a Darwinist racial clash for survival.

Inevitably, many questions remain about Lea's exploits and the full extent of his influence. Major Shelton was probably right when he remarked that "the full story of the accomplishments of Homer Lea will probably never be told, and may never be known."[120] Van Loan also was probably right when he observed: "It is impossible to guess what he might have done had he lived ten years longer. His ambition was limitless. His belief in himself was absolute."[121] However, enough is known about Lea to recognize that his accomplishments were often built on a defiance of conventional wisdom, a sense of destiny, and a serene indifference to criticism. Although the significance of his contributions to the Chinese reform and revolutionary movements and importance of his writings may remain the subjects of debate, and although questions will remain about his exploits, there can be no doubt that Homer Lea left an indelible mark on the history of his times.

APPENDIXES

Appendix A

Translation of Homer Lea's letter of introduction from Tom Tsai Hin of Los Angeles to the leading revolutionists, which appeared on the front page of the *San Francisco Call*, April 22, 1900:

Dear Sir: There is a white man here by the name of Mr. Lea. He is an American living just now in Los Angeles. He is a Stanford man, well up in war ways. He is about to travel and talks well. His people are all great warriors, many of them having figured in the war of North and South in America. He feels greatly for China on account of her weakness and does not like to see things unequal. He wants to teach Chinese to become soldiers, so as to become free. He is willing to go up to the interior of China to get up a school to teach 2000 soldiers. He is going to visit different parts of China, calling at Hongkong, Macao and different cities—together with Jeong Googg Sing, who is a Yung Wing man, also living at this city, and learning war methods on sea and at land at a big school. It is to be hoped that all of our party who should meet him should get much pleasure and good in every way. This letter of introduction is given to him, so as to make his going and coming easier. The moment you see him you can form new societies and let him see we have one object before us, and that is to protect the Emperor. Give him all the help needed. It will be to the good of China. With regards.

Tom Tsai Hin

Appendix B

Letter from Ho Yow, Chinese imperial consul general in San Francisco, which appeared on the front page of the *San Francisco Call,* April 22, 1900:

Through the courtesy of the Call certain letters and papers of a most incriminating character and great importance to my Government have been placed in my hands—documents which prove beyond a doubt that a young American citizen has been plotting with the leaders among the Chinese revolutionists and hopes to become the commander in chief of the insurrectionists in China. The news comes to me as a shock, but I must compliment the Call upon the completeness of this expose and the careful manner in which every thread of the plot has been drawn together, weaving a net in which I find all of the conspirators fairly caught. The Chinese plotters, both here and in China have all been placed under the most watchful surveillance, but we hardly thought that we should be troubled by ambitious Americans desirous of self-aggrandizement and grasping for riches stained with blood of misguided rebels; it now seems that we must be prepared for even this. It is unfortunate that an American should submit to be made the tool of these insurrectionists, under the guise of reforming China, but we have taken precautions against things of this character, and if ever attempted these people will find themselves well met at every step.

Appendix C

K'ang Yu-wei's April 7, 1905, proclamation disavowing Richard Falkenberg:

To the American People—

I desire to announce that General Homer Lea of Los Angeles is the only one recognized and appointed by me as the General of all Chinese military schools in America, and furthermore I have appointed no one such as "General Commanding" or any officer of the so-called "Chinese Imperial Reform Army" which is not in existence, and any person claiming such rank or position in the "Imperial Reform Army" is considered an imposter.

Kang Yu Wei
Grand President,
Chinese Empire Reform Association

NOTES

1. Charismatic Dreamer

1. Accounts of Dr. Lea's history vary considerably in accuracy. For the most authoritative accounts, see Watson Clark Lea to Charles O. Kates, January 18, 1940, Charles O. Kates Personal Papers, Mr. Brian Kates, Pomona, N.Y.; "Captain Joseph C. Lea," in *The Bronco, 1902*, 41–43; Claudine Chandler, "About Thomas C. Lea," November 22, 1959, box A241-1F38, Jackson County Historical Society, Independence, Mo.; and Dolly Breitenbaugh, "Doctor Pleasant Lea and Other Doctors," n.d., box 8, Jackson County Historical Society. For Dr. Lea's involvement in the establishment of Cleveland, Tennessee, see also *Acts Passed the First Session of the Twenty-second General Assembly of the State of Tennessee, 1837–8*, 271–74. For Dr. Lea's involvement with running a post office in Jackson County, Missouri, see also Leech, *List of Post Offices in the United States*, 14. Dr. Lea was born on November 6, 1807, in Jefferson County, Tennessee, and married Lucinda Frances Calloway on April 3, 1838. For his genealogical background and marriage, see http://www.familysearch.org/. His history in Cleveland, Tennessee, is covered in *History of Tennessee*, 802. For additional information on Lea's family, see *United States Census of 1850*, roll M432-402, 257, http://www.ancestry.com/, which indicates that in 1850, Dr. Lea (age forty-two) was married to Lucinda F. Lea (twenty-nine), and they had six children born in Tennessee: Thomas C. (eleven); Joseph C. (nine); Frank E. (seven); Alfred E. (five); Elvira C. (three); and Mary S. (two). For a Lea family background, see Fleming, *Captain Joseph C. Lea*, 3–6. Dr. Lea and Tom C. Lea, his eldest son, are listed as miners in the *1860 Nebraska Territorial Census*. For Dr. Lea's establishment of a sawmill in Boulder, see *History of Clear Creek and Boulder Valleys*, 394.

2. Watson Clark Lea to Charles O. Kates, January 18, 1940, Kates Papers. Accounts that attribute Dr. Lea's death to Kansas border raiders, which include *The History of Jackson County, Missouri*, 271–72, are likely in error. *The History of Jackson County* implies that Colonel Charles R. Jennison's Kansas Volunteer Cavalry Regiment likely murdered Dr. Lea, but Jennison's regiment, under a new commander, was serving in Mississippi in September 1862, according to Seventh Regiment (Jennison's Jayhawkers) Kansas Volunteer Cavalry. It is more likely that Colonel William R. Penick's Missouri state militia unit, referred to in "Captain Joseph C. Lea,"

in *The Bronco 1902,* 42, carried out the murder, since that unit served in the Jackson County vicinity from August 1862 to June 1863, according to Schnetzer, "The Hounds of Old Pennock." See also Padgitt, "Captain Joseph C. Lea," 50–52; "Vivid Story in Civil War Mural," *Independence Examiner,* June 1939, article in files of the Jackson County Historical Society; and "Post Office Mural Up," *Pleasant Hill Times* (Missouri), May 26, 1939, 1. For the James A. Shaw quote, which misspells Dr. Lea's name as Lee, see *The History of Jackson County, Missouri,* 345. Shaw also states: "Lee's Summit, the largest town in Prairie Township, derived its name from Dr. Lee, and from the fact of its location being the highest point between Kansas City and St. Louis on the Missouri Pacific Railroad." The town of Lee's Summit, Missouri, acquired its name in 1868, and generally recognized Dr. Lea as its namesake. See Watson Clark Lea, "It's Lea's Summit, He Says," *Kansas City Star,* April 27, 1908, 1; "American Prophet of War," *Kansas City Star,* March 14, 1942, 14. There is uncertainty about the naming, according to *History of Lee's Summit,* attraction brochure of the Lee's Summit Chamber of Commerce, www.lschamber.com, which indicates the town could have been named in honor of Confederate General Robert E. Lee or Dr. Pleasant Lea.

3. Accounts differ about Alfred Lea's age and early history. The best authority is *History of Clear Creek and Boulder Valleys,* 650–51, which gives his birth date as March 26, 1845. His obituary also lists 1845 as his year of birth; see "Gentleman of Old School," *Los Angeles Times,* August 18, 1909, 2:3. "Tom Lea, Jr., Questions / Ermal Lea Green Answers," circa April 1942, 1, Personal Papers, Mr. and Mrs. James D. Lea, Houston, Tex.; see Carroll H. Coberly, "Reminiscences," 1962, 42, MSS# 125, Colorado Historical Society, Denver, for reference to Alfred's 1864 enlistment with Company B, Third Colorado and participation in the Sand Creek Indian battle. Also see "Alfred E. Lea Biography," unclassified MSS, Colorado Historical Society. For a brief biography of Edward McCook, see "Edward Moody McCook," Territorial Governors Collection, Colorado Department of Personnel and Administration, http://www.colorado.gov/dpa/doit/archives/govs/mccook.html. For J. U. Marlow being the proprietor of the American Hotel in Denver, see an advertisement for the hotel in *Rocky Mountain News* (weekly), February 9, 1870, 1. For Alfred serving as the treasurer of Boulder County, see "Vox Populi," *Boulder News and Courier,* December 29, 1882, 1. For Alfred's early life, see also Thomas C. Lea's unpublished manuscript, "Homer Lea," Spring 1942, El Paso, 2–3, Thomas Calloway Lea Papers, Harry Ransom Humanities Research Center, University of Texas, Austin, Tex.; Mary Roberts, "Oregon Relative Tells of War Prophet," *Oregon Journal,* March 22, 1942, D4; unattributed and untitled Homer Lea manuscript (possibly written by Charles O. Kates), box 3, Joshua B. Powers Papers, Hoover Institution on War, Revolution and Peace, Stanford University, Stanford, Calif.; Robert Sullivan, "Nobody Listens to a Prophet," *New York Daily News,* December 28, 1941, 40; Boothe, "Ever Hear of Homer Lea?" part 1,

70. For Alfred's involvement with the establishment of Steamboat Springs, Colorado, see Leckenby, "The Founding of Steamboat Springs," 95; Leckenby, *The Tread of Pioneers,* 16. For Alfred's involvement with the establishment of Roswell, New Mexico, see Fleming, *Captain Joseph C. Lea,* 118–19. For a listing of some of Alfred's real estate holdings, see Power of Attorney, Homer Lea, et al. to Emma W. Lea (Property in Chavez Co., N.M.), October 1909, and Power of Attorney, Homer Lea, et al. to Emma W. Lea (Property in Boulder Co. Col.), October 1909, Robert G. Wilson Personal Papers, copy in the author's files.

4. Coberly, "Reminiscences," 41–43; *History of Clear Creek and Boulder Valleys,* 651. Hersa's first husband, Colorado Cavalry captain Silas Soule, participated in the infamous 1864 Sand Creek Indian massacre. He married Hersa on April 1, 1865, and was murdered later that month. For a record of their marriage, see Colorado Marriages, 1858–1939, Colorado Historical Society, Denver. For details about Captain Soule's death, see "The Homicide Last Night," *Denver Daily Rocky Mountain News,* April 24, 1865, 2. For background on Hersa Soule, Ivan, and Pete, see Hoover, *Castle o'Montgomery,* 101–3. For the naming of Homer, see Tom Lea manuscript, 3; "Tom Lea, Jr., Questions / Ermal Lea Green Answers," 1. For Hersa's death, see "Death," *Denver Daily Rocky Mountain News,* May 18, 1879, 4, which also indicates that she was thirty-four years, two months, and sixteen days old when she died; "Death of Mrs. A. E. Lea," *Boulder News and Courier,* May 16, 1879, 3; and *Boulder News and Courier,* June 20, 1879, 3. There is uncertainty as to Hersa's age. Her tombstone, which likely has the correct dates, lists her birth as February 1843, which indicates she would have been thirty-six when she died. See Hersa Lea tombstone, Riverside Cemetery, Denver, Colo. Ermal Lea Green to Charles O. Kates, November 19, 1940, Kates Papers, contains reference to Hersa's two oldest children dying in infancy and to Homer, Ermal, and Hersa being raised after their mother's death. The children who died in infancy, Ivan and Mary, are buried next to their mother in an unmarked grave in plot number 5, the Riverside Cemetery, according to a Riverside Cemetery (Coberly/Lea plot) chart furnished the author. See also Perkins, "Silas Soule, His Widow Heresa, and the Rest of the Story."

5. Tom Lea manuscript, 4; Ermal Lea Green to Charles O. Kates, February 14, 1940, Kates Papers. Harry Carr, a close friend of Lea in later life, also attributed Lea's deformity to being dropped as a child: "When he was a baby, he was dropped by a careless nurse, his spine being hopelessly injured. For the rest of his life he wore a steel harness." See Carr, *Riding the Tiger,* 169. In the 1940s, a relative of Hersa Lea, a Mr. Coberly, who resided in Boulder, Colorado, related to Agnes Wright Spring, the state historian of Colorado, that Homer "was on a porch in a highchair when he began rocking it and the chair fell off the porch injuring the boy's back." See Spring, *Near the Greats,* 95–96.

6. Marco Newmark, "Early Boyhood," statement on Homer Lea, unti-

tled folder, box 3, Powers Papers; J. B. Powers, untitled Homer Lea manuscript, 7–8, Powers Papers. The various "statements" on Homer Lea in the Powers Papers are excerpts from letters, which are no longer available, in the Charles O. Kates Papers that were shared with Joshua Powers.

7. Ermal Lea Green to Charles O. Kates, February 14, 1940.

8. Ella Lea Dow to Charles O. Kates, March 15, 1940, Kates Papers.

9. Tom Lea manuscript, 4; Newmark, "Early Boyhood."

10. "Tom Lea, Jr., Questions / Ermal Lea Green Answers," 2.

11. Ermal Lea Green to Charles O. Kates, November 19, 1940. Homer was about ten years old when his grandmother moved to San Jose, according to Newmark, "Early Boyhood." Homer's grandmother, Mrs. Sarah A. Start, likely moved to San Jose in 1887, when in July of that year she purchased 6,755 acres of land for $4,500. She lived on McGlaughlin Avenue in east San Jose. See *San Jose Evening News,* July 20, 1887, 4; "Homer Lea, Napoleon of China, a San Josean," *San Jose Evening News,* May 7, 1912, 5.

12. "Tom Lea, Jr., Questions / Ermal Lea Green Answers," 2. According to Block, "The Old Arapahoe School," 119–21, Homer attended the Arapahoe School, which served as a grammar school from 1882 to 1890. J. B. Sturtevant, "Central School Students, 1886," photograph 210-2-18, and J. B. Sturtevant, "Central School Students, 1887," photograph 210-2-28, Carnegie Branch Library for Local History, Boulder Public Library, Boulder, Colo.

13. Ermal Lea Green to Charles O. Kates, February 14, 1940; Ermal Lea Green to Charles O. Kates, November 19, 1940; "Tom Lea, Jr., Questions / Ermal Lea Green Answers," 1; Newmark, "Early Boyhood"; untitled Homer Lea manuscript, 7–8; Coberly, "Reminiscences," 43. For a description of the National Surgical Institute, established in 1858, see brochure *National Surgical Institute.*

14. [Blanche M.] Mullen, "Youth Stepmother," statement on Homer Lea, untitled folder, box 3, Powers Papers. For the date of Alfred and Emma's marriage, see "Ancestor Chart—Family Group No. 36," December 1, 1987, Wilson Personal Papers, copy in author's files. See also "The First Presbyterian Church of Danville, KY" program of April 24, 1887, which lists Emma Wilson's address as the Deaf Mute Institute, Wilson Personal Papers, copy in author's files. For Alfred knowing Emma during his youth, see Watson Clark Lea to Charles O. Kates, January 18, 1940.

15. John Cory to Charles O. Kates, November 29, 1939, Kates Papers; Newmark, *Jottings in Southern California History,* 134. See "A Chinese General from Los Angeles," *Los Angeles Times,* April 13, 1901, 1, for a reference to the Lea family living in Denver. Alfred Lea's address is listed as 1892 Pennsylvania Avenue in the *Denver City Directory, 1892,* 662.

16. Boothe, "Ever Hear of Homer Lea?" part 1, 70.

17. Mrs. Edith Merrill Hurd to Charles O. Kates, December 19, 1939, Kates Papers.

18. Marshall Stimson, draft article, untitled (on Homer Lea), circa 1942,

2, Genl. Homer Lea folder, Marshall W. Stimson Papers, Huntington Library, Art Collections, and Botanical Gardens, San Marino, Calif.; Frederic Chapin interview with Marshall Stimson, "Boyhood—Denver," circa November 1948, Kates Papers.

19. Tom Treanor, "The Home Front," *Los Angeles Times,* March 24, 1942, 2; Tom Lea manuscript, 4.

20. Treanor, "The Home Front."

21. Lea to Stanford, June 2, 1897, untitled folder, box 3, Powers Papers. The University of the Pacific high school classes were conducted under a program known as the Academy, whose functions were: "First, as a preparatory school of high order, in which students may be prepared for the Freshman class in any first-class college. Second, the course has been so arranged that it will give all the advantages of the best city High School." Homer Lea, San Jose, is listed as one of twenty-five irregular students of the Academic department. See *Catalogue of the University of the Pacific, 1893–1894,* 58–59, 66, Holt-Atherton Special Collections, University of the Pacific, Stockton, Calif. Ermal and Hersa also attended the University of the Pacific. See *Catalogue of the University of the Pacific, 1896–1897,* 76, 78.

22. "Tom Lea, Jr., Questions / Ermal Lea Green Answers," 1; untitled Homer Lea manuscript, 7–8; Roberts, "Oregon Relative Tells of War Prophet," 4; Mullen, "Youth Stepmother." The Lea home is described in "Report Brisk Demand," *Los Angeles Times,* October 3, 1909, 5:4.

23. Stimson, "Great American Who Saw It Coming," 6; McLaughlin, "Los Angeles High School Lyceum League," statement on Homer Lea, untitled folder, box 3, Powers Papers.

24. Newmark, *Jottings in Southern California History,* 134. In Marco Newmark, "Los Angeles High School," statement on Homer Lea, untitled folder, box 3, Powers Papers, he added: "There is nothing very startling about the wording of his declination of the office; nevertheless, his manner in expressing himself had, without exaggeration, an electrical effect, and he immediately became the outstanding leader of the organization."

25. McLaughlin, "Los Angeles High School Lyceum League"; Stimson, "A Los Angeles Jeremiah," 6; Marshall Stimson to Charles O. Kates, December 6, 1939, Kates Papers; Herbert F. True to Charles O. Kates, February 29, 1940, Kates Papers; Marshall Stimson to Hon. James H. Pope, December 3, 1941, Genl. Homer Lea folder, Stimson Papers. Lea is cited as president of the Los Angeles High School Lyceum in a photograph in Scrapbook No. 1, dated March 1896, 12, Stimson Papers.

26. Marshall Stimson, "Los Angeles High School Election," statement on Homer Lea, untitled folder, box 3, Powers Papers.

27. Stimson, "Los Angeles Jeremiah," 7.

28. Marco Newmark to Charles O. Kates, December 26, 1939, Kates Papers; see also Harry Carr, "Death Overpowers Odd World Figure," *Los Angeles Times,* November 2, 1912, 2:1–2.

29. Green, "She Knew Him Well"; Chella Cady Jones to Charles O. Kates, January 22, 1940, Kates Papers.

30. Green, "She Knew Him Well."

31. For reference to Lea's high school romances, see Frederic Chapin to Charles Kates, November 5, 1948, Kates Papers; Newmark, "Los Angeles High School"; [Paul G.] Clark, statement on Homer Lea, untitled folder, box 3, Powers Papers. One childhood sweetheart Homer adored was a girl named Alice Honeywell, according to [Louise] Houghton, statement on Homer Lea, untitled folder, box 3, Powers Papers.

32. Newmark, "Los Angeles High School."

33. Carr, "Death Overpowers Odd World Figure"; Marshall Stimson, "True War Predictions by L.A. Boy Who Upset an Empire," *Los Angeles Evening Herald and Express,* February 25, 1942, B10.

34. Stimson, "A Los Angeles Jeremiah," 7.

35. Greene, *America's Heroes,* 68–78, 108–9; O'Neill, *The Progressive Years,* 14–18; Heilbroner and Singer, *The Economic Transformation of America,* 155–65, 172–91. See also Wiebe, *The Search for Order;* Ginger, *Age of Excess;* Wecter, *The Hero in America,* 342–44.

36. Wecter, *Hero in America,* 115–17.

37. Ibid., 140, 115–19; Gregory, "Unavailing Wealth"; "Tom Lea, Jr., Questions / Ermal Lea Green Answers," 3.

38. Homer Lea to Stanford, June 2, 1897, Powers Papers; Ermal Lea Green to Charles O. Kates, February 14, 1940.

39. Van Loan, "General Homer Lea"; Boothe, "Ever Hear of Homer Lea?" part 1, 70; Stimson, "A Los Angeles Jeremiah," 7.

40. Van Loan, "General Homer Lea."

41. Ibid. For Homer's interests in reading about great military commanders, see "Tom Lea, Jr., Questions / Ermal Lea Green Answers," 3.

42. Sullivan, "Nobody Listens to a Prophet," 52; Huang Chi-lu, *Kuo Fu Chun-shih Ku-wen-Ho-ma Li Chiang-chun (Ch'u Kao),* 12.

43. Stimson, "A Los Angeles Jeremiah," 6; Frederic Chapin to Charles Kates, November 5, 1948, Kates Papers.

44. "A Chinese General from Los Angeles." For Rev. Ng Poon Chew's background, see W. A. Corey, "The Chinese Quarter," *Los Angeles Times,* November 13, 1898, A5; "Curled Their Queues," *Los Angeles Times,* December 24, 1898, 11; Bertha H. Smith, "Wa Mi San Po: Los Angeles' Chinese Newspaper and Its Busy Editor," *Los Angeles Times,* July 23, 1899, 15; "Dr. N. P. Chew Dead; Chinese Editor," *Los Angeles Times,* March 15, 1931, 27; Hyung-chan, *Distinguished Asian Americans,* 56–59. The Chinese Presbyterian Mission was located at 214 North San Pedro Street, according to Phillips, *Los Angeles,* 119.

45. Stimson, "A Los Angeles Jeremiah."

46. Homer Lea to Stanford, June 2, 1897. See [E. W.] Oliver, "Los Angeles High School," statement on Homer Lea, untitled folder, box 3, Pow-

ers Papers, for a brief explanation of Lea's failure to complete high school; Ermal Lea Green to Charles O. Kates, May 7, 1940, Kates Papers. Marshall Stimson told Frederic Chapin that Homer failed to graduate due to receiving a failing grade in one of his classes. Chapin explained to Kates: "It appears that the room teacher of the class had it in for both Lea and Stimson and failed both of them. Stimson protested to the headmaster and forced the teacher to give him an examination in English history which was his failing subject." See Frederic Chapin to Charles Kates, November 5, 1948, Kates Papers.

47. Newmark, "Early Boyhood"; Ermal Lea Green to Charles O. Kates, November 19, 1940.

48. For Homer having Bright's disease, see Carr, *Riding the Tiger*, 174. Bright's disease may have run in the Lea family. Homer's uncle Tom Lea reportedly died from it, according to Chandler, "About Thomas C. Lea," 17. Diabetes runs in the Lea family, according to James D. Lea. See James Lea, e-mail message to author, December 3, 2007. For Lea possibly having diabetes, see Dr. M. Urbanek, medical report on Lea, April 6, 1912, box 4, Powers Papers, which indicates Lea was treated for a diabetic-like condition. For an example of period treatments of Bright's disease, see Edebohls, *The Surgical Treatment of Bright's Disease*.

49. Homer Lea to Stanford, June 2, 1897; Sullivan, "Nobody Listens to a Prophet," 40.

50. [Lydia] Kellam, "Occidental College," statement on Homer Lea, untitled folder, box 3, Powers Papers.

51. Grace M. Lowder, "Occidental College," statement on Homer Lea, untitled folder, box 3, Powers Papers.

52. C. Fred Schoop, "Passing Recalls Homer Lee Story," *Pasadena Star-News,* January 13, 1965, C5.

53. R. Morgan Galbreth to Charles O. Kates, January 19, 1940, Kates Papers; Rev. Guy W. Wadsworth, Occidental College, to Stanford University, June 4, 1897, untitled folder, box 3, Powers Papers; Boothe, "Ever Hear of Homer Lea?" part 1, 70; Glick, *Double Ten,* 35.

54. Ermal Lea Green to Tom Lea Jr., April 7, 1942, James Lea Papers; Schoop, "Passing Recalls Homer Lee Story."

55. "Lyceum Convention," *Los Angeles Times,* June 27, 1897, 26; "Tom Lea, Jr., Questions / Ermal Lea Green Answers," 3.

56. "Lyceum Convention."

57. Irwin, *The Making of a Reporter,* 5–7; Wadsworth to Stanford University, June 4, 1897.

2. In the Dragon's Lair

1. See Homer Lea Grade Transcript, 1897–1899, Stanford University (Registrar), Stanford, Calif.; *Daily Palo Alto,* January 25, 1898, 4.

2. *Daily Palo Alto,* January 25, 1898, 4. See Dr. H. W. Hunsaker to Stanford, May 18, 1898, box 3, Powers Papers.

3. Homer Lea Grade Transcript; Boothe, "Ever Hear of Homer Lea?" part 1, 71; Irwin, *Stanford Quad,* 170. See "Euphronia Society's Election," *San Francisco Call,* September 9, 1902, 3, which refers to the society being "the most prominent debating organization" in Stanford.

4. Irwin, *The Making of a Reporter,* 19.

5. The quote is from Boothe, "Ever Hear of Homer Lea?" part 1, 71. In addition to Lea conducting vicarious military campaigns on maps in his room, Newton Cleaveland, a fellow Stanford student, recalled that he also had "a habit of holding solo military maneuvers with imaginary troops dealing with imaginary situations in the hills behind the campus." See Cleaveland, *Bang! Bang!* 24–25. See also Glick, *Double Ten,* 35–36; "Lea's Career That of a Hero of Romance," *New York Sun,* 3. Lea resided in Encina Hall, a two hundred–room male dormitory with accommodation for three hundred men. See Christopher M. Bradley to Charles O. Kates, March 5, 1940, Kates Papers. For a description of Encina Hall, see Robert W. Harwell, "Dormitory Life at Stanford," *San Francisco Chronicle,* April 22, 1900, 31.

6. Boothe, "Ever Hear of Homer Lea?" part 1, 71.

7. Burns, *The American Idea of Mission,* 267–68.

8. "Lea's Career That of a Hero of Romance," 3.

9. "Obituary," *New York Evening Post,* November 2, 1912, 7.

10. Willard Huntington Wright, "Homer Lea Sorely Stricken," *Los Angeles Times,* August 4, 1912, 5:21.

11. "Lea's Career That of a Hero of Romance," 3; *Daily Palo Alto,* May 5, 1898, 5.

12. Hofstadter, *Social Darwinism,* 178; Burns, *The American Idea of Mission,* 262–66.

13. Hofstadter, *Social Darwinism,* 188–89; Bannister, *Social Darwinism,* 232–34.

14. "An End to Chinese Reform," *Washington Post,* September 23, 1898, 7.

15. "Yuan Shih-Kai on the Crisis," *Times* (London), November 21, 1911, 8; "Where Is Kang, China's First Rebel?" *New York Times,* October 30, 1911, 5; Martin, *Strange Vigour,* 74–75; Vare, *The Last Empress,* 181–91; Waley, *The Remaking of China,* 5–9; Fairbank, *The United States and China,* 180–91; Ponce, *Sun Yat-Sen,* 8–12; Jung-Pang Lo, *K'ang Yu-wei,* 125–44; Ting-i Li, *A History of Modern China,* 243–46.

16. Charles F. Riddell to Charles O. Kates, March 4, 1940, Kates Papers; "White Leader of Chinese," *New York Sun,* June 28, 1905, 2; "Lea's Career That of a Hero of Romance," 3; Wright, "Homer Lea Sorely Stricken"; Boothe, "Ever Hear of Homer Lea?" part 1, 71; Stimson, draft article on Homer Lea, untitled, 3, Stimson Papers.

17. Stanford University registrar letter, n.d., box 3, Powers Papers; the

letter notes that Lea's last paper was filed on May 11, 1899. There is also a statement from Dr. Thomas Denison Wood, professor of hygiene and organic training and the university physician. See also J. Mitchell to Charles O. Kates, October 18, 1939, Kates Papers, which cites Dr. Wood's statement. Homer Lea's transcript notes he was granted a leave of absence on May 12, 1899.

18. Clark, statement on Homer Lea; Newmark, *Jottings in Southern California History,* 135; Boothe, "Ever Hear of Homer Lea?" part 1, 71; "A Chinese General from Los Angeles"; Ermal Lea Green to Charles O. Kates, May 7, 1940, Kates Papers; "McLean Hospital," *Los Angeles Times,* July 9, 1899, B3; "Fire Consumes Disease Germs," *San Francisco Chronicle,* July 10, 1899, 7; Jordan to Editor, *Army and Navy Register,* September 2, 1912, folder 20, box 62, David Starr Jordan Papers, Hoover Institution on War, Revolution and Peace, Stanford University, Stanford, Calif. There is no evidence to support Jordan's assertion that Lea was given six months to live in 1899. In his memoirs (*The Days of a Man,* 32), Jordan altered his assertion, writing that Lea "was warned that he had only three months more to live."

19. "A Chinese General from Los Angeles"; Jung-Pang Lo, *K'ang Yu-wei,* 180–88; Armentrout Ma, "Chinese Politics in the Western Hemisphere," 140–41; Armentrout Ma, *Revolutionaries, Monarchists, and Chinatowns,* 45–51.

20. Jung-Pang Lo, *K'ang Yu-wei,* 180–88; Armentrout Ma, "Chinese Politics in the Western Hemisphere," 140–41; Armentrout Ma, *Revolutionaries, Monarchists, and Chinatowns,* 45–51.

21. "A Chinese General from Los Angeles"; Stimson, "True War Predictions by L.A. Boy Who Upset an Empire," B1.

22. Worden, "A Chinese Reformer in Exile," 76–77; Jordan, *The Days of a Man,* 32. See Emma Wilson Lea quote on Homer's claims of kinship with Robert E. Lee in Treanor, "The Home Front."

23. Chen Lusheng to Tom Leung, May 19, 1900, in Larson, "New Source Materials on Kang Youwei and the Baohuanghui," 158–59.

24. "A Chinese General from Los Angeles."

25. Lea checked into the Palace Hotel on Saturday, March 3, 1900. See "Hotel Arrivals," *San Francisco Call,* March 3, 1900, 11. See also "Young Californian Is Plotting to Become Commander-in-Chief of Chinese Rebel Forces," *San Francisco Call,* April 22, 1900, 1. The Pao Huang Hui headquarters was located on Stockton Street, between Jackson and Washington streets. See "With a Band of Music Chinese Greet Leader," *San Francisco Call,* September 26, 1903, 1.

26. Rev. Ng Poon Chew to David Starr Jordan, December 6, 1912, "Homer Lea" folder, box 62, Jordan Papers. Lea also joined one of the most powerful Chinese secret societies in the United States, the Chinese Free Masons, or Chih-kung t'ang. See Armentrout Ma, "Chinese Politics in the Western Hemisphere," 163–64; Armentrout Ma, *Revolutionaries, Monarchists, and Chinatowns,* 59.

27. Boothe, "Ever Hear of Homer Lea?" part 1, 71; "Young Californian Is Plotting to Become Commander-in-Chief of Chinese Rebel Forces."

28. "Lea's Career That of a Hero of Romance," 3.

29. Boothe, "Ever Hear of Homer Lea?" part 1, 71.

30. Carr, *Riding the Tiger*, 169–70.

31. Charles Van Loan, "Homer Lea's Short Life an Inspiration—His Name Will Rank among Immortals," *Los Angeles Examiner*, November 4, 1912, 11; Van Loan, "General Homer Lea," 7.

32. Carr, *Riding the Tiger*, 170–71; Harry Carr, "The Story of Homer Lea," *Los Angeles Times Magazine*, November 15, 1931, 16.

33. Marco Newmark, "Motives behind China Interest 'Destiny'" statement on Homer Lea, untitled folder, box 3, Powers Papers. Newmark, among others, is in error about a Chinese student attending Stanford. The Stanford archivist found no students with Chinese surnames listed in university directories from 1897 to 1899. Chinese servants, however, were employed on campus. See Margaret Kimball, e-mail message to author, October 31, 2007. According to "Homer Lea, Napoleon of China, a San Josean," Lea employed a Chinese servant at Stanford.

34. "Young Californian Is Plotting to Become Commander-in-Chief of Chinese Rebel Forces." For background on Charles "Chinese" Gordon, see Keegan and Wheatcroft, *Who's Who in Military History*, 139.

35. "Young Californian Is Plotting to Become Commander-in-Chief of Chinese Rebel Forces"; "A Chinese General from Los Angeles."

36. "Young Californian Is Plotting to Become Commander-in-Chief of Chinese Rebel Forces."

37. Ibid.

38. Ibid.; "Homer Lea, a Stanford Student, Sails for China with a Big Sum of Money Collected for the Purpose of Raising an Army to Outwit the Dowager Empress," *San Francisco Call*, June 23, 1900, 1.

39. Hsu, *The Rise of Modern China*, 542–44; Schiffrin, *Origins of the Chinese Revolution*, 37–48; Esterer and Esterer, *Sun Yat-Sen*, 131–32.

40. Jansen, *Japan and China*, 169; Martin, *Strange Vigour*, 92; MacNair, *China in Revolution*, 7–9; Hsu, *Sun Yat-sen*, 29–30; Bruce, *Sun Yat-Sen*, 35; "Sun Yat Sen and the Rising, Proposed Return to China," *Times* (London), October 16, 1911, 8.

41. Hsu, *Rise of Modern China*, 460–73; Fairbank, *The United States and China*, 187, 297.

42. Jung-Pang Lo, *K'ang Yu-wei*, 194–97; Esterer and Esterer, *Sun Yat-Sen*, 182; Sun, *Memoirs of a Chinese Revolutionary*, 152–53.

43. Jung-Pang Lo, *K'ang Yu-wei*, 194–97. Word of Lea's plans to raise a contingent of Americans to fight in the uprising probably did filter back to the Pao Huang Hui leadership in Asia. Dr. Yung Wing, a noted reform party member in China, told the British authorities that K'ang Yu-wei expected four hundred seasoned American veterans to join his military forces and fight

for his cause in the uprising. While Lea may have had access to American soldiers of fortune, the logistics, cost, and problems of commanding and integrating such a group into existing Pao Huang Hui plans far exceeded the resources and capabilities of Lea and the San Francisco Pao Huang Hui. See Armentrout Ma, "Chinese Politics in the Western Hemisphere," 163–64.

44. "Homer Lea, a Stanford Student, Sails for China with a Big Sum of Money." For an example of Lea's solicitations of fellow Stanford students to join his military venture in China, see Christopher M. Bradley to Charles O. Kates, March 5, 1940, Kates Papers. Lea sold his cousin William D. Coberly real estate valued at $475; see "Real Estate Transactions," *San Jose Evening News,* May 9, 1900, 2.

45. Christopher M. Bradley to Charles O. Kates, March 5, 1940, Kates Papers; "Homer Lea, a Stanford Student, Sails for China with a Big Sum of Money"; "Going to China to Fight Empress," *New York Herald,* June 24, 1900, 1:4.

46. Gabriel, *The Course of American Democratic Thought,* 339–40. For the good-bye quote see "Lea's Career That of a Hero of Romance," 3; Homer Lea, "How I Was Made a General in the Chinese Army," *San Francisco Call,* April 21, 1901, 1. For the route of the Pacific Mail Steamship Company's steamship *China,* which included stops in Honolulu, Yokohama, Kobe, Nagasaki, Manila, and Hong Kong, see "Will Carry a Large Cargo to the Orient," *San Francisco Call,* May 5, 1906, 7.

47. "Homer Lea, a Stanford Student, Sails for China with a Big Sum of Money."

3. A Don Quixote in China

1. K'ang Yu-wei to Tom Leung, June 27, 1900, in Larson, "New Source Materials on Kang Youwei and the Baohuanghui," 163–64.

2. See Chen Guoyong (Chen Lusheng), Yokohama, Japan, to Zhangziao (Tom Leung), July 25, 1900, in Larson, "New Source Materials on Kang Youwei and the Baohuanghui," 161; postcard, Homer Lea to Ermal Lea, July 15, 1900, James Lea Papers, in which Lea stated he met Dr. Jordan the previous night; Dr. Jordan dates meeting Lea in Nagasaki in 1900, *Days of a Man,* 32. Alfred E. Buck was the envoy extraordinary and minister plenipotentiary in Tokyo; see *Official Congressional Directory for the Use of the United States Congress,* 278.

3. See Homer Lea to Ermal, July 15, 1900, in which Lea stated he was leaving for Shanghai the following day.

4. For Lea seeing K'ang Yu-wei in Singapore, see Chen Guoyong (Chen Lusheng), Yokohama, Japan, to Zhangziao (Tom Leung), July 25, 1900; postcard, "Greetings from Hongkong," Homer Lea to Ermal, n.d., James Lea Papers, in which Lea stated he "will leave for Singapore in a few days"; Tom Chong's statement in Lea, "How I Was Made a General in the Chinese

Army," which claimed Lea traveled from Singapore to Hong Kong some-time during his Asian trip; and Lea's reference to meeting K'ang Yu-wei in "Homer Lee, the Student, Now a Chinese General," *San Francisco Call,* April 9, 1901, 12. For the convening of a Pao Huang Hui war council in Hong Kong and Macao, see "Chinese Reformers Would Aid Allies," *San Francisco Call,* July 31, 1900, 2; and Governor Henry A. Blake to Foreign Office, August 3, 1900, no. 17/1718, 365–66, Foreign Office Records, Public Record Office, Kew, Richmond, Surrey, U.K.

5. "Prominent Chinamen Quarrel," *New York Times,* July 30, 1900, 2; "Wordy War in Chinatown," *Washington Post,* July 30, 1900, 2; "Dispute between Chinamen," *Boston Globe,* July 30, 1900, 5.

6. Governor Henry A. Blake to Foreign Office, August 3, 1900, no. 17/1718, 365–66, Foreign Office Records.

7. Jung-Pang Lo, *K'ang Yu-wei,* 194–97; Worden, "A Chinese Reformer in Exile," 98–103.

8. Petition, Chinese Empire Reform Association to President McKinley, July 18, 1900, Record Group (RG) 59, Miscellaneous Letters of the Department of State, M179, roll 1077, no. 0282, National Archives and Records Administration (hereafter cited as NARA).

9. Jung-Pang Lo, *K'ang Yu-wei,* 186.

10. *Stanford Alumnus,* February 1901, 75; "Emperor's Death May Loosen Revolution," *Los Angeles Examiner,* November 14, 1908, 7; Lea, "How I Was Made a General in the Chinese Army," 1, 3.

11. Lea, "How I Was Made a General in the Chinese Army."

12. The Chinese inscription on the baton reads: "To General Lea, China, Kwangtung Province, the Emperor Kwang Hsu, Year 26, August 13, 1900." The baton, composed of wood with a dark green finish and blued steel fittings, was in the possession of Joshua B. Powers when the author interviewed him at his Manhattan apartment, New York City, June 8–9, 1985. It has since been stripped of its green and blued finishes and is currently in the possession of the Lea family, South Royalton, Vermont. Lea may have received a commission document making him a lieutenant general. Robert J. Belford, Lea's friend, claimed knowledge of such a document, although he mistook Lea's rank to be a major general: "I have time and again read the document that confers on Homer Lea the office of major-general in the reform army of China." See Belford, "A Cowardly Attack," *Los Angeles Times,* July 19, 1911, 2:6.

13. Jung-Pang Lo, *K'ang Yu-wei,* 187; Armentrout Ma, "Chinese Politics in the Western Hemisphere," 182–83; Worden, "A Chinese Reformer in Exile," 100–107; Chapin, "Homer Lea and the Chinese Revolution," 20–23; "Viceroys Appeal to America," *New York Times,* August 12, 1900, 2; "Disturbance on the Yangtze," *Chicago Daily Tribune,* August 13, 1900, 2; "Tatung Riots Not Anti-foreign," *Chicago Daily Tribune,* August 17, 1900, 2.

14. "Emperor's Death May Loosen Revolution"; "Homer Lea," *Book-*

man, April 1908, 130; "Chinese Gathering to Attack Pekin," *Chicago Daily Tribune,* August 27, 1900, 5; "12 Conspirators Beheaded," *Boston Globe,* August 28, 1900, 2; "Reformers Prepare to Rise," *New York Times,* August 30, 1900, 2.

15. "Homer Lea," *Bookman.*

16. Ibid. The *Bookman* article indicated there reportedly were twenty thousand reform troops at Hankow.

17. "Empire Maker Seeks Health," *Los Angeles Times,* May 8, 1912, 2:11; see also Harry Carr's reference to the same episode in "Death Overpowers Odd World Figure."

18. Jung-Pang Lo, *K'ang Yu-wei,* 187; Carr, "Death Overpowers Odd World Figure"; Thomas, *Born to Raise Hell,* 175–77. For Lea's travels in China, see Lea, "How I Was Made a General in the Chinese Army"; Van Loan, "General Homer Lea," 7.

19. O'Reilly, *Roving and Fighting,* 232.

20. RG 59, Consular Correspondence of the Department of State, Dispatches from U.S. Consuls in Canton, China, 1790–1906, October–December 1900, M101, roll 4, NARA. See also reference to a memento Lea picked up on the Po-Lo battlefield in Harrison Gray Otis to Homer Lea, May 24, 1909, box 1, Powers Papers; and postcard, "Greetings from Canton," Homer Lea to Ermal, n.d., James Lea Papers, in which Lea stated, "Arrived here today from the Interior. This place is expecting to be attacked at any hour."

21. Lea, "How I Was Made a General in the Chinese Army."

22. Ibid.; "Chinese General a Stanford Man," *San Francisco Examiner,* April 9, 1901, 4.

23. "Reformers Are Badly Beaten," *San Francisco Call,* November 25, 1900, 1; "Chinese Reformers Lose Fifteen Hundred Men in a Treacherous Ambush," *San Francisco Call,* December 26, 1900, 1; "Massacre of Reformers," *Washington Post,* December 26, 1900, 1; Consular Dispatches, Canton, October–December 1900, NARA.

24. Lea's escaping China disguised as a Frenchman is attributed to Hersa Lea. See Houghton, statement on Homer Lea.

25. Irwin, quoted in "Lea's Career That of a Hero of Romance," 3.

26. Irwin, *The Making of a Reporter,* 19.

27. Carr, "Death Overpowers Odd World Figure," 1.

28. Clare Boothe, "The Valor of Homer Lea," introduction to Homer Lea, *The Valor of Ignorance,* 16–17; Van Loan, "General Homer Lea," 7. Although their respective reports contain errors, both Boothe and Van Loan place Lea in Hong Kong sometime after leaving China.

29. According to K. Aishi to Homer Lea, January 11, 1901, box 1, Powers Papers, Lea stayed at the Grand Hotel in Yokohama. For Lea's claim to having met Baron Yamagata, see "Gloomy Foreboding of Gen. Homer Lea," *Los Angeles Times,* February 9, 1908, 2:1; Lea, "How I Was Made a General in the Chinese Army," 1, 3; Jung-Pang Lo, *K'ang Yu-wei,* 178–79; Worden,

"A Chinese Reformer in Exile," 63; Jansen, *The Japanese and Sun Yat-Sen*, 78.

30. Lea, "How I Was Made a General in the Chinese Army," 1, 3.

31. Marshall Stimson claimed to have seen letters Marquis Ito wrote to Lea. See Stimson, "A Los Angeles Jeremiah," 5. Ito reportedly helped Liang Ch'i-ch'ao, a cofounder of the Pao Huang Hui, escape arrest in China for safe haven in Japan in 1898. See "A Chinese Reformer," *New York Tribune*, April 28, 1901, 3.

32. For the quote, see "Oriental Notes," *Hawaiian Gazette*, May 31, 1901, 3. See also "Homer Lee, the Student, Now a Chinese General," 12.

4. General without an Army

1. For a list of hotel arrivals, see *San Francisco Call*, April 7, 1901, 25.

2. "Homer Lee, the Student, Now a Chinese General," 12; "Chinese General a Stanford Man," 4; "Plans to Do Big Things in China," *San Francisco Chronicle*, April 9, 1901, 2. For a reprint of the *Examiner* article ("Chinese General a Stanford Man"), see the *Santa Cruz Surf*, April 9, 1901, 1.

3. "Homer Lee, the Student, Now a Chinese General."

4. "Chinese General a Stanford Man."

5. "A Chinese General from Los Angeles."

6. Ibid.

7. Ibid.

8. Armentrout Ma, "Chinese Politics in the Western Hemisphere," 160–61, 197–98; Armentrout Ma, *Revolutionaries, Monarchists, and Chinatowns*, 71–83.

9. Irwin, *The Making of a Reporter*, 19–20.

10. K'ang Yu-wei to Tom Leung, July 5, 1901, in Larson, "New Source Materials on Kang Youwei and the Baohuanghui," 166–67.

11. Carr, "Death Overpowers Odd World Figure."

12. Marco Newmark, "After Return from China (First Visit)," statement on Homer Lea, untitled folder, box 3, Powers Papers.

13. Lea, "How I Was Made a General in the Chinese Army," 1.

14. Ermal Lea Green, "Anecdotes," circa April 1942, 2, James Lea Papers.

15. "Empire Maker Seeks Health"; Carr, "Death Overpowers Odd World Figure"; Marco Newmark, "At Westlake Park," statement on Homer Lea, untitled folder, box 3, Powers Papers; Houghton, statement on Homer Lea; Glick, *Double Ten*, 220.

16. Emma Lea, quoted in Treanor, "The Home Front."

17. Newmark, *Jottings in Southern California History*, 138–39.

18. Armentrout Ma, "Chinese Politics in the Western Hemisphere," 55, 204–6; Armentrout Ma, *Revolutionaries, Monarchists, and Chinatowns*, 82–83.

19. O'Banion's reference to Lea writing the Army of the War Department

cannot be verified in existing U.S. Army records. Such correspondence likely would have gone to the adjutant general. There is no record of Lea's correspondence in the Records of the Adjutant General's Office, RG 94, NARA, nor is there a record group for an auditor of the War Department. The correspondence is referenced in Glick, *Double Ten,* 21–23, 27.

20. Ibid., 12, 21–24.

21. Ibid., 22.

22. Ibid.

23. Ibid.

24. Carr, "Death Overpowers Odd World Figure"; "Honors for Liang Chao," *Los Angeles Express,* October 21, 1903, 3. On August 6, 1903, the same day Lea wrote President Roosevelt, representatives of the Chinese Empire Reform Association's New York branch telegraphed the State Department asking for American support of the reform news editors; see RG 59, Miscellaneous Letters of the Department of State, August 1–11, 1903, M179, roll 1180, NARA.

25. "Silken Robes to Be Worn," *Los Angeles Times,* October 21, 1903, 3; "Occident and Orient Feast," *Los Angeles Times,* October 24, 1903, 7; "Real Chinese Feast, All Native Viands," *Los Angeles Times,* October 25, 1903, 8; "He Voiced a Nation's Woe," *Los Angeles Times,* October 30, 1903, 4; "Pay Official Call," *Los Angeles Times,* October 31, 1903, 2; "Surprise by Wong Whuy," *Los Angeles Times,* November 1, 1903, C11; "Honors for Liang Chao," *Los Angeles Express;* "Chinese Reformer Here," *Los Angeles Express,* October 22, 1903, 1; "Leung with Friends," *Los Angeles Express,* October 24, 1903, 5; "Leung Is Well Pleased," *Los Angeles Express,* October 29, 1903, 11; "Greeted Leung Ki Chu," *Los Angeles Express,* October 30, 1903, 12; "Leong Kai Cheu Formally Welcomed by Municipal Officials and Citizens," *Los Angeles Herald,* October 23, 1903, 3; "Banquet Given Leong Kai Cheu," *Los Angeles Herald,* October 24, 1903, 8; "Banqueted by His Old Classmate," *Los Angeles Herald,* October 25, 1903, 11; "Merchants Greet Liang Chi Chao," *Los Angeles Herald,* October 30, 1903, 11.

26. For background information on Liang Ch'i-ch'ao, see Hao Chang, *Liang Ch'i-ch'ao and the Intellectual Transition in China 1890–1907;* Huang, *Liang Ch'i-ch'ao and Modern Chinese Liberalism.*

27. "Leung Kai Chow's Mission," *New York Tribune,* March 7, 1903, 7.

28. Armentrout Ma, "Chinese Politics in the Western Hemisphere," 20, 62, 233–34; Armentrout Ma, *Revolutionaries, Monarchists, and Chinatowns,* 89–92; "Respects to President," *Boston Globe,* June 21, 1903, 2.

29. Armentrout Ma, "Chinese Politics in the Western Hemisphere," 235–37. "Consul General and Reformers," *New York Tribune,* July 30, 1900, 3, reported allegations made by the Chinese imperial consul general in San Francisco with regard to the Pao Huang Hui's practice of selling commissions and titles. According to the consul general, the reform party "proclaims that any one contributing $100 to the Reform Association fund

shall be made a general; any one contributing $1,000 shall be made a vice-roy, and that any one giving $10,000 shall be made a prince of the royal blood." George B. Cortelyou, Secretary to the President, to Alvey A. Adee, Assistant Secretary of State, September 7, 1900; see enclosure, letter from R. A. Falkenberg to President McKinley, signed R. A. Falkenberg, General C. E. R. A. August 31, 1900, RG 59, Miscellaneous Letters of the Department of State, M179, roll 1081, no. 0307, NARA.

30. The *1910 United States Census* cites Falkenberg's estimated dates of birth and birthplace, series T624, roll 101, part 1, 106B, http://www.ancestry .com/. Falkenberg's early days in Los Angeles as a miner and amateur boxer known as Captain Dick were the subject of several news articles: see "Capt. Dick's Story," *Los Angeles Times*, March 25, 1892, 2; "Attempted Assassination," *Los Angeles Times*, April 18, 1892, 2; "Capt. Dick's Romance," *Los Angeles Times*, November 25, 1892, 9; "Capt. Dick's Whereabouts," *Los Angeles Times*, November 26, 1892, 4; "Capt. Dick's Latest Freak," *Los Angeles Times*, December 4, 1892, 4; "Sporting Notes," *Los Angeles Times*, November 12, 1894, 8; "Says It Is an Untruth," *Los Angeles Times*, November 14, 1894, 8; "Sporting Gossip," *Los Angeles Times*, November 19, 1894, 3; "A Rough and Tumble," *Los Angeles Times*, November 21, 1894, 7; "Prof. 'Billy' Biffs 'Joot,'" *Los Angeles Times*, May 7, 1905, 3:3.

31. The January 29, 1891, *New York Tribune* article and related U.S. diplomatic correspondence are cited in *Papers Relating to the Foreign Relations of the United States*, 83–89.

32. Capt. R. A. Falkenberg to War Department, December 6, 1893; First Endorsement, William J. Volkmar, Assistant Adjutant General, to Commanding Officer, Seventh Cavalry Regiment, December 15, 1893; Second Endorsement, First Lieut. J. F. Bell, Adjutant, Seventh Cavalry, to Capt. Charles A. Varnum, Seventh Cavalry, December 27, 1893; Third Endorsement, Capt. Charles A. Varnum, Seventh Cavalry, to Adjutant, Seventh Cavalry, December 30, 1893; Final Endorsement, Assistant Adjutant General, February 5, 1894, all in RG 94, Records of the Adjutant General's Office (hereafter cited as AGO Records), War Department, no. 20754, NARA; Capt. R. A. Falkenberg to War Department, January 25, 1894, RG 94, AGO Records, no. 1819, NARA; William J. Volkmar, Assistant Adjutant General, to R. A. Falkenberg, February 6, 1894, RG 94, AGO Records, no. 20754, NARA; Capt. R. A. Falkenberg to William J. Volkmar, Assistant Adjutant General, February 13, 1894, and Adjutant General's Office Endorsement, February 3, 1894, RG 94, AGO Records, no. 2924, NARA. The above correspondence is all filed with no. 20754.

33. Capt. R. A. Falkenberg to William J. Volkmar, Assistant Adjutant General, February 13, 1894.

34. Letters of R. A. Falkenberg to President McKinley, March 7, 1899, April 24, 1899, June 1, 1899, and June 23, 1899, RG 94, AGO Records, no. 223380, NARA. The March 7, 1899, and June 1, 1899, letters were origi-

nally in file no. 235372 and are filed with file no. 223380, which contains Falkenberg-related correspondence. For additional information on Falkenberg's alleged background, see "Army Has Hopes," *Portland Oregonian,* August 27, 1905, 9.

35. In one instance Falkenberg arranged to send a telegram to Secretary of War Elihu Root's home allegedly signed by seven prominent Californians, including U.S. senator George C. Perkins. This telegram recommended him highly in light of his service as a major with the First Regiment, South California Volunteer Cavalry during the Spanish-American War, but the telegram was unclear regarding exactly what type of service Falkenberg had performed. When the War Department examined Falkenberg's implied claims further, it discovered he had no legitimate war service, and concluded after consulting with Senator Perkins, who did not know him, that he had fraudulently used the names of the prominent Californians in the telegram to Root. Perkins advised the War Department that one of the telegram's signers, Congressman Russell J. Waters, did endorse Falkenberg. See Capt. R. A. Falkenberg to George B. Cortelyou, July 18, 1899; Adjutant General H. C. Corbin to Senator George C. Perkins, August 30, 1899; Senator George Perkins to H. C. Corbin, August 30, 1899, RG 94, AGO Records, no. 223380, NARA.

36. Mrs. R. A. Von Falkenberg to War Department, November 4, 1899, RG 94, AGO Records, no. 292577, NARA; Assistant Adjutant General John S. Johnson, War Department, to Mrs. Von Falkenberg, December 4, 1899, RG 94, AGO Records, no. 292577, NARA. This correspondence is filed with file no. 223380, which contains Falkenberg-related correspondence.

37. Maj. R. A. Falkenberg to Secretary of War Root, November 1, 1899, RG 94, no. 223380, NARA.

38. Secretary of War Private Secretary to Maj. R. A. Falkenberg, November 8, 1899, RG 94, no. 266040, NARA.

39. Representative R. J. Waters to Secretary of War Root, August 10, 1900, RG 94, no. 338997, NARA; Adjutant General to R. J. Waters, August 16, 1900, RG 94, AGO Records, no. 338997, NARA.

40. "Consul General and Reformers."

41. General R. A. Falkenberg to President McKinley, August 27, 1900, RG 59, Miscellaneous Letters of the Department of State, M179, roll 1081, nos. 0308–16, NARA.

42. Ibid.

43. General R. A. Falkenberg to Secretary of State Hay, October 6, 1900, RG 59, Miscellaneous Letters of the Department of State, M179, roll 1084, nos. 0327–29, NARA.

44. Armentrout Ma, "Chinese Politics in the Western Hemisphere," 197–98; Worden, "A Chinese Reformer in Exile," 104.

45. Major R. A. Falkenberg to Governor Pardee, January 23, 1903, folder 8, box 25, George C. Pardee Papers, Bancroft Library, University of California, Berkeley.

46. Governor Pardee to R. A. Falkenberg (unsigned copy), January 26, 1903, folder 7, box 86, Pardee Papers.

47. Governor Pardee to Col. R. A. Falkenberg (unsigned copy), July 21, 1903, folder 8, box 92, Pardee Papers.

48. Major R. A. Falkenberg to Governor George C. Pardee, July 27, 1903, folder 8, box 25, Pardee Papers. For background of the Standard Rock Oil Company, which was incorporated in Arizona on April 17, 1901, see "Articles of Incorporation of the 'Standard Rock Oil Company,'" *Tucson Daily Citizen*, May 10, 1901, 3; Standard Rock Oil Company, "Asphaltum Refinery Bulletin No. 2," San Francisco, Calif., November 29, 1901, author's files; "Certificate of Increase of Capital Stock," *Tucson Daily Citizen*, August 22, 1902, 7; and Board of Directors, Standard Rock Oil Company, "Annual Statement of the Standard Rock Oil Company and Manager's Report," May 21, 1903, author's files.

49. Major R. A. Falkenberg to Governor George C. Pardee, July 27, 1903, Pardee Papers.

50. Ibid. Governor Pardee's private secretary acknowledged receipt of Falkenberg's letter, but there was no further correspondence on the matter. See Governor Pardee Private Secretary to Col. R. A. Falkenberg, July 28, 1903, folder 10, box 92, Pardee Papers.

51. Liang Ch'i-ch'ao arrived in San Francisco on September 25, 1903. See "With a Band of Music Chinese Greet Leader," 3; "Chinese Reformer Arrives," *New York Times*, September 26, 1903, 6. For Falkenberg's military ties, see "Falkenberg's Crown Badly Tilted," *San Francisco Chronicle*, April 3, 1905, 4. For the banquet being on October 5, see "Banquet Given to Leong Cheu," *San Francisco Call*, October 6, 1903, 9. For Falkenberg's alliance with Dr. T'an Shu-pin, see "Recruiting Army to Reform China: Americans Banding Subjects of Flowery Kingdom Together in All Large Cities," *Pittsburg Dispatch*, February 5, 1905, 2:2.

52. The first news articles mentioning Falkenberg as a reform army general appeared in 1905.

53. "Leong Kai Cheu Formally Welcomed by Municipal Officials and Citizens."

54. "Chinese Reformer Here." See also "Leong Kai Cheu Formally Welcomed by Municipal Officials and Citizens"; and "Mayor of Los Angeles Greets Chinese Reformer," *San Francisco Call*, October 23, 1903, 5.

55. See "Banquet Given Leong Kai Cheu"; "Banqueted by His Old Classmate"; "Merchants Greet Liang Chi Chao"; "Leung with Friends"; "Leung Is Well Pleased"; "Greeted Leung Ki Chu"; "Occident and Orient Feast"; "Real Chinese Feast, All Native Viands"; "He Voiced a Nation's Woe."

56. "Leung with Friends"; "Leung Is Well Pleased."

57. "Surprise by Wong Whuy."

58. "Banquet Given to Leong Cheu."

59. For information concerning the Commercial Corporation, see Armen-

trout Ma, "Chinese Politics in the Western Hemisphere," 204–6; Armentrout Ma, *Revolutionaries, Monarchists, and Chinatowns*, 82–83; 109–12.

60. For Liang Ch'i-ch'ao's itinerary after leaving Los Angeles, see Armentrout Ma, *Revolutionaries, Monarchists, and Chinatowns*, 93. The Pao Huang Hui filed articles of incorporation in Los Angeles on December 8, 1903; see "Reform Society: Chinese Organize One," *Los Angeles Times*, December 9, 1903, 2.

5. The Imperial Reform Army

1. See excerpt from George W. West diary for his involvement with Lea in Eline West to Lee Shippey, April 4, 1945, A. E. O'Banion, 1945–1950 Correspondence, box 1, Carl Glick Papers, University of Iowa, University Libraries, Iowa City; and Lee Shippey, "Leeside," *Los Angeles Times*, April 10, 1945, 4.

2. See "Welcome to a Member of the Royal Family of China," *San Francisco Chronicle*, April 18, 1904, 14, which indicates the San Francisco military company was established in March 1904; and see "Why Drilling of Chinese?" *Los Angeles Times*, May 18, 1904, 1, for the first public references to Lea's cadets in San Francisco and Los Angeles.

3. "To Revivify the Old China," *Los Angeles Times*, January 3, 1904, 5. The solid gold medal, which was in the private collection of Joshua Powers, is suspended from a ribbon with red, white, and blue vertical stripes. Its actual translated inscription reads: "To Comrade General Lea, Loyalty & Honesty, the comrades of this association gives this medal to General Lea."

4. R. A. Falkenberg to Governor George Pardee, February 17, 1904, folder 8, box 25, Pardee Papers. Falkenberg misspelled Wong Kim as Wong Kin. Most of Wong Kim's cadets were American-born Chinese. They had a drill hall and armory at 719 and 721 Sacramento Street. See "Will the Great Chinese Revolution Begin in San Francisco?" *San Francisco Chronicle*, March 6, 1904, 4. For reference to the Shueng Mo Hok Tong Military Association and Falkenberg's affiliation with it, see "All Chinatown Hold Feasts," *San Francisco Call*, June 18, 1904, 2.

5. Governor Pardee's private secretary responded to Falkenberg that his request was being referred to the state adjutant general. There is no further correspondence in the file relating to Falkenberg's request. See Pardee Private Secretary to R. A. Falkenberg, February 21, 1904, folder 2, box 97, Pardee Papers. Anschel, *Homer Lea, Sun Yat-Sen and the Chinese Revolution*, 53–54, 229, asserts that Falkenberg also sought the governor's permission to organize a National Guard company of "American Born Chinese Military Cadets" in a May 7, 1904, petition he drew up that had about forty signatures, including the imperial Chinese consul general, the vice consul general, and several American professional and businessmen. There is no record, however, of the petition correspondence in the Pardee Papers.

6. "Welcome to a Member of the Royal Family of China," 4. See also "He Spends the Day Viewing Wonders of the Great City, and Expresses Amazement—Leaves for the East," *San Francisco Chronicle,* April 19, 1904, 16, for a summary of events covering the prince's first day in the city.

7. "Welcome to a Member of the Royal Family of China."

8. See West's diary entry in Eline West to Lee Shippey, April 4, 1945; and Shippey, "Leeside."

9. "Why Drilling of Chinese?"

10. Ibid.

11. For information on West and Dessery's business partnership, see West's obituary in "Two Killed in Fearful Fall," *Los Angeles Times,* October 26, 1912, 2:1. For Dessery's war service, see a reference to his being a private in H Battery, Third U.S. Artillery in "Our Boys," *Los Angeles Times,* March 4, 1899, 8.

12. "Want Yankees to Drill Them," *San Francisco Call,* July 10, 1904, 40. See also 'Chinese," *Los Angeles Times,* July 10, 1904, 3; and "Discuss Offer of Army Posts," *San Francisco Call,* July 11, 1904, 4.

13. See West's diary entry in Eline West to Lee Shippey, April 4, 1945; and Shippey, "Leeside," which noted on July 7, 1904, that the company was outfitted with "uniforms ill fitting and not too good material."

14. Lea enlisted several members of the National Guard First Brigade Signal Corps. See Harvey Waterman and [Eugene] Griffes, "Reform Cadets," statement on Homer Lea, box 3, Powers Papers.

15. Ibid.

16. Ibid. Waterman also recalled that some British officers were interested in the cadet training and conferred with Lea. Eugene Griffes related the following conversation he had with John York about Lea meeting with British officers: "One incident he [York] mentioned which aroused the curiosity of L.A. was Lea accompanied by two high rank British naval officers, with York boarded—or left a British gun boat at San Pedro harbor & three salutes were fired and much curiosity was aroused just who they were for." See Eugene V. Griffes to Charles O. Kates, December 19, 1939, Kates Papers.

17. Chapin, "Homer Lea and the Chinese Revolution," 41–42; West's final diary entry, referenced in Eline West to Lee Shippey, April 4, 1945, and Shippey, "Leeside," is on July 27, 1904. O'Banion's memory of the chronology of events forty years after the fact again offers a flawed reconstruction. He claimed to join Lea in the summer of 1903, when it is more likely he joined Lea in the summer of 1904. See Glick, *Double Ten,* 25–26, 46.

18. Glick, *Double Ten,* 50–57, 72.

19. Ibid. O'Banion received his deputy sheriff appointment in May 1905. See "Tuesday Topics," *Norfolk Weekly News-Journal* (Nebraska), May 26, 1905, 6.

20. Glick, *Double Ten,* 62–67.

21. For Schreiber's and Nerney's role in the CIA, see Chapin, "Homer

Lea and the Chinese Revolution," 40–41, 115. For Schreiber's National Guard duties, see "Serious Row in the Militia," *San Francisco Call*, January 1906, 14. For Thomas Nerney's affiliation with the naval militia, see "Men Discharged from the Guard," *San Francisco Call*, October 4, 1903, 31. For recruitment of National Guard Signal Corps personnel, see Eugene V. Griffes to Charles O. Kates, December 7, 1939.

22. See Articles of Incorporation of the Western Military Academy, filed November 28, 1904, in the Secretary of State, California State Archives, Sacramento; Glick, *Double Ten*, 67.

23. O'Banion later noted that the board of directors did not know the true purpose of the school, but believed its support could lead to financial concessions in China. He also noted that York served as the academy's attorney. See "Original Notes for Double Ten," Double Ten folder, box 3, Glick Papers. Roger Page is cited as a high school classmate of Lea's in "Thirtynine Harvests; Garnered Bloom Again," *Los Angeles Times*, June 29, 1913, 19. See also Chapin, "Homer Lea and the Chinese Revolution," 34; Glick, *Double Ten*, 59–68; Frederic Chapin to Charles Kates (circa October 1948, on Stanford letterhead,), Kates Papers.

24. Glick, *Double Ten*, 61–62.

25. Ibid.

26. "To Open up a Chinese School in the Windy City," *La Crosse Tribune*, December 2, 1904, 7. On Wan Chew, the editor in chief of the Chineselanguage *Chicago World* newspaper published in San Francisco, claimed to be an organizer of the Chicago cadet company and told a journalist that the company was part of an army expected to number five thousand that could eventually see service in China. He also explained that one of the Chicago company's goals was to provide "athletic exercise" to "the merchants of our race"; see "Chicago Chinese to Drill," *Dallas Morning News*, September 11, 1904, 17.

27. Chapin, "Homer Lea and the Chinese Revolution," 115–16; Glick, *Double Ten*, 66–77; Marquis, *Who's Who in America*, 1129; "Drill Nucleus Here for Chinese Army," *New York Times*, January 22, 1905, 16. There also was a cadet company in Butte, Montana; see "Chinese Are Drilling Like Old Hands at It," *Anaconda Standard* (Montana), August 25, 1905, 1; and "Chinese Reform Party Is Going to Spokane," *Anaconda Standard* (Montana), September 30, 1905, 7. According to "Chinese Drilling in All Countries," *Washington Times*, June 19, 1905, 3, there were reportedly cadet companies in New Orleans, Omaha, and Ogden.

28. For U.S. Army pay scales of the period, see Adjutant General's Office, War Department, *Official Army Register for 1904*, 536.

29. Glick, *Double Ten*, 63; see also CIA uniform regulations and prices in General Orders no. 8, November 1, 1904, box 3, Powers Papers.

30. Glick, *Double Ten*, 222; see also photos of O'Banion drilling cadets at the Sunset and Vermont property on December 19, 1904, in Scrapbook no. 68026-8M.02, Powers Papers.

31. Lea referred to cynical news stories about his school in "Not a Queue in the Line," *Los Angeles Times,* December 31, 1904, 6; Glick, *Double Ten,* 117–18.

32. Adjutant General J. B. Lauck to Roger S. Page, Secretary, Western Military Academy, December 18, 1904, box 3, Powers Papers.

33. "Not a Queue in the Line"; Glick, *Double Ten,* 101.

34. "Flags and Flowers, Throngs and Glory," *Los Angeles Times,* January 3, 1905, 2:1; "Envoy Wong Comes to See," *Los Angeles Times,* January 4, 1905, 2:1. For a biographical background of Envoy Wong Kai Kah, see "Social Advent of the Wongs in America," *Washington Times,* October 11, 1903, 6.

35. "Flags and Flowers, Throngs and Glory." The *Los Angeles Herald* described the cadets' participation as the "crowning feature of the parade," but mistakenly identified them as Japanese. See "Rose Festival Draws Thousands," *Los Angeles Herald,* January 3, 1905, 1.

6. The Falkenberg Comedy

1. "Envoy Wong Comes to See."

2. Glick, *Double Ten,* 112–16; "To Overturn China's Throne," *Chicago American,* December 28, 1904, 1; "Conspiracy against Throne of China: Plot to Slay Chinese Princess," *Chicago American,* December 29, 1904, 1; "Armory in Race St. for Chinese Revolutionists," *Philadelphia Inquirer,* December 28, 1904, 1–2.

3. See "Americans for Chinese Army," *New York Times,* May 15, 1904, 2; and "Yankee Officers Sought to Serve in Chinese Army," *Atlanta Constitution,* May 15, 1904, 4.

4. For reference to ranks and positions of Falkenberg, Parmentier, and English, see Parmentier to Secretary of State Hay, July 1, 1904, RG 59, Miscellaneous Letters of the Department of State, I, M179, roll 1216, nos. 0047–52, NARA; Glick, *Double Ten,* 139; "Whose Army Falkenberg's?" *Los Angeles Times,* March 30, 1905, 2:1. For biographical information on Fernand Parmentier, see *Press Reference Library: Notables of the Southwest,* 286; *One Thousand American Men of Mark,* 231; "Loved Soldier Slain by Turk," *Los Angeles Times,* January 25, 1916, 2:1. English, a real estate dealer, also was commander of the local Grand Army of the Republic Civil War veteran's organization and a brigadier general in the state's Union Veteran's Union. For English's background, see "Yankton Man Grows Famous," *Omaha World Herald,* May 14, 1904, 7; for English's prior affiliation with Falkenberg, see R. A. Falkenberg to President McKinley, April 24, 1899, NARA; for English commanding the CIRA Cavalry Division, see "Headquarters Cavalry Div" letterhead in Edmond F. English to Cary T. Ray, August 12, 1904, CIRA folder, Cary T. Ray Papers, Chicago History Museum. For Falkenberg soliciting contributions from his officers, see "Falkenberg's Crown Badly Tilted."

5. "China Gets Local Men," *Bellingham Herald*, April 28, 1905, 1; "Americans Will Serve in China," *San Francisco Call*, May 7, 1904, 1; "Americans for Chinese Army," *New York Sun*, May 14, 1904, 1; "Going to China," *Aberdeen Daily News* (South Dakota), May 14, 1904, 4; "Americans for Chinese Army," *New York Times*, May 15, 1904, 2; "Prince Pu Lun Wants Americans for Army," *Washington Times*, May 15, 1904, 6; "Yankee Officers Sought to Serve in Chinese Army"; "Recruiting Americans," *San Francisco Call*, May 24, 1904, 3; "Chinese Reform Army Is Seeking Recruits," *Washington Times*, May 29, 1904, 5. English told a journalist on May 19 that Prince Pu Lun had "nothing to do" with his recruiting effort, and issued a subsequent statement on May 31 that he had received no orders from Prince Pu Lun sanctioning his recruiting efforts. See "American Soldiers Wanted by the Chinese," *Tucson Daily Citizen*, May 19, 1904, 1; and "Chinese Reform Army," *Aberdeen Daily News* (South Dakota), June 2, 1904, 6. For an interview English gave in November that highlighted some of his recruiting endeavors, see W. R. R., "Dowager Empress Wants Some Western Ideas," *Omaha World Herald*, November 6, 1904, 14.

6. "No Jobs Are Open in Chinese Army," *Washington Times*, May 13, 1904, 3.

7. Chentung Liang Cheng to Secretary of State Hay, May 25, 1904, RG 59, Notes from the Chinese Legation in the U.S. to Department of State, 1868–1906, M98, roll 6, no. 125, NARA. See also "Chinese Imperial Reform Army a Myth," *San Francisco Chronicle*, May 30, 1904, 4.

8. Chentung Liang Cheng to Secretary of State Hay, May 25, 1904; Chapin, "Homer Lea and the Chinese Revolution," 61. For an example of an American militia officer serving with the imperial Chinese army in China, see "Will Instruct Chinese Forces," *San Francisco Chronicle*, April 11, 1904, 3.

9. E. H. Conger to Secretary of State Hay, June 24, 1904, RG 59, Dispatches from U.S. Ministers to China, 1843–1906, M92, roll 126, no. 1642, NARA.

10. For a representative correspondence between English and a prospective CIRA officer, see Edmond F. English to Cary T. Ray, August 12, 1904, Ray Papers; Edmond F. English to Cary T. Ray, August 22, 1904, CIRA folder, Ray Papers. See also "Georgia Officer in Chinese Army," *Atlanta Constitution*, February 21, 1906, 3.

11. "Falkenberg's Crown Badly Tilted."

12. Parmentier to Hay, July 1, 1904, RG 59, NARA.

13. Ibid.

14. "Pig-tailed Warriors Go through Maneuvers," *San Francisco Call*, July 25, 1904, 5.

15. "For Revolution in China," *New York Sun*, November 14, 1904, 1. See also "China Seeks Drill Masters," *San Francisco Call*, October 14, 1904, 4; "Officers for Reform Army," *Washington Post*, November 25, 1904, 1.

16. Publicity surrounding Falkenberg's CIRA spread throughout 1905 among members of the U.S. Army, state national guards, and other American military organizations, whose members wrote U.S. consuls in China seeking to join a soon-to-be-formed CIRA. The State Department advised the applicants to have nothing to do with "any such scheme." See "Would Go to War: Oregon Militia Officers to Join Chinese Army," *Portland Oregonian,* November 24, 1904, 10; "A Warning to Americans," *New York Tribune,* January 20, 1906, 2.

17. "Chinese Reform Plan," *Washington Post,* January 8, 1905, E12. The article also included references to several of Falkenberg's associates:

> Working actively with Gen. Falkenberg in this great reform movement to rehabilitate China, are many prominent Americans, who hold important positions on his staff.
>
> The Intelligence Department, which is really the most important office in the general staff, was turned over by the commanding general to that noteworthy American officer, Lieut. Gen. Fernand Parmentier, who is conceded to be a clever tactician, well versed in all departments of the army, but whom Gen. Falkenberg considers a military genius and a Napoleon in artillery and engineer branches of the service.
>
> Gen. Parmentier holds the office of chief of staff and adjutant general besides, though only a trifle over forty years of age.
>
> Brig. Gen. George B. Cole, now of Seattle, Wash., ex–United States Commissioner of California, and a true friend of the reformers, is judge advocate general, and Col. R. R. Rogers has charge of the ordnance department.

18. "To Overturn China's Throne"; "Armory in Race St. for Chinese Revolutionists."

19. Wilkie likely visited Los Angeles in early 1905, despite O'Banion's later recollection that Wilkie visited Los Angeles in midsummer 1905 and conferred with Lea; Lea at that time was traveling with K'ang Yu-wei and could not have been present. See "Original Notes for Double Ten," Double Ten folder, box 3, Glick Papers; Glick, *Double Ten,* 120–21; Major George Gibbs to General Lea, January 6, 1905, box 1, Powers Papers.

20. Glick, *Double Ten,* 122–24. Wilkie may have whitewashed his investigation into the Western Military Academy on instruction from President Roosevelt. See Frederic Chapin to Charles Kates, November 5, 1948, Kates Papers. A search of Secret Service records in the National Archives and Records Administration revealed no information on Wilkie's investigation.

21. Glick, *Double Ten,* 124–25.

22. Ah Mow, the deceased, was a staunch Pao Huang Hui supporter; see "Weird Rites for Ah Mow," *Los Angeles Times,* January 20, 1905, 2:1; "Ah

Mow Buried with Pomp," *Los Angeles Herald,* January 20, 1905, 1–2; and "Only Son to China's Cause," *Los Angeles Times,* June 23, 1905, 2:5.

23. Jung-Pang Lo, *Kang Yu-wei,* 195–98; Worden, "A Chinese Reformer in Exile," 109–20.

24. "Kong Yu Wei Comes Today," *Los Angeles Times,* March 13, 1905, 3; Glick, *Double Ten,* 126.

25. "Kong Yu Wei Long on Way," *Los Angeles Times,* March 14, 1905, 2:10; "Mr. Kong Storm-Bound," *Los Angeles Times,* March 15, 1905, 2:1; "Chinese Reformer Here," *Los Angeles Times,* March 16, 1905, 2:8; "Cannot Locate Kang Yu Wei," *Los Angeles Express,* March 14, 1905, 11; "Kang Yu Wei Finally Reaches Los Angeles," *Los Angeles Express,* March 15, 1905, 2; "Chinese Reformer Stormbound at Bakersfield," *Los Angeles Examiner,* March 15, 1905, 6; "Secretary Formerly High in Councils of Chinese Emperor Comes to Investigate Conditions," *Los Angeles Examiner,* March 16, 1905, 6.

26. "Kang Yu Wei Finally Reaches Los Angeles"; "Secretary Formerly High in Councils of Chinese Emperor Comes to Investigate Conditions."

27. "Secretary Formerly High in Councils of Chinese Emperor Comes to Investigate Conditions."

28. "Kowtow to Kang Yu Wei," *Los Angeles Times,* March 19, 1905, 6; "Roosevelt's Ways Are Admired by Kang Yu Wei," *Los Angeles Examiner,* March 17, 1905, 6; "Declares in Favor of Restoration of Kwank Hsu," *Los Angeles Examiner,* March 19, 1905, 23; Glick, *Double Ten,* 126–27. Among Lea's guests were Judge Waldo M. York, Colonel C. M. Moses, Colonel W. J. Fife, Harrison Gray Otis, newsmen Jack London, Harry Carr, and Charles Van Loan, and Chamber of Commerce representatives John Alton, G. G. Johnson, Archibald C. Way, and Newman Essick.

29. "Kowtow to Kang Yu Wei." See also "Col. Hotchkiss Dead," *Los Angeles Times,* April 2, 1905, 1:6.

30. "Kong Wu Wei Visits Mayor," *Los Angeles Herald,* March 22, 1905, 5.

31. "Chinese Diplomat Entertained," *Los Angeles Times,* March 25, 1905, 2:2.

32. Glick, *Double Ten,* 137–39.

33. Ibid., 139–41.

34. The dinner was held Monday evening, March 27, and included Mr. and Mrs. Hotchkiss, K'ang Yu-wei, Chou Kuo-hsien, General and Mrs. Falkenberg, Lieutenant General Parmentier, and Miss Daisy Daugherty (Mrs. Falkenberg's niece), among other ladies. See "Distinguished Guests Dined," *Los Angeles Times,* March 29, 1905, 2:10; and Grace Grundy, "Social Diary and Gossip," *Los Angeles Herald,* March 28, 1905, 6.

35. Glick, *Double Ten,* 141–43.

36. "Whose Army Falkenberg's?"

37. Ibid.

38. Ibid.

39. Glick, *Double Ten,* 145–46.

40. "Kong Cables to Find Out," *Los Angeles Times,* March 31, 1905, 1:7; Chapin, "Homer Lea and the Chinese Revolution," 68. For Allen Chung being the general secretary of the local Pao Huang Hui, see "To Revivify the Old China."

41. "Whose Army Falkenberg's?"

42. Ibid.

43. Ibid.

44. Ibid.; "Falkenberg's Crown Badly Tilted."

45. "Falkenberg's Crown Badly Tilted."

46. "Kong Cables to Find Out" reported that Falkenberg made Hotchkiss a brigadier general in his army, and on March 30, Hotchkiss "had been taken to his bed sick, as a result of the unkind aspirations cast upon his triumphant banquet to the rampant leader of this army." See also, "Col. Hotchkiss Dead"; "Pioneer Lawyer Called by Death," *Los Angeles Herald,* April 2, 1905, 2:9. General Falkenberg was among the pallbearers at the Hotchkiss funeral: see "Notables Bear Remains of Hotchkiss to Grave," *Los Angeles Examiner,* April 6, 1905, 3; "'Excellency' Shakes Dust," *Los Angeles Times,* April 3, 1905, 4.

47. "Extortion Charged in Chinese Army," *Los Angeles Examiner,* April 7, 1905, 2; "'Blackmail,' Says Gen. Faulkenberg," *Los Angeles Herald,* April 7, 1905, 1; "Wei Stops the War between Chinese Generals," *Los Angeles Examiner,* April 8, 1905, 14; "'Generals' in Tangled Web," *Los Angeles Times,* April 7, 1905, 2:12.

48. "Extortion Charged in Chinese Army"; "'Blackmail,' Says Gen. Faulkenberg"; "Wei Stops the War between Chinese Generals"; "'Generals' in Tangled Web."

49. "'Generals' in Tangled Web."

50. "Wei Stops the War between Chinese Generals."

51. Ibid.

52. "Tries to Sort Out Generals," *Los Angeles Times,* April 8, 1905, 2:6.

53. "'Gen.' Falkenberg Packs His Traps," *Los Angeles Times,* April 11, 1905, 2:1.

54. For an example of Falkenberg's ongoing recruiting CIRA efforts, see "Reform Army Gets Hildebrand," *Bellingham Herald,* May 13, 1905, 8.

7. Resourceful Schemer

1. "Wei Stops the War between Chinese Generals." Lea arrived in San Francisco on April 12, 1905, during his tour. See "Personal," *San Francisco Call,* April 13, 1905, 5.

2. "Unlawful Militia," *Fresno Morning Republican,* April 21, 1905, 10; "Incorporated by State," *Fresno Evening Democrat,* April 21, 1905, 2; "Chinese Company Incorporated," *Fresno Morning Republican,* April 22, 1905,

12; "Imperial Army Gets Setback," *San Francisco Call,* April 22, 1905, 4; "Was Drilling a Chinese Squad," *San Francisco Chronicle,* April 22, 1905, 3; "Guards Suppressed," *Fresno Morning Republican,* May 16, 1905, 5; "Hard Lines for Lea," *Fresno Morning Republican,* June 17, 1905, 10; "Inspection Report," *Fresno Morning Republican,* September 19, 1905, 6; "Talks Plainly of National Guard," *San Francisco Chronicle,* September 19, 1905, 9. For the quote, see W. D. Crichton to Governor Pardee, May 5, 1905, folder 9, box 18, Pardee Papers. For Crichton's prior service as a judge advocate officer, see "For Congressman," *San Francisco Call,* September 9, 1900, 23, Pardee Papers.

3. W. D. Crichton to Governor Pardee, May 5, 1905, Pardee Papers.

4. Telegram, Homer Lea to Governor Pardee, April 25, 1905, folder 14, box 41, Pardee Papers.

5. Anschel, *Homer Lea, Sun Yat-Sen and the Chinese Revolution,* 64, cites a telegram (231n56) in the Stanford University archives with an added note, dated April 25, 1905, from Lea to Dr. David Starr Jordan, claiming that Lea invited Jordan and several army and navy officers to the dinner. Stanford University archives have no record of the telegram and note, but it is likely Lea may have invited other distinguished guests to the dinner. Jordan's memoirs, *The Days of a Man,* recount his accepting a dinner invitation from Lea on at least one occasion.

6. "Lea Will Continue His Trip to the East," *St. Louis Republic,* May 20, 1905, 2; "General Lea Speaks Up," *Fresno Morning Republican,* May 24, 1905, 5; "Hard Lines For Lea"; Governor Pardee to Dr. Chester Rowell, May 10, 1905, folder 6, box 105, Pardee Papers; Governor Pardee to W. D. Crichton, May 10, 1905, folder 6, box 105, Pardee Papers.

7. "Provost Guard May Seize Arms," *San Francisco Chronicle,* May 4, 1905, 9. See also "Funston Calls Down Homer Lea," *San Francisco Call,* May 3, 1905, 16.

8. "Provost Guard May Seize Arms."

9. Ibid.; "Governor After Chinese Army," *San Francisco Chronicle,* May 18, 1905, 9.

10. "Governor After Chinese Army."

11. Governor Pardee to W. D. Crichton, May 4, 1905, folder 5, box 105, Pardee Papers; W. D. Crichton to Governor Pardee, May 5, 1905, folder 9, box 18, Pardee Papers; Dr. Chester Rowell to Governor Pardee, May 5, 1905, folder 1, box 63, Pardee Papers. For Dr. Rowell's background, see biographical entry in Harper, *Who's Who on the Pacific Coast,* 492. See also "Obituary Notes," *New York Times,* May 25, 1912, 13. For Crichton's Democratic Party ties, see "For Congressman."

12. K'ang Yu-wei's entourage stopped for a layover in Kansas City, Missouri, on May 13 and left for St. Louis on the evening of May 14; see "Kang Yu Wei in Town," *Kansas City Star,* May 14, 1905, 8. While in Kansas City, K'ang Yu-wei addressed a group of Chinese; see "Chinese Reformer

246 • Notes to Pages 109–114

on America," *Chicago Daily Tribune,* May 15, 1905, 3. Also, when K'ang Yu-wei arrived in St. Louis, "Chinese Reformer Here with Suite," *St. Louis Republic,* May 16, 1905, 1, reported that the reform movement was establishing "drilling clubs" in "every Chinese community in the United States."

13. Governor Pardee to G. W. Jones, May 10, 1905, folder 6, box 105, Pardee Papers.

14. "Puts an End to Company D," *San Francisco Call,* May 17, 1905, 3; Governor Pardee to Dr. Chester Rowell, May 10, 1905, folder 6, box 105, Pardee Papers; Governor Pardee to W. D. Crichton, May 10, 1905, folder 6, box 105, Pardee Papers.

15. "Will Disband the Chinese Reformer," *St. Louis Globe-Democrat,* May 19, 1905, 1; G. W. Jones to Governor Pardee, May 17, 1905, folder 32, box 37, Pardee Papers; Worden, "A Chinese Reformer in Exile," 137.

16. Lea to G. W. Jones, May 18, 1905, enclosure in Geo. W. Jones to Hon. Geo. C. Pardee, May 22, 1905, folder 32, box 37, Pardee Papers; see also "Guards Suppressed"; "Governor After Chinese Army"; "California Routs China's Reformers," *St. Louis Republic,* May 19, 1905, 1.

17. Lea to G. W. Jones, May 18, 1905, Pardee Papers.

18. "Lea Will Continue His Trip to the East."

19. "General Lea Speaks Up"; G. W. Jones to CERA, Fresno, May 22, 1905, enclosure in Geo. W. Jones to Hon. Geo. C. Pardee, May 22, 1905, Pardee Papers.

20. R. A. Falkenberg to Governor Pardee, May 18, 1905, folder 8, box 25, Pardee Papers.

21. Ibid.

22. "Governor After Chinese Army."

23. "'Modern Sage of the Flowery Kingdom' Gathering Mighty Force to Hurl against the Walls of Stagnation and Retrogression in China," *St. Louis Republic,* May 21, 1905, 4:1. See also "California Routs China's Reformers," which cited the reform party's efforts to raise a large war chest.

24. "Will Disband the Chinese," *St. Louis Globe-Democrat,* May 20, 1905, 3; "Baptists Favor Modified Exclusion Laws at Chinese Reformer's Request," *St. Louis Republic,* May 20, 1905, 3.

25. "Cadets to Drill at Big Horse Show," *St. Louis Republic,* May 18, 1905, 5; "Big Horse Show to Be Repeated," *St. Louis Republic,* May 20, 1905, 9.

26. "'Modern Sage of the Flowery Kingdom' Gathering Mighty Force."

27. "American Hopes to Be Lafayette of China; Leads Army," *St. Louis Post Dispatch,* May 19, 1905, 13.

28. "'Modern Sage of the Flowery Kingdom' Gathering Mighty Force."

29. "Chinese Reformer Leaves St. Louis," *St. Louis Republic,* May 23, 1905, 3.

30. "Says Empress Took Bribe," *Chicago Daily Tribune,* May 24, 1905, 7; "Chinese Reformer Comes to Chicago," *Inter Ocean,* May 24, 1905, 5;

"Kang Yu Says American Vim and Ideas Would Revive China," *Chicago Daily Journal,* May 25, 1905, 8; "Feast for Chinese Reformer," *Chicago Daily Tribune,* May 26, 1905, 6. "Kang Will Depart Tonight," *St. Louis Republic,* May 22, 1905, 3, reported that Lea would inspect three cadet companies in Chicago.

31. "Homer Lea on China," *Los Angeles Times,* June 11, 1905, 1:4. For information on K'ang Yu-wei's visiting Ohio, see Worden, "A Chinese Reformer in Exile," 156; "Kang Yu Wei Is a Visitor Here," *Washington Times,* June 9, 1905, 1; "Progress in China, a Man Who Works for Reform," *Washington Evening Star,* June 9, 1905, 7.

32. After arriving in Baltimore and checking into the Hotel Rennert, K'ang Yu-wei's party dined at a local Chinese restaurant. K'ang Yu-wei and Lea both made after-dinner speeches; in his Lea praised the work of his reform cadets who were training across the country. See "Kang Yu Wei Arrives," *Baltimore Sun,* June 11, 1905, 16. See also "Noted Chinese Leader Coming," *Baltimore American,* June 10, 1905, 8; "Kang Yu Wei in Baltimore," *Baltimore American,* June 11, 1905, 8; "Reformer Wei Talks of China," *Baltimore American,* June 12, 1905, 12; "Kang Yu Wei Comes Today," *Baltimore Evening Herald,* June 10, 1905, 10.

33. For Lea's initial meeting with Roosevelt, see Desk Diaries [appointment book], "Homer Lea, Introduced by Genl. H. G. Otis," June 15, 1905, reel no. 430, series 9, Theodore Roosevelt Papers, Library of Congress Manuscript Division, Washington, D.C. K'ang Yu-wei likely met Roosevelt and Loomis at the State Department rather than the White House since there is no record of the meeting in the White House appointment book. For K'ang Yu-wei's statement about meeting Roosevelt, see "Former Chinese Premier Is Here as a Reformer," *Pittsburg Dispatch,* June 18, 1905, 2; and "Aid Chinese Reform," *Pittsburg Dispatch,* June 19, 1905, 3. An American Asiatic Association delegation met with President Roosevelt on June 12, 1905, to lobby against the exclusion laws. See "Appeal for the Chinese," *New York Times,* June 13, 1905, 8; and Jung-Pang Lo, *Kang Yu-wei,* 198.

34. "Aid Chinese Reform."

35. "Chinese Reformer Here," *New York Tribune,* June 28, 1905, 3; "Chinese Reformer to Be Here Today," *Philadelphia Inquirer,* June 24, 1905, 7; Worden, "A Chinese Reformer in Exile," 161; Desk Diaries [appointment book], "Mr. Kang Yu Wei, at Request of Mr. Chew Kok Hean," June 24, 1905, reel no. 430, series 9, Theodore Roosevelt Papers.

36. "Man Who Wants to Reform China Given a Warm Welcome," *Philadelphia Inquirer,* June 25, 1905, 2.

37. "Chinese Reformer Given Glad Welcome," *Philadelphia Public Ledger,* June 25, 1905, 9.

38. "American May Lead Chinese," *Philadelphia Inquirer,* June 26, 1905, 1.

39. Ibid.

40. Ibid., 2. For more press coverage of K'ang Yu-wei and Lea's Phila-

delphia visit, see "Chinese Reformer at Picnic," *Philadelphia Inquirer,* June 27, 1905, 10; "Chinese Reformer Pleased with Order," *Philadelphia North American,* June 26, 1905, 4; "Chinese Reformer to Visit Mayor Today," *Philadelphia North American,* June 27, 1905, 3; "Mayor Receives Kang Yu Wei," *Philadelphia Inquirer,* June 28, 1905, 7; "Chinese Reformer Shakes Mayor's Hand," *Philadelphia North American,* June 28, 1905, 16; "Exiled Chinese Reformer Given a Great Reception," *Philadelphia Press,* June 25, 1905, 3; "Chinaman Lauds Mayor Weaver," *Philadelphia Press,* June 28, 1905, 5; "Chinese Reformer Given Glad Welcome," *Philadelphia Public Ledger,* June 25, 1905, 9; "Exile from China Arouses Chinese," *Philadelphia Public Ledger,* June 26, 1905, 2.

41. Jack Parkerson, "15,000 Armed Chinese in the United States Preparing on American Soil for War of Conquest," *Los Angeles Herald,* June 25, 1905, 1, 4.

42. "Confirms Report of Intended Encampment," *Los Angeles Herald,* June 25, 1905, 4; see also "Contends Soldiers Are Merely Students," *Los Angeles Herald,* June 25, 1905, 4; "Government Official Offered Big Inducement," *Los Angeles Herald,* June 25, 1905, 4; "Speaker of Legislature Po Wong Wuey Member," *Los Angeles Herald,* June 25, 1905, 4; "Fresno Company Is Stopped from Drilling," *Los Angeles Herald,* June 25, 1905, 4.

43. "Assistant United States Attorney Talks," *Los Angeles Herald,* June 25, 1905, 4.

44. "Chinese Reformer Here"; "Kang Yu Wei Arrives; Reviews Chinese Troops," *New York Times,* June 28, 1905, 2; "Chinatown Greets Apostle; His Doctrine Is a New China," *New York American and Journal,* June 28, 1905, 8; "Head Reformer: Chinese Welcome Kang Yu Wei," *Lowell Sun* (Massachusetts), June 29, 1905, 2.

45. W. H. Eckley to Governor Pardee, May 24, 1905, folder 61, box 24, Pardee Papers; Worden, "A Chinese Reformer in Exile," 142–43. See also "Chinese Are Being Drilled," *Atlanta Constitution,* May 28, 1905, 2:4; "'Chinks' Must Not Drill in the United States," *La Crosse Tribune,* June 17, 1905, 8.

46. Governor Pardee to W. H. Eckley, May 30, 1905, folder 9, box 105, Pardee Papers; R. A. Falkenberg to Governor Pardee, June 15, 1905, folder 8, box 25, Pardee Papers.

47. Pardee to R. A. Falkenberg, June 16, 1905, folder 1, box 106, Pardee Papers.

48. W. H. Eckley to Governor Frank Higgins, May 25, 1905; Frank E. Perley, Secretary to Governor Higgins, to William Loeb, Jr., Secretary to the President, May 27, 1905, both in RG 94, Records of the Adjutant General's Office, Department of War, no. 1019722, NARA.

49. William Loeb, Jr., to War Department, n.d., received by War Department May 29, 1905; Second Indorsement, War Department to Judge Advocate General, May 31, 1905; Third Indorsement, Judge Advocate General's

Office to Military Secretary, War Department, June 3, 1905; Fourth Indorsement, Military Secretary Office to Chief of Staff, June 5, 1905; memo, Lieutenant General Chaffee, Chief of Staff, to Military Secretary, June 7, 1905; Fifth Indorsement, Military Secretary to L.A. Police Chief, June 8, 1905; W. A. Hammel, L.A. Chief of Police, to Military Secretary's Office, June 20, 1905; Sixth Indorsement, Military Secretary's Office to the Chief of Staff, June 26, 1905; Seventh Indorsement, memo, Lieutenant General Chaffee to Military Secretary, June 27, 1905; Eighth Indorsement, Military Secretary to Judge Advocate General, June 28, 1905; Ninth Indorsement, Judge Advocate General to Military Secretary, June 30, 1905; Acting Secretary of War to Secretary of State, July 3, 1905; Tenth Indorsement, Military Secretary to Governor Higgins, July 3, 1905; Acting Secretary of State to Acting Secretary of War, July 14, 1905; Acting Secretary of War to Secretary of State, July 18, 1905, all found in RG 94, Records of the Adjutant General's Office, Department of War, no. 1019722, NARA. The War Department resolved that unless Lea violated sections 5281, 5282, or 5286 of the neutrality laws, then there could be no basis for the federal government to take action. Section 5281 prohibited Americans from accepting foreign commissions against a friendly state; section 5282 prohibited enlisting or procuring enlistment in foreign service within the United States; section 5286 prohibited military expeditions against friendly states that began in the United States. See also McClenon and Gilbert, *Index to the Federal Statutes,* 727.

50. W. A. Hammel, L.A. Chief of Police, to Military Secretary's Office, June 20, 1905. See also "Police Watch Cadets," *Los Angeles Times,* June 23, 1905, 2:7.

51. "Drill Nucleus Here for Chinese Army"; "A Chop Suey Waterloo," *New York Evening Post,* June 20, 1905, 1; "Chinese Cadets Frowned on by Governor," *New York World,* June 20, 1905, 1; "The Chinese Are Drilling," *New York Times,* June 21, 1905, 4; "Police Rout Chinese Soldiers," *Pittsburg Dispatch,* June 21, 1905, 6. The press reported that the cadets had been drilling for ten years. This is probably mistaken and more likely refers to George McVickar's drill team of Chinese boys at the St. Bartholomew's Boys Club, which began training in the summer of 1902, rather than the Pao Huang Hui, which had been in existence only five years. See "Chinese Sunday School Boys Form Military Corps," *Boston Globe,* July 22, 1902, 8; "Chinese Military Corps," *Washington Post,* September 11, 1904, E2; "Chinese Reformers Are Drilling," *New York Tribune,* January 24, 1905, 7; "Chinese Militant," *Galveston Daily News,* February 6, 1905, 12; "New York Chinamen Trained to Fight," *New York Tribune,* June 11, 1905, 8; Worden, "A Chinese Reformer in Exile," 146n66.

52. "Sir Liang Cheng Ridicules Stories of Chinese Army," *Washington Times,* June 27, 1905, 12. See also "Want China to Imitate America," *New York Herald,* June 26, 1905, 2; "That Los Angeles Army," *Los Angeles Times,* June 26, 1905, 2.

53. "Chinese Reformer Here"; Worden, "A Chinese Reformer in Exile," 146; "Kang Yu Wei Arrives; Reviews Chinese Troops"; "Head Chinese Reformer Here," *New York Sun*, June 28, 1905, 7.

54. "Kang Yu Wei Received by Mayor M'Clellan," *New York World*, June 29, 1905, 5. The article also indicated that Lea assisted Chou Kuo-hsien as K'ang Yu-wei's interpreter.

55. "White Leader of Chinese," *New York Sun*, June 28, 1905, 2.

56. Ibid.

57. "The Man of the Week: Prince Kang Yu Wei," *Los Angeles Herald Magazine*, July 23, 1905, 1. See also "Chinese Reformer Talks to Weaver," *Washington Times*, June 27, 1905, 12. K'ang Yu-wei also asserted his belief in "peaceful revolution" in "Chinatown Greets Apostle."

58. "China's Greatest Need," *New York Tribune*, July 5, 1905, 4.

59. Irwin, *The Making of a Reporter*, 20–21.

60. "Kang Yu Wei Is Pleased with Edict," *Hartford Courant*, July 19, 1905, 8. Captain Ben O. Young is also referred to as Captain Ben Oyang, business manager of the *Chinese World* newspaper. See "Beautiful Chinese Girl Becomes the Bride of a Newspaper Man," *Los Angeles Herald*, October 17, 1906, 3. While in New York, Lea gave an interview to the *New York Sun* in which he discussed his views on China's desires to participate in the Russo-Japanese War peace settlement. See "Pleads China's Cause: General Lea Says She Has Right at Peace Conference," *New York Sun*, July 23, 1905, 4.

61. Jung-Pang Lo, *K'ang Yu-wei*, 199–204; "Boston Institutions," *Boston Globe*, July 7, 1905, 14; "Emancipation Ideals for Chinese," *Boston Globe*, July 7, 1905, 26; "Calls on the Governor," *Boston Globe*, July 10, 1905, 3; "Kang Yu Wei Better," *Boston Globe*, July 11, 1905, 14; "Herb Tea and Fan Saves Kang Yu Wei," *Boston Journal*, July 13, 1905, 12; "On Recruiting Errand," *Boston Journal*, July 6, 1905, 6; "Gen. Kang Snubs Chief Executive," *Boston Journal*, July 7, 1905, 8; "Oriental Grandee Talks to Boston Celestials at Park Street Church," *Boston Journal*, July 10, 1905, 3; "Kang Yu Wei Calls on Governor," *Boston Journal*, July 11, 1905, 12; "Chinese Reformer Coming This Week," *Hartford Courant*, July 11, 1905, 4; "Chinese Reformer Comes Tomorrow," *Hartford Courant*, July 14, 1905, 8; "When Kang Yu Wei Fled from China," *Hartford Courant*, July 15, 1905, 3; "Kang Yu Wei Here for a Week," *Hartford Courant*, July 17, 1905, 11; "Miss Kang Tung Pek Fires Machine Gun," *Hartford Courant*, July 18, 1905, 11; "Kang Yu Wei Is Pleased with Edict," *Hartford Courant*, July 19, 1905, 8; "Kang Yu Wei Departs," *Hartford Courant*, July 20, 1905, 18.

62. Lea sent Ermal several postcards from Canada. There are photographs of the fronts of three postcards, undated, that were mailed from Canada to Ermal in the James Lea Papers. A postcard from the Quebec Citadel states that Lea met with Sir Bryan Leighton and visited the Quebec Citadel. There are also two cards from Halifax, Nova Scotia, one of which indicates that Lea planned to visit Cape Breton Island. For Sir Thomas Lipton reportedly acting

as Lea's host in Nova Scotia, see Frederic Chapin to Charles Kates, February 26, [1949], Kates Papers. Lea mentioned that Sir Bryan Leighton had invited him on a fishing trip in Quebec, according to a reference to a postcard in Ermal Lea Green to Tom Lea Jr., April 7, 1942, James Lea Papers. For reference to the Toronto postcard, see "Notes on Conversation with Newmark," circa 1948, Kates Papers. For the quote, see "Let Bygones Be Bygones," *Los Angeles Times,* December 6, 1906, 1:7.

63. R. A. Falkenberg to Governor George Pardee, August 30, 1905, folder 8, box 25, Pardee Papers.

64. R. J. Faneuf to Governor Pardee, September 28, 1905, folder 39, box 27, Pardee Papers. Faneuf's company numbered forty-five cadets and trained at 367 Ninth Street. See "American Drill Master Teaches Young Chinese Idea How to Shoot," *San Francisco Call,* March 1, 1905, 5; "Chinese Study Manual of Arms," *San Francisco Chronicle,* March 1, 1905, 13.

65. "Drilled Chinese Leaving San Francisco for Home," *Washington Times,* February 13, 1906, 9.

66. O'Banion to Glick, circa 1946, Correspondence regarding Double Ten Movie folder, box 3, Glick Papers.

67. Waterman and Griffes, "Reform Cadets"; see also undated article enclosed with Falkenberg letter to State Department, October 30, 1905, RG 59, Miscellaneous Letters of the Department of State, M179, roll 1266, nos. 0848–49, NARA.

68. Lea to Governor Pardee, October 7, 1905, folder 14, box 41, Pardee Papers.

69. Ibid.

70. Ibid.

71. Governor Pardee to Homer Lea, October 13, 1905, folder 2, box 108, Pardee Papers.

72. "Chinese Establish School," *Los Angeles Herald,* October 13, 1905, 7; "Chinese Military School," *Los Angeles Times,* October 13, 1905, 1:13.

73. R. A. Falkenberg to Department of State, October 30, 1905, RG 59, nos. 0848–49, M179, roll no. 1266, NARA.

74. "Eminent Visitors Royally Welcomed," *San Francisco Call,* January 13, 1906, 1; "Order of the Dragon China's Hope for Reform," *Washington Times,* March 16, 1906, 9; "Would Open China to World," *Washington Post,* March 17, 1906, F1; "Dick Has Drag On," *Los Angeles Times,* July 12, 1906, 11; "Secret Military Order Is to Be Investigated," *San Francisco Call,* July 14, 1906, 9; "Americans Rule Armies of China: General R. A. Falkenberg Will Be Imperial Commander-in-Chief," *Washington Times,* July 31, 1906, 2; "Another Boost of Falkenberg," *Los Angeles Times,* August 1, 1906, 1:4; "'Old Dutchman' Mine," *Nevada State Journal,* January 4, 1907, 6; "Ready to Build New Railroad," *Reno Evening Gazette,* March 29, 1907, 6. For Governor John Sparks being Falkenberg's business partner, see Articles of Incorporation of Wild Horse Mining and Milling Company, April 1, 1907,

folder 53, SS Corp-0068, Secretary of State Corporation Files, Nevada State Library and Archives, Carson City. Falkenberg's military appointment on the governor's staff is referred to in "Wild Horse Mines Are Very Rich," *Nevada State Journal*, May 1, 1907, 6. See *Appendix to Journals of Senate and Assembly of the Twenty-fourth Session of the Legislature of the State of Nevada, 1909*, 39, for the official appointment date of May 17, 1907, when Falkenberg became "Aide-de-Camp on staff of Governor, with rank of Lieutenant-Colonel." Records also indicate that Governor John Sparks appointed Falkenberg a lieutenant colonel on May 20, 1907, among nine other lieutenant colonel appointments from March to June 1907. See Governor's Appointment Book, 1887–1914, 160, Gov-1330, Nevada State Library and Archives, Carson City. For Falkenberg's eventual return to California, see R. A. von Falkenberg to Tasker L. Oddie, February 4, 1911, folder 86, box 3, Tasker A. Odie Papers, Huntington Library, Art Collections, and Botanical Gardens, San Marino, Calif.; "Hotel Manager Missing," *Los Angeles Times*, May 6, 1913, 2:7.

8. The Quill and the Sword

1. "Homer Lea Loses His Peacock Feather," *San Francisco Chronicle*, December 30, 1905, 14.

2. "Reform Chinese Ignore Trouble," *Los Angeles Herald*, March 6, 1906, 2:1.

3. The last extant CIA document is an acknowledgment of a receipt for the purchase of military items from the Pettibone Brothers military supply house in October 1906. See Pettibone Bros. Mfg. Co., Cincinnati, Ohio, to Western Military Academy, October 30, 1906, box 2, Powers Papers.

4. According to Armentrout Ma, "Chinese Politics in the Western Hemisphere," 301–3, the reorganization began in late 1906, but the Hartford, Connecticut, branch, for example, did not change its name until March 1907, see "Chinese Reform Meeting Sunday: Empire Constitutional Party of China, That Is the New Name That Reformers Will Adopt," *Hartford Courant*, March 16, 1907, 5; Hsu, *Rise of Modern China*, 493–95; Fairbank, *The United States and China*, 189–92; Bruce, *Sun Yat-Sen*, 34–35. After Sun Yat-sen consolidated and reorganized his party into the Tung Meng Hui in the summer of 1905, his organization seriously began to challenge K'ang Yu-wei and the reformers. The growing momentum of Sun Yat-sen's revolutionary party and serious financial reverses suffered by the Reformers' Commercial Corporation ultimately signaled the decline and eventual eclipse of the Pao Huang Hui. See Martin, *Strange Vigour*, 103; Armentrout Ma, "Chinese Politics in the Western Hemisphere," 332, 343–44, 406–87; Armentrout Ma, *Revolutionaries, Monarchists, and Chinatowns*, 116–17; and Hensman, *Sun Yat-sen*, 47.

5. "Chinese Regiment Disbands" *New York Times*, May 28, 1907, 4. See

also "Chinese Reformers to Celebrate," *New York Tribune,* May 24, 1907, 14.

6. Glick, *Double Ten,* 223. See Pettibone Bros. Mfg. Co., Cincinnati, Ohio, to Western Military Academy, October 30, 1906, as the last dated document confirming cadet activity. One of the last public appearances of Lea's cadets may have been during the visit in March 1906 of Chinese prince Tsai Tse to New York City. See "Chinese Prince Here; Will See Roosevelt," *New York Times,* March 10, 1906, 11, which noted that a cadet honor guard greeted the prince at a restaurant in Chinatown: "The Imperial Guard of the Chinese Reform Association, fifteen strong, under the command of Col. Lee Ling, were lined up on the sidewalk at present arms when the Prince and his party alighted." See also "Home Boys in Chinese War," *Los Angeles Times,* November 16, 1908, 16, which noted: "The Chinese boys of the cadet company that used to drill at night around the alleys of our Chinatown, are now said to be in China organizing and drilling a revolutionary army." Also see "Empire Maker Seeks Health," which noted how suddenly the cadet training ceased: "Within a week every member of these companies had melted away." For Lea's picture hanging in a Pao Huang Hui assembly room, see "Hot Debates in Chinatown," *New York Sun,* November 29, 1908, 9.

7. Glick, *Double Ten,* 186–89, 223–26, 278; Chapin, "Homer Lea and the Chinese Revolution," 98. In early January 1915, O'Banion was tried and convicted of smuggling Chinese and sentenced to eighteen months in the federal prison at McNeil's Island, California. See "Discouraging Smugglers," *Los Angeles Times,* November 14, 1914, 2:3; "Pleases Inspectors," *Los Angeles Times,* November 15, 1912, 2:13; "Runs the Gamut of Criminality," *Los Angeles Times,* July 4, 1913, 2:8; "Smuggler Testifies," *Los Angeles Times,* May 1, 1914, 2:5; "Smuggling Charge Fails," *Los Angeles Times,* May 6, 1914, 2:5; "Jurors Disagree," *Los Angeles Times,* May 9, 1914, 2:5; "Not Guilty Plea of Indicted Men," *Los Angeles Times,* July 7, 1914, 2:2; "Smuggling Case on Trial Again," *Los Angeles Times,* October 3, 1914, 2:2; "Alleged Smuggler's on Trial," *Los Angeles Times,* October 8, 1914, 2:10; "Defense Laconic," *Los Angeles Times,* October 17, 1914, 2:5; "McNeil's Island for Them," *Los Angeles Times,* January 6, 1915, 2:3. See also O'Banion's comments about his treatment in prison in letter he wrote Albert H. Powers, May 9, 1943, Capt. Ansel E. O'Banion folder, box 2, Powers Papers.

8. "Refuses to Fight a Duel," *Los Angeles Herald,* July 2, 1906, 1; "Flexner May Fight with Pie," *Los Angeles Herald,* July 4, 1906, 1.

9. "Refuses to Fight a Duel."

10. See Homer Lea, preface to *The Valor of Ignorance.* Lea states he completed the partial draft subsequent to the signing of the Portsmouth Treaty (September 1905).

11. "Homer Lea Passes After Life Full of Effort," *Los Angeles Tribune,* November 2, 1912, 3.

12. See Emma Wilson Lea quote in Treanor, "The Home Front."

13. Ella Lea Dorr to Charles O. Kates, March 15, 1940, Kates Papers; "Leaves Sword for the Pen," *Los Angeles Times,* January 28, 1907, 2:1. See Lea's notebook with a thirty-chapter outline sketch for a political history of China entitled "The Re-awakening of China," dated August 7, 1906, box 3, Powers Papers. For Lea's proficiency in Chinese, as well as French, German, Spanish, Latin, and Greek, see "Tom Lea, Jr., Questions / Ermal Lea Green Answers," 2; and see Lea's undated notebook that contains a short vocabulary list of English and Chinese that indicates he had some proficiency in Chinese and wrote it fairly well, Notebook, box 3, Powers Papers. Lea may have begun learning Chinese in high school. On his return from China in 1901, the April 13, 1901, *Los Angeles Times* article "A Chinese General from Los Angeles" credited him with being an excellent linguist who learned Chinese in Chinatown while attending high school. See also "Gen. Homer Lea's Career That of a Hero of Romance," which cited Lea learning Chinese from his acquaintance with Chinese at Stanford.

14. See Lea's notebook with a chapter outline sketch for "The Re-awakening of China." "Leaves Sword for the Pen" credited Lea with having written three articles, one in Chinese, one on the Chinese Exclusion Act in the February 1907 issue of *World's Work Magazine,* and "Can China Fight?" in the February 1907 issue of *World Today Magazine.* There is no record of either a Chinese-language article or the *World's Work* article. See Lea, "Can China Fight?" 137–46. Lea reportedly wrote some books, of which there is no record, in Chinese. See "Books and Authors," *New York Sun,* February 14, 1908, 5.

15. Ermal Lea Green to Tom Lea Jr., April 7, 1942, James Lea Papers.

16. Ella Lea Dorr to Charles O. Kates, March 15, 1940, Kates Papers.

17. Ibid.

18. For Robert Belford's help with Lea's writing, see "Tom Lea, Jr., Questions / Ermal Lea Green Answers," 3. Lea's illness and the title of his adventure novel, "Ling Chee," is discussed in "Leaves Sword for the Pen." His illness is also discussed in Marco Newmark, "1906–1907 Trip through Mountains for Valor Data," statement on Homer Lea, box 3, Powers Papers. An advertisement for Lea's adventure novel in "January McClure Fiction," *McClure's Magazine,* November 1907, 230, referenced the upcoming book's title as "The Lyngchee." See author's interview with Joshua B. Powers about his mother's secretarial role with Lea. Before Ethel Powers assisted Lea, she and Ellen Leech attended the Southern California Editorial Association annual excursion trip to Honolulu, Hawaii, in September 1906. See "California Editors in Honolulu," *Los Angeles Herald,* September 20, 1906, 6.

19. Irwin, *The Making of a Reporter,* 21.

20. "Leaves Sword for the Pen."

21. For the types of literature and ideas that may have influenced Lea's thinking, see Bannister, *Social Darwinism,* 236–38; Millis, *Arms and Men,* 171–72; Asahi Shimbun staff, *Pacific Rivals,* 59–61; David Starr Jordan, "The

Decay of Races," *Current Literature*, July 1901, 59–61; Mallan, "Roosevelt, Brooks Adams, and Lea," 217–19; Jaher, *Doubters and Dissenters*, 3–11, 18.

22. Neuman, *America Encounters Japan*, 121–27; Asahi Shimbun staff, *Pacific Rivals*, 59–61; Millis, *Arms and Men*, 171–72; Millett and Maslowski, *For the Common Defense*, 318.

23. Neuman, *America Encounters Japan*, 121–27; Asahi Shimbun staff, *Pacific Rivals*, 59–61; Millis, *Arms and Men*, 171–72; Millett and Maslowski, *For the Common Defense*, 318.

24. "Arm against Japan," *Washington Post*, January 31, 1907, 1; see also Akira Iriye, "Japan as a Competitor, 1895–1917," in Iriye, *Mutual Images*, 79–80.

25. Neuman, *America Encounters Japan*, 124–27; Stephen Chalmers, "The Great War of 1908 Vividly Described," *New York Times*, July 28, 1907, 5:9. Articles highlighting concerns of a war with Japan began appearing in 1905 during the Russo-Japanese War. See "The Great Naval Battle of August 17, 1919 off the Bay of Manila between the American and Japanese Navies," *Washington Times Magazine*, June 11, 1905, 1, 4; Arthur H. Dutton, "If Japan Should Attack Us," *San Francisco Call*, September 23, 1906, 3; Edwin H. Summers, "Why Our Navy Guarantees Peace with Japan," *San Francisco Call*, January 6, 1907, 5; "Japan's War Preparations," *Washington Post*, March 16, 1907, 3; "The 'Next War' as Seen by German Eyes," *New York Times*, April 28, 1907, 5:1; "Steel Rails and Friendship," *San Francisco Call*, May 21, 1907, 8; Hamilton Wright, "If Japan Should Seize the Philippines," *San Francisco Call*, July 21, 1907, 3; Rodic, "Military Conditions in the United States and Japan"; *Current Literature*, August 1907, 126–29; "The Americanization of Japan Now a Menace to America," *Washington Times Magazine*, August 25, 1907, 2; Richmond P. Hobson, "America Is Defenseless in the Far East," *Washington Times Magazine*, October 27, 1907, 6; R. P. Hobson, "Japan May Seize the Pacific Slope, Says Hobson," *Washington Times Magazine*, November 3, 1907, 6–8; "Japanese War Is Predicted," *Los Angeles Times*, November 12, 1907, 1; Richmond Pearson Hobson, "Billions of Defenseless America Lure Japs," *Washington Times Magazine*, November 17, 1907, 3, 9; Bristol, "The Japanese Invasion"; Richmond Pearson Hobson, "Japanese Press Clamors Loudly for War with America, Asserts Hobson," *Washington Times Magazine*, May 10, 1908, 2. See letter to the editor, "War Scare Stories," *New York Times*, July 13, 1907, 6, for a condemnation of widespread war scare articles in New York newspapers.

26. See Lea, *The Valor of Ignorance;* Lea, "The Aeroplane in War"; Lea, *The Day of the Saxon.*

27. Kennedy, "Homer Lea and the Peace Makers," 478; Bannister, *Social Darwinism*, 236–38; Jaher, *Doubters and Dissenters*, 3–11; Mallan, "Roosevelt, Brooks Adams, and Lea," 217–19; see also Lears, *No Place of Grace*, for a discussion on advocates of militarism as part of a reactionary group to America in transition.

28. Van Loan, "General Homer Lea," 7.

29. Newmark, "1906–1907 Trip through Mountains for Valor Data."

30. Ibid.

31. Ermal Lea Green to Charles O. Kates, May 7, 1940, Kates Papers.

32. Van Loan, "Homer Lea's Short Life an Inspiration."

33. "Music and the Stage," *Los Angeles Times,* September 18, 1907, 2:5. Lea copyrighted "The Crimson Spider" on November 20, 1909. See Copyright Office, Class D Drama Deposits, unpublished 1909, registration no. D17518, shelf no. 20,301, reel no. 405, Library of Congress Manuscript Division, Washington, D.C. Lea gave copyrights of his romance novel, published as *The Vermilion Pencil,* and the dramatized version, "The Crimson Spider," to his wife in 1912; see Copyright Document, July 30 1912, box 1, Powers Papers.

34. "Music and the Stage."

35. "Observations by a First Nighter," *Los Angeles Herald,* December 1, 1907, 6.

36. Author's interview with Joshua B. Powers. According to Ethel's obituary in 1934, she was fifty-eight at the time of her death. See "Lea Death Recalls Past," *Los Angeles Times,* March 10, 1943, 2. There is some ambiguity about Ethel's birth date. See also Carolien Maynard (Ethel's granddaughter), e-mail message to author, December 5, 2007, which indicates Ethel was likely born on July 30, 1875. The e-mail also contains a brief biographical sketch of A. D. Powers, Ethel's first husband, written by Tom Powers, Ethel's grandson. See also Joshua Powers III, e-mail message to author, March 26, 2008, which contains information about the Bryant family genealogy that indicates Ethel was born on July 31, 1875.

37. Marco Newmark, "Attitudes towards Women," statement on Homer Lea, untitled folder, box 3, Powers Papers; see also Green, "She Knew Him Well."

38. Newmark, "Attitudes towards Women."

39. Author's interview with Joshua B. Powers.

40. "Gloomy Foreboding of Gen. Homer Lea." Lea's prophesy about a Japanese surprise attack on America was likely based on Japan's use of such a strategy at the start of the Russo-Japanese War.

41. "Novelist Writes of Chinese Life," *New York Times,* March 14, 1908, 138.

42. "New Books Reviewed," *Los Angeles Times,* April 19, 1908, 6:1. Other positive reviews included "New Literature," *Boston Globe,* March 20, 1908, 2; "The World of Books," *Washington Herald,* March 22, 1908, 14.

43. Lea, *The Vermilion Pencil.*

44. Marco Newmark, "Aversion to Missionaries—Personality," statement on Homer Lea, box 3, Powers Papers; Lea, *The Vermilion Pencil.*

45. Display advertisement, *New York Times Book Review,* March 21, 1908, 164; display advertisement, *New York Sun,* March 21, 1908, 7.

46. Lea, "How Socialism Failed in China." This article marked the first

time Lea published using the title of "General." Also, Jack London's wide popularity in the California press as an advocate of socialism may have influenced Lea to address socialism, possibly in the hope of gaining similar public recognition as London.

47. See "Love Wins o'er Pen and Sword," *Los Angeles Times,* August 14, 1911, 1:8; Carr, "Death Overpowers Odd World Figure," 2. For the first indication of Lea residing at Laguna Beach, see Homer Lea to C. B. Booth, April 7, 1908, folder 4, box 1, Charles B. Boothe Papers, Hoover Institution on War, Revolution and Peace, Stanford University, Stanford, Calif.; Lea wrote Boothe he was "situated on the Long Beach car at Vista del Mar," with the phone number "Main 4659 Long Beach," and a return mailing address of "Long Beach, R.F.D. 2 Box 163," in Lea to Boothe, August 26, 1908, folder 4, box 1, Boothe Papers.

48. Author's interview with Joshua B. Powers.

49. Lea to Ethel Powers, September 20, 1908, Powers Private Collection.

9. The Red Dragon Plan

1. Lea to Ethel Powers, September 20, 1908, Powers Private Collection.

2. Lea to Boothe, September 21, 1908, folder 4, box 1, Boothe Papers.

3. Ibid.; see also Lea to Boothe, October 5, 1908, folder 4, box 1, Boothe Papers; Yung Wing to Lea, December 4, 1908, folder 7, box 1, Boothe Papers.

4. Charles B. Boothe lived at 824 South Bonnie Brae Street. See the *Los Angeles City Directory, 1901,* 141; and "Died," *Los Angeles Herald,* April 14, 1906, 6. In October 1904 Boothe purchased land in South Pasadena with plans to build a residence on North Garfield Avenue, where he eventually moved. See "Alhambra," *Los Angeles Times,* October 13, 1904, 2:11. For Boothe's St. Louis visit, see "Visitors at St. Louis Hotels," *St. Louis Republic,* May 16, 1905, 6. K'ang Yu-wei returned to America in March 1907; see "Dinner to Kang Yu Wei," *New York Times,* March 18, 1907, 4. See also Lea to Boothe, April 7, 1908, Boothe Papers; and Boothe to Lea, September 11, 1908, folder 4, box 1, Boothe Papers. For Boothe's background, see "Boothe, C. B.," in *Who's Who in the Pacific Southwest,* 50; "Death's Swift Call Comes," *Los Angeles Times,* April 12, 1913, 2:1; *History of California,* 701–3; and Moody, "Makers of Los Angeles," 322.

5. "Boothe, C. B."; "Death's Swift Call Comes"; *History of California,* 701–3; Moody, "Makers of Los Angeles," 322. See Julian Hartt, "Americans' Plot for Chinese Revolt Revealed," *Los Angeles Times,* October 13, 1966, 2:1, 10–12; Worthy, "Yung Wing in America," 265–87; Lea, "How I Was Made a General in the Chinese Army," 1. Yung Wing was previously the official guardian of K'ang Yu-wei's favorite daughter, who resided in Hartford; see Armentrout Ma, "Chinese Politics in the Western Hemisphere," 337; Armentrout Ma, *Revolutionaries, Monarchists, and Chinatowns,* 85.

6. See Lea to Boothe, October 5, 1908, Boothe Papers, for an indication of Yung Wing's favorable support for Lea. For Yung Wing's involvement in the failed 1902–3 Kwangtung revolutionary effort, see Armentrout Ma, "The Canton Rising of 1902–1903."

7. Yung Wing to Lea, December 4, 1908, folder 7, box 1, Boothe Papers.

8. Ibid.; Yung Wing to Boothe, December 5, 1908, folder 1, box 1, Boothe Papers.

9. Boothe to Lea, September 11, 1908, Boothe Papers; Lea to Boothe, September 21, 1908, folder 1, box 1, Boothe Papers; Yung Wing to Boothe, October 9, 1908, folder 1, box 1, Boothe Papers.

10. Lea to Boothe, September 21, 1908, Boothe Papers. Boothe went to Washington, D.C., in mid-September as a delegate to the Tuberculosis Congress. See South Pasadena section in "Los Angeles County—Its Cities and Towns," *Los Angeles Times*, September 17, 1908, 2:8.

11. Lea to Boothe, September 21, 1908, Boothe Papers.

12. Ibid.

13. Boothe to Allen, November 18, 1908, folder 2, box 1, Boothe Papers; Boothe to Yung Wing, December 28, 1908; folder 1, box 1, Boothe Papers. When Boothe contacted Allen to join the conspiracy, Allen was a consulting engineer in New York City; see letterhead on Allen to Boothe, January 21, 1909, folder 2, box 1, Boothe Papers.

14. "Emperor's Death May Loosen Revolution." For the death of the emperor and empress, see also "Chinese Announce Death of Emperor," *New York Times*, November 15, 1908, 1; "Tsi-An, Ruler of China, Dead," *New York Times*, November 16, 1908, 1.

15. Lea to Boothe, November 17, 1908, folder 4, box 1, Boothe Papers; Boothe to Allen, November 18, 1908, folder 2, box 1, Boothe Papers; Yung Wing to Lea, December 4, 1908; Yung Wing to Boothe and Lea, December 5, 1908, folder 1, box 1, Boothe Papers.

16. Boothe to Allen, November 18, 1908, Boothe Papers.

17. Ibid.

18. Yung Wing to Boothe, December 6, 1908, folder 1, box 1, Boothe Papers; Yung Wing to Boothe, December 14, 1908, folder 1, box 1, Boothe Papers; Boothe to Yung Wing, December 28, 1908, folder 1, box 1, Boothe Papers; Allen to Boothe, January 21, 1909, folder 2, box 1, Boothe Papers.

19. "China Dismisses Head of Army," *New York Times*, January 3, 1909, 3:4; Yung Wing to Boothe, January 4, 1909, folder 1, box 1, Boothe Papers; Yung Wing to Boothe, January 16, 1909, folder 1, box 1, Boothe Papers; Allen to Boothe, January 21 1909, Boothe Papers.

20. Yung Wing to Boothe, January 16, 1909, Boothe Papers.

21. Allen to Boothe, January 21, 1909, Boothe Papers.

22. Yung Wing to Boothe, January 16, 1909, Boothe Papers; Boothe to Allen, February 3, 1909, folder 2, box 1, Boothe Papers.

23. Allen to Boothe, January 21, 1909, Boothe Papers; Allen to Boothe, February 1, 1909, folder 2, box 1, Boothe Papers.

24. Allen to Boothe, January 21, 1909, Boothe Papers. Allen believed that $9,000,000 would be necessary for the Red Dragon plan.

25. Boothe to Allen, February 3, 1909, Boothe Papers.

26. Mowry, *The Era of Theodore Roosevelt,* 190–91; Chong, "The Abortive American-Chinese Project for Chinese Revolution," 57–58.

27. Mowry, *The Era of Theodore Roosevelt,* 190–91.

28. Ibid.

29. Allen to Boothe, February 6, 1909, folder 2, box 1, Boothe Papers.

30. Allen to Boothe, February 13, 1909, folder 2, box 1, Boothe Papers.

31. Chaffee to Lea, May 18, 1909, box 1, Powers Papers.

32. Boothe to Allen, February 3, 1909, folder 2, box 1, Boothe Papers.

33. Chaffee to Lea, May 18, 1909, Powers Papers.

34. Otis to Lea, May 24, 1909, Otis folder, box 1, Powers Papers; Rodman, *History of the Bench and Bar of Southern California,* 134; Boothe to K'ang Yu-wei, June 14, 1909, folder 6, box 1, Boothe Papers.

35. Boothe to Allen, February 3, 1909, Boothe Papers; Lea, "The Valor of Ignorance," *Harper's Weekly.*

36. Yung Wing to Boothe, September 14, 1909, folder 1, box 1, Boothe Papers. For Lea's planned Hawaiian vacation, see Boothe to Yung Wing, October 2, 1909, folder 1, box 1, Boothe Papers. For Alfred Lea's obituary, see "Gentleman of Old School," *Los Angeles Times,* August 18, 1909, 2:3. Emma Lea sold the house on Bonnie Brae Street in early October. See "Report Brisk Demand," *Los Angeles Times,* October 3, 1909, 5:24. During the fall months Lea also completed a dramatized version of *The Vermilion Pencil;* see Library of Congress card receipt for "The Crimson Spider," dated November 20, 1909 (copyright date), in Scrapbook, box 9, Powers Papers. A copy of the fifty-page play is on file at the Library of Congress.

37. Lea, *The Valor of Ignorance;* see also Roberts to Lord Grenfell, November 28, 1909, no. 7101-23-122-11-83, Field Marshal Lord Frederick S. Roberts Papers, National Army Museum, London; Sir D. Probyn to Roberts, December 16, 1909, no. 7101-23-122-8-31, Roberts Papers; Roberts to Robert Blatchford, December 17, 1909, no. 7101-23-122-11-84, Roberts Papers; Sir Arthur Balfour to Roberts, December 17, 1909, no. 7101-23-122-8-31, Roberts Papers; Roberts to Lea, March 5, 1910, no. 7101-23-122-125-1, Roberts Papers.

38. For the Japanese edition, see Lea, *General Homer Lea's "The Valor of Ignorance,"* trans. Ike. "'Gen.' Homer Lea Says He Is Chief of Staff," *China Press* (Shanghai), December 28, 1911, article enclosure in American Consulate-General, Shanghai, China, to Secretary of State, Washington, December 30, 1911, RG 59, Notes from the Chinese Legation in the U.S. to Department of State, 1868–1906, January 12, 1904–July 7, 1906, M98, roll 1008, no. 893.00, NARA; Neuman, *America Encounters Japan,* 127.

39. "War Scares on the Pacific Coast," *San Francisco Call,* November 16, 1909, 6.

40. Lea, *The Valor of Ignorance,* 306–7.

41. "Books," *Spectator,* December 25, 1909, 1101–2. For other period reviews see "'General' Homer Lea's Sensational Book," *San Francisco Chronicle,* November 13, 1909, 8; "Japan's Control of the Pacific," *Literary Digest,* November 13, 1909, 823; "A Guide to the New Books," *Literary Digest,* November 27, 1909, 962; "The Year's Curriculum in Fiction," *Independent,* November 27, 1909, 1149; "As to Our Foreign Relations," *American Review of Reviews,* December 1909, 764; "Most Valorous in Our Ignorance," *New York Times,* January 8, 1910, 2:16; "Fresh Literature—The Newest Books Reviewed," *Los Angeles Times,* February 27, 1910, 3:19; "Books and Periodicals," *Infantry Journal,* March 1910, 770–71; "Concerning *The Valor of Ignorance,*" *Infantry Journal,* May 1910, 885–86.

42. For a closer examination of Lea and his critics, see Kennedy, "Homer Lea and the Peace Makers."

43. Boothe to Yung Wing, December 23, 1909, folder 1, box 1, Boothe Papers.

10. Final Crusade

1. Schiffrin, *Reluctant Revolutionary,* 139–40; Hsu, *Sun Yat-sen,* 70–74; Boothe to Yung Wing, December 23, 1909, Boothe Papers; Boothe to Yung Wing, December 31, 1909, Boothe Papers.

2. Sun Yat-sen to Lea, September 5, 1910, folder 8, box 1, Boothe Papers; Sun Yat-sen to Lea, February 24, 1910, folder 8, box 1, Boothe Papers; Yung Wing to Boothe, March 4, 1910, folder 1, box 1, Boothe Papers; detailed plan on revolutionary forces within China and proposals of the revolution, March 12, 1910, folder 3, box 1, Boothe Papers; Allen to Boothe, March 14, 1910, folder 2, box 1, Boothe Papers; Sun Yat-sen to Boothe, March 21, 1910, folder 3, box 1, Boothe Papers; Yung Wing to Boothe, March 28, 1910, folder 1, box 1, Boothe Papers; Sun Yat-sen to Boothe, November 8, 1910, folder 3, box 1, Boothe Papers; "Says Rebels Have Called Sun Yat Sen," *New York Times,* November 18, 1911, 3.

3. Chun-tu Hsueh, *Huang Hsing and the Chinese Revolution,* 79–80.

4. Boothe to Sun Yat-sen, May 12, 1910, folder 3, box 1, Boothe Papers; see also Sun Yat-sen to Boothe, May 24, 1910, folder 3, box 1, Boothe Papers; Lea to Allen, June 13, 1910, folder 9, box 1, Boothe Papers; Lea to Boothe, June 21, 1910, folder 4, box 1, Boothe Papers; Sun Yat-sen to Boothe, June 22, 1910, folder 3, box 1, Boothe Papers; Sun Yat-sen to Boothe, July 15, 1910; folder 3, box 1, Boothe Papers; Boothe to Allen, July 19, 1910, folder 2, box 1, Boothe Papers; Allen to Boothe, July 23, 1910, folder 2, box 1, Boothe Papers; Sun Yat-sen to Boothe, September 4, 1910, folder 3, box 1, Boothe Papers; Sun Yat-sen to Lea, September 5, 1910,

folder 3, box 1, Boothe Papers; Sun Yat-sen to Boothe, November 8, 1910, folder 3, box 1, Boothe Papers.

5. When Ethel Powers returned to Lea, her son Joshua came with her. He stayed for his sophomore year in high school in Long Beach with his mother and Lea. This information comes from the author's interview with Joshua B. Powers. See also Lea, "The Aeroplane in War."

6. Ibid. For other period works on military aviation, see also Wells, *War in the Air;* Maxim, "Warfare of the Future"; Hersey, "Menace of Aerial Warfare"; Tulloch, "Aerial Peril"; Crutcher, "Military Possibilities of Aeroplanes"; Todd, "What War Will Be with Flying Machines."

7. Lea, "Aeroplane in War," part 1, 8.

8. Carr, "Death Overpowers Odd World Figure"; Carr, "The Story of Homer Lea."

9. Carr, *Riding the Tiger,* 173.

10. "Gen. Lea Foresees a War with Japan," *Washington Times,* August 14, 1910, 13. See also "Predicts Japanese War," *Los Angeles Times,* August 14, 1910, 2:5.

11. For a transcript of the speech, see U.S. Congress, *Congressional Record,* 6551–60. The quote is on page 6558. See also Hon. James McLachlan, of California, "Defenselessness of the Pacific Coast: A Speech in the House of Representatives, May 19, 1910," *Infantry Journal,* July 1910, 1–32.

12. McLachlan, "Defenselessness of the Pacific Coast"; Major George H. Shelton to Gen. Lea, October 18, 1910, box 1, Powers Papers. For Lea's ideas being publicized in the *Infantry Journal,* see [Major George H. Shelton, ed.], "Concerning *The Valor of Ignorance,*" *Infantry Journal,* May 1910, 885–86; Shelton, "A Notable Speech in Congress—And the Result," *Infantry Journal,* July 1910, 117–19; Shelton, "Mr. McLachlan and the McGlachlan Resolution," *Infantry Journal,* September 1910, 303–4; Shelton, "Professional Reading," *Infantry Journal,* September 1910, 330–37; Shelton, "The Problem of the Pacific Coast," *Infantry Journal,* November 1910, 440–47; Shelton, "Concerning Some Aerial Articles," *Infantry Journal,* November 1910, 459–60; Shelton, "Concerning Some Expressions of Pacific Coast Opinion," *Infantry Journal,* November 1910, 463–64. See also Major General Arthur Murray, chief of coast artillery, who seized upon Lea's arguments in warning of Pacific Coast vulnerability to attack in "Admits Coast Needs 80,000 Soldiers," *San Francisco Examiner,* November 15, 1910, 1. See also Congressman Richmond Hobson's remarks on war games conducted at the Army War College in "Hobson Says We Are Defenseless against Japan," *New York Times,* February 5, 1911, 38. Lea's book also helped inspire Army Chief of Staff Major General Leonard Wood's preparedness campaign. In a September 1912 letter to Lea, Wood referred to Lea's interests in military matters and added, "I bespeak your assistance in waging a campaign of education along the lines laid down." See Wood to Lea, September 14, 1912, box 2, Powers Papers; and see also Holme, *The Life of Leonard Wood,* 158–63. For Lea's

indirect influence on armed forces defense policy, also see Tuttle, "The Army War Maneuvers in California."

13. Lea to Roberts, April 15, 1910, no. 7101-23-122-47-73, Roberts Papers.

14. Major R. C. Croxton, 20th Infantry, to Gen. Lea, November 3, 1910, box 1, Powers Papers; Major General Wm. P. Duvall, Commander, Philippines Division, to Theodore Roosevelt, November 2, 1910, *Valor* correspondence folder, box 3, Powers Papers. Roosevelt was critical of *The Valor of Ignorance* in a December 28, 1910, letter he wrote to British general Ian S. Hamilton, in which he stated: "The trouble with Homer Lea is that having a good case he proceeded to destroy it by hysterical overemphasis and exaggeration." See Morison, *Letters of Theodore Roosevelt*, 194. There were two versions of "The Great Symbol." Ethel Lea copyrighted a revised adaptation of *The Vermilion Pencil*, by Homer Lea and Ethel Lea, entitled "The Great Symbol," on February 13, 1913. See "The Great Symbol," Copyright Drama Deposits, 1913, registration no. D32291, shelf no. 20,849.2, reel no. 307, Library of Congress Manuscript Division, Washington, D.C. Lea's friend U.S. Army major Richard C. Croxton also copyrighted a revised adaptation of *The Vermilion Pencil*, entitled "The Great Symbol," by Homer Lea and R. C. Croxton, which also included Ethel Lea as one of the copyright holders, on June 13, 1913. See "The Great Symbol," Copyright Drama Deposits, 1913, registration no. D32291, shelf no. 20,849.3, reel no. 345, Library of Congress Manuscript Division.

15. "Gatherings of Representatives of Pacific Coast Interests in This City Next Thursday Will Be Important Event," *San Francisco Chronicle,* November 15, 1910, 10; "All Parts of Coast Are Sending Their Representatives," *San Francisco Chronicle,* November 16, 1910, 16; "Pacific Coast Congress Opens," *San Francisco Chronicle,* November 17, 1910, 3; "Permanent Organization to Further the Interests of This Coast," *San Francisco Chronicle,* November 18, 1910, 1–2; "'Who Will Rule the Pacific?' Asks the Governor," *San Francisco Call,* November 18, 1910, 3; "Noted Men Gather at Banquet," *San Francisco Call,* November 19, 1910, 1; "Hearty Indorsement Given to Exposition and Better Defenses Demanded," *San Francisco Call,* November 19, 1910, 2.

16. The San Diego speech is referenced in "An Eloquent Note of Warning," *Army and Navy Journal,* December 32, 1910, 501–2.

17. Marquis, *Who's Who in America,* 1129.

18. Sun Yat-sen to Boothe, December 16, 1910, folder 3, box 1, Boothe Papers; see also Boothe to Sun Yat-sen, September 26, 1910, folder 3, box 1, Boothe Papers; Boothe to Sun Yat-sen, October 21, 1910, folder 3, box 1, Boothe Papers; Sun Yat-sen to Boothe, November 8, 1910, folder 3, box 1, Boothe Papers.

19. Boothe to Hill, January 12, 1911, folder 5, box 1, Boothe Papers; see also Hill to Boothe, March 3, 1911, folder 5, box 1, Boothe Papers. The

Red Dragon conspirators believed the popular misconception that China was a great economic market yet to be exploited by the West. See Varg, *The Making of a Myth;* and Crow, *Four Hundred Million Customers.*

20. Sun Yat-sen to Boothe, March 6, 1911, folder 3, box 1, Boothe Papers; Boothe to Sun Yat-sen, April 13, 1911, folder 3, box 1, Boothe Papers.

21. Sir John G. Tollemache Sinclair to Lea, May 3, 1911, box 1, Powers Papers; Carr, "Death Overpowers Odd World Figure"; Carr, *Riding the Tiger,* 173–74; Major George H. Shelton, ed., "Concerning Homer Lea," *Infantry Journal,* November–December 1912, 403; Van Loan, "Homer Lea's Short Life an Inspiration."

22. Carr, "Death Overpowers Odd World Figure," 2; "General Homer Lea Is Dead, Helped Create a New China—Work There Shortens Life," *Los Angeles Examiner,* November 2, 1912, 4; author's interview with Joshua B. Powers; Stimson, "A Los Angeles Jeremiah," 9; Van Loan, "General Homer Lea," 7.

23. Lea's friend Robert Belford discussed employing Lea in a newly organized typewriter company. The letterhead of Belford's stationary reads "Typewriter Silencer Mfrs. Inventors—Owners—Silencer Typewriters + Add Machines." See Belford to Leas, July 8, 1911, box 1, Powers Papers; Carr, *Riding the Tiger,* 173–74; Carr, "Death Overpowers Odd World Figure," 2; Lea to H. H. Evert of *Van Norden's Magazine,* April 3, 1911, box 1, Powers Papers.

24. Lea sent documents on May 3, 1911 to Koki H. Ike, a journalist and supporter of Sun Yat-sen, transferring the copyright of *The Valor of Ignorance* for a Japanese edition. See Ike to Lea, June 1, 1911, box 1, Powers Papers.

25. "Personal," *Los Angeles Times,* June 10, 1911, 2:6.

26. See "Says Rebels Have Called Sun Yat Sen"; Trevor Dawson to Lord Edward Grey, November 13, 1911, box 4, Powers Papers.

27. Carr, *Riding the Tiger,* 174.

28. "Love Wins o'er Pen and Sword"; "General Homer Lea Weds Stenographer," *San Francisco Chronicle,* August 14, 1911, 1. For Lea wearing his mother's wedding ring, see Green, "Anecdotes," 3.

29. The Leas' passport, dated June 22, 1911, is in box 5, Powers Papers. For Lea's contact with Root, see Senator Elihu Root to Lea, September 19, 1911, box 1, Powers Papers; Lea to Root, circa November 1, 1911, box 1, Powers Papers. For Stimson's meeting with Lea, see Stimson's February 10, 1942, diary entry in Henry L. Stimson Diaries, reel 7:512, Henry L. Stimson Papers, 1846–1966, MS 465, Yale Manuscripts and Archives-Collections, Sterling Memorial Library, New Haven, Conn.; Mowry, *The Era of Theodore Roosevelt,* 281–82. After Washington, the Leas spent a weekend with inventor Hudson Maxim and his wife at their Lake Hopatcong, New Jersey, residence. See "Lake Hopatcong Had a Fine Fourth," *Philadelphia Inquirer,* July 9, 1911, 11.

30. Homer Lea to unidentified friend, August 18, 1911, box 1, Powers

Papers. For Dr. Karl Meurer being an ophthalmologist in Wiesbaden, see "New Items."

31. Homer Lea to unidentified friend, August 18, 1911, Powers Papers; Captain Samuel Shartle, U.S. Military Attaché, Berlin, to Lea, August 9, 1911, box 1, Powers Papers; "Kaiser Likes Lea's Book," *New York Times*, August 20, 1911, C2. There is some question whether Lea ever met with Kaiser Wilhelm. In Ermal Lea Green to Charles O. Kates, February 14, 1940, Ermal claimed that while the Leas were in Paris, Lea received an invitation from the kaiser to be his guest for two weeks at the imperial palace in Berlin, which Lea accepted, and they discussed *The Valor of Ignorance* in the kaiser's study. In S. G. Shartle to Charles Kates, March 28, 1940, Kates Papers, Samuel Shartle states his belief that it was unlikely Lea met the kaiser in Berlin, but acknowledged he could possibly have met him at Mainz:

> As I did not attend the maneuvers of the XVIII Corps in 1911, I would not know about the General's activities in it, nor about the courtesies extended him. To be perfectly frank, I rather doubt the story about his being a guest at the palace for two weeks. If the palace in Berlin is referred to, I would have known of it and been sufficiently impressed with such an honor to a fellow countryman to remember it. And I think I would have heard of it, if at one of the other palaces. If the Kaiser attended that maneuvers, he doubtless received the General, for that was his custom in the case of foreign observers. And it is quite probable that because of General Lea's fame, the Kaiser granted him several audiences in order to widen his knowledge of world affairs, as he was wont to do.

The veracity of the claim that Lea met the kaiser is uncertain due to the chronology of events and lack of any verification in other firsthand accounts that such a meeting occurred. The Leas had not yet visited Paris, and neither Lea nor Ethel ever made any mention of an event as important as meeting the kaiser in their respective correspondence. Also, since Lea was not an accredited foreign observer, he would not automatically have been received by Kaiser Wilhelm. Furthermore, Joshua Powers, in his interview with the author, stated that as far as he knew, Lea never met the kaiser. In all likelihood, Lea's actual account, of seeing the kaiser from a distance at the Mainz maneuvers, was distorted by his family and friends after the fact.

32. Reid, *Manchu Abdication and the Powers*, 242–44; Eberhard, *History of China*, 300–301; Hsu, *Sun Yat-sen*, 77–81; Harold Schiffrin, "The Enigma of Sun Yat-Sen," in Wright, *China in Revolution*, 470–72; Glick, *Double Ten*, 272–74; Esterer and Esterer, *Sun Yat-Sen*, 123; Ethel Lea to David Starr Jordan, December 31, 1912, Homer Lea folder, box 62, Jordan Papers. The quote is from "Kaiser Likes Lea's Book," *New York Times*, August 20, 1911, C2.

33. Hsu, *Sun Yat-sen,* 78–80. The full version of the text reads:

At that time, I could have come home in disguise by way of the Pacific Ocean, and I could have reached Shanghai in twenty days. Then I could have directed the revolutionary war myself; that would have given me the greatest satisfaction of my life. But my second thought was that my contribution to the revolutionary work was not in the battle field but in diplomatic circles. So I decided to devote myself to diplomatic work and not return until the diplomatic questions were solved.

At that time, the American government stood for the open-door policy in China. It had no settled opinion about the Chinese Revolution. On the other hand, American public opinion was favorably inclined towards our side. In France, both government and the people were favorable toward the Chinese Revolution. In England, the people were sympathetic toward us; but the China policy of the government largely followed the lead of Japan. Germany and Russia were more or less pro-Manchu, and our own Party had very little connection with either the people or the governments in Germany and in Russia. So we had no way of changing the policy of Russia and Germany.

Japan was very intimate with China. The Japanese people were not only sympathetic toward us, but many of them had even sacrificed their lives to assist the Chinese Revolution. On the other hand, the policy of the Japanese government was not favorable. It had expelled me landing in Japan, and had once refused me landing in Japan. These actions plainly indicated the attitude of the government towards the Chinese Revolution. By virtue of the Treaty of 1900, however, Japan could not act independently.

In brief, of the six Foreign Powers that have most intimate relations with China, America and France were sympathetic with the Chinese Revolution. Germany and Russia were opposed to us. The people in England were sympathetic toward us, but the government policy was not definite. So the key of our diplomacy would be the attitude of the British government because it would determine in a large measure the success or failure of our Revolution. If the British government was for the revolution, the Japanese government would not need be feared.

34. Hsu, *Sun Yat-sen,* 77–81.
35. Ethel Lea to Agnes Bryant, October 23, 1911, box, 1, Powers Papers.
36. See untitled partial manuscript, 276, box 4, Powers Papers; Lea to Roberts, October 19, 1911, no. 7101-23-122-47-72, Roberts Papers.
37. Untitled partial manuscript, 276–77, Powers Papers.

38. Ibid., 277–78; see Lea publishing contract with Harpers for *The Day of the Saxon,* October 25, 1911, box 2, Powers Papers.

39. Homer Lea to Ethel Lea, October 26, 1911, Kates Papers.

40. Ibid.

41. Sun Yat-sen to Lea, October 31, 1911, box 1, Powers Papers.

42. Sun Yat-sen to Lea, November 1, 1911, box 1, Powers Papers,

43. Lea to Roberts, November 1, 1911, no. 7101-23-122-47-71, Roberts Papers.

44. Lea to Root, n.d., box 1, Powers Papers. After writing to Root the first time from London, Lea wrote him again on November 21, 1911, with an offer to act as an advisor for the authorities of the revolution in China. Root graciously declined since it would have posed a conflict of interest with his duties as a U.S. senator. See Root to Lea, December 19, 1911, box 1, Powers Papers.

45. See Reid, *Manchu Abdication and the Powers,* 301–2; Schiffrin, *Reluctant Revolutionary,* 155–57.

46. Untitled partial manuscript, 279, Powers Papers.

47. Ibid.; Roberts to Lea, November 8, 1911, box 1, Powers Papers.

48. For Lea's invitation to join the Imperial Maritime League, see Harold F. Wyatt, Honorary Secretary, Imperial Maritime League, to Gen. Lea, Wiesbaden, October 4, 1911, box 1, Powers Papers. The league's goals are outlined in "The Imperial Maritime League," *Times* (London), January 28, 1908, 6. For Lea's quote, see "The Declaration of London," *Times* (London), November 11, 1911, 8; untitled partial manuscript, 284–85, Powers Papers.

49. Dawson to Grey, November 13, 1911, box 4, Powers Papers; Schiffrin, *Reluctant Revolutionary,* 156–57.

50. Wu, *Sun Yat-Sen,* 143–45; Schiffrin, *Reluctant Revolutionary,* 155–56.

51. As quoted in Schiffrin, *Reluctant Revolutionary,* 156.

52. Ibid.

53. "Imperial Unity and Defence," *Times* (London), November 15, 1911, 7.

54. Ethel Lea to Agnes Bryant, November 16, 1911, Powers Papers.

55. The *Daily Graphic* story also appeared in "Says Rebels Have Called Sun Yat Sen."

56. Roberts to Lea, November 15, 1911, box 1, Powers Papers; untitled partial manuscript, 274–80, Powers Papers; Col. F. N. Maude to Lea, November 17, 1911, box 1, Powers Papers; Maude to Lea, November 19, 1911, box 1, Powers Papers. Before leaving London, Sun Yat-sen and Lea conferred with James Deitrick, a railroad engineer with experience in Mongolia, about the possibilities of launching a revolution there. Deitrick offered to send a man there to explore the possibilities for $1,000. Nothing developed from their talks. See Deitrick to Lea, November 20, 1911, box 1, Pow-

ers Papers; untitled partial manuscript, 288, Powers Papers. Before leaving London, Sun Yat-sen and Lea had lunch with Lord Charles Beresford, who recalled that Lea intended to reorganize the Chinese army. See Beresford, *Memoirs*, 441.

57. Ethel Lea to Agnes Bryant, November 16, 1911, box 1, Powers Papers; E. C. Grenfell to Lea, November 17, 1911, box 1, Powers Papers; Schriffin, *Reluctant Revolutionary*, 157.

58. Sun Yat-sen, "My Reminiscences," 304. Sun Yat-sen later acknowledged being introduced to Lea through Yung Wing and then meeting Lea for the first time in Los Angeles. See "Homer Lea Dead; A Tribute to Him by Dr. Sun Yat Sen," *China Press* (Shanghai), November 6, 1912, Scrapbook, box 5, Powers Papers. Lyon Sharmon, the author of *Sun Yat-sen: His Life and Its Meaning*, believed Lea may have collaborated with Sun Yat-sen in preparing for the article. He wrote Charles Kates: "I came to believe— without any possibility of verification—that Lea was the author, or main collaborator of the article 'My Reminiscences by Sun-Yat-sen' published in the *Strand* March 1912. This is the article responsible for gross error that Sun Yat-sen's father was a Christian and an employee of the London Missionary Society, and it is the article in which Homer Lea's connection with Sun Yat-sen is exploited." See Lyon Sharmon to Charles O. Kates, November 28, 1939, Kates Papers. Ethel Lea later wrote a brief summary of Lea's career in which she noted: "It was not until the death of Kuang Hsu that he [Lea] agreed to join Sun Yat-sen in his revolutionary plans, although Sun had approached him with that end in view some years previously." See Ethel Lea letter, in Gowen and Hall, *Outline History of China*, 352. There is no documentation to verify Ethel's claim that Sun Yat-sen approached Lea to join him before the emperor's death. Her allegation is likely based on the unreliable *Strand* article.

59. Schiffrin, *Reluctant Revolutionary*, 157–58; Cheng, "The T'ung-Meng-Hui," 183; untitled partial manuscript, 298, Powers Papers; "Sun Yat Sen's Plans for China Republic," *New York Times*, November 25, 1911, 12. For Li Yuan-Hung's background, see S. S. Knabenshue, "Li Yuan-Hung, President," *Los Angeles Times*, June 18, 1916, 3:22; "Li Yuan-Hung Dead, Ex-President of China." *New York Times*, June 4, 1928, 3; "China's Lafayette," *Coshocton Morning Tribune*, November 28, 1911, 4.

60. Ethel Lea to Agnes Bryant, November 26, 1911, box 1, Powers Papers.

61. Ethel Lea letter, in Gowen and Hall, *Outline History of China*.

62. Chien-fu Ch'en, *Kuo-Fu-Ch'uan*, 201; Huang Chi-lu, *Kuo Fu Chun-shih Ku-wen-Ho-ma Li Chiang-chun* (publishing data unavailable; text referred to from University of Chicago Library no. 2298.41-4447, 16).

63. See *Singapore Free Press*, December 18, 1911, article enclosed in dispatch of American Consulate General, Singapore, December 30, 1911, to the Secretary of State, RG 59, Notes from the Chinese Legation in the

U.S. to Department of State, 1868–1906, January 12, 1904–7 July 1906, M98, roll 1808, no. 893.00/985, NARA; also sent in Vice Consul General, Shanghai, to Secretary of State, December 30, 1911, RG 59, Records of the Department of State relating to the Internal Affairs of China, 1910–1929, M329, roll 9, no. 893.00/985, NARA. For Lea's Penang interview, which has the wrong arrival date of December 15, see "Sun Yat Sen Nearing China, Arrival at Penang," *Manchester Guardian,* December 16, 1911, 9. For Lea and Sun Yat-sen arriving at Penang on December 14, see "China to Launch Republic," *Washington Post,* December 15, 1911, 1.

64. Earl Hamilton Smith, "China in Grip of Feudal War," *New York Times,* September 7, 1924, 8:5.

65. See George E. Anderson, American Consul General, Hong Kong, report to the Secretary of State, December 21, 1911, RG 59, Records of the Department of State relating to the Internal Affairs of China, 1910–1929, M329, roll 8, no. 893.00/801, NARA. Sun Yat-sen and Lea arrived in Singapore on December 16, 1912. See "Chinese to Fix Terms of Peace," *San Francisco Chronicle,* December 17, 1912, 39.

66. Anderson, American Consul General, Hong Kong, report to the Secretary of State, December 21, 1911.

67. Ibid.

68. Ibid.

69. Wells, *Blood on the Moon,* 34.

70. "Dr. Sun Yat Sen at Shanghai," *New York Times,* December 25, 1911, 1; "Manchus Bow to Will of People," *New York Times,* December 27, 1911, 1; "Accept Sun as Leader," *New York Times,* December 28, 1911, 1; "Dr. Sun Is Elected President of China," *New York Times,* December 29, 1911, 1; McCormick, *Flowery Republic,* 273.

71. McCormick, *Flowery Republic,* 273.

72. Ibid.; Selle, *Donald of China,* 188–211; Crow, *China Takes Her Place,* 68.

73. In the interview Lea disavowed any affiliations with the U.S. Army and claimed that he had earned his general's title leading four divisions in the 1900 attempt to rescue the emperor. He added that he had been involved with the revolutionary movement for the past twelve years, during which time he had commanded all Chinese troops in America and become well known as a military strategist through his writing. See "'Gen.' Homer Lea Says He Is Chief of Staff." Lea's photo shows him wearing two Pao Huang Hui medals; the medal on his chest, given him in January 1904; and a gold medal, an eight-pointed star, suspended from his neck on a crimson ribbon, which he received from K'ang Yu Wei during their 1905 cross-country tour. Lea's medal was reportedly inscribed: "To Homer Lea from Kang Yu Wei," according to a description of the medal in the *Bookman,* June 1908, 338. K'ang Yu-wei presented a dozen or so similar silver eight-pointed star medals, the "Order of Kwang Hsu," to Lea's CIA officers and other reform officials during his 1905 cross-country tour. The medal had an image of the emperor

on the obverse, and on the reverse were two crossed flags, one with a Chinese dragon, representing the Chinese imperial flag, and one the Pao Haung Hui flag with its three stars representing liberty, education, and equality. There was an inscription around the medal's border saying the medal was presented by the emperor in his thirty-fourth year through K'ang Yu-wei. Beneath the reform flag were the Chinese words "Pao Huang Hui." See "Order of Kwang Su for Rev. Mr. Poole," *Philadelphia Inquirer,* July 13, 1905, 6.

74. "'Gen.' Homer Lea Says He Is Chief of Staff."

75. Records of the U.S. District Court action against Lea in Shanghai have not survived in the National Archives. See Chapin, "Homer Lea and the Chinese Revolution," 108. See "Foreigners Guard the Way to Peking," *New York Times,* January 1912, 3:4, which noted: "General Homer Lea, the American officer who accompanied Dr. Sun Yat Sen to China for the purpose of taking a responsible position with the revolutionaries as a military adviser, has received official notification that there is a penalty of death attached to the participation by an American in the insurrection in China"; William Calhoun, U.S. Minister, Peking, to Secretary of State, December 28, 1911, RG 59, Records of the Department of State relating to the Internal Affairs of China, 1910–1929, M329, roll 8, no. 893.00/822, NARA.

76. Lea's quote is translated from a Chinese-language Shanghai newspaper that probably appeared between December 29–31, 1911, as cited by Huang Chi-lu, *Kuo Fu Chun-shih Ku-wen-Ho-ma Li Chiang-chun,* 15.

77. Charles L. Boynton, "Concerning General Homer Lea—A Memorandum," 1951 or 1952, Homer Lea folder, box 3, Charles L. Boynton Papers, Hoover Institution on War, Revolution and Peace, Stanford University, Stanford, Calif.

78. Nelson T. Johnson to Charles O. Kates, March 6, 1940, Kates Papers. The *Chung Sai Yat Po,* a San Francisco–based Chinese-language newspaper, reportedly carried the story of the U.S. District Court injunction against Lea. See Chapin, "Homer Lea and the Chinese Revolution," 108.

79. *Singapore Free Press,* December 16, 1911; Vice Consul General, Shanghai, to Secretary of State, December 18, 1911, RG 59, Records of the Department of State relating to the Internal Affairs of China, 1910–1929, M329, roll 9, no. 893.00/984, NARA; F. A. Duneka to General Lea, December 1, 1911, box 1, Powers Papers; F. A. Duneka to General Lea, December 14, 1911, box 1, Powers Papers.

80. Hall, *Eminent Asians,* 48–50; see also "Obituary," *New York Evening Post,* November 2, 1912, 7; Newmark, *Jottings in Southern California History,* 142; see commemorative medal in Powers Private Collection inscribed "Presidential Palace of the Republic of China Commemorating the Independence Ceremony January 1, 1912." For details of Sun Yat-sen's inauguration, see McCormick, *Flowery Republic,* 276–78.

81. Lea to R. J. Belford, "Draft I. The Story Letter," circa November 1912, box 1, Powers Papers.

82. McCormick, *Flowery Republic,* 294–95.

83. Linebarger, statement on Homer Lea, box 3, Powers Papers.

84. Hui-Min Lo, *Correspondence of G. E. Morrison,* 731.

85. "To Abdicate by Tomorrow Morning," *New York Times,* January 28, 1912, 3:3, 5; "Chinese Truce Ends, No One to Fight," *New York Times,* January 29, 1912, 3; "Manchus to Go with $2,000,000 a Year," *New York Times,* January 31, 1912, 1; "Abdication Edict of Manchus Signed," *New York Times,* February 1, 1912, 5; "China's Empress Decrees a Republic," *New York Times,* February 5, 1912, 3; "Dual China Government," *New York Times,* February 6, 1912, 3; "Yuan to Be Elected President of China," *New York Times,* February 14, 1912, 5; "Yuan to Be Made President Today," *New York Times,* February 15, 1912, 5.

86. "Gen. Homer Lea Loses His Job," *Syracuse Journal,* February 7, 1912, 4.

87. "'Peace or War,' Says Sun," *Washington Post,* February 12, 1912, 3. Lea was reported in a "dying condition," in "Gen. Homer Lea Very Ill," *New York Times,* February 13, 1912, 5.

88. "China Calls Author-Soldier, Gen. Lea Longs to Return," *Los Angeles Examiner,* August 23, 1912, 4:21–22.

89. Urbanek, medical report on Lea; "China a Republic by Edict Tomorrow," *New York Times,* February 12, 1912, 3; "Yuan, Fearing Ruin, Wants to Resign," *New York Times,* February 18, 1912, 3:5; Ethel Lea to Agnes Bryant, February 23, 1912, box 1, Powers Papers. For Dr. Henri Fresson being a physician and surgeon, see "Liste générale des membres de l'association." The *Army and Navy Journal* article did not specify who arranged for Dr. Fresson's train from Shanghai. Sun Yat-sen did visit Lea and conferred with Drs. Urbanek and Fresson. See *Army and Navy Journal,* April 6, 1912, 977.

90. For Ethel's arrangements to keep their arrival secret in San Francisco, see Ethel to Agnes Bryant, March 31, 1912, box 1, Powers Papers. See also "Gen. Homer Lea Broken Physically by Labors in the Orient," *San Francisco Chronicle,* May 7, 1912, 3; *San Francisco Call,* May 7, 1912, 6. For reference to the Japanese delegations welcoming Lea at each port, see Ethel Lea to David Starr Jordan, January 14, 1913, folder 20, box 62, Jordan Papers.

91. Wright, "Homer Lea Sorely Stricken," noted that Lea's Santa Monica cottage overlooked the sea. The street address is cited in several obituaries. See "L.A. Boy Buried Who Liberated the Chinese," *Los Angeles Evening Herald,* November 2, 1912, 2; "General Homer Lea Is Dead, Helped Create a New China."

92. Newmark, "Homer Lea," 184.

93. "General Homer Lea Is Dead, Helped Create a New China."

94. Ibid.

95. Lea stated his intent to write the third volume of his trilogy in the

preface to *The Day of the Saxon*. For the quote, see Lea, *The Day of the Saxon*, 5. See also Jaher, *Doubters and Dissenters*, 85. Lea probably submitted a reworked excerpt from *The Valor of Ignorance* to *North American Review* for publication. The article appeared as "The Legacy of Commodore Perry."

96. See book reviews in "*The Day of the Saxon*," *Athenaeum*, June 22, 1912, 707–8; "End of England," *New York Times*, July 21, 1912, 6:419; Willard Huntington Wright, "The New Books and the Book News," *Los Angeles Times*, July 28, 1912, 3:20; "Book Reviews," *Infantry Journal*, July–August 1913, 164–65; "*The Day of the Saxon*," *Spectator*, August 24, 1912, 274; Graham Berry, "Homer Lea's *The Day of the Saxon*," *Bookman*, September 1912, 73–75; "Other Books Worth While," *Literary Digest*, October 19, 1912, 686; F. J. Mather Jr., "An Apostle of War," *Nation*, October 24, 1912, 385–86; Edward B. Krehbiel, "A Would-be Disturber of the World's Peace," *Dial*, November 1, 1912, 334–35; "War and Peace," *Independent*, September 26, 1912, 725–26; Perkins, *The Great Rapprochement*. For Japanese interest in *The Day of the Saxon*, see "Among the Authors," *New York Times Book Review*, November 17, 1912, 670; "Congress Is Stirred by Assault on Sims," *Atlanta Constitution*, April 20, 1913, 3. In 1914 Ethel Lea gave Sun Yat-sen and Koki H. Ike permission and rights to translate *The Day of the Saxon* into Japanese, allowing Sun Yat-sen to retain the profits, but there is no indication that a translation was done. See Mrs. Lea to Sun Yat-sen, May 1, 1914, box 1, Powers Papers. *The Day of the Saxon* went into three German editions prior to World War II, in 1913, 1917, and 1919. In 1925 an English edition also came out in Germany.

97. Lea to Sun Yat-sen, July 27, 1912, as cited in Chapin, "Homer Lea and the Chinese Revolution," 126. In the letter Lea also wrote Sun Yat-sen that he had heard there were plans to use American officers in the Chinese army. He asked Sun Yat-sen for information about such plans and added, "[S]hould you wish these officers I can see the Secretary of War and get permission for whatever number you might need." He also advised Sun Yat-sen that he was prepared to go to Washington, London, and Paris as Sun Yat-sen's representative before returning to China.

98. Wright, "Homer Lea Sorely Stricken." See also "Masterpiece of Strategy," *Los Angeles Times*, July 28, 1912, 3:20.

99. Wright, "Homer Lea Sorely Stricken." Harry Bowling, "The Unwritten Sequel," *Los Angeles Times*, December 12, 1922, 2:4, asserted that Lea's third volume was to be a book on Russian expansionism entitled "The Swarming of the Slav." There is no evidence to validate Bowling's assertion, which is inconsistent with the Wright interview.

100. "Lan Tien Wei to See Los Angeles," *Los Angeles Examiner*, August 7, 1912, 3; "For Protection Only, Army Needed to Repel Invaders," *Los Angeles Times*, August 16, 1912, 2:2; "General Homer Lea Entertaining Party of Prominent Chinese," *Venice Vanguard*, August 16, 1912, 1; "China Not Actually in Need of a Loan, Says General Lan," *Christian Science Monitor*,

October 8, 1912, 1. Lea discussed his plans to return to China with other Chinese visitors. For example, his plans were reported in "General Homer Lea to Return to China," *San Francisco Chronicle,* August 29, 1912, 1.

101. Albert H. Powers to Captain Ansel O'Banion, March 16, 1943, Capt. Ansel E. O'Banion folder, box 2, Powers Papers; Albert Powers, statement about Homer Lea, untitled folder, box 3, Powers Papers.

102. Van Loan, "Homer Lea's Short Life an Inspiration."

103. Lea to R. J. Belford, "Draft I. The Story Letter."

104. Stimson recalled seeing Lea four days before his death, October 29, which is incorrect. He most likely saw Lea on October 27, before Lea was completely incapacitated by his stroke. See Stimson, draft article, untitled (on Homer Lea), 5, Stimson Papers.

105. "Homer Lea Dead; A Tribute to Him by Dr. Sun Yat Sen"; Ethel Lea to David Starr Jordan, December 31, 1912, Homer Lea folder, box 62, Jordan Papers; Sun Yat-sen to Lea, October 13, 1912, as cited in Chapin, "Homer Lea and the Chinese Revolution," 127.

106. "General Homer Lea Is Dead, Helped Create a New China," 1.

107. "Homer Lea Passes After Life Full of Effort."

108. "General Homer Lea Is Dead, Helped Create a New China," 1.

109. Ibid., 4.

110. Ibid., 1; Newmark, *Jottings in Southern California History,* 144; Newmark, "Homer Lea," 184. Newmark neglected to include Belford as one of the attendees, but Belford is cited in "Silently Impressive," *Los Angeles Times,* November 3, 1912, 1:14. Ermal was living in Alaska and could not attend her brother's funeral. See Carr, "Death Overpowers Odd World Figure."

111. Newmark, *Jottings in Southern California History,* 144; Newmark, "Homer Lea," 184.

112. "Silently Impressive"; "Homer Lea Passes After Life Full of Effort"; "L.A. Boy Buried Who Liberated the Chinese."

Conclusion

1. "Tom Lea, Jr., Questions / Ermal Lea Green Answers," 4.

2. Newmark, "Homer Lea," 178.

3. Van Loan, "Homer Lea's Short Life an Inspiration."

4. Ethel Lea and Ansel O'Banion burned bundles of Lea's papers in the backyard of Ethel's Santa Monica residence two weeks after Lea's funeral. See Glick, *Double Ten,* 277.

5. Ibid.

6. Shelton, "Concerning Homer Lea."

7. Ethel Lea, 1913 diary of Europe trip, entry June 17, 1913, Powers Private Collection.

8. Albert H. Powers to Captain Ansel O'Banion, March 16, 1943, Powers Papers.

9. "Tom Lea, Jr., Questions / Ermal Lea Green Answers," 4.

10. Newmark, "Aversion to Missionaries—Personality."

11. Quoted in Lee Craig, "Hunchback Genius of Revolution," *Long Beach Independent-Press-Telegram, Southland Magazine,* June 26, 1955, 76.

12. Robert Belford to Ethel Lea, August 8, 1913, box 1, Powers Papers.

13. Van Loan, "Homer Lea's Short Life an Inspiration."

14. "A Chinese General from Los Angeles."

15. Ermal Lea Green to Charles O. Kates, February 14, 1940.

16. Green, "Anecdotes," 3.

17. "Refuses to Fight a Duel." For Lea's interest in football, see "The Old Sport's Musings," *Hartford Courant,* November 5, 1912, 16.

18. "Shriners Kowtow to Great Dragon," *Los Angeles Herald,* May 9, 1907, 5. See Lea's membership receipt for the F. & A. M. (Free & Accepted Masons) Pentalpha Lodge No. 202, December 5, 1910, box 5, Powers Papers.

19. The Knave, "General Homer Lea's Wit," *Oakland Tribune,* February 18, 1912, 26.

20. "Homer Lea's Estate Totals Only $4000," *Oakland Tribune,* November 16, 1912, 20. The first indication Lea owned an automobile is an article citing an auto mishap. See "Auto Balks in Bad Place," *Los Angeles Times,* October 11, 1909, 18.

21. "Homer Lea's Estate Totals Only $4000"; "The Old Sport's Musings"; membership card, Automobile Club of Southern California, August 1, 1910, Documents folder, box 5, Powers Papers.

22. Author's interview with Joshua B. Powers.

23. Marshall Stimson discussed Lea's high school romances with Chapin, and implied that Lea possibly may have visited prostitutes in Los Angeles's Chinatown. See Frederic Chapin to Charles Kates, November 5, 1948, Kates Papers.

24. Edwin Janss to Charles O. Kates, March 5, 1940, Kates Papers.

25. Frederic Chapin to Charles Kates, November 5, 1948, Kates Papers.

26. Green, "Anecdotes," 1–2.

27. Carr, "Death Overpowers Odd World Figure."

28. Newmark, "Aversion to Missionaries—Personality."

29. "Morgan's Best Outclassed," *Los Angeles Times,* January 12, 1913, 2:9. Joshua Powers confirmed that Sun Yat-sen gave rare gifts to Lea and his mother. When the author interviewed him, he had in his possession a rare imperial Chinese porcelain bowl given his mother by Dr. Sun Yat-sen. See also "Empire Maker Seeks Health," which reported: "Shortly after the Boxer rebellion Lea returned to Los Angeles supplied with what seemed to be unlimited funds."

30. "American Hopes to Be Lafayette of China."

31. Lea to Boothe, circa December 1908, Powers Private Collection. Lea wrote Boothe the following:

My Dear Mr. Boothe;

The Cheng-kwa plate, photographs of which I gave you some days ago, was given to me in 1905 by his Excellency, Kang Yu Wei, for services which I had rendered him in endeavoring to bring about the restoration of the late Emperor Kwang Hsu. Kang Yu Wei was the Emperor's chief adviser, prior to his deposition in 1898. This plate was given to Kang Yu Wei by the Emperor, having been in the Imperial palace for some two hundred years. It was very highly valued by both the Emperor and Kang Yu Wei. Its estimated value in money, is from ten to fifteen thousand dollars. Full information concerning this ware, its rarity and great value, can be found in the works of any author on Chinese antiques. Have already referred you to Captain Brinkley's work, Vol. IX, pp 116 to 122. I believe there are other English authorities, that go more fully into the matter. As to the authenticity of this piece of ware, it speaks for itself.

Lea, for reasons unknown, did not sell the plate for the Red Dragon conspiracy, but eventually took it to Europe in 1911 and unsuccessfully tried to sell it in London. He wrote Ethel (see Homer Lea to Ethel Lea, October 26, 1911, Kates Papers): "I could do nothing with the plate. Sir Tollemache went with me to the dealers. They all insisted that is was not Ching Kwa but didn't know what it is. So we will keep the plate until they pay what it is worth."

32. Albert H. Powers to Captain Ansel O'Banion, March 16, 1943, Powers Papers.

33. A. E. O'Banion to Albert H. Powers, March 22, 1943, Capt. Ansel E. O'Banion folder, box 2, Powers Papers.

34. "Homer Lea's Estate Totals Only $4000."

35. Green, "Anecdotes," 3.

36. Irwin, *The Making of a Reporter,* 19–20.

37. "Morgan's Best Outclassed."

38. According to Ermal, Ethel Lea sold Lea's art objects and personal belongings at a public auction in New York City. See "Tom Lea, Jr., Questions / Ermal Lea Green Answers," 5.

39. Van Loan, "General Homer Lea."

40. D. S. Jordan to Gen. Homer Lea, December 7, 1909, box 1, Powers Papers.

41. Stimson, draft article, untitled (on Homer Lea), 3, Stimson Papers.

42. Ibid.

43. David Starr Jordan, "'General' Homer Lea," *San Francisco Chronicle,* January 3, 1912, 6.

44. Jordan's letter is reprinted in Young, *The Impudence of Charlatanism,* 5–6.

45. Ibid., 1–6.

46. David Starr Jordan to Ralph Lane, April 26, 1912, folder 20, box 62, Jordan Papers.

47. Young, *The Impudence of Charlatanism*, 1.

48. Editor, "Impudence of Charlatanism," *Army and Navy Register,* August 24, 1912, 1675.

49. David Starr Jordan to Editor, *Army and Navy Register,* September 2, 1912, folder 20, box 62, Jordan Papers.

50. David Starr Jordan, draft, "The Valor of Ignorance," n.d., folder 20, box 62, Jordan Papers.

51. Charles Zeublin to Dr. David Starr Jordan, September 4, 1912, folder 20, box 62, Jordan Papers.

52. "War and Peace," *Independent,* September 26, 1912, 726, reprinted the footnote.

53. Boynton, "Concerning General Homer Lea."

54. Frederic Chapin examined post-1907 *Chung Sai Yat Po* files with the assistance of a Chinese translator and observed that the newspaper was "very hostile to Lea." He cited the headline as an example and added that the newspaper had a "very short paragraph" on Lea's return and death. See Fred Chapin to Charles Kates, [February 1, 1949], Kates Papers.

55. Ng Poon Chew to Jordan, December 6, 1912, folder 20, box 62, Jordan Papers.

56. "The Late 'General' Lea," *New York Evening Post,* December 19, 1912, 6; Ng Poon Chew, "The Real Homer Lea," *Oriental Review,* January 1913, 171–72.

57. Ethel Lea to David Starr Jordan, December 31, 1912, folder 20, box 62, Jordan Papers.

58. Ethel Lea to David Starr Jordan, January 14, 1913, folder 20, box 62, Jordan Papers; David Starr Jordan to Ethel Lea, January 22, 1913, folder 20, box 62, Jordan Papers.

59. Jordan, *Days of a Man,* 34.

60. Ibid., 32.

61. Ibid., 32–34. Jordan's biographical narrative includes erroneous and misleading claims that Lea never got to China in 1900; that Sun Yat-sen first began working with him in Hong Kong in 1900; and that Lea subsequently returned to California, cut off ties with the reformers, and proclaimed himself a general in training Chinese cadets.

62. Ethel Lea, 1913 diary of Europe trip, entry August 23, 1913, Powers Private Collection. John Russell Kennedy was an Associated Press correspondent stationed in Japan. For a brief biography of Russell, see O'Connor, "Japan's Irish Publicists," 14. Ethel left New York for her European trip on May 17, 1913. See "Beware, Pacific Coast! Says Mrs. Homer Lea," *San Francisco Chronicle,* May 18, 1913, 33.

63. Ethel Lea, 1913 diary of Europe trip, entry September 15, 1913, Powers Private Collection.

64. The October 23, 1918, letter from Sun Yat-sen is no longer available, but is quoted by Charles O. Kates in a summary of his research entitled "Homer Lea," circa 1949, Kates Papers. The full quote is: "I think it would be a good idea for you to write a biography of the General. Since the War, he is ever so much admired, and his foresight and genius recognized. How I wish that he were with us now to see his prophecies come true! The life of such a brilliant man must not remain ignorant to the world."

65. Ethel Lea letter, in Gowen and Hall, *Outline History of China*.

66. Boynton, "Concerning General Homer Lea."

67. "Gen. Homer Lea Dead," *Boston Globe*, November 2, 1912, 11.

68. "Tom Lea, Jr., Questions / Ermal Lea Green Answers," 1.

69. "Emperor's Death May Loosen Revolution."

70. Ibid.; Hsu, *Rise of Modern China*, 572–76, 643–49.

71. "Gloomy Foreboding of Gen. Homer Lea"; "Predicts Japanese War." See Lea, *The Valor of Ignorance*, 252–53, for the forecast of the Japanese main attack on the Philippines; and for results of the December 1941 attack, see Matloff, *American Military History*, 433.

72. "Berlin Swelters, Americans at Home," *New York Times*, June 8, 1913, C2.

73. "Homer Lea's Book Interests Germans," *New York Times*, November 24, 1912, 3:3; "Book News," *Los Angeles Times Book Review*, December 15, 1912, 3; Lea, *Des Britischen Reiches Schicksalsstunde;* "May Muzzle Crown Prince," *New York Times*, July 17, 1914, 1; "Rap Crown Prince," *Washington Post*, August 9, 1914, 7; "War Book That Got Kaiser's Heir into Trouble," *New York Times*, September 6, 1914, 4:7; an English-language translation of *Des Deutchen Reiches Schicksalsstunde* appeared as H. Frobenius, *The German Empire's Hour of Destiny* (New York: McBride, Nast, 1914).

74. Marcu, "American Prophet of Total War," 474.

75. Lea referred to the Japanese publication numbers for *The Valor of Ignorance* in "'Gen.' Homer Lea Says He Is Chief of Staff." The *New York Times Book Review* cited the Japanese translation going through twenty editions during its first month of publication. See "Books and Authors," *New York Times Book Review*, February 11, 1912, 68.

76. For a reference to Sato's articles, see "Japs Don't Want War," *Los Angeles Times*, September 26, 1920, 1. See Kojiro Sato, *If Japan and America Fight*, 24, 96, 222, for references to Lea.

77. "Yamamoto Planned Assault; Seeks to Take White House," *Christian Science Monitor*, December 16, 1941, 7.

78. For the quote, see General Tomoyuki Yamashita, as told to Captain Lowell M. Limpus, "Strategy Must Change," *Infantry Journal*, April 1946, 17.

79. Fukudome, "Hawaii Operation," 1317.

80. George Van Horn Moseley, "One Soldier's Journey," 4:3, box 14, George Van Horn Moseley Papers, MSS33712, Library of Congress Manuscript Division, Washington, D.C.

81. "Among the Authors," *New York Times Book Review,* August 6, 1910, 6. See also "Among the Authors," *New York Times Book Review,* October 22, 1910, 8. In 1916 Harper and Brothers responded to demands for cheaper editions of *The Valor of Ignorance* and *The Day of the Saxon* by reducing the price of each rather than bringing out a less expensive edition. See Fanny Butcher, "Tabloid Book Review," *Chicago Daily Tribune,* July 9, 1916, 8:6.

82. Commander Ward Winchell, U.S. Navy Recruiting Officer, "Navy's Call for Men Needs Quick Answer," *Los Angeles Times,* March 27, 1917, 2:1.

83. Lieutenant Colonel George S. Patton Jr., General Staff Corps, "The Causes of War: A Comparative Study of the Similarity of Conditions Existing in 1913 and 1935," November 27, 1935, 10, George S. Patton Jr. Papers, box 70, folder 12, Library of Congress Manuscript Division, Washington, D.C.

84. Willoughby and Chamberlain, *MacArthur,* 17, 19.

85. Stimson diary entry for February 10, 1942, H. L. Stimson Papers.

86. Robert E. Runser, "Lea the Prophet," *Washington Post,* March 22, 1942, 4:10.

87. For examples of newspaper articles, many of which were syndicated nationwide, see Robert W. Reed, "Japan Rose to Power against Our 'Valor of Ignorance,'" *Kansas City Star,* January 11, 1942, 1C–3C; "Another Japanese War Prophesy, Dating from 1909, to Be Reprinted," *Galveston Daily News,* February 1, 1942, 25; Stimson, "True War Predictions by L.A. Boy Who Upset an Empire"; Stimson, "Great American Who Saw It Coming"; John Grover, "West Coast Invasion Pattern?" *Oakland Tribune,* March 7, 1942, 2; Willis Thornton, "Will U.S. Be Invaded?" *Montana Standard Magazine,* March 22, 1942, 1; Treanor, "The Home Front"; "Homer Lea's 1909 Jap War Prophecy Now Popular at Library," *Galveston Daily News,* March 29, 1942, 21. Marshall Stimson appeared on the Columbia Broadcasting System radio program, *I Was There,* which discussed Lea, on March 30, 1942. See Script, "I Was There," Homer Lea Spot, Columbia Broadcasting System, March 30, 1942, Genl. Homer Lea folder, Stimson Papers; Marshall Stimson to Joshua B. Powers, May 14, 1942, Genl. Homer Lea folder, Stimson Papers. Charles Laughton portrayed Lea in "Profit without Honor" on the National Broadcasting Company radio program *Cavalcade of America,* which aired on August 31, 1942. See "Radio Today," *New York Times,* August 31, 1942, 31; "Laughton Will Be Starred in Original Drama," *Fresno Bee,* August 31, 1942, 7. For examples of magazine articles, see "Battle of America: Invasion of the U.S.?"; "Prophesies of Homer Lea"; Marcu, "American Prophet of Total War"; "Jap Fantasy?"; Larrabee, "Pacific Prophets Come to Judgment." Lea's life also received coverage in a comic book. See "The Amazing Homer Lea."

88. Boothe, "Ever Hear of Homer Lea?"

89. Green, "She Knew Him Well."

90. Boothe, "Ever Hear of Homer Lea?" part 2, 27, 38.

91. Green, "She Knew Him Well."

92. Albert Powers to Captain [O'Banion], March 16, 1943, Capt. Ansel E. O'Banion folder, box 2, Powers Papers.

93. A. E. O'Banion to Albert Powers, March 22, 1943, Capt. Ansel E. O'Banion folder, box 2, Powers Papers.

94. "Books Published Today," *New York Times,* March 18, 1942, 27; John Chamberlain, "Books of the Times," *New York Times,* April 1, 1942, 19.

95. Tom Lea Jr. to Ermal Lea Green, March 28, 1942, James Lea Papers.

96. Tom Lea Jr. to Ermal Lea Green, circa March 1942, James Lea Papers; Tom Lea Jr. to Ermal Lea Green, March 28, 1942, James Lea Papers; Ermal Lea Green to Tom Lea Jr., March 30, 1942, James Lea Papers; Tom Lea Jr. to Ermal Lea Green, April 2, 1942, James Lea Papers; Tom Lea manuscript.

97. Ermal Lea Green to Tom Lea Jr., March 26, 1942, James Lea Papers; Ermal Lea Green to Tom Lea Jr., March 30, 1942, James Lea Papers.

98. Carl Glick to Captain Ansel O'Banion, May 5, 1943, Origins of Double Ten folder, box 3, Glick Papers; A. E. O'Banion to Albert H. Powers, May 9, 1943, Capt. Ansel E. O'Banion folder, box 2, Powers Papers; Albert Powers to Captain [O'Banion], March 16, 1943; A. E. O'Banion to Albert Powers, March 22, 1943. Glick, *Double Ten.* Glick explained how he came to write *Double Ten* in Carl Glick to Dr. Orient Lee, April 16, 1970, Notes on Translation of Double Ten to Chinese folder, box 3, Glick Papers.

99. "Letters to the Times," *Los Angeles Times,* December 6, 1939, 2:4. For a review of Kates's history on researching Homer Lea, see "Homer Lea," circa 1949, Kates Papers; Charles O. Kates to Carl Glick, February 13, 1948, Correspondence (Double Ten) folder, box 3, Glick Papers; Glick to Kates, February 14, 1948, Correspondence (Double Ten) folder, box 3, Glick Papers; C. O. Kates to Joshua B. Powers, June 10, 1952, Kates Papers; Joshua B. Powers to Major C. O. Kates, June 12, 1952, Kates Papers; Frederic Chapin to Charles Kates, September 18, 1952, Kates Papers; C. O. Kates to John Schaffner, September 25, 1952, Kates Papers; Charles Kates to Frederic Chapin, September 25, 1952, Kates Papers; John Schaffner to C. O. Kates, March 31, 1953, Kates Papers; Charles Kates to Frederic Chapin, April 11, 1953, Kates Papers; Frederic Chapin to Charles Kates, May 25, 1953, Kates Papers. See Chapin, "Homer Lea and the Chinese Revolution." See also Frederic L. Chapin to Marshall Stimson, October 31, 1948, Genl. Homer Lea folder, Stimson Papers.

100. C. O. Kates to Joshua Powers, September 20, 1955, Kates Papers.

101. For background on the donation of the Powers and Boothe papers to the Hoover Institution, see John T. Ma to Hon. Chi-lu Huang, December 20, 1968, H. Lea folder, box 78, Howard P. Jones Papers, Hoover Institution on War, Revolution and Peace, Stanford University, Stanford, Calif. For the quote, see Anschel, *Homer Lea, Sun Yat-Sen and the Chinese Revolution,* xv.

102. "Picture Plays and People," *New York Times,* January 8, 1922, 71; Mae Tinee, "Hello Bessie! Glad to See You Once More!" *Chicago Daily Tribune,* March 9, 1922, 14; "*Vermilion Pencil,*" *Atlanta Constitution,* May 28, 1922, E4; "Pan Bill Is Chaos with Highlights," *Los Angeles Times,* July 4, 1922, 2:11.

103. Louella O. Parsons, "Life Story of Hunchback Military Genius Who Served China Attracts Filmdom," *Fresno Bee,* February 27, 1942, 8.

104. Edwin Schallert, "Deanna Goes Dramatic; 20th Gets Joan Bennett," *Los Angeles Times,* April 15, 1942, 12. Upton Close was the pen name of foreign correspondent Josef Washington Hall, who had wide experience covering Asian affairs. See also Marshall Stimson to Jack Warner, April 23, 1942, Genl. Homer Lea folder, Stimson Papers.

105. See "General Homer Lea," Literary File, Plays, folder 15, box 327, Clare Boothe Luce Papers, Library of Congress Manuscript Division, Washington, D.C., 1–69. See reference to Boothe's screenplay in Louella O. Parsons, "Fred Allen Signs Contract, Gets Full Power to Decide Cost, Direction and Stories," *Fresno Bee,* March 5, 1942, 9.

106. Jack Warner of Warner Brothers told Marshall Stimson he had decided not to do a Lea film. See Marshall Stimson to Joshua B. Powers, May 14, 1942, Genl. Homer Lea folder, Stimson Papers; Louella Parsons, "Paul Muni Is Selected to Play Role of Dr. Sun Yat Sen, Chinese Patriot," *Fresno Bee,* October 27, 1942, 7.

107. Claire Primus to Carl Glick, December 17, 1947, Correspondence concerning Lester Fuller Interest in a Double Ten Movie folder, box 3, Glick Papers; Glick to Captain [O'Banion], December 21, 1948, Proposal for a Screenplay folder, box 3, Glick Papers; Glick to Captain [O'Banion], March 17, 1949, Proposal for a Screenplay folder, box 3, Glick Papers.

108. A. E. O'Banion to Carl Glick, January 14, 1958, Other Biographies of Homer Lea folder, box 3, Glick Papers.

109. For the William Schorr film, see Thomas M. Pryor, "Homer Lea's Life Planned as Film," *New York Times,* August 26, 1955, 10; Hedda Hopper, "Marjorie Main to Co-star with Gary Cooper," *Chicago Daily Tribune,* August 26, 1955, A6; Hedda Hopper, "A Submarine Will Be Setting for Cary Grant's Next Film," *Chicago Daily Tribune,* September 16, 1955, A11; Charles O. Kates to William W. Schorr, August 28, 1955, Kates Papers. For Joshua Powers's apprehensions about the Schorr film, see author's interview with Joshua B. Powers. For the quote, see Joshua B. Powers to O'Banion, September 6, 1955, Miscellaneous (Double Ten) folder, box 3, Glick Papers.

110. A. E. O'Banion to Carl Glick, January 14, 1958, Other Biographies of Homer Lea folder, box 3, Glick Papers; A. E. O'Banion to Carl Glick, March 3, 1958, Other Biographies of Homer Lea folder, box 3, Glick Papers.

111. For the proposed television episode, see Julian Lesser to J. B. Powers, July 7, 1959, box 2, Powers Papers. In July 2002 the author, a U.S. Army Center of Military History historian at the time, gave an interview

to the *Baltimore Sun* newspaper discussing his work for the army, and in the course of the interview mentioned his research on a Homer Lea biography. The article appeared on the Internet and came to the attention of Bob Nessler of ABC television, who had a personal interest in Homer Lea. He contacted the author to discuss the possibility of doing a television miniseries or movie about Lea's life based on *Homer Lea: American Soldier of Fortune,* but the author's incomplete research precluded further discussion about producing such a project at that time. For the article, see Tom Bowman, "Do You Need Any History?" *Baltimore Sun,* July 24, 2002, 2A.

112. "Literary Notes," *Christian Science Monitor,* November 4, 1912, 7.

113. Suez, "Chinese-American Bonds of Trade and Friendship," 7. The author, Juming C. Suez, is incorrectly identified in the article citation as I. C. Suez.

114. For details on the 1914 Chinese delegation visit, see Newmark, untitled notes on Homer Lea, Powers Papers. For the donation of Lea's papers by Joshua Powers to the Hoover Institution with a condition to fulfill Lea's burial wishes, see John T. Ma to Hon. Chi-lu Huang, December 20, 1968, Jones Papers; for additional background on Lea's will and burial in Taiwan, see Dr. John Ma, e-mail message to author, December 29, 2002; for Ethel and Joshua Powers keeping Lea's ashes, see Carolien Maynard, e-mail message to author, November 14, 2007.

115. Memorandum, John T. Ma to Dr. W. Glenn Campbell, Professor Sworakowski, Ambassador Jones, Mr. Joshua B. Powers, January 25, 1969, H. Lea folder, box 78, Jones Papers.

116. Ibid.; "Homer Lea Back," *China Post,* April 19, 1969, 4.

117. "Homer Lea Back."

118. "Homer Lea Laid to Rest," *China Post,* April 21, 1969, 4.

119. Joshua Powers, in his interview with the author, had some misgivings about presenting Lea's sword to President Chiang Kai-shek, believing that the president did not particularly appreciate its historic significance. For press accounts about Lea's ashes eventually being taken to Nanking, see "Homer Lea Back"; "Homer Lea Laid to Rest"; "Homer Lea at Home Again in China," *Chicago Daily Tribune,* April 22, 1969, 18; "Dr. Sun's American Advisor Laid to Rest in Free China," *Free China Weekly,* April 27, 1969, 4. For the quote, see Joshua B. Powers to Ambassador Howard P. Jones, June 5, 1969, H. Lea folder, box 78, Jones Papers.

120. Shelton, "Concerning Homer Lea."

121. Van Loan, "General Homer Lea."

BIBLIOGRAPHY

Primary Sources

Archival Sources

Bancroft Library, University of California, Berkeley, California.
    George C. Pardee Papers.
California State Archives, Sacramento, California.
    California National Guard Personnel Records.
Carnegie Branch Library for Local History, Boulder Public Library, Boulder, Colorado.
Chicago History Museum, Chicago, Illinois.
    Cary T. Ray Papers.
Colorado Historical Society, Denver, Colorado.
    Colorado Marriages, 1858–1939.
    Papers relating to the Lea Family.
Foreign Office Records. Public Record Office, Kew, Richmond, Surrey, United Kingdom.
Harry Ransom Humanities Research Center, University of Texas, Austin, Texas.
    Thomas Calloway Lea Papers.
Holt-Atherton Special Collections, University of the Pacific, Stockton, California.
    Lea Family School Records and Documents.
Hoover Institution on War, Revolution and Peace, Stanford University, Stanford, California.
    Charles B. Boothe Papers.
    Charles L. Boynton Papers.
    Howard P. Jones Papers.
    David Starr Jordan Papers.
    Joshua B. Powers Papers.
Huntington Library, Art Collections, and Botanical Gardens, San Marino, California.
    Tasker A. Odie Papers.
    Marshall W. Stimson Papers.
Jackson County Historical Society, Independence, Missouri.
    Papers relating to the Lea Family.

Mr. Brian Kates, Pomona, New York.
　　Charles O. Kates Personal Papers.
Mr. and Mrs. James D. Lea, Houston, Texas.
　　Personal Papers.
Library of Congress Manuscript Division, Washington, D.C.
　　"The Crimson Spider." Copyright Office, Class D Drama Deposits, 1909.
　　"The Great Symbol." Copyright Drama Deposits, 1913.
　　Clare Boothe Luce Papers.
　　George S. Patton Jr. Papers.
　　Theodore Roosevelt Papers.
　　George Van Horn Moseley Papers.
National Archives and Records Administration, Washington, D.C.
　　Consular Correspondence of the Department of State, Dispatches from U.S. Consuls in Canton, China, 1790–1906, October–December 1900. Record Group 59.
　　Dispatches from U.S. Ministers to China, 1843–1906. Record Group 59.
　　Miscellaneous Letters of the Department of State. Record Group 59.
　　Notes from the Chinese Legation in the U.S. to Department of State, 1868–1906. Record Group 59.
　　Numerical and Minor Files of the Department of State, 1906–1910. Record Group 59.
　　Records of the Adjutant General's Office, Department of War. Record Group 94.
　　Records of the Department of State relating to the Internal Affairs of China, 1910–1929. Record Group 59.
National Army Museum, London, United Kingdom.
　　Field Marshal Lord Frederick S. Roberts Papers.
Nevada State Library and Archives, Carson City, Nevada.
　　Governor's Appointment Book, 1887–1914.
　　Secretary of State Corporation Files.
Powers Family, South Royalton, Vermont.
　　Joshua B. Powers Personal Papers.
Stanford University (Registrar), Stanford, California.
　　Homer Lea Grade Transcript, 1897–1899.
University of Iowa, University Libraries, Iowa City, Iowa.
　　Carl Glick Papers.
Robert G. Wilson, Wichita, Kansas.
　　Personal Papers.

Other Primary Sources

Abbott, James F. *Japanese Expansion and American Policies.* New York: Macmillan, 1916.

Acts Passed the First Session of the Twenty-second General Assembly of the State of Tennessee, 1837–8. Nashville: S. Nye, 1838.

Adjutant General's Office, War Department. *Official Army Register for 1904.* Washington, D.C.: Adjutant Generals' Office, War Department, 1903.

Angell, Norman. *Arms and Industry: A Study of the Foundations of International Polity.* New York: G. P. Putnam's Sons, 1914.

————. *The Great Illusion: A Study of the Relation of Military Power to National Advantage.* New York: G. P. Putnam's Sons, 1910.

Appendix to Journals of Senate and Assembly of the Twenty-fourth Session of the Legislature of the State of Nevada, 1909. Vol. 1. Carson City: State Printing Office, 1909.

Brinkley, Frank. *China: Its History, Arts and Literature.* Vol. 9. Boston: J. B. Millet, 1902.

Bristol, Gilbert C. "The Japanese Invasion." *Army and Navy Life and the United Service,* November 1907, 517–27.

The Bronco, 1902. Roswell: New Mexico Military Institute, 1902.

Builders of Our Nation: Men of 1914. Chicago: Men of Nineteen-Fourteen, 1915.

California Death Index, 1940–1997. http://www.ancestry.com/ (accessed October 5, 2004).

Cantlie, James, and C. Sheridan Jones. *Sun Yat Sen and the Awakening of China.* New York: Fleming H. Revell, 1912.

Childe, Cromwell. "American Kings." *Adventure,* August 1913, 100–106.

Chisholm, Hugh, ed. *The Britannica Year Book, 1913.* New York: Encyclopedia Britannica, 1913.

Colby, Frank M., ed. *The New International Year Book: A Compendium of the World's Progress for the Year 1912.* New York: Dodd, Mead, 1913.

Crocker-Langley San Francisco Directory for the Year Ending October 1908. San Francisco: H. S. Crocker, 1908.

Crutcher, P. "Military Possibilities of Aeroplanes." *Scientific American,* August 15, 1908, 107.

Denver City Directory, 1892. Denver: Ballinger and Richards, 1892.

De Tessan, François. *Promenades au Far-West.* Paris: Plon-Nourrit, 1912.

Dingle, Edwin J. *China's Revolution, 1911–1912: A Historical and Political Record of the Civil War.* New York: McBride, Nast, 1912.

Edebohls, George M. *The Surgical Treatment of Bright's Disease.* New York: Frank F. Lisiecki, 1904.

1880 United States Census. http://www.ancestry.com/ (accessed May 19, 2004).

1860 Nebraska Territorial Census, Free Inhabitants in the Gold Hill Settlement

(Colorado), Post Office: Denver City. http://ftp.rootsweb.com/pub/usgenweb/ne/state/census/1860/f0134.txt (accessed April 13, 2007).

The Encyclopedia Americana. Vol. 17. New York: Encyclopedia Americana, 1919.

Family Search (genealogy). http://www.familysearch.org/ (accessed April 23, 2007).

"Foreign Affairs." *Military Engineer,* September–October 1954, 377–79.

Grane, William L. *The Passing of War: A Study in Things That Make for Peace.* London: Macmillan, 1912.

Gregory, Eliot. "Unavailing Wealth." *Century,* June 1903, 242.

Hanna, Captain Matthew E. "The Valor of Ignorance." *Journal of the United States Cavalry Association,* March 1910, 1025–27.

Harper, Franklin, ed. *Who's Who on the Pacific Coast: A Bibliographical Compilation of Notable Living Contemporaries West of the Rocky Mountains.* Los Angeles: Harper, 1913.

Hersey, H. B. "Menace of Aerial Warfare." *Century,* February 1909, 627–30.

History of California and an Extended History of Los Angeles and Environs: Biographical. Vols. 2–3. Los Angeles: Historic Record, 1915.

History of Clear Creek and Boulder Valleys, Colorado. Chicago: O. L. Baskin, 1880.

The History of Jackson County, Missouri, Containing a History of the County, Its Cities, Towns, Etc. Kansas City, Mo.: Union Historical, Birdsall, Williams, 1881; repr., Cape Girardeau, Mo.: Ramfre, 1966.

Irwin, William H., ed. *Stanford Quad—1900.* Palo Alto: Stanford University, 1900.

Jordan, David Starr. *Unseen Empire: A Study of the Plight of Nations That Do Not Pay Their Debts.* Boston: American Unitarian Association, 1912.

Jordan, David Starr, and Edward E. Krehbiel. *Syllabus of Lectures on International Conciliation Given at Leland Stanford Junior University.* Boston: World Peace Foundation, 1912.

Laing Chi-Ch'ao. *The Great Chinese Philosopher K'ang Yu-Wei.* 1903; repr., San Francisco: Chinese World, 1953.

Lea, Homer. "The Aeroplane in War: Some Observations on a Military Delusion." *Harper's Weekly,* August 20, 1910, 8–9; August 27, 1910, 11, 26.

———. *Des Britischen Reiches Schicksalsstunde, Mahnwort eines Angelsachsen* [The British Empire's Fateful Hour: The Warning of an Anglo-Saxon General]. Translated by Graf Ernst zu Reventlow. Berlin: E. S. Mittler and Sohn, 1913; repr., 1917, 1919.

———. "Can China Fight?" *World Today,* February 1907, 137–46.

———. *The Day of the Saxon.* 1912; repr., New York: Harper and Brothers, 1942.

———. *The Day of the Saxon.* Bielefeld / Leipzig: Velhagen and Klasing, 1925.

———. *General Homer Lea's "The Valor of Ignorance": The War between*

Japan and America. Translated by Koki H. Ike. Tokyo: Hakubun-Kwan, 1911.

————. "How Socialism Failed in China." *Van Norden's Magazine,* September 1908, 107–13; October 1908, 81–85.

————. *If America Fights with Japan: The Pacific War Foretold Thirty-three Years Ago.* Tokyo: Hokuseido, 1942.

————. "The Legacy of Commodore Perry." *North American Review,* June 1913, 741–60.

————. *The Valor of Ignorance.* 1909; repr., New York: Harper and Brothers, 1942.

————. "The Valor of Ignorance," *Harper's Weekly,* September 18, 1909, 7; September 25, 1909, 15; October 2, 1909, 13; October 9, 1909, 13; October 16, 1909, 15–16; October 23, 1909, 13; October 30, 1909, 11–12; November 6, 1909, 11–12.

————. *The Vermilion Pencil: A Romance of China.* New York: McClure, 1908.

Leech, D. D. T. *List of Post Offices in the United States with the Names of Postmasters on the 1st of July 1855.* Washington, D.C.: George S. Gideon, 1855.

"Liste générale des membres de l'association, arrêtée au 15 Juin 1908." *Bulletin du Comité de L'Association Amicale des Internes et Anciens Internes en Médecine des Hôpitaux & Hospicos civils de Paris,* February 15, 1908, 90.

Los Angeles City Directory, 1901. N.p.

Marquis, Albert Nelson, ed. *Who's Who in America: A Biographical Dictionary of Notable Living Men and Women of the United States.* Vol. 6, *1910–1911.* Chicago: A. N. Marquis, 1910.

Maxim, Hiram. "Warfare of the Future." *Science,* December 11, 1908, 826–31.

McClenon, Walter H., and Wilfred C. Gilbert. *Index to the Federal Statutes, 1874–1931.* Washington, D.C.: Government Printing Office, 1933.

McCormick, Frederick. *The Flowery Republic.* New York: D. Appleton, 1913.

Moody, Charles Amadon, ed. "Makers of Los Angeles." *Out West: A Magazine of the Old Pacific and New,* April 1909, 311–420.

The National Cyclopedia of American Biography. Vol. 2. New York: James T. White, 1921.

National Surgical Institute. Indianapolis: Baker-Randolph, n.d.

"New Items." *Ophthalmic Record: A Monthly Review of the Progress of Ophthalmology,* February 1910, 111.

Ng, Poon Chew. "The Real Homer Lea." *Oriental Review,* January 1913, 171–72.

1910 United States Census. http://www.ancestry.com/ (accessed May 19, 2004).

1920 United States Census. http://www.ancestry.com/ (accessed October 5, 2004).

Official Congressional Directory for the Use of the United States Congress: Fifty-sixth Congress. Washington, D.C.: Government Printing Office, 1900.

One Thousand American Men of Mark of Today. Chicago: American Men of Mark, 1916.

O'Reilly, Edward S. *Roving and Fighting: Adventures under Four Flags.* New York: Century, 1918.

Papers Relating to the Foreign Relations of the United States. 52nd Cong., 1st sess., House of Representatives. Washington, D.C.: Government Printing Office, 1892.

Patterson, Homer L., ed. *Patterson's College and School Directory of the United States and Canada.* Chicago: American Educational, 1905.

Phillips, Alice Mary. *Los Angeles: A Guide Book.* Los Angeles: Neuner, 1907.

Press Reference Library: Notables of the Southwest. Los Angeles: Los Angeles Examiner, 1912.

Rodic, Captain Ignez. "Military Conditions in the United States and Japan." *Journal of the Military Service Institution of the United States,* July–August 1907, 12–27.

Rodman, Willoughby. *History of the Bench and Bar of Southern California.* Los Angeles: William J. Porter, 1909.

Runkle, Ben P. "The Valor of Ignorance." *National Guard Magazine,* January 1910, 553–56.

Sato, Kojiro. *If Japan and America Fight.* Tokyo: Meguro Bunten, 1921.

Seventh Regiment (Jennison's Jayhawkers) Kansas Volunteer Cavalry. Kansas State Historical Society. http://www.kshs.org/genealogists/military/7thks.htm (accessed September 9, 2007).

Suez, I. C. "Chinese-American Bonds of Trade and Friendship." *Far Eastern Fortnightly,* October 11, 1920, 7–8.

Sun Yat-sen. "My Reminiscences." *Strand,* March 1912, 301–7.

Territorial Governors Collection. Colorado Department of Personnel and Administration. http://www.colorado.gov/dpa/doit/archives/govs/mccook.html (accessed April 16, 2007).

Todd, F. "What War Will Be with Flying Machines." *World's Work,* November 1908, 10911–22.

Townley, Susan. *My Chinese Note Book.* London: Methuen, 1904.

Tulloch, T. G. "Aerial Peril." *Nineteenth Century and After,* May 1909, 800–809.

Tuttle, Oliver W. "The Army War Maneuvers in California." *Overland Monthly,* October 1912, 313–23.

United States Census of 1850. http://www.ancestry.com/ (accessed October 5, 2004).

U.S. Congress. *Congressional Record.* 61st Cong., 2nd sess., May 19, 1910. House Resolution 707, 45:6. Washington, D.C.: Government Printing Office, 1910.

Van Loan, Charles E. "General Homer Lea: November 17, 1876–November 1, 1912." *Harper's Weekly,* January 4, 1913, 7.

Wells, H. G. *War in the Air.* London: G. Bell and Sons, 1908.

Who's Who in America (1910–1915). Chicago: A. N. Marquis, 1910–15.

Who's Who in the Pacific Southwest: A Compilation of Authentic Biographical Sketches of Citizens of Southern California and Arizona. Los Angeles: Times-Mirror, 1913.

"The Yellow Peril." *National Guard Magazine,* December 1909, 553–56.

Young, Robert. *The Impudence of Charlatanism.* World Peace Foundation Pamphlet Series. Boston: World Peace Foundation, 1912.

Secondary Sources

Abrahamson, James L. *America Arms for a New Century: The Making of a Great Military Power.* New York: Free Press, 1981.

Alexander, Tom. "'Ambitious Little Romancer'—or Visionary Genius?" *Smithsonian,* July 1993, 103–4, 106–15.

"The Amazing Homer Lea." *True Comics,* March 1943, 48–53.

Anderson, Wing. *War's End: Including Cudmore's Prophesy of the Twentieth Century.* Los Angeles: Kosmon, 1944.

Anschel, Eugene. *Homer Lea, Sun Yat-Sen, and the Chinese Revolution.* New York: Praeger, 1984.

Armentrout Ma, L. Eve. "The Canton Rising of 1902–1903: Reformers, Revolutionaries, and the Second Taiping." *Modern Asian Studies* 10 (1976): 83–105.

———. "Chinese Politics in the Western Hemisphere, 1893–1911: Rivalry between Reformers and Revolutionaries in the Americas." Ph.D. diss., University of California–Davis, 1977.

———. *Revolutionaries, Monarchists, and Chinatowns: Chinese Politics in the Americas and the 1911 Revolution.* Honolulu: University of Hawaii Press, 1990.

Asahi Shimbun staff. *The Pacific Rivals: A Japanese View of Japanese-American Relations.* New York and Tokyo: Weatherhill / Asahi, 1972.

Bannister, Robert C. *Social Darwinism: Science and Myth in Anglo-American Social Thought.* Philadelphia: Temple University Press, 1979.

"Battle of America: Invasion of the U.S.?" *Time,* December 23, 1941, 8–19.

Bendersky, Joseph W. *The "Jewish Threat": Anti-Semitic Politics of the U.S. Army.* New York: Basic, 2000.

Bennett, Henry G. "The Valor of Ignorance." *Scabbard and Blade Journal,* October 1935, 6–8.

Beresford, Charles. *The Memoirs of Admiral Lord Charles Beresford.* Vol. 2. Boston: Little, Brown, 1914.

Block, Augusta Hauck. "The Old Arapahoe School." *Colorado Magazine,* May 1945, 119–25.

Bonner, Arthur. *Alas! What Brought Thee Hither? The Chinese in New York, 1800–1950.* Cranbury, N.J.: Fairleigh Dickinson University Press, 1997.

Boothe, Clare. "Ever Hear of Homer Lea?" *Saturday Evening Post,* March 7, 1942, 12–13, 70–72; March 14, 1942, 27, 38–40, 42.

Brill, Heinz. "Vergessene Weltpolitische Einsichten von Homer Lea" [Forgotten Insights into World Politics by Homer Lea]. *Zeitschrift fur Politik* (West Germany) 28 (1981): 196–99.

Bruce, Robert. *Sun Yat-Sen.* London: Oxford University Press, 1969.

Burns, Edward. *The American Idea of Mission: Concepts of National Purpose and Destiny.* Piscataway: N.J.: Rutgers University Press, 1957.

California: A Guide to the Golden State, Compiled and Written by the Federal Writers' Project of the Works Progress Administration for the State of California. New York: Hastings House, 1939.

Carr, Harry. *Riding the Tiger: An American Newspaper Man in the Orient.* New York: Houghton Mifflin, 1934.

Carroll, Bernice A. *Design for Total War: Arms and Economics in the Third Reich.* The Hague: Mouton, 1968.

Chapin, Frederick L. "Homer Lea and the Chinese Revolution," AB Honors thesis, Harvard University, 1950.

Cheng, Shelly Hsien. "The T'ung Meng Hui: Its Organization and Finances, 1905–1912." Ph.D. diss., University of Washington, 1962.

Chien-fu Ch'en. *Kuo-Fu-Ch'uan* [The Complete Biography of the National Father]. Tai-pei, Taiwan: Great Western, 1970.

Chong, Key Ray. "The Abortive American-Chinese Project for Chinese Revolution, 1908–1911." *Pacific Historical Review* 41 (1972): 54–70.

———. *Americans and Chinese Reform and Revolution, 1898–1922.* New York: University Press of America, 1984.

Chun-tu Hsueh. *Huang Hsing and the Chinese Revolution.* Stanford: Stanford University Press, 1961.

Cleaveland, Norman. *Bang! Bang! In Ampang: Dredging Tin during Malaya's "Emergency."* San Pedro, Calif.: Symcon, 1973.

Cohen, Warren. *America's Response to China: An Interpretative History of Sino-American Relations.* New York: John Wiley and Sons, 1971.

Craver, Rebecca, and Adair Margo, eds. *Tom Lea: An Oral History.* El Paso: Texas Western Press, 1995.

Crow, Carl. *China Takes Her Place.* New York: Harper and Brothers, 1944.

———. *Four Hundred Million Customers.* New York: Harper and Brothers, 1937.

Daniels, Roger. *The Politics of Prejudice: The Anti-Japanese Movement in California and the Struggle for Japanese Exclusion.* Berkeley: University of California Press, 1962.

D'Auvergne, Edmund B. *Pierre Lotti: The Romance of a Great Writer.* New York: Kennikat, 1970.

"Dr. Sun Yat-Sen's Advisor Buried in Taipei." *Cosmorama Pictorial,* April–May 1969, 12–13.

Duke, David C. *Distant Obligations: Modern American Writers and Foreign Causes.* New York: Oxford University Press, 1983.

Eberhard, Wolfram. *A History of China.* Berkeley: University of California Press, 1960.

Edgerton, Robert B. *Warriors of the Rising Sun: A History of the Japanese Military.* New York: W. W. Norton, 1997.

Egbert, Doris Sloan. "Homer Lea: A Military Leader." M.A. thesis, University of South Dakota, 1967.

Esterer, Arnulf, and Louise Esterer. *Sun Yat-Sen: China's Great Champion.* New York: Julian Messner, 1970.

Fairbank, John King. *The United States and China.* 1948; repr., Cambridge, Mass.: Harvard University Press, 1975.

Fleming, Elvis E. *Captain Joseph C. Lea: From Confederate Guerilla to New Mexico Patriarch.* Las Cruces, N.M.: Yucca Free Press, 2002.

Fleming, Thomas. "Homer Lea and the Decline of the West." *American Heritage,* May–June 1988, 98–104.

Fukudome, Shigeru. "Hawaii Operation." United States Naval Institute *Proceedings* 81 (December 1955): 1315–31.

Gabriel, Ralph. *The Course of American Democratic Thought: An Intellectual History since 1815.* New York: Ronald, 1940.

Gatzke, Hans. *Germany and the United States: A "Special Relationship."* Cambridge, Mass.: Harvard University Press, 1980.

Ginger, Ray. *Age of Excess: The United States from 1877 to 1914.* New York: Macmillan, 1975.

Glick, Carl. *Double Ten: Captain O'Banion's Story of the Chinese Revolution.* New York: Whittlesey House, 1945.

Glick, Carl, and Hong Sheng-Hwa. *Swords of Silence: Chinese Secret Societies—Past and Present.* New York: McGraw-Hill, 1947.

Gowen, Herbert, and Josef W. Hall. *An Outline History of China.* New York: D. Appelton, 1929.

Green, Ermal Lea. "She Knew Him Well." *Saturday Evening Post,* May 23, 1942, 4.

Greene, Theodore P. *America's Heroes: The Changing Models of Success in American Magazines.* New York: Oxford University Press, 1970.

Grieder, Jerome B. *Intellectuals and the State in Modern China: A Narrative History.* New York: Free Press, 1981.

Hall, Josef W. *Eminent Asians.* New York: D. Appleton, 1929.

Hao Chang. *Liang Ch'i-ch'ao and the Intellectual Transition in China, 1890–1907.* Cambridge, Mass.: Harvard University Press, 1971.

Hardie, Raymond. "Homer." *Stanford Magazine,* June 1990, 44–47.

Heilbroner, Robert, and Aaron Singer. *The Economic Transformation of America: 1600 to the Present.* New York: Harcourt Brace Jovanovich, 1977.

Hensman, C. Richard. *Sun Yat-sen.* London: SCM, 1971.

Herwig, Holger. *Politics of Frustration: The United States in German Naval Planning.* Boston: Little, Brown, 1976.

Hibbert, Christopher. *The Dragon Wakes: China and the West, 1793–1911.* New York: Harper and Row, 1970.

Hickman, W. Z. *History of Jackson County, Missouri.* Topeka, Kans: Historical Publishing, 1920.

"History of Lee's Summit" Attraction brochure, Lee's Summit, Missouri, Chamber of Commerce. www.lschamber.com (accessed April 13, 2007).

History of Tennessee: From the Earliest Times to the Present. Chicago: Goodspeed, 1887; repr., Nashville: Charles and Randy Elder, 1972.

Hofstadter, Richard. *Social Darwinism in American Thought.* Philadelphia: University of Pennsylvania Press, 1944; rev. ed., Boston: Beacon, 1970.

Holme, John G. *The Life of Leonard Wood.* New York: Doubleday, Page, 1920.

Hoover, Frances Montgomery. *Castle o'Montgomery.* Nashville: Parthenon, 1974.

Hsu, Immanuel C. Y. *The Rise of Modern China.* New York: Oxford University Press, 1975.

Hsu, Leonard S. *Sun Yat-sen: His Political and Social Ideals.* Los Angeles: University of Southern California Press, 1933.

Huang, Carol. "The Chinese Western Military Academies in the United States." In *Chartered Schools: Two Hundred Years of Independent Academies in the United States, 1727–1925,* edited by Nancy Beadie and Kim Tolly. New York: Routledge Falmer, 2002.

Huang Chi-lu. *Kuo Fu Chun-shih Ku-wen-Ho-ma Li Chiang-chun (Ch'u Kao)* [The Military Consultant of the National Father—General Homer Lea]. N.p.

Huang, Philip C. *Liang Ch'i-ch'ao and Modern Chinese Liberalism.* Seattle: University of Washington Press, 1972.

Hudson, Valerie M., and Hyler, Eric. "Homer Lea's Geopolitical Theory: Valor or Ignorance?" *Journal of Strategic Studies* 12 (September 1989): 324–48.

Hui-Min Lo, ed. *The Correspondence of G. E. Morrison, 1895–1912.* Cambridge: Cambridge University Press, 1976.

Hyer, Eric, and Valerie M. Hudson. "Homer Lea and the Chinese Contras: The Chinese Imperial Reform Army in America, 1901–1911." *Chinese Studies in History* 26 (Fall 1992): 63–85.

Iriye, Akira, ed. *Mutual Images: Essays in American-Japanese Relations.* Cambridge, Mass.: Harvard University Press, 1975.

———. *Pacific Estrangement: Japanese and American Expansion, 1897–1911.* Cambridge, Mass.: Harvard University Press, 1972.

Irwin, William H. *The Making of a Reporter.* New York: G. P. Putnam's Sons, 1942.

Jaher, Frederick C. *Doubters and Dissenters: Cataclysmic Thought in America, 1885–1918.* London: Free Press of Glencoe, Collier Macmillan, 1964.

Jansen, Marius. *Japan and China: From War to Peace, 1894–1972*. Chicago: Rand McNally College, 1970.

———. *The Japanese and Sun Yat-Sen*. Cambridge, Mass.: Harvard University Press, 1954.

"Jap Fantasy?" *American Rifleman*, September 1942, 10–13, 16.

Jordan, David Starr. *The Days of a Man: Being Memories of a Naturalist, Teacher and Minor Prophet of Democracy*. Vol. 2, *1900–1921*. New York: World Book, 1922.

Jung-Pang Lo, ed. *K'ang Yu-Wei—A Biography and Symposium*. Tucson: University of Arizona Press, 1967.

Keegan, John, and Andrew Wheatcroft. *Who's Who in Military History: From 1435 to the Present*. New York: William Morrow, 1976.

Kennedy, Thomas C. "Homer Lea and the Peace Makers." *Historian: A Journal of History* 45 (August 1983): 473–96.

Kennedy, William V. "The Wisdom of Homer Lea." Carlisle Barracks, Pa.: Strategic Studies Institute, U.S. Army War College, 1980.

Kern, Daniel J. "Military Prophets." *Military Review*, August 1960, 9–16.

Kim, Hyung-chan, ed. *Distinguished Asian Americans: A Biographical Dictionary*. Westport, Conn.: Greenwood, 2000.

Kimball, John C. "Homer Lea—Interloper on History." United States Naval Institute *Proceedings* 98 (April 1972): 61–67.

Kolb, Captain Avery E. "The Bitter Tea of Homer Lea." *Army Combat Forces Journal*, July 1955, 17–19.

Larrabee, Harold A. "Pacific Prophets Come to Judgment." *Public Opinion Quarterly* 6 (1942): 459–65.

Larson, Jane Leung. "Articulating China's First Mass Movement: Kang Youwei, Liang Qichao, the Baohuanghui, and the 1905 Anti-American Boycott." *Twentieth-Century China*, November 2007, 4–26.

———. "New Source Materials on Kang Youwei and the Baohuanghui." *Chinese America: History and Perspectives, Journal of the Chinese Historical Society of America* 7 (1993): 156–88.

Leang-Li T'ang. *The Inner History of the Chinese Revolution*. London: George Routledge and Sons, 1930.

Lears, T. J. Jackson. *No Place of Grace: Antimodernism and the Transformation of American Culture, 1888–1920*. New York: Pantheon, 1981.

Leckenby, Charles H. "The Founding of Steamboat Springs and of Hans Park." *Colorado Magazine*, May 1929, 92–98.

———. *The Tread of Pioneers: Some Highlights in the Dramatic and Colorful History of Northwestern Colorado*. Steamboat Springs, Colo.: Pilot, 1944.

Lenhaus, Louis. "Born to Battle: The True Adventures of Homer Lea." *Showdown for Men*, February 1958, 39–42.

Lens, Sidney. *The Forging of the American Empire*. New York: Thomas Crowell, 1971.

Levenson, Joseph R. *Liang Ch'-Ch'ao and the Mind of Modern China*. Cambridge, Mass.: Harvard University Press, 1953.

Li Hung Chang. *Memoirs of the Viceroy Li Hung Chang*. London: Constable, 1913.

Libby, Justin H. "An Asian Profile: Homer Lea and the Prophesy of War in the Pacific." *Asian Profile*, October 2001, 407–15.

Lui, Garding. *Inside Los Angeles Chinatown*. [Los Angeles?]: n.p., 1948.

MacNair, Harley F. *China in Revolution: An Analysis of Politics and Militarism under the Republic*. Chicago: University of Chicago Press, 1931.

Mallan, John P. "Roosevelt, Brooks Adams, and Lea: The Warrior Critique of the Business Civilization." *American Quarterly* 8 (Fall 1956): 216–30.

Malone, Dumas, ed. *Dictionary of American Biography*. Vol. 11. New York: Charles Scribner's Sons, 1933.

Marcu, Valeriu. "American Prophet of Total War." *American Mercury*, January–June 1942, 473–78.

Martin, Bernard. *Strange Vigour: A Biography of Sun-Yat-Sen*. New York: Kennikat, 1970.

Matloff, Maurice, ed. *American Military History*. Rev. ed. Washington, D.C.: U.S. Army Center of Military History, 1989.

McClenon, Walter H., and Wilfred C. Gilbert. *Index to the Federal Statutes, 1874–1931*. Washington, D.C.: Government Printing Office, 1933.

McDougall, Walter A. *Let the Sea Make a Noise: A History of the North Pacific from Magellan to MacArthur*. New York: Basic, 1993.

McGroarty, John S. *Los Angeles from the Mountains to the Sea*. Vol. 3. New York: American Historical Society, 1921.

McLanahan, Austin. "'General' Homer Lea, 'Military Consultant': *The Valor of Ignorance—Day of the Saxon*." Baltimore: Maryland Historical Society, 1942.

Millett, Allan R., and Peter Maslowski. *For the Common Defense: A Military History of the United States of America*. Rev. ed. New York: Free Press, 1994.

Millis, Walter. *Arms and Men: A Study in American Military History*. New York: New American Library, 1956.

Monroe, Stephen C. "The Crystal Ball of Homer Lea." *Retired Officer*, April 1982, 34–37.

Morison, Elting E., ed. *The Letters of Theodore Roosevelt*. Vol. 7. Cambridge, Mass.: Harvard University Press, 1954.

Mowry, George E. *The Era of Theodore Roosevelt and the Birth of Modern America, 1900–1912*. New York: Harper and Brothers, 1958; repr., New York: Harper Torchbook, 1962.

Myron, Paul, and Anthony Linbarger. *The Political Doctrines of Sun-Yat Sen*. Baltimore: Johns Hopkins University Press, 1937.

The National Cyclopedia of American Biography. Vol. 2. New York: James T. White, 1921.

Neuman, William L. *America Encounters Japan: From Perry to MacArthur.* Baltimore: Johns Hopkins University Press, 1963.

Newmark, Harris. *Sixty Years in Southern California, 1853–1913.* New York: Knickerbocker, 1916.

Newmark, Marco R. "Homer Lea." *Historical Society of Southern California* 37 (June 1955): 177–84.

———. *Jottings in Southern California History.* Los Angeles: Ward Ritchie, 1955.

Ng, Franklin. "The Western Military Academy in Fresno." In *Origins and Destinations: 41 Essays on Chinese America.* Los Angeles: Chinese Historical Society of Southern California and UCLA Asian Studies Center, 1994.

Niu, Sien-chong. "Two Forgotten American Strategists." *Military Review,* November 1966, 53–59.

O'Connor, Peter. "Japan's Irish Publicists." *Number 1 Shimbun,* June 2007, 14–15.

O'Connor, Richard. *Pacific Destiny: An Informal History of the U.S. in the Pacific.* Boston: Little, Brown, 1969.

O'Neill, William. *The Progressive Years: America Comes of Age.* New York: Harper and Row, 1975.

"On War." *Army,* January 1961, 60.

Padgitt, James T. "Captain Joseph C. Lea, the Father of Roswell." In *West Texas Historical Association Year Book,* vol. 35. Abilene: West Texas Historical Association, 1959.

Pak-wah Leung, Edwin, ed. *Historical Dictionary of Revolutionary China, 1839–1976.* Westport, Conn.: Greenwood, 1992.

Panichas, George A., ed. *Promise of Greatness: The War of 1914–1918.* New York: John Day, 1968.

Perkins, Bradford. *The Great Rapprochement: England and the United States, 1895–1914.* London: Victor Gollancz, 1969.

Perkins, LaVonne. "Silas Soule, His Widow Heresa, and the Rest of the Story." *Denver Westerners Roundup,* March–April 1999, 3–21.

Perleberg, Max. *Who's Who in Modern China: From the Beginning of the Chinese Republic to the End of 1953.* Hong Kong: Ye Olde Printerie, 1954.

Ponce, Mariano. *Sun Yat-Sen: The Founder of the Republic of China.* Manila: Filipino-Chinese Cultural Foundation, 1965.

Possony, Stefan. "General Homer Lea and the Republic of China." *Chinese Culture,* June 1969, 43–45.

Powers, Joshua B., III. "Burying Homer." *Military History,* February 2005, 8.

"Prophesies of Homer Lea." *Newsweek,* April 6, 1942, 66–67.

Rankin, Mary B. *Early Chinese Revolutionaries: Radical Intellectuals in Shanghai and Chekiang, 1902–1911.* Cambridge, Mass.: Harvard University Press, 1971.

Rees, Simon. "The Enigmatic Homer Lea." *Military History,* October 2004, 58–64.

Reid, John G. *The Manchu Abdication and the Powers, 1908–1912: An Episode in Pre-war Diplomacy.* Berkeley: University of California Press, 1935.

Restarick, Henry B. *Sun Yat Sen: Liberator of China.* New Haven, Conn.: Yale University Press, 1931.

Riccardelli, Richard F. "A Forgotten American Military Strategist: The Vision and Enigma of Homer Lea." *Army History,* Winter 1996, 17–22.

Riverside Cemetery (Coberly/Lea Plot) Chart. Denver, Colorado. Copy in author's files.

Robertson, William Glenn. "Homer Lea." In *Dictionary of American Biography,* vol. 2, edited by Roger J. Spiller. Westport, Conn.: Greenwood, 1984.

Rolle, Andrew. *Occidental College: A Centennial History.* Los Angeles: Castle, 1986.

Rottach, Edmund. *La Chine en revolution.* Paris: Perrin, 1914.

Schiffrin, Harold Z. *Sun Yat-Sen and the Origins of the Chinese Revolution.* Berkeley: University of California Press, 1968.

———. *Sun Yat-Sen: Reluctant Revolutionary.* Boston: Little, Brown, 1980.

Schnetzer, Wayne. "The Hounds of Old Pennock." *Blue and Grey Chronicle,* August 2002, 1–2.

Schwartz, Steven. *From West to East: California and the Making of the American Mind.* New York: Free Press, 1998.

Selle, Earl A. *Donald of China.* New York: Harper and Brothers, 1948.

Sharmon, Lyon. *Sun Yat-sen: His Life and Its Meaning.* New York: John Day, 1934.

Slaughter, H. L. "Homer Lea: Patriotic Prophet of the West." *CDL (Christian Defense League) Report,* September 1983, 1–6.

Spring, Agnes Wright. *Near the Greats: Prominent People Known to Agnes Wright Spring.* Frederick, Colo.: Platte'N Press, 1981.

Standard Rock Oil Company. "Annual Statement of the Standard Rock Oil Company and Manager's Report," May 21, 1903. Copy in author's files.

———. "Asphaltum Refinery Bulletin No. 2." San Francisco, November 29, 1901. Copy in author's files.

Starr, Kevin. *Inventing the Dream: California through the Progressive Era.* New York: Oxford University Press, 1985.

Stephan, John J. *Hawaii under the Rising Sun: Japan's Plans for Conquest after Pearl Harbor.* Honolulu: University of Hawaii Press, 1984.

Stimson, Marshall. "Great American Who Saw It Coming." *Christian Science Monitor Weekly Magazine,* March 7, 1942, 6.

———. "A Los Angeles Jeremiah—Homer Lea: Military Genius and Prophet." *Historical Society of Southern California Quarterly* 24 (March 1942): 5–13.

Sun Yat-Sen. *Memoirs of a Chinese Revolutionary: A Programme of National Reconstruction for China.* Tai-pei, Taiwan: China Cultural Service, 1953.

Thomas, Lowell. *Born to Raise Hell: The Life Story of Tex O'Reilly, Soldier of Fortune.* New York: Doubleday, Doran, 1936.

Thomson, John Stuart. *China Revolutionized*. Indianapolis: Bobbs-Merrill, 1913.

Ting-i Li. *A History of Modern China*. Dartmouth, N.H.: Oriental, 1970.

Turner, Justin G. "General Homer Lea." *Manuscripts* 22 (Spring 1970): 96–102.

U.S. Military Academy. *Register of Graduates and Former Cadets, 1802–1960*. West Point, N.Y.: West Point Alumni Foundation, 1960.

Vagts, Alfred. *A History of Militarism*. Greenwich, Conn.: Meridian, 1959.

Vare, Daniele. *The Last Empress*. New York: Doubleday, Doran, 1938.

Varg, Paul. *The Making of a Myth: The United States and China, 1897–1912*. East Lansing: Michigan State University Press, 1968.

Waley, Adolf. *The Remaking of China*. New York: E. P. Dutton, 1915.

Webster's American Military Biographies. Springfield, Mass.: G. and C. Merriam, 1978.

Wecter, Dixon. *The Hero in America: A Chronicle of Hero-Worship*. New York: Charles Scribner's Sons, 1941.

Weigley, Russell F. *Towards an American Army: Military Thought from Washington to Marshall*. New York: Columbia University Press, 1962.

Welcome, Henry. "The California Connection (or: How Two Americans from Southern California Played a Significant Role in China's Revolution in 1911)." *Chinese Historical Society of Southern California,* December 1983, 4–11.

Wells, Linton. *Blood on the Moon: The Autobiography of Linton Wells*. New York: Houghton Mifflin, 1937.

Who Was Who in American History—The Military. Chicago: Marquis Who's Who, 1975.

Wiebe, Robert. *The Search for Order, 1877–1920*. New York: Hill and Wang, 1967.

Willoughby, Charles A., and John Chamberlain. *MacArthur, 1941–1951*. New York: McGraw-Hill, 1954.

Worden, Robert Lee. "A Chinese Reformer in Exile: The North American Phase of the Travels of K'ang Yu-Wei, 1899–1909." Ph.D. diss., Georgetown University, 1972.

Worthy, Edmund H. "Yung Wing in America." *Pacific Historical Review* 34 (August 1965): 265–87.

Wright, Mary C., ed. *China in Revolution: The First Phase, 1900–1913*. New Haven, Conn.: Yale University Press, 1968.

Wu, John C. H. *Sun Yat-Sen: The Man and His Ideas*. Taipei, Taiwan: Commercial, 1971.

INDEX

Newmark, Marco R. *(cont.)*
  on Lea's deformity, 12
  on Lea's feelings about
    missionaries, 142
  at Lea's funeral, 188
  on Lea's health, 21–22
  on Lea's intent to go to China,
    33, 34–35
  on Lea's personality, 16, 191
  on Lea's views of women and
    marriage, 140–41
New York City
  Lea and K'ang Yu-wei in, 118,
    121–22, 123
  reform army controversy, 118,
    119–21
New York Evening Post, 199
New York Herald, 39
New York Sun, 91–92, 121, 250n60
New York Times
  on American fears of war with
    Japan, 137
  on the disbanding of Vickar's
    Chinese regiment, 131
  on the influence of *The Valor of
    Ignorance,* 168, 203, 204
  on Lea's influence in Germany,
    202
  on *The Vermilion Pencil,* 142
New York Tribune, 66, 122
Ng Poon Chew, 21, 33, 35, 191, 199

Oakland Tribune, 192, 195
O'Banion, Ansel E.
  biography of Lea and, 207
  burns Lea's papers after his death,
    189, 272n4
  Chinese Imperial Army and, 83
  on the demise of the reform army,
    130
  deputy sheriff appointment,
    238n19
  the Falkenberg controversy and,
    96, 100–102

  government investigation of the
    Western Military Academy and,
    92–93
  joins Lea's cadet cadre plan,
    63–64, 79, 80, 238n17
  on Lea and money, 195
  at Lea's funeral, 188
  on Lea's personality, 206
  the Sager incident and, 100–102
  smuggling Chinese and, 131, 253n7
  at the Tournament of Roses
    Parade, 84
  Western Military Academy and, 81
Occidental College, 22–23
Okuma Shigenobu, 51–52, 61
On Wan Chew, 239n26
Open Door policy, 38, 113, 136
O'Reilly, Edward "Tex," 48, 49
Oriental Review, 199
Otis, Harrison Gray, 115, 125, 154
"Our Country" (Strong), 29

Pacific Coast Congress, 164
Pacific Lyceum League, 23
pacifism/pacifists, 27, 28, 157
Page, Roger S., 80, 83
Palace Hotel, 55, 106, 192
Pao Huang Hui (Protect the
  Emperor Society)
  the Boxer Rebellion and, 38
  Commercial Corporation, 72
  creation and goals of, 3, 31
  demise of, 252n4
  elevation of Lea's position in, 58
  factionalism in, 57–58
  failed uprising of, 46–49
  Richard Falkenberg and, 65,
    67–70
  Fresno cadet company crisis,
    105–10
  gold medals awarded to Lea,
    75–76, 237n3, 268–69n73
  incorporation in Los Angeles,
    237n60